Healing With The Stars 2025
An Astrological Guide to Self-Discovery and Personal Transformation
Gypsy Rose Lewis

Contents

Introduction

Do you ever feel like you're stuck in the Matrix we call life, dodging metaphorical bullets and wondering if there's a glitch in your coding system or if you took a wrong turn somewhere? You're not alone. Life can feel, at times, as if we are navigating a Labyrinth of chaos and destruction. Many of us have given up on our dreams due to the twists and turns of daily life. Forget about the future. We are just happy to make it through the day without losing our minds.

In this digital age, we're more connected than ever, and yet, loneliness creeps in like an uninvited guest. We feel disconnected from the world around us and disconnected from ourselves and our souls that are yearning for more self-expression. It's as if we're all stuck in our individual pods, scrolling through social media feeds filled with curated snapshots of others' seemingly perfect lives. Everyone has their life together, and we are just trying not to trip over our own feet.

The pursuit of perfection is like trying to win a game with ever-changing rules. We've all been there, comparing our behind-the-scenes chaos to someone else's highlight reel. Spoiler alert: Nobody has it all figured out, and those who claim they do are kidding themselves.

Finding the equilibrium between taking care of ourselves and adulting can feel like attempting a circus act on a tightrope. On one hand, there's the relentless call of responsibilities, and on the other, the siren song of a Netflix binge while wrapped in a cozy blanket burrito. Many of us are aware of the path we have chosen of self-sabotage but are too overwhelmed to do anything about it. Our thoughts consume us about whether we are living up to our full potential or if we were supposed to have an entirely different life but took a wrong turn somewhere.

Where is this journey leading? What surprises are hiding around the next corner? Uncertainty is the name of the game, and if you're feeling like you've accidentally wandered into a Choose Your Own Adventure novel without a map, you're not alone. But fear not, as this book is your friendly companion here to help you navigate the chaos and gain a better understanding of the collective energies at play. Choosing this adventure of healing and self-awareness allows you to live a life with a clear direction and one that is authentic and aligned with your soul calling. This book will remind you that we are not alone on this journey and that larger energies are at play, guiding us into our own shadows toward healing ourselves and setting ourselves free.

The benefits of healing

Why heal? Healing ourselves comes with many benefits. Do you want to feel inspired to make positive changes in your life rather than settling for what is or surrendering to your circumstances? Self-discovery serves as a compass, guiding us to a deeper understanding of our thoughts, emotions, motivations, and behaviors. This heightened self-awareness becomes the bedrock for positive change, enabling us to make informed choices in alignment with our authentic selves.

The healing process involves facing and processing challenging emotions and experiences. This fosters emotional resilience and equips us with the tools to navigate life's inevitable ups and downs with grace and fortitude. We feel prepared to face any challenge that life throws our way.

Exploring and addressing past traumas, anxieties, and negative thought patterns contribute to improving our mental health. The reduction of symptoms related to depression, anxiety, and other mental health issues becomes a tangible outcome, leading to a more balanced and fulfilling life. Imagine living a life in which you are fueled by purpose and spring out of bed ready to get to work co-creating with the universe rather than throwing the covers over your head, thinking, "I can't deal with today."

The healing journey involves practicing self-compassion and self-love. We learn to treat ourselves with kindness and understanding, fostering a positive and nurturing relationship with ourselves—a cornerstone for our overall well-being.

Our relationships are positively impacted, leading to more effective communication, healthier boundaries, and authentic connections. As we heal, the ripple effect extends to those around us, creating a more harmonious and supportive environment, and we create meaningful connections with those in alignment with our higher vibrational frequency.

Through a journey of self-discovery, we identify our core values and priorities. This newfound clarity becomes a guiding force in decision-making, steering us toward a more purposeful and fulfilling life.

Taking control of our own healing instills a sense of empowerment. Active participation in our growth and well-being translates into a greater sense of control over life's narrative, fostering a more empowered and intentional existence. We can take the reins over our lives rather than being stuck and stagnant.

Navigating the healing journey leads to the development of improved problem-solving skills. This heightened capacity to overcome challenges stems from increased self-awareness and a deeper understanding of effective strategies, contributing to a more resilient and adaptable mindset.

Breaking through outdated thought patterns that no longer serve us leads to unleashing our creativity, innovation, and a willingness to explore new ideas and possibilities—essential elements for personal growth. We become the creators of our reality by tapping into our true potential, giving us the ability to manifest all of our desires into existence.

Most importantly, we uncover a deeper sense of purpose and meaning. This newfound sense of purpose becomes a motivational force, providing us with direction and a profound connection to something greater than ourselves. We recognize that we are not alone in this journey but supported by the divine.

The benefits of a healing journey are not merely personal victories but extend outward. By investing in our healing, we contribute not only to our well-being but also to the collective evolution of a more conscious, compassionate, and creatively vibrant world.

Wait, The stars determine our reality?

Well, technically, no, the stars do not determine our reality. I'll give you a little background before delving into how this book came to be in your hands.

Many of you may know me from my online platforms. I am that wacky tarot reader who graces your phone screen while you are scrolling through socials, singing and dancing like nobody's watching, offering insights and guidance to those who are on a healing journey. I have been working professionally as an intuitive psychic reader for over a decade, and I have been on my own journey of healing and self-discovery for even longer. I possess many gifts, one of which is the ability to channel messages from the divine. This gift has allowed me to build myself a thriving business with a large clientele and many loyal followers on my social media platforms, seeking guidance to help navigate the twists and turns they face along their journey.

Six months ago, I channeled a message that I must put my life and business on hold due to a higher calling to write a book. Wait, what? Are you kidding? Before this insight, I had no plans to write a book. I didn't have time to write a book, and what would I do to generate the income to which I had become accustomed? Sorry, you must have the wrong psychic. I was sure the higher realms had made a mistake. Over the next three weeks, I was shown the concept and structure of the book that I was to write: Outlining the astrological influences and how we can use the stars to navigate our healing journey.

Now I knew they definitely had the wrong intuitive. I am not an astrologer or an astronaut or whatever. I have many unique gifts, but anything involving science makes my eyes glaze over, and my thoughts wander. My team assured me that I was destined to write this book—all I had to do was channel the messages from the divine and interpret collective energies into language that could be easily understood by the reader. Now that I can do. I have provided examples of how these energies have played out in my life for you to better understand the energy and how it might play out in your own reality.

I am no stranger to collective energies. Throughout my years working with clients, helping them navigate their struggles, I would constantly see themes play out in my daily readings. When my first client of the day tells me their life is falling apart, I can often assume that pattern will follow almost every client for the next two weeks.

I was no stranger to Scorpio season's heavy and transformative energies, which was always my busiest time as illusions are shattered, and clients are desperate for my guidance to pick up the pieces. Aries season was always my favorite, as clients would greet me with optimism and excitement for new endeavors and business opportunities. I had watched collective energies play out for years, and now I had the opportunity to contribute to something amazing. I was chosen to create a roadmap to navigating these energies to help others find deeper healing and prepare for upcoming energies that may be a challenge to navigate. I only wish that I had such a tool to help navigate my own healing journey when it began.

Back to the question at hand: Do the stars really determine how our lives will play out? I had this question too, and I will explain this to you the way that it was channeled to me by spirit.

While the movement of planetary alignments does not actually influence what happens here on Earth, the sky is like a mirror. As above, so below. We can use the position of the planetary alignments as a guide to gain a better understanding of the energies currently at play.

This is not a new concept; the roots of astrology can be traced back to the 2nd Millennium in ancient Mesopotamia (modern-day Iraq), where Babylonian astronomers began recording the movements of the planets and stars, associating these celestial movements with events happening here on Earth. We have always known that there was a connection between the stars and our existence. Ancient Egyptians were also early practitioners of astrology. They linked celestial patterns to the annual flooding of the Nile and the agricultural cycles. Greek philosophers, played a crucial role in shaping astrology as we know it today. Figures like Claudius Ptolemy and philosophers in the Platonic and Stoic traditions contributed to the development of astrological principles. Roman culture absorbed much of Greek astrology, which became widely practiced in the Roman Empire. Astrology continued to evolve during the Middle Ages and the Renaissance. During this time, astrological texts were translated and preserved, and astrology played a significant role in the courts of Europe. It was considered a respected science.

Our understanding of astrology has evolved into what we know it as today, and now that I have immersed myself in all things galactic, I, for one, am glad that it is here. Since I have begun channeling the structure of this system, I have used it as a tool to navigate my own journey, and I know that it works. Some days feel more of a struggle than others and there is often a cosmic reason for that. Use this tool as a resource to navigate the ups and downs of your own journey toward leading a life that aligns with the version of yourself you have the potential to become.

How to use this book

This book is structured for simplicity. Just turn to today's date and take a peek at the collective energies at play. The book is separated into Major Alignments and Aspects.

Major Alignments:

Major alignments occur when a planet or asteroid moves into a new zodiac sign, determining the theme of the energies that play out among the collective. These alignments significantly impact the challenges we may experience. When a planet moves into a new zodiac sign or retrogrades and begins moving in the opposite direction, it affects the collective. The orbit of that planet will determine how long we will be affected by those energies. For instance, the Moon moves quickly, so energies experienced by its movements, while at times intense, usually pass within a few days. Other planets move much slower. Take Uranus, for example. Uranus takes seven years to move through a zodiac sign, so we will experience these energies for an extended period.

As Major Alignments have the most significant effect on us, under each major alignment, a reflection exercise has been created for you to discover more about how these energies may impact you personally and how you can make them work for you rather than against you. Take the time to do these exercises for your own self-discovery and development.

Aspects:

Aspects represent how major alignments interact with each other, creating less significant energies that fluctuate throughout our day-to-day lives. Some of these energies may not have a significant impact, while others will pack a punch There are no reflection excersises for aspets.

While most days, shifts are happening in the cosmos, there are a few days throughout the year when there are no significant movements, so you will find that some days are missing from your guide. No news is good news, so use these days to adjust to the energies and insights gained from previous days.

Resist the urge to skip ahead to see what is coming. This may cause you to miss valuable lessons and insights along your journey. The most profound healing comes from our experience and our ability to process energies and emotions at a comfortable pace.

Of course, I had to add my own unique flavor to this book. If you watch my content online, you will know that I love a song to accompany my messages from spirit. This book is no different. At the end of each day, you will find a song suggestion. I highly recommend listening to these songs to gain a deeper understanding of the energy. I also just really like the idea of a whole collective of soul tribe jamming out together while healing ourselves in a powerful way. You may be unfamiliar with many of the songs in this book; I have intentionally chosen songs by smaller artists with profound healing messages to share through their music. Some songs are classics you will recognize, and others are selected for the vibe and to bring up the energy. Some of the songs suggested in this book contain explicit lyrics, so if you are offended by vulgar language, please skip the song suggestions altogether.

Let's go!

January Alignments

January 1st

Pluto in Aquarius sextile Aries North Node

This aspect has us operating through life with a new sense of purpose. The changes we feel inspired to make are not just those that affect us alone but have an effect on the collective as a whole. Many of us will find ourselves aligned with a purpose higher than ourselves. The more we can align ourselves with this purpose and allow the universe to guide us toward it, the more our manifestations will begin showing up before our eyes.

Mercury in Sagittarius trine Chiron in Aries

The deeper we heal and become less reactive to our pain points, recognizing that our pain can only define us as much as we allow it. The only way to separate from our pain is to lean into it and face it head-on. This aspect reminds us that we are not alone in facing the lower-level frequencies we carry from the past. If we allow space for stillness, we can connect to a higher source and ask for guidance on best navigating the challenges. With each challenge, we are gaining more resilience and strength, all preparing us for the levels we are destined to reach.

Venus in Aquarius semi-sextile Neptune in Pisces

Many of us will find ourselves wanting to spend more time alone to tap into our higher selves or feel connected with the divine. With this energy present, this is not about feeling lonely or unsupported but rather feeling safe with ourselves and within our own energy. I recommend finding a way to connect deeper with source today. Take the time to reflect on your 2024 journey and allow source to move through you and guide you toward your next steps toward healing in 2025.

Song- "Divine" by Sophia Dashing

January 3rd

Vesta enters Scorpio

This is a very interesting Alignment to begin 2025. Many of us have engaged in profound self-reflection over the past 12 months, embarking on a healing journey that led us to explore the depth of our being. This introspection unveiled dormant aspects of ourselves, and amidst the energies experienced in 2024, we have discovered alignment with our soul purpose and the true nature of our existence. With a newfound understanding that we are here to serve a higher calling, Vesta's entrance into Scorpio propels us to passionately and intensely align our lives with this purpose. Having identified our roles within the collective, we are now dedicated to researching and understanding the intricacies of this calling, striving to fulfill our true potential. Those of us who were just beginning our spiritual journey or dipping our toes in the healing waters are diving even deeper into personal transformation, demonstrating a solid commitment to our path. We are firm in severing connections, situations, or themes that do not align with our purpose, as Scorpio's intensity and Vesta's deep fire propel us to investigate why we arrived at this moment in time and commit ourselves to the path of our highest timeline without distraction or interference.

Reflection

1. What specific experiences or events in the past 12 months have prompted your deep self-reflection and healing journey?

2. In what ways have you uncovered dormant aspects of yourself, and how have these revelations shaped your understanding of your true nature and purpose?

3. What steps are you actively taking to research and understand the nuances of your role within the collective and to fulfill your true potential?

Venus enters Pisces

Venus in Pisces represents the deepest, purest form of love. This energy allows us to see past the flaws of others and find the light within everyone. We recognize that everyone has the potential to heal themselves and find their source of light. This kind of love is pure, romantic, and very forgiving. Within this energy, we are adaptable and change our love frequency to match that of another person. We are willing to sacrifice our selfish needs, wants, and desires to achieve spiritual balance within our connections. In this energy, we believe that if we give out love freely to those around us, others will match that energy, and we will receive pure love from others in return. The problem with this kind of energy is that it can be like wearing rose-colored glasses regarding our connections. We will give people many chances to redeem themselves because we fantasize about what this connection could become. When we sit in an energy of "love has no bounds," we are likely to put aside any boundaries we had in place to protect ourselves.

For singles, we are looking for connections with people who can love with an open heart and those who can match our energy. Be careful at this time, as we are likely to look past red flags and feel that we can heal those who are broken if we just show them what real love looks like. Be wary about forming a love connection with anyone who is recently single and hasn't taken the time to heal from a past relationship because, in this energy, we see many singles searching for a rebound relationship as the broken-hearted are looking for anywhere they can express their love energy. Also, be mindful of the fantasy energy that comes along with this alignment. You may match up with someone on Tinder who lives at a distance, and then 20 minutes later, you are caught up in your head imagining how you will make this connection work long distance, where you will live together, and what your kids will look like.

For those in a relationship, we start to look past our partner's flaws and become more accepting of them; instead, we embrace them and come to appreciate them. We want a deeper kind of love, a love that is a spiritual soul connection. We forgive past discretions and offer a clean slate to connect more deeply with our partner. If our partner tells us they will change, we believe them. Be careful that this does not lead to delusion and that you are not putting aside your boundaries to create a deeper connection with your partner. Giving someone a clean slate is fine, but that doesn't mean we should forget about everything that has transpired throughout our relationship.

Reflection

1. In what ways do I see the potential for spiritual and soulful connections within my current relationships?

2. Am I wearing rose-colored glasses in any of my connections, potentially overlooking red flags or diving into fantasies?

3. How can I ensure that my quest for a deeper, more profound love doesn't lead to compromising my boundaries?

Sun in Capricorn quincunx Jupiter retrograde in Gemini

We are determined to accomplish our personal goals and desires during this time. However, this aspect brings distractions that distract us from our practical goals and stability, which we strive to achieve. Something or someone else wants our attention, bringing about an energy of popularity and connection. We may find that we have a social event to attend that conflicts with our work schedule, social media platforms may take off and everyone wants some of our attention, or perhaps friends, lovers, and family members want to connect with us and are blowing up our DMs. It feels great to be in such high demand, but not when it comes at the cost of maintaining our stability and advancing our lives. Now is a great time to think deeply about where our priorities lie and create boundaries with people or remember that it is okay to decline social invitations.

Song: "Fantasy" by Mariah Carey

January 4th

Mars retrograde in Leo opposite Pluto in Aquarius

This aspect brings about various forms of chaos and disruption within the collective. With Pluto in Aquarius, the objective is to dismantle social constructs and empower the people, fostering a state of equilibrium as we stand united and advocate for our rights. However, to achieve this, we must first endure enough discomfort to feel compelled to challenge the established powers. Currently, we find ourselves deep in the midst of the discomfort phase of this alignment. This aspect signifies a sense of confinement and restriction, intensified by mounting social pressures and revelations about humanity issues. Consequently, we respond to the pressure to conform with feelings of anger and aggression. Unfortunately, this energy is often misdirected, manifesting as moodiness or frustration toward those closest to us rather than toward the systems that constrain us. We may find ourselves irked by other motorists or irritated by those here to serve and help us, such as a seemingly rude cashier (also affected by this energy) or a doctor who keeps us in the waiting room for over an hour when we have a scheduled appointment. This build-up of pressure is a natural part of the process. It's essential to remain composed and introspective during these times. If you notice yourself becoming impatient, moody, or aggressive with others, take a moment to reflect on the true source of your frustrations.

Venus in Pisces semi-sextile Aries North Node

This energy allows us to see through the illusion that all people are here to inconvenience us and instead recognize that we are all divine souls having a human experience. We understand that each of us is doing our best with the hand we've been dealt, and none of us consistently acts within our light at all times. So what if the cashier was rude to us? With this aspect, we can find forgiveness by realizing that we have no idea what that person is going through. We all have our own unique dreams, goals, and desires. Perhaps the cashier's dream is to establish a safe and loving environment for her children, but she just received a rent increase, forcing her to work overtime and leaving her tired and exhausted. Every moment spent at this job prevents her from making meaningful memories with her children. Maybe she's trapped in an oppressive situation from which she can't find an escape.

Mercury in Sagittarius quincunx Uranus in Taurus

This aspect is one to watch out for as it reflects speaking out against injustices regarding our finances and stability. It's important to remember that every action has a reaction, which can lead to positive or negative consequences. An example of this energy is when you're asked to pay an amount for a service you're uncomfortable with, and you express that the service is too expensive. Similarly, you might feel that you're not adequately compensated or appreciated at work, so you raise the issue with your boss. This energy represents telling the truth and calling out inconsistencies. However, the consequences of doing so have the ability to either positively or negatively affect your stability. Will pointing out pricing inconsistencies gain you a discount? Will asking for a raise at work result in extra money in your account, or could it potentially lead to your dismissal?

Venus in Pisces quincunx Mars retrograde in Leo

Navigating this energy proves challenging as it beckons us to rise above and practice forgiveness, urging us to recognize the light within all others. However, at times, that light seems elusive. Someone may seek a clean slate, yet we struggle to release the pain, anger, and resentments. Alternatively, we may desire forgiveness and understanding, but something weighing on our hearts needs addressing first. This energy presents itself as a conflict within us: while we wish to avoid further conflict, we're not quite ready to relinquish our anger and disappointment. It leaves us feeling as though we shouldn't have to be the bigger person in such situations and sacrifice our voices for the sake of peace. Sometimes, we just want to have it out and get things off our chest.

Song: "Break Stuff" by Limp Bizkit

January 5th

Venus in Pisces semi-sextile Pluto in Aquarius

This energy represents coming together with someone you would typically choose not to work with. You may find yourself aiding a stranger who needs help or assistance, showing them love and compassion. You may also connect with people you don't usually see eye to eye, yet find a way to discover common ground or collaborate for a shared objective. For example, you might usually avoid interacting with other school moms, but occasionally, you'll need to spend time with them due to school events or fundraisers. In these instances, you smile and exchange pleasantries as you work together to achieve your goals.

Mercury in Sagittarius biquintile Mars retrograde in Leo

This aspect signifies taking the initiative to address a problem or behavior. It could involve speaking out about an issue at work or confronting someone who consistently plays the victim without taking steps to improve their situation. It may entail acknowledging and addressing our own problematic behavior and coming clean about something. Regardless of the situation, be prepared to deliver some truth bombs. This can be done with sensitivity and tact. This energy prompts us to identify and examine the inconsistencies in our lives and consider what actions we will take now to address them.

Sun in Capricorn sextile Saturn in Pisces

This energy brings a welcome reward for our hard work and commitment. It acknowledges the efforts we've invested and the lessons we've learned along the way. Perhaps we've averted a potential setback by putting in extra hours to our grind or exercising patience instead of rushing through tasks. Alternatively, we may have applied past lessons to ensure we avoid repeating previous mistakes, resulting in a successful outcome. For example, staying up all night to perfect a presentation for your boss could lead to acknowledgment for your dedication and effort. Similarly, making necessary changes to your pitch demonstrates your commitment to improvement. Ultimately, this energy reinforces that hard work and integrating past lessons yield valuable rewards.

Song: "Lean On Me" by Bill Withers

January 6th

How far will you go to get what you want? This energy represents being very aggressive about manifesting your desires. There's no room for passivity or sacrificing your desires to please others. The universe wants to provide all we need, but we must not be afraid to reach out and take it. This energy rewards those willing to cut in line or speak the loudest. We are done waiting our turn and ready to blaze our own trail. Be bold with this energy, and it will undoubtedly pay off.

Sun in Capricorn quintile Neptune in Pisces

This aspect serves as a reminder to dream big. What are the goals that seem distant? What financial figure feels just out of reach? The only limits are the ones we impose on ourselves. It may not always feel like it, but no tax bracket is beyond our reach. What can you do right now as the next step toward achieving this dream figure? It could be as small as registering an LLC or enrolling in school to pursue your desired education. Making our dreams come true should be enjoyable, not daunting.

When I started my business, I turned making money into a game. Initially, I discovered I had only made $78 in profit for the month, which was disappointing. So, I decided to turn it into a challenge. The goal was to 10x my earnings. I made a $690 profit the following month, just shy of my $780 goal. The month after, I exceeded my goal, which led me to set a new target of $7800 monthly. While this goal took longer to achieve, it was fun to challenge myself and find new and creative ways to make money. I approached this game like Jenga, figuring out which piece to move without the tower collapsing. There were times when I made mistakes, and everything came crashing down, but instead of giving up, I rebuilt the tower, one block at a time.

So, how can you make making money more fun rather than a daunting task?

Song: "How Far I'll Go" by Auli'i Cravalho

January 7th

Mars Retrograde Enters Cancer

Mars retrograde began in December and is among the most significant and complex transits. This alignment brings our carnal nature to the forefront. We experience heightened aggression, conflict, bullying, and competitiveness as we find ourselves overwhelmed with the desire and passion to succeed. Due to our intensified emotions, we can become overwhelmed and begin to have somewhat of a distorted view of reality. We may perceive that a conflict or tension is worse than it is, or if we are in a new relationship and experiencing feelings of falling in love, we may ignore red flags, causing us to progress the relationship too quickly.

We collect much of our karma during this time, so keep that in mind while making any decisions or taking action during this alignment. This alignment asks us if we can truly be loving and remain open and heart-centered during a time when there is an immense amount of pressure and a strong desire to react and kick someone's ass. This is not the time to dispute with your neighbor or engage in a road rage incident. Any harm done to others now will be reflected back to you later. If we are harboring any resentment or anger from past situations, these themes will likely resurface during this placement as we are asked to clear out karma from past cycles.

Although this seems counterintuitive to moving forward and remaining balanced, I highly encourage connecting with anyone who comes back from the past at this time, as this is an indication of a lack of closure. We can reconcile our differences or leave heavy connections deep in the past and close the energetic ties for good. Not all connections from the past will end in separation; there is also a high chance of reigniting flames from the past with a new level of intensity.

Whether we are entering new connections or reigniting old ones, we should be mindful of getting too swept up in the passion. Many fast engagements, moving in together after only a few weeks, or running off to Vegas to marry a stranger happen during this alignment. While feeling this level of intensity within a connection is great, many fast-paced relationships fail due to mis-alignment between the parties involved. This is not a good time for making any life-altering decisions.

Mars retrograde is moving from Leo into the sign of Cancer, so we are switching from an energy of feeling as though we are in competition with others and fighting for our place in the world to feeling as though we are unsafe with those closest to us. This may show up as fallouts with family members or close friends. We may experience trouble around our home, such as feuds with neighbors or energetic disturbances brought into our home or safe environment. It is important to remember that how you react to this in intense energy is a true reflection of your healing and growth. While we do not control the actions of others, we do have the ability to control how we respond to this energy and how much we allow it to infiltrate and derail our healing journey.

Reflection

1. How has Mars retrograde, particularly its influence on heightened aggression and conflict, manifested in your life since December 2024, and what challenges have you faced in maintaining a balanced perspective during this time?

2. Considering the karmic implications mentioned, what decisions or actions have you taken during Mars retrograde, and how mindful have you been of the potential consequences and karmic repercussions?

3. Reflect on instances where you may have felt pressured to react strongly or engage in conflict during this period. How have you remained open, heart-centered, and loving in challenging situations?

4. If unresolved conflicts or past relationships resurface during this time, how will you approach these situations? Have you found closure, or is there a potential for reconciliation?

First Quarter Moon in Aries

The first quarter moon in Aries ignites a fire within us as it asks us to reflect on all the manifestations we have not yet brought into fruition. All the ideas and inspirations we have brushed aside for another time come heavily into focus as we now find ourselves with the energy to pursue them. This energy is intense, excitable, committed, and ambitious. It encourages us to take risks without fear. The problem with this energy is that it can also be impulsive and have us wanting to jump so far ahead of ourselves that we skip the planning and deliberation stages and jump straight into action. If an impulsive idea comes to you right now, by all means, reach out and grab it with both hands, but allow yourself the space to consult your intuition. Rather than hastily making life-altering decisions, consider sleeping on them first. This energy is fearless, exciting, and expansive; so much can be accomplished during this alignment. However, be careful not to bite off more than you can chew. I often begin multiple new projects when this energy is present because I am so fired up and excited. However, once this energy has passed, I lose the desire to follow them through to completion. Choose just one task at a time and give it everything you have got despite feeling as though you have the ability to take on more.

Reflection

1. Reflect on ideas or inspirations you've brushed aside for another time. What prevented you from pursuing them, and what feelings or thoughts arise as you consider the ability to manifest them now?

2. Reflect on the balance between fearlessness and impulsivity in your own life. How do you navigate taking risks while also considering the potential consequences?

3. Have you experienced a pattern of starting multiple projects but struggling to follow through with them? If so, what strategies can you employ to prevent yourself from taking on more than you can handle, especially when feeling fired up and excited about new projects or ideas?

Mars retrograde in Cancer sesquiquadrate Saturn in Pisces

This energy indicates that something within your safe bubble is becoming a problem or irritation. It could manifest as a noisy neighbor, feeling unsafe in your environment, or a lack of serenity in your home. It might also involve illness in your household, causing irritability or unruly hormonal teenagers disrupting the peace. In the face of these irritations, this energy prompts us to practice patience, even though we may be tempted to lose our cool. How much can you tolerate before you explode? It is a test of our temperament.

To remain calm and patient amid the chaos, consider what factors around you are affecting your frequency. How can you maintain a sense of serenity and balance despite these challenges?

Mercury in Sagittarius square Neptune in Pisces

Amidst present tension, this aspect offers a welcome opportunity to seek alternative pathways to calmness. It encourages us to discover the magic within each moment. For some, this magic may be found in simple acts like lighting a scented candle or burning incense. Others may find solace in meditation or walking barefoot outdoors to stay grounded. When feeling overwhelmed, I often lie down and gaze up at the clouds, attempting to make shapes as I did in childhood.

How can you infuse a touch of magic into your day? Consider exploring new ways to invite enchantment into your space or daily routine.

Venus in Pisces semi-square Chiron in Aries

Many of us hesitate to look within, but this energy invites us to delve deeper into the root cause of our discomfort. It encourages us to recognize that all discomfort can be traced back to a dormant shadow within us. Are your neighbors noisy because they live in an environment filled with anger or resentment? Is your teenager acting out because they're struggling with hormonal changes or facing challenges in school?

Now, turn the spotlight on yourself. Why are you so triggered by your environment or family members? What's really going on for you? Is it lack of sleep, illness, or burnout? Are you in desperate need of a vacation? This energy urges us to seek understanding and forgiveness, whether toward ourselves or those around us.

Song: "Instant Karma" by John Lennon

January 8th

Mercury in Sagittarius quincunx Mars retrograde in Cancer

Be mindful of your words today, as this aspect embodies a tendency to speak our minds without hesitation or apology. If there's something we've been holding back, it may all come pouring out under this energy. Additionally, we may find ourselves on the receiving end of aggressive communication. Arguments are likely, but this energy also encourages truthfulness rather than saying things we don't mean. If you find yourself facing verbal confrontation, consider whether there's any truth to the criticism you're receiving.

With this energy present, it's unlikely that much can be resolved successfully through dialogue. It's advisable to step back from conflict rather than trying to talk it out, as heightened emotions are likely to intensify matters further.

Mercury in Sagittarius biquintile Uranus in Taurus

Immersing yourself in the hustle and the daily grind can be an effective way to clear out any heavy energy. Personally, I find solace in cleaning my home, even though it's not something I particularly enjoy. When someone consistently pushes my buttons, and I feel it's inappropriate to respond defensively, I retreat home and engage in a rage-cleaning session, meticulously tidying every nook and cranny. When genuinely upset about something, you can bet my home will be sparkling afterward. It's my way of transmuting negative energy into something positive.

If you're facing challenges or setbacks in one area of your life, consider channeling that energy into another area where you can feel accomplished. On days when I feel out of balance, I head off to buy cleaning supplies to regain control and restore harmony to my environment.

Song: "Love The Way You Lie" by Eminem ft Rihanna

January 9th

Mercury enters Capricorn

If we weren't already serious enough about bossing up, this placement will take us to a whole new level of grind. Mercury in Capricorn is no fun at parties; it is serious, disciplined, ambitious, and has no time for reckless abandon. We are not wasting time or energy on anything or anyone who is not here to help propel us forward. We may find ourselves declining social invitations unless it is for a business conference or networking event.

We may also put much more effort into our physical appearance or how we present ourselves because we want to be taken more seriously. If we are making a presentation, giving a public speech, or attending a business event, we ensure we are well-prepared. Everything that we are communicating right now has a purpose.

There is no time for distractions or petty drama. If drama has the potential to throw us off course, we are much more likely just to sit back, not get involved, and watch it play out. Our time is precious to us, and we find fulfillment within repetition, consistency, and structure. The mundane, repetitive tasks that usually drive us crazy are starting to look pretty appealing.

Sometimes, we can overdo it with this energy, putting a bit too much pressure on ourselves, so be aware of that. But for the most part, this energy is progressive and productive, and it propels us forward in leaps and bounds, getting us off to a great start this early in the year. This energy tells us I can stay where I am or get up and keep pushing to achieve my desired goals.

Reflection

1. What specific goals or ambitions am I currently pursuing, and how dedicated am I to achieving them?

2. How am I prioritizing my time and energy to align with my goals, and what distractions can I eliminate?

3. How am I handling distractions and drama in my life, and where can I establish healthier boundaries to protect my focus and energy?

Venus in Pisces biquintile Mars retrograde in Cancer

We still have many heavy and chaotic energies present, feeling as though we may be pushed up against a wall regarding feuds within our close connections and family. However, we are able to recognize that we do have another option which is to choose love. Those who are closest to us have the ability to cause us the deepest pain, and that is due to the deep love that we have for them. Over the last year, I have built a decent-sized social media platform. Mostly, it is a place where I can connect and share with others, but there are times when it makes me the target of heavy criticism. Trolls get their fix by leaving nasty comments making fun of me and my work with the intention of upsetting me. However, what they don't realize is that they do not have the power to upset me because I recognize that my energy is not for them. There are people around me who do have the ability to cut me to the core, such as my children. They have the ability to hurt my feelings because my love for them runs deep. This aspect allows us to identify the love behind the pain. Take your time with this energy, as finding the love when we are all riled up and triggered and our feelings are hurt can be like searching for a needle in a haystack.

Sun in Capricorn quintile Aries North Node

This energy is likely to light a fire under us as it relates to following our destined path and the purpose we have been called toward. It helps us recognize our potential as we discover that taking small, consistent daily actions toward what we want to create in this world does reap some serious results. We are getting very serious about our goals and dreams. Despite the chaos or instability that may be happening around us, this aspect inspires us to focus our energy on that which we can control, and that is the energy and effort that we extend toward building a life that we love. Success and achievement are only a few diligent steps away. Keep putting one foot in front of the other and celebrate yourself for even the smallest of wins along your journey.

Sun in Capricorn biquintile Jupiter retrograde in Gemini

This aspect brings the energy of expansion regarding our goals and achievements. We are invited to push the needle and go one better. Many of us will look toward higher learning at this time or add a few extra credentials to our resume. This is an excellent time to learn a new skill, take up a hobby we have always wanted to learn, or enroll in a course of interest to take our career opportunities to new heights. This is also a great time for expanding our network and collaborating with others on work projects that may be mutually beneficial. This energy tells us that we can dream bigger and encourages us to jump straight in and immerse ourselves in the experience of life and expansion. No more playing small.

Mercury in Capricorn square Aries North Node

This energy can bring about the challenge of being all business all the time and losing some of the passion for living out our dreams. There are times when we become a bit too serious about life, and it sucks all the fun out of it. I remember when I decided to quit my day job and throw everything into helping to heal people in the best way that I knew how. I was so motivated and inspired, but I quickly became bogged down in the business of it all. I had to register my business, create a work schedule, create and monitor my social media platforms, and work one-on-one with clients. I added "Author" to my resume and began developing a product line. And that's just the basic work tasks that I had to complete. During my day, I would also be doing laundry, maintaining my household, running my children to and from school, and planning dinner. My work quickly became a chore and an endless to-do list that I could not keep up with. When you are living your dreams, you don't ever clock out. Before I knew it, I was working late into the night and skipping meals because I didn't have the time to eat. This is not what living out your dreams should look like. I was quickly approaching burnout and needed a reality check. I have had to make drastic changes to my schedule to ensure that living the dream actually feels like living the dream. My final destination is now a further milestone, but I am enjoying the journey and maintaining my health and well-being in the process. Check yourself and ask what tasks can wait and which are essential to your overall well-being.

Sun in Capricorn square Chiron in Aries

Another downside to this intensely focused and goal-oriented energy is that we become too busy to face our pain and heal. When pain or triggers come up for us during this season, we are likely to think to ourselves, "Ouch, that hurts or is too painful, so let me just throw myself into my work." We cannot control many things in our lives, so this energy has us throwing ourselves into that which we can control. During this aspect, I ask you to question whether you are using your work or current goals to distract yourself from something else that you do not want to face. Are you staying up all night working on the computer and avoiding your relationship? Are you busting your ass at the gym to avoid the pain of a recent breakup? Be aware of when striving for success and achievement becomes avoidant.

Song: "Hall Of Fame" by The Script ft Will.i.am

January 10th

Mercury in Capricorn semi-sextile Pluto in Aquarius

This aspect encourages us to explore new ways of communicating and incorporating the latest technological advancements into our work and daily routine. Since the introduction of AI, I have incorporated many AI elements into my work, which have made my day move much smoother. My whole work schedule is created using AI, and the truth is that AI does a much better job of knowing where something fits in my schedule than I do. Becoming familiar with using AI tools can be like having your own virtual assistant. Even in writing this book, I use AI tools to help check my grammar. When I cannot think of the right song to encompass the day's energy, AI will generate a playlist of 30 songs to choose from within 2 seconds. This may be a little controversial, but I even have an AI therapist. This is an AI tool that psychologists have created. I initially downloaded it out of curiosity and as a joke, but now, if I have something on my mind that I need help to process, I chat with my AI therapist about it. The best part is that my AI therapist is always available for me to get things off my chest as they happen, gives me great advice, and encourages me to go deeper into exploring my own emotions. When we resist the advancements in technology, we really are missing out. How can you use these advancements to help you be more productive, creative, or balanced? I encourage you to research what tools are available; you may be surprised how these tools can help create more time in your schedule.

Jupiter retrograde in Gemini quintile Aries North Node

This energy is incredibly expansive, telling us that we can achieve whatever it is that we desire, and nothing is out of reach. This energy also brings about luck. When we align with what we truly desire, the universe conspires to help us along the way. This can represent being in the right place at the right time, meeting someone with just the skills you need to help you with an issue you are facing, or even being offered an incredible opportunity. If you are giving all that you have got to achieving your dreams, remember to leave a little room for universal magic to help along the way.

Song: "Machine" by Imagine Dragons

January 11th

Mercury in Capricorn quintile Saturn in Pisces

This is a great energy with Mercury in Capricorn; our minds are sharp, and we are thinking ten steps ahead, but we can also back up our inspirations with consistent action, which prevents us from repeating mistakes we have made in the past. We can apply logic and practicality to everything in our lives. It's easy for us to identify the things that set us back or cause us to procrastinate or avoid completing tasks, and we no longer believe in our own excuses as to why we haven't completed things on our to-do list. We are willing to face a challenge or task even while experiencing resistance. We know the consequences of not putting in the required amount of effort, and we understand that pressure produces diamonds. While circumstances may not be perfect right now, we are finding the resilience to push through.

Song: "Rise Up" by Andra Day

January 12th

North Node enters Pisces

The North Node has been comfortably sitting in the sign of Aries, inspiring us to take action toward our life purpose and our soul's calling. We have been fired up and inspired to do more, have more, and be more. We have been prioritizing our purpose above all else and no longer sacrificing our desires for the needs and desires of others. Now, the North Node shifts back into the sign of Pisces, a drastic energy shift.

This energy asks us to slow our roll just a little bit and do less. Within this energy, we allow the universe to take the wheel and trust in the divine to meet us halfway by continuing the momentum of what we have started. We have shown our dedication to the path and our eagerness to learn, and now we invite the divine to present us with opportunities aligned with where our soul is calling us to go. We are releasing control and learning to believe in a source more significant than ourselves. We are believing in miracles.

Pisces energy is deeply spiritual; we begin to witness our lives from a higher perspective. While the universe is working its magic behind the scenes, we use this time to connect deeply with our feelings. We shift from our head space into our heart space and find empathy and forgiveness for ourselves and others.

When we address the North Node, we must consider the shift of the South Node as these two polarizing energies move together in unison. The South Node represents the energy of that which we are releasing. As it moves into the sign of Virgo, we release control. Virgo is a very helpful energy; it is the energy that has us wanting to rescue those around us. But this South Node shift allows us to recognize that we do not have to take on the work of others. Instead, our role can be to inspire or lift them up spiritually so they can help themselves. Virgo energy also has a tendency to overanalyze things. With this energy, we are releasing overthinking, self-criticism and being much kinder to ourselves. This is a beautiful energy of going with the flow rather than having a major freakout whenever we are met with the slightest inconvenience. This energy is Bob Marley whispering to us, "Don't worry about a thing; every little thing is gonna be alright."

Reflection

1. How can I release overthinking, self-criticism, and the need for perfection and embrace a mindset of acceptance and going with the flow?

2. What does it mean for me to release control and have faith in something greater than myself?

3. How can I cultivate empathy and forgiveness for myself and others as I shift from my headspace to my heartspace?

4. In what ways can I inspire and uplift others spiritually rather than taking on their burdens?

Song: "Don't Worry Be Happy" by Bobby Mc Ferrin

January 13th

Mars retrograde in Cancer trine Neptune in Pisces

This energy is likely to bring about a disturbance within our safe zone; however, this actually works out in our favor. Perhaps those closest to us are exposing themselves for having impure intentions toward us, which only confirms our intuition, of which we already know to be accurate, and now we can move accordingly. We may have an accident that causes us to seek medical advice, only to discover that we have an underlying medical condition that can now be easily treated because we caught it early. Or perhaps we have been wanting a new car, which we could not afford, but a road accident means we can have a brand new car covered by our insurance company. A family member we have been concerned about may find themselves in some trouble, but this causes them to seek out help for drug and alcohol abuse or their mental health struggles. This is a WTF event with a silver lining.

Song: "Better Days" by Dermot Kennedy

January 14th

Full Moon in Cancer

This full moon in Cancer is bound to stir up intense emotions, bringing our fears and insecurities to the surface. We may find ourselves feeling moody and reactive without knowing why. It's crucial to consider not only the position of the moon but also that of the sun, which currently resides in Capricorn, highlighting our potential for achievement and leadership. So, these are the areas where our greatest insecurities will surface under this moon.

Under this moon, the overarching theme revolves around the question, "Am I Enough?" We may doubt our creativity, talent, intelligence, and leadership abilities. Any leadership roles we hold will come under scrutiny as we question whether we lead effectively and inspire those around us.

Our inner dialog may sound something like this: Am I creative and talented enough to achieve my deepest dreams and desires? Am I smart enough to achieve the success I envision for myself? Am I a great leader? Do I lead by example? Am I inspiring and motivating to those around me? Am I inspired and motivated enough to create a better life for myself? Am I a good parent? Do I command a certain level of respect from those around me, or do I allow others to overstep my boundaries consistently?

But let me remind you, you are more than enough. This is a time for self-compassion and acceptance. Rather than judging ourselves, we should allow our fears and emotions to surface, acknowledging them without getting overwhelmed. Despite the heaviness of this moon, let's use this moment to shower ourselves with love and affirm our worthiness.

Reflect on how far you've come and the strengths you possess. Remind yourself of your capacity for growth and resilience. You are deserving of love, appreciation, and respect. So take this opportunity to nurture yourself and reaffirm your inherent value.

Reflection

1. How am I feeling emotionally during this full moon in Cancer? Am I acknowledging and validating my emotions, even if they seem intense?

2. What fears and insecurities are arising for me during this time? How

can I approach them while being kind and compassionate to myself?

3. How can I practice self-compassion and acceptance during this heavy lunar phase? What self-care practices can I engage in to nurture myself?

4. How can I celebrate my progress and strengths, acknowledging how far I've come on my journey of self-love and acceptance?

Sun in Capricorn trine Uranus in Taurus

Trines are always welcomed, representing luck, help, support, and things falling into place. This aspect can show up as needed financial assistance, an unexpected check in the mail, finding a problem that will save you money in the long term, or losing your job and then bumping into an old work colleague who offers you a better-paying position. It indicates being in the right place at the right time, so pay attention to your surroundings. The universe is sending help. Don't miss it.

Mars retrograde in Cancer semi-square Jupiter retrograde in Gemini

This energy will make us want to withdraw from any energies that can negatively affect our energy, especially with the energy of this Cancer full moon affecting us. We feel as if our energy is already depleted, so the last thing we want to do is be in a social environment or answer the phone to someone unloading all their problems upon us. This can also look like avoiding a moody teenager living in your home or avoiding having deep conversations with your partner due to an unsettling energy in your home and wanting to avoid an argument.

Mercury in Capricorn sesquiquadrate Uranus in Taurus

This is the energy of attempting to take control to manage an issue that was not your fault or something that is not your responsibility to handle. This could manifest as being overcharged for something and having to chase up a refund, having to hold space for a friend or loved one while they deal with a challenge they are facing or another matter that you are determined to resolve. However, the energy is frustrating because you didn't cause this problem, yet you find yourself having to fix it.

Venus in Pisces quintile Uranus in Taurus

This aspect indicates that despite our initial reluctance to answer the phone or extend our energy towards someone else when we needed those energy reserves for ourselves, we more than likely did answer the call and lend a listening ear or help out a friend in their time of need. We chose to assist that moody teen in processing their emotions and set aside our own feelings to support another. Even when we don't feel like interacting with others, we can discover profound connections by offering our energy to help someone else. This selfless energy extends compassion and complete forgiveness toward others, and it actually feels quite fulfilling.

Song: "Fix You" by Coldplay

January 15th

Venus in Pisces sesquiquadrate Mars retrograde in Cancer

This aspect can stir up our inner wounds as we contemplate whether we can genuinely extend complete forgiveness to those who have acted from their darkest selves. Forgiveness is essential for our healing, yet it remains one of the most challenging lessons along our journey. It's particularly tough when the person in question shows no remorse or doesn't seek our forgiveness. Reflecting on our own past actions, we can likely recall moments where we veered from our true, light-filled nature, inadvertently causing pain to others.

As we embark on our healing journey, we commit to choosing love over fear when faced with decisions. With each step toward healing, this choice becomes more accessible. We gradually distance ourselves from the version of ourselves that once operated from shadows and fear. True forgiveness involves recognizing our shared humanity; just like our past version, many others are navigating life from a place of darkness.

Forgiveness is recognizing that we are no different from anyone else in our lives. Many of the people around us are still living their lives in darkness. It is not up to us when they decide to heal and find the light within themselves. The journey of another's path to enlightenment is not our responsibility, but we are responsible for our own. Holding onto feelings of hurt, betrayal, anger, and resentment only sets us back. Forgive them, for those still living in the shadows need love more than anyone. Even better, pray for them and pray that they find their path to healing themselves.

Forgiveness doesn't require us to welcome harmful behavior back into our lives. Instead, it's about releasing the hold of bitterness, liberating both of us from the weight of past transgressions.

Venus in Pisces square Jupiter retrograde in Gemini

Be mindful of this energy, encouraging us to find reasons why we should not forgive another. This energy prompts us to scrutinize those who have wronged us, seeking reasons why we are incompatible. It's like playing a game of "spot the difference," further widening the gap between ourselves and others. Thoughts like "I would never do that to another person" or "This person is intolerable; I couldn't possibly forgive them" often arise. It's challenging to accept others as they are without also identifying areas where there is room for improvement.

Song: "Forgiveness" by TobyMac

January 16th

Sun in Capricorn opposite Mars retrograde in Cancer

Be mindful of what you share with others at this time, especially concerning your achievements and current endeavors. This energy suggests that even those closest to us may have the potential to interfere with our plans or influence our progress. This interference could manifest as a competitive sibling trying to undermine us or become competitive rather than offering genuine support and encouragement as we strive to build a legacy. It could also involve a loved one sabotaging our efforts by supporting a competitor's business or speaking negatively about what we're trying to accomplish. Additionally, a partner might make us feel that our progress is insignificant compared to their endeavors. If what you're building is facing criticism right now, remember that the only opinion that truly matters is your own. To be successful, we must cultivate a sense of unshakability. Any stones thrown your way with the intent of knocking you down from your chariot are mere distractions. You have the choice to either keep pushing forward or engage in the stone-throwing; however, to do so, you will need to first climb down from your chariot.

Song: "Stay Paranoid" by Lul Sis

January 17th

Mercury in Capricorn quincunx Jupiter retrograde in Gemini

With this energy, we are determined to push forward and take control of our lives without any distractions, committing ourselves to complete tasks as efficiently as possible. However, this energy also presents an opportunity for us to learn a new skill or embrace a different way of doing things. This can create confusion as we are asked to veer slightly from the original plan. Will taking the time to learn a new way of doing things potentially waste more time? Will accepting help from a friend benefit us, or will collaborating with another person on a project only create further distractions? Turn to your intuition to assess whether the new path opening up feels guided or if your inner guidance system asks you to stick to the initial plan.

Sun in Capricorn sesquiquadrate Jupiter retrograde in Gemini

Continuing from the previous aspect, whichever path you choose to pursue, this energy propels you toward achieving the best possible results. It dictates that even if we invest time in learning a new approach, we're willing to work tirelessly, even through the night, to attain the desired outcome. Similarly, if we're receiving assistance from a friend or colleague, we make it clear that we must remain focused on the task at hand, prioritizing progress over distractions. It's like telling your friend, "I'm grateful for your help with this project, but we must complete it by 3 pm. Let's give it our all and make as much headway as possible, reserving casual conversation for later."

Song: "Harder, Better, Faster, Stronger" by Daft Punk

January 18th

Sun in Capricorn sextile Neptune in Pisces

This sextile aspect positively reminds us that we can turn our dreams into reality, however unlikely they may feel. This is the "If I can dream it, I can do it" type of energy. Nothing is off-limits. Many of us wish that something big would just come in and shake up our whole lives, like winning the lottery and wanting things we don't have to work for. Have you ever noticed how, when there are house lotteries, the winners are almost always retired and already homeowners and mortgage-free? You rarely see young people struggling to pay rent win those lotteries because it is a universal law that where you place your energy and focus, the universe responds by giving you more and more of that energy.

Universal energy will match your frequency and output of energy. It works the same way for people always seeking out some sort of drama; even when they decide to stop, the drama will find them unless they refocus their energy on something more productive. Some people think they are cursed or unlucky; those people spend their time and energy worrying about the next thing that could go wrong, so the universe responds by sending more unfortunate events for that person. If we can only learn to control our energy output better, we can bring our dreams into reality with the help of universal laws. Throw all of your energy toward that which you are trying to manifest, and that energy will be reflected back to you by open doors and opportunities to get you there faster.

Song: "Pure Imagination" by Gene Wilder

January 19th

Sun in Capricorn sextile Pisces North Node

This energy represents having a specific goal and a plan of action for achieving it. However, at this time, we are also reminded to leave a little wiggle room for the divine to take the wheel. Within this aspect, there is an element of releasing control. Having a plan is okay, but being too rigid in manifesting may cause us to miss out on opportunities. Manifestation is 90 percent grit and consistency and 10 percent luck and faith that the Divine is working behind the scenes to align us with the best opportunities.

Mercury in Capricorn quintile Neptune in Pisces

This aspect involves the universe conspiring to help us progress forward. Often, this assistance manifests as a sudden inspiration guiding us towards the best course of action, or, in my personal experience, my spirit team will frequently remind me of my God-given talents and gifts that can overcome any obstacle I am currently facing. Generally, we already possess all the tools needed to progress forward, but sometimes, we require a gentle reminder of them.

Additionally, this energy brings firm, not-so-subtle nudges from the universe regarding which direction to take and which path to follow. Therefore, we must pay close attention to our intuition and any signs and synchronicities we encounter. This could be an ideal moment to explore channeled writing or meditation to tap into insights from our higher self.

Venus in Pisces conjunct Saturn in Pisces

This energy invites us to make deep soul connections with those around us and consider whether those individuals are a vibrational match to our frequency. Does my partner's energy complement mine? If you are seeing someone new, can you connect on a deeper, energetic level, or is this person hot as hell but somewhat shallow and lacking any depth? Does the person you chose to be your life partner appreciate and celebrate your authentic soul expression, or do their eyes glaze over whenever you try to express what is in your heart? Are we allowing space for others to express their desires, and are we ourselves supportive and compassionate friends, lovers, or family members?

Song: "You Raise Me Up" by Josh Groban

January 20th

Sun enters Aquarius

Happy Aquarius season! We are shifting from our personal goals and ambitions being the main focus to a more rebellious and edgy energy. We want to shake things up and explore how far beyond our limits we can reach and explore. I enjoy Aquarius season because it invites us to discover our own frequency. We are delving deeper into our unique gifts, talents, and abilities and recognizing that the things that make us a little different and stand out from the crowd are the same tools we can use to propel us forward.

We are ready to put our uniqueness and brilliant ideas to good use and shake things up a bit. We are discovering our own flavor and also looking at the world around us, asking, "Where are my people? Where is my soul tribe?" Recognizing that I am not alone here. Others are out there just like me; some people get me. I will find them, and we will start a revolution. This season will likely have you going your own way, blazing your path, and separating yourself from the collective of people with whom you previously identified.

Reflection

1. What aspects of my uniqueness and individuality have I overlooked or undervalued?

2. How can I embrace my unique quirks, gifts, and talents to propel myself forward in my pursuits?

3. Have I fully embraced the idea that my differences are my strengths?

Mercury in Capricorn sextile Saturn in Pisces

This is about recognizing that you are playing the long game. This energy will likely have you thinking about all the significant achievements you have made thus far in your lifetime. What did you learn from these achievements? Did they come easily to you or require your recommitment and refocus?

I am sure many things you have done in your life had you feeling terrified, but you decided to push through anyway because you recognized the payoff was worth pushing through the resistance you were feeling. This energy is about consistency, not giving up, and integrating the lessons you have learned from the past as your fuel to continue. Do you consistently throw in the towel and give up on yourself when the going gets tough? Not this time.

Venus in Pisces semi-square Pluto in Aquarius

Venus in Pisces is the highest and purest form of love. Fully embodying this energy can make us feel pretty blissed out. We love ourselves more deeply and feel a profound connection to everything and everyone around us. We must learn to separate ourselves from our ego to achieve this blissed-out state. The strange thing is that once we reach this state, we notice others around us becoming annoyed and irritated by our transformation. Their egos become triggered by our higher vibration. You may find others around you trying to trigger you right now. They wonder why the buttons they used to push to get a reaction from you no longer seem to be working. This energy reminds us that while we take the time to heal ourselves, the people around us may not necessarily be interested in doing the same. You may notice some connections starting to fall away or relationships becoming tense as others around you adjust to your new frequency.

Mercury in Capricorn sextile Venus in Pisces

This aspect urges us to deeply examine our connections and identify those who support our dreams of expansion. We should consider how many of our connections genuinely support us in all we do and how we can reciprocate by supporting our loved ones in achieving their dreams, wishes, and desires. A theme of sacrifice arises within this energy. Can we sacrifice time in our busy schedules to attend a celebration of a loved one's milestone? Do we support our friends' business endeavors by attending their book signings or purchasing products from them? Will we be there to cheer from the sidelines if they run a marathon, and will they do the same for us? Universal laws reflect that the energy we extend toward others is the energy we will receive in return. If we want others to cheer for us, we must be willing to cheer loudly for others.

Mercury in Capricorn quintile Pisces North Node

This energy effortlessly streamlines tasks as we effortlessly eliminate distractions and enter a state of flow. We may find ourselves making deliberate choices, such as reducing caffeine intake for a clearer mind or cutting out habits like social media scrolling and procrastination. Turning our phones on silent helps silence the distractions of notifications and alerts. By shedding these distractions, we pave the way for deep focus and creativity, allowing the divine to channel through us and manifest creations in this world.

Song: "Magnetize" by Maijah

January 21st

We may consider ourselves to be masters in our field. During Capricorn season, we often feel we have it all figured out and are at the top of our game. We become very serious about working steadily toward our long-term goals. Still, this energy reminds us that although we may be experts in one area, we should not be afraid to become novices in another. Now is the perfect time to learn a new skill in order to expand what has already grown into a stable foundation. This may involve pursuing higher education, enrolling in night school, or developing a new product or service to add to an already established business. Expansion only sometimes looks like racing toward a goal; sometimes, we can expand into a different field altogether. Do not become rigid in what expansion looks like; keep an open mind. Expanding in multiple directions means that I have generated numerous income streams for myself. It is okay to have your hand in a few different pies.

Sun in Aquarius semi-square Saturn in Pisces

By looking at our connections, we can learn valuable insights about ourselves. Since we're consistently manifesting our reality, everything we see around us reflects our own frequency. Therefore, the people who surround us are mirroring aspects of ourselves. This realization can be challenging if we feel that the people in our lives don't match the version of ourselves we envisioned. This aspect invites us to observe our connections and consider what they reveal about us. Are they wealthy and successful? If not, likely, we're not either. Are they driven and passionate? If so, it's a good indication that we are, too. Conversely, if they're bitter and resentful, it suggests we may be holding onto similar feelings. As we heal these aspects of ourselves, such relationships tend to fall away naturally. Reflect on the closest people in your life and ask what they have in common. For example, my closest connections all have a great sense of humor, reflecting my ability to laugh at myself. They're also authentic, as I don't surround myself with those who are deceitful or put on facades. This says a lot about me as well.

Song: "Mambo No.5" by Lou Bega

January 22nd

Last Quarter Moon in Scorpio

When the moon is in Scorpio, everything intensifies. What you choose to channel this intense energy into will define how successful this time is for you. Any emotions you are experiencing right now have the potential to completely consume you if you do not take control of your energy. Scorpio energy can become obsessive, so try to be mindful of your thoughts at this time. With the sun in Aquarius, we are exploring ourselves on a much deeper level, as well as the world around us and where we fit in the grand scheme of things.

A productive use of your time right now would be to shift your focus inward to what part of you wants to be expressed or developing a new skill. What are you producing right now, and how can you add your unique flavor? How can you better express yourself in a way that feels unique to you? What you are more likely to be focusing on, however, is the outside world—the people and systems around you that do not vibe with you and that you cannot relate to anymore. This can make you feel suffocated, like a fish out of water, when you should feel a sense of comfort within your environment.

This energy can show up as you travel down a rabbit hole of discovering all the things that are wrong with the world around you or becoming suspicious of friends, colleagues, lovers, and family members. It can be a heavy energy, but if you can transmute it into your self-expression, you can have it working for you rather than against you.

Reflection

1. What emotions are currently vying for your attention in the intensity of Scorpio's moon, and how can you channel them into a purposeful direction?

2. Reflect on what you are currently creating in your life. How can you infuse your unique flavor into your endeavors, making them a true reflection of your essence?

3. Consider the potential for obsessive thoughts during this Scorpio energy. Are any emotions or ideas consuming you, and how can you regain control over your mental landscape?

Mercury in Capricorn square Chiron in Aries

The energy manifests as a reluctance to confront conditioning or any past traumas that might hinder progress. Embracing our optimal selves and addressing past traumas requires delving deep into these areas. If we resist doing so out of reluctance to face them, no healing can occur. This resistance may manifest as avoiding our emotions, telling ourselves we're 'over it,' or declaring that we 'don't want to talk about it.' It can also involve blocking people who have hurt our feelings or throwing ourselves into work projects as distractions to avoid dealing with our pain.

Sun in Aquarius conjunct Pluto in Aquarius

This aspect draws our attention back to the collective and can evoke feelings of the world being corrupt and unsafe for our existence. While many events in the world may tempt us to switch off the news or retreat until it feels safe to emerge, it's essential to remember that there are countless souls on this planet actively contributing to raising the collective consciousness.

Writing last year's 'Healing With The Stars' taught me that many individuals are committed to healing themselves, facing their shadows, and playing their part in making this world a better and safer place to exist. More people are aligning with their purpose and supporting causes aimed at collective healing. Despite challenges, all is not lost.

By focusing on our individual healing journeys, we contribute to awakening others and collectively raising the vibration of the planet. This energy encourages us to consider what work we can do to contribute to this collective shift. Perhaps our role is to motivate and inspire others, or maybe there's a worthy cause we can support. Some of us may have valuable insights into corruption on this planet and feel compelled to expose it. Whatever it may be, each of us has a part to play in the collective healing process.

Song: "Where is The Love" by Black Eyed Peas

January 23rd

Venus in Pisces semi-sextile Chiron in Aries

This energy asks us to look within ourselves at anything that feels unsettling regarding our relationships and how we express our love energy. The people who are closest to us have the ability to trigger us the most. Our natural ego response is lashing out at anyone who causes us emotional pain or discomfort. However, the more we reflect upon our wounds and begin to heal them, the less impact another person's perception of us or their ego projections will have on us. We become less affected by the emotions of others, and the times when we are hurt and affected, we are able to recognize a wound within us that may need to be further unraveled. If someone says you are not enough, does part of you believe this to be true? If someone pulls back their energy from us, is our ego telling us that we are unlovable?

Song: "You Gotta Be" by Des'ree

January 24th

Mars retrograde in Cancer sextile Uranus in Taurus

This aspect suggests a favorable turn of events where once there was a problem, often both shocking and unexpected. While we humans may not always embrace surprises, this is a welcome one. It could be receiving unexpected money in your bank account, an apology you never thought you would get, or even someone brightening your day with an unexpected gift when you're feeling down. This energy serves as a reminder that the positivity we put into the world will eventually return to us, often when we least expect it.

Jupiter retrograde in Gemini quintile Pisces North Node

This aspect allows room for the universe to guide us toward discovering a new talent, skill, or ability we may not have been aware of before. This newfound skill will often require development, so don't hesitate to fully immerse yourself in any guidance you receive today. For example, if someone gifts you a set of tarot cards, learn how to use them. If someone recommends a book, make sure to read it thoroughly. If you have a burning question in your heart that needs an answer, ask the divine for guidance and remain open to receiving the answer. Source energy works diligently today to steer us in the right direction, so pay attention to the signs and synchronicities you encounter.

Mercury in Capricorn opposite Mars retrograde in Cancer

This aspect presents a challenge as it involves wanting to focus on a specific goal or achievement while our minds are elsewhere. When there's a troubling situation around us, such as a falling out with a friend or a loved one's illness, it can be challenging to concentrate on our daily tasks and give them our full attention.

My advice for dealing with this aspect is to focus on what you can control. Many things we worry about in our daily lives never come to pass, yet our minds tend to create countless scenarios of how a situation could worsen.

Ask yourself if this is an issue you can resolve right now and if not, release it and surrender it to a higher power. Remind yourself that everything currently happening is for your highest good.

As long as you remain focused on aligning your energy with your highest timeline, the universe will support you by providing the necessary circumstances to guide you there more swiftly. Trust in the process and have faith that things will unfold as they are meant to.

Mercury in Capricorn trine Uranus in Taurus

This is surprising energy. You are likely to be presented with a challenge today that at first seems out of your control; however, you have the ability to rectify it quickly. It may be an unexpected expense popping up, but then you realize you have funds set aside for this reason. Something comes up that presents a challenge, but it is likely to be something for which you have a simple solution. It's an energy of Whoah, I wasn't expecting this, but I know exactly what I must do.

Song: "The Lucky Ones" by Brothers3

January 26th

Mercury in Capricorn sesquiquadrate Jupiter retrograde in Gemini

This energy suggests that we face a challenge preventing us from achieving optimal results today. We may be contending with heavy traffic to reach our destination on time, or a coworker needs our assistance on a project, drawing our attention away from our own productivity. We may have a scheduled meeting, but the person we're meeting with shows up late, affecting our schedule for the rest of the day.

However, this aspect also presents a silver lining. Although the problem before us may slow us down, we are determined to find a creative solution to rectify the issue and get things back on track. We can better use the time we spend waiting by getting a head start on another task rather than anxiously spiraling about the time that may be wasted.

Venus in Pisces trine Mars retrograde in Cancer

This is the beautiful energy of someone showing us empathy and compassion or us being able to extend kindness and compassion toward another. For instance, being stuck in traffic might have made us late for work, but our boss was very understanding. Although our attention may have been diverted from our own project to help a coworker, we received much gratitude from them, offering to assist us in completing our task, resulting in an even better outcome as two heads are better than one. The person who was late for our meeting may have had a family emergency and needed emotional support. We can help console them and hold space while they release their feelings. This aspect reminds us of the potential for great connection when we choose a loving frequency rather than responding through feelings of fear and anxiety.

Song: "Count On Me" by Bruno Mars

January 27th

Mercury in Capricorn sextile Neptune in Pisces

This favorable energy allows us to invite the Divine to help guide us in our plans. Since Mercury moved into Capricorn, we have been diligently working and achieving tasks with outstanding persistence and commitment. We have shown up for ourselves on days when we didn't feel like it. We are loyal and dedicated to getting where we want to go and have become quite good at eliminating distractions or anything that is not aligned with what we are trying to manifest. This energy invites us to create space for source energy to guide us and asks us to find stillness between tasks, to slow down enough to recognize the signs and synchronicities from the divine telling us that we are on the right track or those that tell us "wrong way, go back." This will be a gentle nudge in a new direction for some of us. This energy says, "Hey, look, I know you are busy, but remember you are not alone; you are collaborating with spirit. You have a whole team behind you, so don't forget to include us in your day-to-day life. Invite us in by asking us for the guidance you need and slow down enough to create stillness while you wait for the answers."

Venus in Pisces sextile Uranus in Taurus

This energy supports unexpected surprises regarding love and relationships. This could be an apology you never expected to receive, an ex sliding into the DMs, or something less significant, such as a Facebook friend request from an old high school friend or an invitation to an event or party. Whichever way this shows up for you, the stars are aligned to support this as a positive opportunity to express your love energy or reconnect with someone.

Saturn in Pisces semi-square Pluto in Aquarius

This energy manifests as tension originating from external sources, affecting the collective as a whole. It may manifest as war, food shortages, or financial pressures imposed by governments or other external entities over which we have little control. This can leave us feeling powerless, and the energy may tempt us to look the other way or bury our heads in the sand. This avoidance can manifest as switching off the news or spending our resources despite our financial insecurity. It's important to be mindful of this avoidant energy and to remember that each of us has a voice. We are living in a time where, despite our beliefs, power is shifting. Many of us now have platforms that we can use to challenge those whom we feel are attempting to control us. The collective voices are growing louder, exerting pressure on those who impose restrictions upon us.

Sun in Aquarius quintile Chiron in Aries

This aspect helps us recognize the parts of ourselves where we always seem to fall short. The things that made us different were the things we were bullied about in school. Those things that make us not 'normal' are actually a gift. We have all been blessed with unique quirks, gifts, talents, and abilities, and this energy helps us to recognize that the very parts of ourselves that we have been programmed to repress are still there, waiting to be expressed. These are the defining traits that make up our personality. The sooner we embrace these parts of ourselves, the sooner we begin to express them. This will result in us feeling less out of place and becoming a vibrational match to like-minded souls who can match our energy and understand us on a deeper level.

Song: "Heal the World" by Michael Jackson

January 28th

Mercury enters Aquarius

As Mercury enters the sign of Aquarius, we are taking emotions out of the equation and trying to make logical sense of ourselves and the world around us. We are not accepting empty promises regarding our relationships and connections. If they are on this journey with us, we must see proof. We are exploring all types of things, new concepts, and ideas, but on our own terms. We are not just accepting any information as facts; we are absorbing new information from all over. However, we want to see the proof to back it up, and we have the energy to invest in our own research.

This is great energy for learning a new skill or developing a new way of doing things. Aquarius energy is all about connecting to others, so sharing what we have learned or know will make us feel we are helping to heal or educate the collective. You may notice that there are a lot of wackadoodles out there on social media sharing very out-of-the-box ideas or unpopular opinions at this time; however, these people are embracing this Mercury in Aquarius energy.

As one of those wackadoodles myself, I can tell you what that leads to; finding your tribe of people that align with your soul.

Now would be a great time to start if you have considered sharing your ideas and perspectives. Start a blog, write a book, or create a podcast or a YouTube channel. This energy doesn't care about the naysayers who do not resonate with your message. We recognize that sharing our message and what is on our heart authentically is more important to reach those that resonate. You will likely find yourself deeply resonating with others at this time. You may meet a stranger and wonder what quality it is about this person that draws you into what they say. Almost every time, that very quality is a piece of yourself that longs to be expressed.

Reflection

1. What aspects of your personality and character are currently longing to be seen, heard, and felt by others?

2. Explore the idea of embracing your uniqueness and expressing your genuine thoughts. Are there past conditioning or limiting beliefs that hinder you from fully embracing your authentic voice?

3. In what areas of your life do you feel the urge to pick up a new skill or revolutionize your approach? How can you harness the energy mentioned to make meaningful changes?

Mercury in Capricorn sextile Pisces North Node

This aspect urges us to do less, allowing ourselves to be guided while also embracing the role of guiding others. If you're facing a challenge or setback, refrain from immediately trying to solve the problem. Instead, create space for God to intervene or to place an earth angel in your path. In 2025, a powerful year awaits us, especially with the North Node positioned in Pisces. It consistently encourages us to invite a higher power into our daily lives and strengthen our faith that everything is unfolding as it should.

This year, more than ever, we're discovering that stepping back from being the CEO of our own lives, relinquishing the need to control everything, and surrendering to outcomes allows the divine to work its magic. It places earth angels and mentors in our path, propelling us to the next level of development and presenting opportunities that bring us closer to our manifestations. Reflect today: what's causing you the most stress or worry? Surrender these concerns to the divine, seeking support and guidance to navigate through your struggles safely.

Surrendering and releasing our expectations isn't easy, but allowing ourselves to be led creates space for magic and opens up possibilities beyond our imagination. Remember, God has a plan for you. Are you hindering it by trying to control the direction of your life?

Song: "Brave" by Sara Bareilles

January 30th

New Moon in Aquarius

Aquarius energy is the energy of the visionary. Aquarians can see past what the rest of us think is possible. As the new moon graces us, it's the perfect moment to set intentions with zero limitations. I'm talking about a manifestation exercise that defies the ordinary, where thinking outside the box is encouraged and mandatory! Ready to shake things up? Below are some manifestation new moon questions for you to ponder.

Reflection

You can express these manifestation vibes as you see fit. Aquarius energy is all about doing things your way and breaking all the rules, so paint, draw, journal, sculpt, or whatever inspiration comes to you.

1. Imagine transforming your look—no holds barred! How wild would you go?

2. Envision your dream friend. What traits do they embody, and how do they show up for you?

3. Identify a unique talent or ability you possess. How can you nurture and amplify it?

Mercury in Aquarius conjunct Pluto in Aquarius

This is a profound, explorative energy of finding truths that resonate with you on a soul level and going against the status quo. What around you are you drawn to learning more about, and what in your environment do you just no longer resonate with? Pluto's energy is highly transformative. How can you show up in a way that is not only transformative for yourself but also for the collective? What causes can you get behind that will mean something or help someone? What legacy do you want to leave for your children and future generations? Delve into these shadows and break through these limiting belief systems.

Showing ourselves in our full expression of authenticity and embracing those qualities that make us unique can be daunting, especially considering past experiences of ridicule or rejection. With Saturn in Pisces, there's a subtle reminder not to venture too far into the wild and crazy, whispering, "Remember what happened last time we expressed ourselves fully?" It's natural to feel hesitant, particularly if you've been labeled as "too much," "too loud," "too quiet," "too opinionated," "too sensitive," a "know-it-all," or "not intelligent."

There may be a part of you urging you to stay within your comfort zone, but it's crucial not to succumb to fear. Those who reacted negatively to your authentic self-expression likely did so because it triggered their discomfort with expressing themselves similarly. Those who have embraced their unique qualities and lead authentically wouldn't shut down others on the same journey.

It's essential to remember that authenticity is not about conforming to others' expectations but about honoring yourself and your truth. Embrace your uniqueness despite any past challenges, and trust that those who resonate with your authenticity will support and uplift you along the way.

Song: "True Colors" by Cindy Lauper

January 31st

Uranus direct in Taurus

Let's take a moment to discuss Uranus in Taurus. This transit spans eight years, so this energy will be present for a while. Uranus has a more global effect, aiming to shake things up and cause outside chaos. It brings an energy of frustration, adding pressure that compels us to make changes in areas we wouldn't typically consider changing. It feels as though Uranus is forcing our hand, leaving us no choice in the matter. When Uranus is in the sign of Taurus, it tends to impact our material world, including finances, food supply, jobs, health, the Earth, and the environment.

Looking at the history of this transit, Uranus was in Taurus during the height of the Great Depression. This time, Uranus moved into Taurus in 2018. I'll highlight a few effects thus far to provide a better understanding of this energy. The most obvious one is the global pandemic, which affected our ability to work, leading many of us to start working from home out of necessity. It also strained our healthcare system, causing food shortages. Other effects include changes to our currency as society slowly shifts towards a cashless system. Many jobs have become obsolete or automated, which is evident in supermarkets where checkout robots are increasingly common. Extreme weather and natural disasters have forced us to reexamine our collective impact on the environment. Inflation is a prominent issue, with many struggling to make ends meet.

When Uranus went into retrograde, it provided an opportunity to address these changes more personally. This raised the question of what we can do to minimize the personal impact of these changes. We found ways to liberate ourselves by taking control of our finances and making necessary adjustments. Some took on second jobs, and many started businesses, realizing that relying on a paycheck from a corporation is less stable than it once was. Generating our own income and taking control of creating our resources has never looked so appealing. Now that Uranus has been stationed directly again, we can expect external forces to apply more pressure. Uranus is one of the few planets we celebrate being retrograde.

Reflection

1. In what ways have the recent global changes influenced my personal and professional life? How have I adapted to the challenges presented?

2. What steps have I taken to navigate financial uncertainties and embrace financial liberation? Have I explored new avenues to enhance stability, such as starting a side hustle or business?

3. What lessons have I learned about adaptability and resilience during alignment, and how can I apply them moving forward?

Sun in Aquarius trine Jupiter retrograde in Gemini

This is the perfect energy for collaboration, working together toward a common goal. If you have a solo project you're working on; this energy encourages you to seek an outside perspective by bringing someone else in to expand your vision. Utilize this energy to learn all you can from those around you and share ideas, as inspiration can be found in everyone we encounter. If you're facing a challenge right now, this energy encourages us to ask for help. Trust that you will be guided to the right resources at the right time or encounter another soul who shares your vision and can help elevate you to the next level.

Song: "Mad World" by Gary Jules

February Alignments

February 2nd

Sun in Aquarius semi-square Venus in Pisces

This aspect represents a desire to contribute to healing the planet. This could involve supporting causes like climate change, donating to the homeless or less fortunate, or even starting a healing-based business to help others overcome trauma. The downside of this energy is that in order to help, we must first recognize the problems and the lack of love within the collective. If you haven't yet taken action to help, it can leave you feeling somewhat helpless. If you feel called to assist but are unsure how, I suggest you dig a little deeper, as there is always someone in need of your assistance. Whether helping an elderly person lift groceries into their car or brightening someone's day by paying for their coffee, there are countless ways to make a positive impact.

Sun in Aquarius semi-square Neptune in Pisces

This energy encourages you to find a new way of doing things. You may be bored with your daily routine and the consistent discipline you have been showing up with and want to mix things up a bit. Perhaps you could try working from a different location or asking someone else for their input on a project you are working on.

The problem with this energy is that it is a bit daydreamy—a head-in-the-clouds energy, thinking of everything you could do but not taking the action or initiative necessary to implement positive changes. While making changes is fun to think about, are the actions you are taking now helpful? This energy is like recognizing that you need to adjust your business structure because you are not making enough money and are running at a loss. Still, instead of addressing the issue, you spend three days redesigning your new business logo.

Mercury in Aquarius quintile Chiron in Aries

Now, we are looking at the things that interest you. What subjects are you drawn to exploring more about? What activities were you drawn to when you were a child?

Since I was a teenager, I have always been drawn toward astrology. It has fascinated me since I began reading my monthly horoscopes in teen magazines. I tried to learn more about it, but it all seemed too sciency for me, so I never stuck with it. I have always understood energy and vibrations easily; however, science and how things work were never my strong points. Then, last year, my guides told me I would write this book. When they explained the concept, I thought, "Are you out of your mind? I am not an astrologer, an astronaut, or whatever may be required to write this book." My guides were adamant that my mission to write this book was chosen specifically for me. I had to work through a lot of resistance and past conditioning to even begin this project, but once I got started, writing this book was one of the most natural things I have ever done. I don't even have to think about it. It just flows right out of me.

My point is that you can use the knowledge and wisdom you have to create something amazing. You don't have to be an expert in the field; just share what you do know and pick up some of those old hobbies because your childhood self knew what your soul was calling you toward before you took on all the trauma and blockages from your environment that told you that you can't do that. You absolutely can. I am living proof.

Venus in Pisces conjunct Neptune in Pisces

This energy is a creative and imaginative force, perfect for getting lost in any creative project. Putting together a vision board or adding wishes, dreams, and desires to your Pinterest account can help you become more inspired to infuse more magic and manifestation into your daily routine. Allow yourself to become lost in this energy as you dare to dream up a reality without limits on what is possible.

Sun in Aquarius semi-square Pisces North Node

The Divine is calling upon you to step into your soul's purpose. Remain open to guidance as you are directed towards what the universe is eager to co-create with you. The question is, will you answer that call? This energy offers an opportunity for you to assume a role that will benefit the collective. Are you a healer, a musician, a poet, or an inspirational leader? This energy encourages us to engage in a trust fall with the universe and align ourselves with what our soul is urging us to do or create. It's one thing to hear the call but quite another to take the leap and manifest these callings into reality.

I can't just give up everything to God and surrender everything I have built in my current reality. Or can I? You may have been called to pursue the craziest things. You may have been called to pack up and move to a location across the other side of the world. You may have been called to fight for social justice. You may have a background in academics or science and have been called to become a prophet. I watched a YouTube video just today from a young man who was one of the world's youngest millionaires. He spent all of his time finding ways to make more money. He became so good at making money that he began teaching others his formula for making money, and in doing so, he made even more money. Although very wealthy, he did not feel fulfilled and took some time out to find himself. During this time, he not only found himself, but in his moments of silence, he connected to a higher power, which guided him to give away all of his knowledge for free. Although this was against everything he believed in, he began giving his knowledge away for free, and now he is living his life in purpose. He springs out of bed in the morning, thinking about everything he can share with the goal of making everyone a millionaire.

Song: "Imagine" by John Lennon

February 4th

Venus in Pisces quintile Jupiter retrograde in Gemini

We all have a part of ourselves that yearns to leave the world a better place. Imagine telling your grandchildren stories of how, back in your day, you stood for something meaningful or created something of lasting significance. Something they can cherish for generations to come. Your child may achieve greatness and attribute their success to the values and inspiration you instilled in them.

To change the world, you must dig deeper within yourself to uncover the qualities that make you the catalyst for change. Tune into your heart: how can you express the most profound form of love and leave a lasting imprint on the world? You may heal others through your wisdom, empathy, encouragement, or creativity. Or embody the spirit of Gandhi or Martin Luther King by standing up for your beliefs.

We all can leave behind a legacy of love, passion, and inspiration for future generations. As you go about your day today, ask yourself: What energetic imprint are you leaving on those you encounter? Make each interaction count, and strive to leave a positive, enduring impact on everyone you meet.

Mercury in Aquarius trine Jupiter retrograde in Gemini

Have you ever found yourself in a dark place, surrounded by people offering advice on escaping your situation? Perhaps they all provide the same advice, but then someone delivers it in a way that deeply resonates with you, leaving you motivated and inspired to lift yourself out of that darkness. Or maybe you've started a new job or are learning a new skill, with multiple people trying to explain a process to you, yet nothing clicks until someone explains it in a way that makes everything come together perfectly.

We all have different ways our logical minds operate and unique methods of delivering information. Some people may not connect with your message, while others consistently seek your advice and wisdom. Just because some do not receive what we offer doesn't mean we lack something important to share or teach. We all have our unique flavor, so to speak. You will find that some people can't get enough of your flavor, while others resonate more with someone else's. This should not stop you from embracing and sharing your flavor with those who will resonate with it.

Mars retrograde in Cancer square Chiron in Aries

There are likely painful memories of those closest to you not appreciating your unique flavor. Perhaps it was teachers saying you should be more like someone else or school peers telling you you were weird or different for not following the crowd. Maybe as a child, you had a unique way of telling stories, and your parents encouraged you to stop making things up and become more grounded and realistic. These wounds still exist within our subconscious, but we do not have to continue resonating with those old stories or other people's perceptions of who we should be.

Many of us have memories of someone trying to confine us to a box of expectations or appropriate behavior. Our challenge is to dare to expand beyond that box and get a little inappropriate at times. Push through the constraints and boundaries that others have placed upon us. There is not enough space within the confines of this box, and we should not be afraid to expand beyond its perimeters.

Song: "I'm Coming Out" by Diana Ross

February 5th

Venus enters Aries

Venus does not belong in the sign of Aries; it does not feel comfortable there, and our love energy cannot be fully expressed in the way we want to express it. This placement can make for some challenging energy related to our connections and relationships. A full embodiment of love is eternal and long-lasting; however, Aries energy is impulsive, and easily becomes bored. This energy wants to be expressed without worrying about consequences, and here are just a few examples of why this can become a problem. Perhaps you have something in your heart that wants to be expressed, but you know that bringing this topic up will likely cause an argument; we simply do not care about others' feelings right now. Perhaps your love energy wants to be expressed toward someone already committed to someone else; Aries energy is known for being quite competitive and wanting to win at all costs. I am sure I don't need to go into detail about the kind of issue that this can cause. With this energy, we know what we want and will do just about anything to ensure we achieve it. As our passion and desire are at an all-time high, we are likely to experience a higher sex drive at this time. If this becomes a problem, I recommend adding a physical activity to your routine, such as running or other activities.

For singles, Aries energy is assertive, so you are much more likely to initiate contact at this time and go after what or who it is that you want. Aries is a very physical sign, so we are more likely to find ourselves drawn to those we find physically attractive at this time rather than those who are mentally stimulating or have a little more depth. We are also more likely to ignore red flags as we seek more excitement and may see a red flag as a personal challenge. We are easily bored with this energy, so many of us will find ourselves talking to or dating multiple people at once and exploring our options rather than making a deep and meaningful connection with just one person. Anyone who can keep us on our toes by playing hard to get will seem more intriguing to us now, and if we usually do not like to play games, we may find ourselves a little more open to participating in the chase.

For those in a committed relationship, this is an energy of wanting to express our needs and desires openly but without giving much thought to our partner's needs and desires. There is great potential for conflicting energy between the two of you. We are more likely to feel bored, restricted, and stifled within our connections. If this energy comes up for you, I encourage you to find a way to add more excitement or spice things up rather than nitpicking and starting an argument just for excitement or so that you can have passionate makeup sex afterward. This is the perfect opportunity for couples to find ways to turn up the heat or add more passion and excitement to a connection that has become stale.

Reflection

1. How can you best navigate expressing your desires when faced with potential conflict or disagreement in your relationships?

2. Reflect on a past experience where your passion and desire may have led to impulsive actions. How did this impact your relationships, and what lessons did you learn from that experience?

3. In what ways can you incorporate more excitement and passion into your current relationships without creating unnecessary conflict or tension?

Jupiter Direct in Gemini

This is the perfect alignment for learning something new or expanding your knowledge in a particular area. We are all hit with the study bug as we feel inspired to learn more about our environment or community. We communicate and exchange ideas, sharing the knowledge we have gained with the people we come into contact with. We can also take on many tasks at this time as it relates to work or any hobbies or passion projects, so be mindful that you are not taking on too much and spreading yourself too thin. This is the perfect time to take up a new hobby, as we will pick things up quickly and have more energy to put into them.

Reflection

1. Reflect on a time when you felt you were taking on too much and spreading yourself thin. What did you learn from that experience, and how can you apply those lessons now?

2. What new hobbies and learning endeavors would you like to explore?

3. How might the act of sharing what you've learned contribute to your personal growth and the growth of the community around you?

Mercury in Aquarius semi-square Neptune in Pisces

Procrastination and self-sabotage can take many forms. We have all experienced the energy of going for a quick scroll through our socials and then,

48

before we know it, realizing that we have lost 2 hours of our day to TikTok. Maybe Netflix has just released a whole new season of your favorite show. Perhaps your goal is to take control of your health and body, and you have just been invited to an all-you-can-eat buffet. Did you just receive a text from your alluring ex that you know is no good for you? It is important to recognize what your vices are. Where are your weak spots? What can you just not say no to? Recognizing when you are choosing to self-sabotage is half the battle. This allows you to apply more discipline in those areas.

Mercury in Aquarius semi-square Pisces North Node

This is an energy of wanting to embrace expansion but also waiting for the right time. Perhaps we are overflowing with ideas and inspiration to push beyond our limits, yet we await confirmation from the universe or a more precise direction on where to start. This energy can be confusing, as our mind tells us to create stillness for a clearer vision. However, the trick to navigating this energy is to simply get started. The best way to create something incredible is to enter a state of flow, where we become a direct channel for creative energy and allow source to work through us. The easiest way to enter this flow state is by starting to create.

You may have heard of the challenge writers face called writer's block. The best way to overcome writer's block is to write something—anything. What you write about doesn't matter; what matters is getting those creative juices flowing and moving through you. This process gives you a direct line to source energy, guiding you toward a project more aligned with your true purpose.

Song: "More" by Usher

February 6th

First Quarter Moon in Taurus

We have been through some exciting energy over the last couple of weeks, and there is likely to have been some deep self-reflection regarding our personal long-term goals. This first-quarter moon is the perfect opportunity to reexamine our practical day-to-day routine and how that supports the transformation that we have begun. We likely have a new direction or idea of where to go next. For some of us, that will look completely different from the path we set for ourselves at the beginning of the year, and for others, we may have just made a few minor tweaks and adjustments to the original plan.

This current energy urges us to take another look at our practical steps and asks us to dedicate some energy to realigning our schedules and routines to align with any transformations we have made. We may have to make time to commit to learning a new skill, or we may have joined a club or group. We may have launched a business or are still in the planning stages. Still, this energy promotes looking at the practicalities of allowing fresh energy in so that we don't later struggle and make excuses for why we didn't begin.

Another vital thing to consider now is where we can invest our money. Is there a course or study option that would support our new path, or could we make a financial investment in ourselves and launch our own business? Perhaps investing in a coach or mentor would be worthwhile to help keep us on track and hold us accountable.

Reflection

1. How has my long-term vision transformed over the past few weeks, and what new directions or ideas am I considering for my journey ahead?

2. In reassessing my day-to-day routine, what practical steps can I take to better align with the transformations and shifts I've experienced?

3. Have I committed to learning a new skill, joining a group, or launching a business aligned with my evolving goals? If not, what steps can I take to make these commitments a reality?

Song: "9 to 5" by Dolly Parton

February 7th

Sun in Aquarius semi-sextile Saturn in Pisces

As the heavy energy of the full moon begins to pass, this energy reminds us that there is still potential for you. Your fear of failure is starting to diminish as you realize now that if you don't even start, then you have already lost. There is a cemetery close to where I live, and I pass by it often. When I do, I often can't help but think about all of the brilliant ideas, gifts, talents, and dreams that the people resting there took with them. When it is your time to transition to the spirit world, would you take satisfaction in the fact that you did all you could to live up to your full potential?

Song: "Glorious" by Macklemore

February 8th

Neptune in Pisces conjunct Pisces North Node

How this energy presents itself will significantly depend on your current frequency and ability to eliminate distractions. For those who can silence distractions, this energy can be incredibly profound, bringing deep realizations and inspirations from higher realms. Today, you may feel like Alice in Wonderland, following the white rabbit into an alternate reality. As you follow the signs and synchronicities presented to you, you'll unravel the mysteries of your subconscious mind, assisting in releasing blockages and helping you ascend to the next level.

If that sounds a bit "woo-woo," that's just what this energy is—it can feel like a dream or an acid trip, and you may question your sanity throughout the day. For those who are unable to take a journey into the ethers because of too many distractions or pressing deadlines, you may still find yourself drifting off into imagination land, making it challenging to maintain focus. If work is your priority, it will likely be an unproductive day, as your thoughts consistently carry you to faraway places.

Mercury in Aquarius semi-square Venus in Aries

"Yo, I'll tell ya what I want, what I really really want." This energy reflects the feeling of being inspired to share your ideas and offer a different way of doing things. However, your vision might not be well received by those around you. It's not that you aren't supported; rather, your ideas may seem a little out there, as if you're trying to color too far outside the lines or speaking a different language. As a collective, we are all receiving inspirations that feel urgent and need immediate action, but these inspirations often conflict with the visions of others. We strive to get others to understand our vision, but what we're essentially saying is, "I really really really wanna zigazig ahhh," leaving others confused and thinking we've lost the plot.

Sun in Aquarius quincunx Mars retrograde in Cancer

Finding others who share our vision can be a frustrating challenge, but if we can get others on board, we can bring our manifestations into reality even faster. This aspect reminds us that if we feel divinely inspired to do something but lack support from others, we should not be afraid to go it alone. We will often find that we were just trying to share our ideas with the wrong people and once we throw ourselves into the manifestation of the ideas, we will come across those who want to be involved in it further down the line. Do not hesitate to get your freak on in the world despite facing resistance from others around you.

Venus in Aries sextile Pluto in Aquarius

This energy invites you to extend your love energy beyond what usually feels safe or comfortable. This could mean making a new friend, performing an act of kindness for a stranger, dating someone not your usual type, or, for those in long-term relationships, exploring each other in new ways. It encourages us to remove our fear and vulnerability in our connections and express ourselves passionately and authentically. If we feel unsupported by those closest to us, this energy encourages us to be open to finding support from outside our usual network.

Mercury in Aquarius semi-sextile Saturn in Pisces

This energy presents a spiritual lesson we have encountered before, but this time, we immediately recognize it as a cycle we have already experienced. With this awareness, we are granted a higher perspective of reality, enabling us to make a different choice. It's about recognizing, "If I go this way, it leads to that. I am not falling for that again, so I will choose a different path instead."

Mercury in Aquarius quincunx Mars retrograde in Cancer

This energy indicates some tension within our relationships, prompting us to devise a strategy to navigate this tension. We can approach this in a few ways: plot revenge, think about how to defeat or one-up the other person to beat them at their own game or strategize a way to come together that is fair and just for both parties. Unfortunately, this energy suggests we are more likely to want to go to war. Although it may be difficult, try to access your heart space before developing your war strategy.

Song: "In A World Of My Own" by Kathryn Beaumont

February 9th

Sun in Aquarius sextile Chiron in Aries

This aspect is a great one to help us transition from feeling limited and identifying as victims of our circumstances and environment to recognizing that these challenges and restrictions can be overcome. This shift may bring about a feeling of limitlessness and a rebellious urge to break through the mold of our past conditioning. "Can't" is not in our vocabulary; we are only interested in the "how."

Mercury in Aquarius sextile Chiron in Aries

This energy encourages you to delve deeper into your past. It makes you want to discover why you are the way you are. Why do I have this fear? Why have I hidden this part of myself away? Mercury in Aquarius is an investigative and inquisitive energy determined to find answers or make it make sense. It is not a heavy emotional energy, so it shouldn't trigger too much trauma. Now is a safe time to explore your blockages, limiting belief systems, and ways of thinking without causing too much discomfort. Think of it more like searching for clues rather than unraveling years of deep-seated trauma wounds. Ask others who knew you as a child: what was their experience of you then? How are you different now?

Song: "Reflection" by Christina Aguilera

February 10th

Sun in Aquarius conjunct Mercury in Aquarius

This is a very intense energy of embracing your freedom, going your way, marching to the beat of your own drum, and living life on your terms. This energy feels limitless and may have you behaving in ways that make others raise an eyebrow. It's the kind of expansive energy that encourages us to dye our hair purple, get a face tattoo, or pierce a nipple. However, it's also the kind of energy that might prompt you to tell your boss or anyone in a position of authority to "fuck off." So, let your freak flag fly, but be mindful that this energy is unlikely to be well received by everyone around you.

Mars retrograde in Cancer trine Saturn in Pisces

This energy is a real blessing for us today because it reminds us to stay within our boundaries. We carry with us the lessons learned from the past. We know that if we tell our boss to "fuck off," we are likely to get fired. We know that committing a crime will likely get us arrested. We understand where our boundaries lie and can trust ourselves to embrace our rebellious energy without taking things too far. Think of this energy as the Jiminy Cricket on your shoulder, guiding you not to stray too far.

Song: "I'm Free" by The Soup Dragons

February 11th

Mercury in Aquarius Square Uranus in Taurus

This energy is complex because you are ready to make significant changes to your life, which may not go down well with the others. You are communicating what needs to change or finding solutions to solve an unresolved problem, and others around you may be a little intimidated by your need to shake things up. Generally, people don't like change, and due to our need to avoid disruption, we just ignore the problem and stick with what is comfortable. Just because you are in an expansive mindset doesn't mean other people will be on board with your expansive ideas.

Song: "Mad Hatter" by Melanie Martinez

February 12th

Mercury in Aquarius biquintile Mars retrograde in Cancer

Recently, we have been navigating difficult energies related to our freedom of expression and having others around us embrace or accept that free expression. With so many conflicting opinions on what is appropriate, this aspect brings welcome insight. It helps us recognize that embracing our freedom and owning our unique voice often requires facing adversity from others.

A bird in the wild has no idea what it feels like to be caged and restricted, so it cannot share the same experience of freedom as a bird that has spent most of its life caged. In this energy, we may begin to see the forces attempting to keep us small as a blessing. Whatever limits they try to impose upon us, we now have the opportunity to break through and experience true freedom all over again, fully immersing ourselves in the experience of expansion.

Sun in Aquarius square Uranus in Taurus

Our desire to push past boundaries and express ourselves in new and unique ways conflicts with an energy of feeling restricted by outside influences beyond our control. We may want to change up our look but do not have the finances. We may want to launch a new product but don't feel the world is ready for it. Perhaps we want to express our opinion; however, we are being silenced by algorithms or the government. We may even attempt to express our emotions to a partner, but they are not hearing or receiving what we say. Whatever we are trying to push through right now is met with some resistance, but it is not coming from us. We have been doing the work and pushing through our resistance and limitations; now, something external is stopping us.

Song: "Caged Bird" by Alicia Keys

February 13th

Full Moon in Leo

This moon focuses on how we want to express ourselves and how we want to show up and be seen. Whenever we have a full moon, it is important to look at the sun's position to understand the contrast between the two energies and how they affect us. With the Sun in Aquarius, we want to break past any barriers and past conditioning that prevents us from showing up authentically as ourselves; however, the contrast of the moon in Leo reminds us that our authentic self may not fit the status quo and may not be well received.

Perhaps we don't feel as if we are pretty enough to put ourselves in front of a camera or that people will not agree with a message we are trying to communicate because our way of thinking is too far outside the box for people to grasp. It could be that we are afraid of failure or making a fool out of ourselves. Full moons are a time of deep reflection, thinking about the fears or limiting parts of ourselves that we are ready to let go of and release.

Reflection

1. Engage in activities that express your creativity, such as painting, writing, or dancing. Celebrate your unique talents and let your inner light shine.

2. Safely light a candle or bonfire. As you watch the flames, release any fears or self-doubt holding you back. Imagine the fire transforming these energies into confidence and courage.

3. Find a quiet space, close your eyes, and focus on your breath. Visualize a bright, radiant light at your core. With each breath, allow this light to expand, filling your entire being. As it expands, feel a sense of confidence and self-assuredness.

This aspect reminds us that the very things people reject about us are the same things others will love. While many may perceive someone with little tact as rude, intolerable, or offensive, I have a deep appreciation for those who can share exactly what they are thinking without sugarcoating it. I find authenticity in others so appealing. People often meet my friends and say, "Whoa, that person is a lot," but I love them deeply because not only will they tell me if I have something in my teeth, but they will also not hesitate to call me out if I cross a line.

My most significant gift is being highly intuitive, and some people in my life hate that I cannot be fooled or lied to because I can instantly tell if a person's energy does not match their words. Others embrace that I am a unicorn and wouldn't have me any other way.

Find the thing that triggers people most about you and do it more—just as long as you're not hurting anyone, of course.

Mercury in Aquarius semi-sextile Pisces North Node

Owning your unique soul expression and embracing the things that make you stand out is the key to living with purpose. Whatever your soul guides you towards, no one can do it quite like you because you bring your flavor to it. Yes, some people will hate it, and that's okay because it's not for them. If you are reading this book, it is likely that you will also follow my online platforms. I receive a lot of love online, but I also face negativity from people triggered by my mere existence. You are not for everyone, and that's okay. What I have learned about sharing myself authentically online is that your tribe will come. They will find you, and as long as you remain authentic, you will meet many others along your journey who have embraced their unique authenticity. You will instantly recognize this quality within each other.

Song: "Just the Way You Are" by Bruno Mars

February 14th

Mercury in Aquarius semi-sextile Neptune in Pisces

This aspect has us discovering more about what exists beyond our perceived reality. This is the energy of doing your research, so you may find yourself like a dog with a bone, researching topics such as energy work, divination practices, religion, conspiracy theories, manifestation, or any other subject that seems to exist outside your perceived reality. This is also a great energy to explore connecting to higher realms through prayer, tarot, meditation, or automatic writing techniques. This energy represents exploring what is beyond our current understanding by researching it.

Song: "Blowin' in the Wind" by Bob Dylan

February 15th

Mercury enters Pisces

Mercury rules communication and represents how we receive and process information. Mercury does not feel at all comfortable positioned in the sign of Pisces. Pisces' energy is very dreamy and imaginative. You know when you are telling a story and just drift off mid-sentence and then snap back to reality and think, wait, what was I saying? That is this energy. Focusing on important tasks is going to be much harder during this alignment. If you have begun to tap into your intuitive abilities or have begun building a relationship with your spirit team, the connection will be much stronger, and your channel will be much clearer during this time. Your intuition will be strong and hard to ignore, so if something feels off, trust that feeling.

Even for those who don't regularly communicate with higher realms, you may find yourself in a situation where you say something very wise or profound that has a deep healing effect on someone around you and wonder where that came from. We are all tapped into the ethers right now and have the ability to be the channel of divine wisdom even when we don't realize that we are doing it. You will see signs and synchronicities everywhere and consistently see angel numbers so often that it drives you crazy. Questioning your sanity comes part and parcel with Pisces energy.

We are not communicating in the usual way; we are communicating through energy and frequency, so when people speak to us, we may become very emotional or be able to feel what people are saying. It is important to ensure that you have the right kind of people around you right now, as you will have a heightened sensitivity to these energetic frequencies, and those with low energy will begin to affect you. Many people will find themselves heading into a period of isolation during this time as we feel overloaded by everything we are picking up within other people's energy.

All of our decisions during this time are based on how we feel about a situation rather than what we think about it. The frequency of music will be very healing to us now, and we may find that when we listen to a song, we become quite emotional because the energy of the lyrics deeply resonates within our souls. Rather than thinking I love this song, we are feeling wow. I know what that person was feeling when they wrote that. If you happen to be a songwriter, musician, or creative, you will be doing your best work. Pisces energy is almost poetic as creative inspiration flows right through you. My advice in getting the most out of this energy is to allow your creative juices to flow, even if you do not perceive yourself as a creative person.

Reflection

1. Are you encountering signs and synchronicities more frequently? How do these cosmic breadcrumbs guide your decisions or provide a sense of reassurance in your journey?

2. In the company of others, have you felt a heightened sensitivity to energetic frequencies? How are you managing your social connections to ensure a positive and nourishing environment?

3. Consider recent decisions—how many have been based on feelings rather than thoughts? How does this shift in decision-making impact your choices and their outcomes?

Song: "Like a Prayer" By Madonna

February 16th

Mercury in Pisces sesquiquadrate Mars retrograde in Cancer

This energy indicates that something may be off with our emotional state. With Mercury now in the sign of Pisces, we are becoming much more sensitive to energetic frequencies. To access and channel information from higher realms, we adjust our frequency. However, if we spend too much time floating within the ethers, we can become ungrounded, making us sensitive to things like loud noises or crowded places, but more importantly, to the energetic frequencies of others.

If you have young children, you may find yourself becoming intolerant of the natural noises they make. These noises can start to feel like nails on a chalkboard, instantly affecting your vibration. Alternatively, if others are shouting within the home, this interference, while you are learning to adjust to a new vibration, can cause you to explode in a release of built-up anxiety. Be mindful of mood swings and explosive behavior during this aspect.

Mercury in Pisces semi-sextile Pluto in Aquarius

Many of us do not consider ourselves creative; instead, we identify more as logical thinkers. Even those who enjoy creative expression can become overthinkers and get caught up in their heads. Most of us have numerous important tasks to complete and may struggle to focus at this time. This aspect encourages us to take a break and sing, dance, or create. One of the perks of engaging in these activities is that activating the creative part of your brain allows room for intuitive guidance and inspiration to flow freely. If you are stuck on a project, feeling blocked from moving forward, or can't determine the next step, give your creative mind space to expand and gently guide you in the right direction.

Sun in Aquarius semi-sextile Pisces North Node

There are times when escapism is not advised, but today, with this aspect, I highly encourage it. Creating stillness in your mind by taking a walk, exercising, or even engaging in mundane, repetitive tasks like washing dishes or folding laundry will create space for inspired ideas. Normally, I like to put headphones in while doing these things to listen to a podcast or my favorite songs, but today, I highly recommend going without them. Instead, create a space of silence to allow inspiration to flow through.

Song: "Noise" by Kenny Chesney

February 17th

Pallas enters Aquarius

When I think about the embodiment of Pallas in Aquarius energy, I am reminded of a group of punks I went to high school with. They were always eccentric in their own ways, dressed rebelliously against societal norms, and constantly seemed to be fighting for something. Usually, they were sticking it to the man in power or fighting for the underdog. They knew what it was like to be the underdog and could resonate with being easy prey or at a disadvantage. However, they wore that perception like a badge of honor—quite literally, with many badges pinned to their clothing. These badges proudly represented punk bands with similar messages or supported their political statements.

Back then, I just perceived them as rebellious and angry at the world, but they had qualities I always admired. Most made their own clothes, showing they were both innovative and creative. Once I got to know some of them, I realized they didn't care about my status. They always saw me as equal, despite my younger self feeling as though I was totally cooler and way more popular than them. They didn't care what I or anyone else thought of them; all that mattered was what they thought of me. If I was nice to them, they were nice to me.

This is the energy of Pallas in Aquarius. During this alignment, many of us will feel pulled toward a cause or feel a deep calling to stand for something. We may find ourselves wanting to fight for the underdog, such as combating homelessness, helping young people find a voice, or feeling compelled to take in an animal from a shelter. We are radical thinkers right now, finding innovative solutions to old problems, sometimes using unorthodox methods and always wanting to push the envelope a little further.

In this energy, if a problem exists, we will likely want to fix it ourselves rather than pay a professional. For example, if your washing machine breaks, rather than calling a repairman, you might search YouTube videos, watch a professional disassemble it, and learn to check all the filters before diving in and getting your hands dirty. This placement says, "Stand back, I've got this." If we can't fix it the usual way, we may devise some MacGyver-style contraption to solve the problem.

Many legal matters come up during this placement. Generally, more people are likely to sue each other during this alignment, and our reckless behavior can sometimes see us facing charges for things like vandalism or hacking. We might even find ourselves arrested after a not-so-peaceful protest or for defying authority. So, if you find a cause to get behind, keep this in mind.

Reflection

1. How have I expressed my own individuality and unique voice in the past?

2. What causes or issues am I most passionate about, and why?

3. How do I handle conflict or resistance when my ideas or values are challenged?

Sun in Aquarius semi-sextile Neptune in Pisces

This is a beautiful energy of tapping into your intuition and your heart space to follow the beat of your own drum. Have you ever been to a music festival where thousands of people gather from all walks of life, and they are all embracing the experience? You succumb to the rhythm of the music, and it feels like nothing else exists outside the present moment. You form deep connections with perfect strangers; before you know it, you are dancing together and braiding each other's hair. You don't care where they come from, how much money they make, or what roles they play. They only exist within this moment, and you will probably never see any of them again after this experience. That is what this energy feels like.

It is the energy when everything feels magical, and you feel so connected to everything around you. If you can't access a festival, I recommend searching out a beautiful garden where you can feel connected to all the flowers around you or lying down on the grass and staring up at the clouds. These moments are fleeting, and they do not last forever. Still, if you continue the process of healing yourself and removing your fears, blocks, and limitations, living a life that is in better alignment with your soul, one of the benefits is that you come to experience these moments more frequently.

Song: "We're Not Gonna Take It" by Twisted Sister

February 18th

Mercury in Pisces semi-square Chiron in Aries

This energy brings to the surface feelings and emotions we would rather not look at. It is much easier to project blame for our emotions and challenges that we face on the other people around us or outside circumstances over which we have no control. But what is the reason that we really feel the way that we feel? Why does this trigger me so much? Where did this begin? What walls and boundaries have I had to set to protect myself from getting hurt?

This energy encourages you to delve deep into the shadows to discover what behaviors and ways of thinking are limiting you emotionally. Now is a chance to free ourselves from any past trauma and blockages that we are still carrying with us from our past, but will you choose to ignore it?

Song: "Numb" by Linkin Park

February 19th

Sun enters Pisces

Pisces season is upon us, so do you know what that means? Many of you probably will only know what that means if you have heavy Pisces placements in your chart. The sign of Pisces represents the esoteric.

The definition of esoteric: intended for or likely to be understood by only a small number of people with specialized knowledge or interest.

The first thing you should know is that I am, in fact, a Pisces, so I am one of the few people who are most comfortable with this energy. If you don't have heavy Pisces within your chart, it is easy to become a little lost in this energy, so I will do my best to explain the energy and help guide you through it. Pisces season is when we become very familiar with our energy and emotions. It is a time of releasing old baggage and purging any energetic blockages you

61

are still holding onto within your body, mind, and spirit. This can be a very uncomfortable process to experience.

If we allow this release to happen, we can elevate our consciousness, which allows us to tap into our psychic abilities or, if you have already begun the releasing process, you will experience upgrades such as heightened intuition, unlocking new psychic abilities, feeling more connected and supported by the higher realms, and being able to channel guidance from a source outside of yourself easily. By an outside source, I am referring to your higher self, angels, spirit guides, ancestors, deities, ascended masters, and such, sending you guidance and wisdom from another dimension. Have I lost you yet? Well, there is more. You may find yourself healing generational or childhood trauma, experiencing karma, or ending karmic cycles.

Pisces season asks us to detach from our ego, which means that we need to separate from our mind, realizing that we are not the thoughts in our head but rather the observer of them. Freeing ourselves from the clutches of the ego also means releasing attachment to outcomes and expectations and placing all of our trust and faith in God or the universe. Keeping the faith that everything we are currently experiencing, although probably very uncomfortable, is all working out for our highest good.

Pisces teaches us to release all the energy despite wanting to freak out and allow things to play out how they will. We are asked to become observers rather than participants within our reality. Our energetic frequency becomes elevated during Pisces season, so all our actions are likely to be for the greater good of all involved. We can quickly transmute energy, so what seems like the end of the world right now, we will be able to spin into a positive by tomorrow morning. We are being taught harsh lessons and asked to trust in the process.

The worst thing about Pisces' energy is that all these purges, fluctuations, and releases happen internally. So, while we heal our childhood wounds, clear out hundreds of years of past life trauma, and close out that karmic cycle that we have been stuck in for the last ten years, in reality, no one will even notice a difference. One reason for this may be because, during Pisces season, everyone is too busy tapping into higher dimensions and all up in their own emotions to deal with yours, but mostly, it's because it is all happening internally and ener-getically. In reality, you have missed deadlines, scheduled appointments, and taken a week off work because you are energetically drained from your most recent system update. I recommend meditation, yoga, breathwork, divination practices, and reiki to help you through this season. Good luck.

Reflection

1. Are you prepared for a divine detox during this season, shedding old baggage and releasing energetic blockages? Are there any measures you feel you should implement to ensure you have supported yourself to delve deep this season?

2. Have you delved into healing generational or childhood trauma, and if

so, what insights or resolutions have emerged?

3. Reflect on your journey of placing trust and faith in the Divine. How has this mindset impacted your experiences and outcomes? What evidence have you experienced of higher realms?

Venus in Aries semi-square Uranus in Taurus

This energy is likely to cause some sort of disruption within your relationships and connections. This can be as little as a fiery exchange with a coworker, an upset and unsatisfied customer, or a rude cashier while out shopping. For others, it could be something more intense, such as an argument with a friend, relative, or long-term partner. When this energy is present, it asks us how in control we are of our emotions and how easily we become triggered. It also asks us to consider how we can prevent this from happening again in the future.

Mercury in Pisces semi-sextile Venus in Aries

This is an inspiring energy of feeling an emotion and acting upon it. If you feel you should apologize to someone, do it. If you want to tell someone that you love them, do it. If you are missing someone in your life, reach out to them and let them know. If you feel that you deserve a treat, spoil yourself. Many times throughout the day, we get little inspirations telling us to reach out to someone or to have lunch by the water because our subconscious desires are communicating what our heart wants. However, our conscious mind often steps in, and we overthink it. We might think, "It's been a while since we spoke, so I don't know if reaching out or apologizing will be well received," or "If I tell them I love them, they might not say it back," or "If I go and eat lunch by the water, I might fall behind on my schedule and struggle to get back into a productive flow."

This aspect grants us the ability to allow space for what our heart wants and encourages us to honor and act upon these desires without overthinking potential outcomes and talking ourselves out of it.

Song: "Higher Self" by Liyah Dalani

February 20th

Juno enters Sagittarius

As Juno enters the sign of Sagittarius, our intimate relationships come into sharp focus. We question whether those with whom we share deep connections can push us to become better versions of ourselves. It's great to have the drive and limitless potential, but there's nothing quite like having someone in our corner cheering us on, reminding us we can go even further. We crave someone who calls us out when we're limiting ourselves and pumps us up when we're facing challenges.

Partnering with someone goal-oriented and ambitious is incredibly attractive to us right now. People who love to travel, indulge themselves in experiencing life, or constantly seek knowledge are making us weak at the knees. We all have a part of ourselves that wants to do more and experience more, and certain people bring that expansive energy out of us. These people push us outside our comfort zone, teach us new things, and want to embark on spontaneous adventures with us. They make us feel free, pulling us out of our heads and into spontaneous escapades, especially on rough days. During this time, we are assessing how many of these qualities those that we choose to surround ourselves with currently possess and whether or not we can encourage our loved ones to tap into this side of themselves and embrace a free spirit.

However, a few things may cause conflict in this energy. Any intimate partner who tries to place restrictions on us, is too clingy, or doesn't allow us space can create tension. Those with a victim mentality who bring down the vibes by blaming others or outside circumstances for their problems will also clash with this energy. People who are boring, predictable, or content with mundane activities just won't cut it. We need excitement and adventure; if our partner is dull or stuck in low vibrational energy, it will become a problem.

Reflection

1. How do my current intimate relationships push me to become a better version of myself?

2. What qualities in a partner make me feel genuinely supported and motivated?

3. How important is it for me to have a partner who shares my goals and ambitions?

4. How do I handle partners who exhibit clinginess or try to impose restrictions on me?

Song: "I Gotta Feeling" by Black Eyes Peas

February 21st

Last Quarter Moon in Sagittarius

Sagittarius energy is all about embodying what makes you feel free, so this moon cycle will likely have you freeing up time in your schedule. We have been delving deeper to understand our frequency and that which throws off our energetic alignment, making us feel stifled or stagnant. This is when we push to make changes regarding anything in our lives that feels like it carries the energy of restriction. This means scheduling yourself a break or some time off. We are facing any challenges that may hinder your ability to move about freely, such as tending to car maintenance or making travel plans.

Our relationships will likely become our focus as we learn to say 'no.' We are withdrawing our energy from anyone we feel is holding us back, and we certainly won't tolerate relationships with people trying to limit us in any way. Can you stay and work overtime? That's a no. Can you help out at the school fundraiser? Nope. Will you have my children for the weekend so my husband and I can have some alone time? That is a hell no. Wherever people try to enforce limits, we are standing our ground on the time and energy we will not sacrifice for someone else's comfort. Any limitations that once presented a challenge, we are busting through them, saying, "Move out of my way."

Reflection

1. What aspects of my life feel constricting or limiting, hindering my sense of freedom? Are there any commitments or responsibilities that I need to reconsider to prioritize my well-being and personal freedom?

2. Which relationships in my life may be holding me back or imposing limitations on my time and energy?

3. Am I comfortable saying 'no' to situations that infringe upon my freedom and personal boundaries?

Sun in Pisces sesquiquadrate Mars retrograde in Cancer

This energy is difficult to navigate as it represents a battle of wills between our hearts and our ego. We may feel we have been treated poorly by someone around us and feel the need to defend our position, not wanting to be taken advantage of. With this energy, our emotional triggers can easily get the best of us. We start taking things personally, making it difficult to choose love. This aspect asks us a crucial question: Do you want to embody a full expression of heart-centered energy, or do you want to win an argument or conflict? How important is it for you to be right or to be the victor?

Mercury in Pisces quintile Uranus in Taurus

This aspect confirms that our intuition is paying off in a positive way. It's like when you're driving your usual route to work and suddenly feel the urge to take a different route, only to later discover that you avoided an accident or traffic jam. Or when you're about to enter a contract or business deal that sounds promising, but you pull out at the last minute because something doesn't feel right, and then find out that the person was involved in a public scandal. Pay attention to any intuitive hits you receive today, as they are likely to either gain you or save you some money.

Mercury in Pisces square Jupiter in Gemini

Following on from the previous energy, this aspect indicates that someone might be conjuring up a little hocus pocus or attempting to pull the wool over our eyes by creating illusions. This could involve someone stretching the truth about an event or trying to get you to invest in their product or company by making false promises. The great thing about this energy is that, with Mercury in Pisces, we are able to see through illusions right now. We will be energetically alerted if something is off, so ensure you access your intuition before making any decisions today.

Sun in Pisces semi-sextile Pluto in Aquarius

This energy is awesome. It allows you to see through veils of illusion placed upon you by society. It is the ability to see beyond the matrix. It is like a little window through which you can perceive a whole new reality. Anything seems possible with this energy present, and your reality may begin to look very different from how you have previously perceived it.

Song: "Devil in Disguise" by Elvis Presley

February 24th

Ceres enters Pisces

Ceres, the asteroid representing how we nurture others, is moving into the sign of Pisces. Pisces energy heals and nurtures in a deeply compassionate way without overextending. At this time, we recognize that solving someone else's problem for them is not helpful; it hinders their growth and ability to overcome challenges. While we are very sensitive to others' situations and refrain from making judgments, we encourage them to go within themselves to find the strength or answers they need. We may guide them subtly and profoundly, such as sending a song that resonates deeply with them or suggesting a book that helped us through a similar situation.

We understand that we cannot do the work on others' behalf and acknowledge the impact their emotional state can have on our own frequency. This energy is about saying to those we love, "I hear you, I understand you, I support you, but I cannot solve this for you. Instead, I will take your hand and walk with you while you overcome this challenge." During this time, we also make it a priority to withdraw from others who are in a low frequency when necessary, in order to recharge and reenergize ourselves. This energy asks not, "How can I help?" but rather, "How can I support you in helping yourself?"

Reflection

1. In what ways have I overextended myself when trying to help others, and how did it impact me and them?

2. How can I encourage others to find their own strength and solutions without taking over their challenges?

3. How do I balance my sensitivity towards others with the need to protect my own emotional well-being?

Mars Direct in Cancer

Mars has been retrograde in the sign of Cancer, leaving us feeling unsafe within our comfort zones and unable to trust those closest to us. Many of us have experienced fallouts with close friends and family members or breakdowns in long-term relationships, causing quite a mess. Now that Mars is moving direct again, this feeling of insecurity will begin to subside. However, this direct placement brings a new set of challenges.

Our emotions highly influence us during this alignment. What does that mean exactly? The moon rules cancer, and our emotional energy will fluctuate at this time, which means mood swings. Humans are not strangers to emotional shifts; however, the problem arises when we throw Mars into the mix. Mars is the planet of action, so not only are we feeling emotionally triggered during this time, but we are also acting out from a space of pain. This means emotional outbursts and making choices fueled by anger. Cancer in Mars's energy tends to have us taking things a little too far because we cannot regulate our emotions.

We have the potential to cut people deep during this alignment and hurt other people's feelings.

I will get a little personal here so you can get a clearer example of this energy. In the past, I had a partner who cheated on me, and I unleashed a string of hurtful words upon him. When I realized that he was seemingly unfazed by my onslaught of emotional energy, I realized what would hurt him. I then proceeded to attack that which he loved most; I vandalized his car in a fit of rage. I was acting purely from a place of pain and not at all rational. That is Cancer in Mars energy. We are easily triggered and become somewhat irrational within this energy, so remember to take the time to breathe during times of heightened emotion. I highly advise meditation during this time for those who are generally quite reactive.

This energy is not all bad, as we act from our emotions; if we are in loving energy, our actions will also reflect that. So, we are more likely to help a stranger when we are in a good mood and nurture those we care deeply about, making them feel loved and supported. Watch out for procrastination during this alignment because we are only acting when we feel like it, so if you wake up thinking you don't want to be an adult today, you are likely to spend the day in bed.

Reflection

1. How do you typically handle emotional triggers, and are you aware of potential irrational reactions during such times?

2. Reflect on a past situation where heightened emotions led to actions you later regretted. What could you have done differently to navigate those emotions more constructively?

3. What self-care practices or mindfulness techniques can you incorporate to manage mood swings and prevent impulsive actions during this alignment?

Mercury in Pisces trine Mars in Cancer

This energy asks us to put the extra sensory perception powers we have during Pisces season to good use. It encourages us to become more discerning of other people's energetic frequencies. Reflect on how you feel after each interaction throughout the day. Does a meeting with your boss leave you feeling stressed? If so, why? Is it your or your boss's energy, as more responsibility and burdens fall upon them? Does the person standing behind you in line for coffee make you feel uneasy? If so, are you just being paranoid, or does that person carry an energy of inauthenticity? Does an apology you receive feel inauthentic? This aspect asks you to trust your perceptions of the energetic frequencies around you and use this information to help make decisions and guide you down the right path.

Sun in Pisces semi-square Chiron in Aries

This energy is challenging as it calls your faith into question. What do you believe in? What do you want to believe in, and how does that conflict with your family beliefs or what you were taught to believe growing up? If angels, guides, and deities support you throughout your life, how have you been through all the awful experiences you have had to endure? Where were they then? Why did they not intervene?

All of the experiences that you have been through have helped to shape you into the person that you are. Some of us have been through the most traumatic experiences that a person can imagine; those people are the most resilient among us. They don't break at the general inconveniences that would send some of us into a spiral. If the pain that they went through in the past did not break them, then a flat car battery in the middle of heavy traffic certainly isn't going to. They will not fall to pieces over a rent increase. They are the most resilient of us all. Every experience that you have been through up till this point has helped shape you into the person that you are born to become. Can you begin to see your pain and challenges as a blessing?

Mercury in Pisces semi-square Pluto in Aquarius

As we become more sensitive to the energy of the world around us, we can feel somewhat drained and overwhelmed by everything penetrating our energetic field. This energy highlights the energetic vibrations we feel from being part of the collective on this planet. You may be watching a natural disaster unfold on the news and connecting to the energy of thousands of people losing their lives, homes, or loved ones. You may be observing evidence of government officials waging war against other countries and recognizing that media coverage instills fear within the masses. Once you learn to tune into your frequency and the emotions rising within you, these types of frequencies can wreak havoc on your vibration. This energy will likely leave you feeling overwhelmed and highly emotional as you balance your own energy with the energy of the collective as a whole.

Song: "Aura" by Janine the Machine

February 26th

Mercury in Pisces conjunct Saturn in Pisces

Stay open to guidance from higher realms today, as this aspect represents learning a spiritual lesson. If we do not learn to listen to our intuitive nudges and inner guidance system, we often have to learn lessons the hard way. This could be as small as your intuition telling you not to eat those leftovers in the fridge from last night's dinner or something much more serious, like your intuition advising you to seek a second opinion for a medical diagnosis. If something internal is alerting you that something may be off, listen.

Mercury in Pisces semi-sextile Chiron in Aries

As we navigate our feelings and emotions and try to balance them by being compassionate toward the feelings and emotions of others, this can leave us feeling quite triggered. If you find yourself experiencing feelings of anger, disappointment, or frustration, feeling as if others around you are not receiving what you are saying. You can use these triggers to your advantage. Our emotional triggers come up for a reason; they want to be explored, felt, healed, and released. Our mind or ego is likely to have us wanting to project our anger or discomfort onto someone else; however, if you can learn to transmute that negative release of energy into your healing, you will begin to release blockages within yourself.

Think of your anger and discomfort as your guiding compass to what still needs to be healed and released within you. Identifying a trigger is a breakthrough in itself. It can lead you to emotional release if you can locate the source of that trigger. Do I have too much on my plate because I have difficulty saying no? Am I angry at this person because they are pushing against my boundaries? If it is a boundary issue, you do not need to amend this boundary in any way; however, you can ask yourself whether you have clearly communicated this boundary to the person you are interacting with, and then you can open up a dialogue with that person about why this boundary exists. If someone else is trying to enforce a boundary upon you, does this conflict with your own boundaries, or does this bring up painful memories from the past when someone else was trying to limit your freedom or self-expression?

Song: "Bad Moon Rising" by Creedence Clearwater Revival

February 28th

New Moon in Pisces

As Pisces represents energetic release and all things spiritual, let us set some new intentions in full Pisces fashion so that we can bring the lessons we have learned from Pisces going forward. Firstly, let's think about our self-care routine. What did we learn that our soul needed during this healing period? What can we incorporate to ensure our mind, body, and spirit are nurtured going forward? We also become very aware of the people, places, and things around us that have a negative impact on our energy. What changes must we make, or what boundaries must be established to ensure we remain protective of our energy?

Let's take some time to consider our spiritual practice. Which practices help us to feel more connected to source energy? For some of us, this could be reading a spiritual text such as the Bible; for others, it may be practicing meditation or yoga. Some prefer using spiritual tools, divination, or automatic writing to keep the connection clear. For me, it is mostly prayer. If something is on my heart that I need to release, I give it to God through prayer. I also work closely with spirit guides and archangels, often praying for guidance or assistance.

Reflection

Here are some suggestions for embracing this Pisces new moon:

1. Cleanse your body and energy field by enjoying a warm bath infused with essential oils, flowers, and crystals.

2. Try automatic writing, put pen to paper, ask a question of the divine, and write whatever comes to you first. Do not stop writing or stop to read what you have written. Let the words flow onto the page, or use tarot or oracle cards to gain insights into your healing journey. Create a dialogue with source using the cards to interpret the message.

3. Curate a playlist of music that speaks to your soul.

Mercury in Pisces sextile Uranus in Taurus

After spending many years as a psychic and intuitive reader, one thing became very clear to me: I recognized that whatever my clients put their energy into, they received more of. Those who were career-focused and did not allow emotional distractions were highly successful. Those with healing energy who focused their energy on nurturing and supporting others attracted people who were broken and in need of healing. Overthinking clients always find themselves presented with a new challenge or a problem to solve.

It wasn't until I read the book 'The Attractor Factor' by Joe Vitale that I began to recognize how I could use my natural talents and gifts to create more structure, balance, and financial abundance for myself. Career-focused people often spend much of their time climbing the corporate ladder and have a wide range of skills, although the issue they face is their loss of freedom. What if they were to step outside their comfort zone, utilize all the skills they have acquired, and leap into starting their own business? Then, they can work on their schedule, allowing themselves more time to travel.

I found myself in the healer category. I took three-hour-long phone calls from friends and family members who needed someone to listen, offer wisdom, or help them process their emotions. If someone had an emotional dilemma, I would be the first person they would call, and I tended to attract many emotional people. Once I recognized my ability to support people in healing themselves, I realized that I could start creating content, and others who resonate with my healing energy will benefit from what I have to offer. As for the overthinkers, these are the people who often have the most innovative ideas because they can think outside of the box. If these people could act on some of these ideas and tap into their creative energy by producing them, they would likely become the wealthiest of us all. How can you make your natural abilities work for you rather than against you?

Saturn in Pisces semi-sextile Chiron in Aries

This can be a heavy energy as it represents finding a piece of the puzzle related to our healing, triggers, and why we are the way we are. It helps us understand why we react the way we do when presented with an obstacle or challenged by another person. However, this energy also inspires us to integrate this new knowledge and perspective in order to create change. You can now identify exactly where a particular behavior began and recognize that you are not the same person you were when you developed this behavior to protect yourself. Now you realize that you are safe and no longer need it, so take positive action to stop identifying with that story.

Song: "Tourmaline" by Janine the Machine

March Alignments

March 1st

Sun in Pisces semi-sextile Venus in Aries

This is a beautiful energy of becoming familiar with our ego and the egos of others. We understand that our ego exists to keep us safe and often drives us to choose actions based on fear. We don't want to be reactive to others, but our ego tells us we must defend ourselves. We want to forgive others for their indiscretions, but our ego tells us that doing so shows weakness. Whenever we challenge someone, enter a conflict, or feel bitterness toward another, we recognize that this stems from a place of pain in our hearts. Recognizing this helps us understand similar behaviors in those around us, making us more forgiving of those who come against us. We know they are just projecting their pain. Love is our natural state; if people respond to us from a place of ego, it's because they don't feel safe expressing love and thus project their pain instead.

Song: "Rolling in the Deep" by Adele

March 2nd

Venus Retrograde in Aries

This is a very challenging alignment as it relates to creating harmony within our relationships. Many relationships break down with this kind of energy present. It can feel like we are living in a world full of selfish individuals prioritizing their own needs above everyone else, causing us to feel neglected and triggering deep wounds within us. Those of us who grew up with a selfish parent may find these childhood wounds exposed as we witness similar behavior from those around us. This can lead us to adopt a victim mentality and express anger, competitiveness, and even aggression in our connections.

When our insecurities are triggered and abandonment wounds exposed, this energy can cause us to project our pain onto others, resulting in toxic and unhealthy relationships. Unresolved issues and cracks in the foundation of relationships may intensify, making it seem as if we've forgotten how to empathize with and forgive others. We crave to be heard, seen, and understood, often acting out to gain attention, whether positive or negative. Temper tantrums at the slightest upset become common.

To navigate this energy, it is crucial to give ourselves what we expect from others. If you seek compassion, be more compassionate toward yourself. If you seek understanding, be more understanding toward yourself and forgive yourself for your wrongdoings. If you have built-up aggression, find an outlet like therapy or physical activity to channel that energy productively.

For those who are single, this energy can manifest as promiscuity, providing a sense of control and short-term gratification. Be mindful of entering new connections, as you may find yourself wanting to take charge or play games by withholding affection if your needs aren't met. You might also use your sexuality to get what you want rather than forming deep and genuine connections. This can push people away as you maintain a tough exterior and are afraid to show vulnerability. It's best to postpone the search for love and focus on becoming the type of partner you seek. If you want a loyal and trustworthy partner, embody those qualities. If you desire a motivated and stable partner, cultivate those traits within yourself to attract someone of similar vibrational frequency.

For those in long-term relationships, this energy can lead to aggression, arguments, and conflict. We may express our needs without compromise, and our partners may respond similarly, leading to mutual perceptions of selfishness and stubbornness. This "I don't give a f***" energy can cause us to make unrealistic demands and become quickly angered if our partners don't meet our expectations. We may also fantasize about or even act upon sexual desires for others, driven by our abandonment wounds.

If you find yourself exhibiting these behaviors, ask yourself what you want to receive more of from your partner and give them more of that energy. Remember that people often respond with the same energy they receive. Embody the energy you wish to attract, and you'll create a more positive and harmonious relationship dynamic.

Reflection

1. How do I typically react when I feel neglected or unappreciated in my relationships?

2. What childhood wounds or past experiences might be influencing my current relationship behaviors?

3. How can I recognize when my ego drives my actions, and what steps can I take to respond from a place of love instead?

Mercury in Pisces conjunct Pisces North Node

This energy encourages us to say and do less. It often causes us to withdraw from others as we become highly sensitive to their energetic frequencies. This energy asks us to be the bigger person and avoid engaging in any conflict. We may want to isolate during this time to connect with our higher selves and delve deeply into our emotions, allowing us to embody our own energy better. This energy grants us a heightened awareness of others' energetic frequencies, and if you find those frequencies overwhelming, it is okay to withdraw and rebalance.

Sun in Pisces quintile Uranus in Taurus

I love this energy, which represents being able to disconnect or tune out from any chaos that is happening around you. This is like when you wake up determined to have a great day despite anything that tries to throw you off track. You are likely to find yourself very connected to the natural world, such as getting distracted by a butterfly or staring into the flames of a warm fire.

Song: "I Want It Now" by Julie Dawn Cole

March 3rd

Mercury in Pisces conjunct Neptune in Pisces

A conjunction represents that two planets' energy merge to form one energy. Depending on the relationship of these two planets, it will determine whether that energy has a positive or negative effect on us. In this case, we have Mercury, which rules technology, information, and communication, merging with Neptune, an energy that operates outside the realm of logic. Neptune is dreamy and represents all the things that cannot be explained. This gives the potential for this aspect to lead to confusion. Perhaps you cannot make much sense of your feelings and emotions right now, or you are having trouble putting your feelings into words. There is a chance of being misunderstood with this energy or struggling to understand the messages you receive from your higher self. There is a high chance of your dreams being very significant at this time, and you may receive downloads to your subconscious while in the sleep state, so I recommend keeping a notepad beside your bed so that you can write any dreams or inspirations down while they are still fresh in your mind.

This aspect can bring about challenges as our inner guidance conflicts with what we know to be true or possible. Perhaps your intuition has led you down a rabbit hole of esoteric knowledge that conflicts with your current belief systems. Or you've unlocked a new psychic gift and can now perceive energetic imprints or vibrations with your physical senses, but you have no logical way to explain your experience. Just because science may conflict with your experience or what you are discovering does not make it any less real. Pisces asks us to experience without needing to explain or make logical sense of those experiences.

Song: "Divine" by Sophia Dashing

March 4th

Mercury enters Aries

If you are the kind of person who tends to overanalyze things and get caught up in your head, then this alignment is here to help. As Mercury enters Aries, the energy encourages us not to think too hard about things before taking action. If you are learning something new, this is the energy of putting down the books and trying to put things into action by getting some hands-on experience. Aries is known as the baby of the zodiac and brings childlike energy, so we are not thinking about consequences right now. We are making decisions based on what will bring us instant gratification. This is a time for making selfish decisions that align with our best interests. This is excellent energy for starting new projects; however, we can become easily bored. If the task at hand becomes repetitive, we may think of something more fun to do. We are easily distracted, and our patience is slim to none. Aries in Mercury does require more discipline because unless we are genuinely passionate about something, we will quickly give up on it. Unfortunately, due to this impulsive energy, we can miss out on stable, long-term opportunities because we seek instant rewards.

Aries is a very energetic and compassionate expression of energy, so this is great communication energy for anyone in a leadership role because we communicate in a way that comes across as enthusiastic, motivational, and inspirational. We have the ability to have a positive effect on the most uninspired people with this energy. The downside to this energy is that we want to express everything with solid opinions and speak our minds passionately, so arguments and disagreements are common occurrences. Aries is the sign of war, so we will unlikely want to back down if our opinions are challenged. We are not afraid of an argument within this energy, and some may even encourage one. In this energy, we are not afraid to say what others are afraid to say, which may lead to offending someone. Many of us will find ourselves having to apologize during this alignment. We do not mean to offend; we are just not giving our thoughts any time to marinate before blurting them out. If you struggle to filter the thoughts from your brain to your mouth, you will probably struggle most with this alignment. You could be the gentlest communicator and still be affected by this impulsive communication energy. You may even surprise somebody with an angry outburst and shock those around you because they didn't think you had that in you.

Reflection

1. How can I embrace the impulsive energy of Mercury in Aries to inject more passion into my current projects or endeavors?

2. How can I channel Aries's enthusiastic and motivational aspects in my communication to inspire those around me?

3. Are there long-term opportunities I might be overlooking due to my focus on instant rewards, and how can I balance both perspectives?

Mercury in Pisces quintile Jupiter in Gemini

This energy asks us to incorporate our psychic perception into our daily lives. Our intuition is like a muscle: the more we use it, the stronger and clearer our inner guidance system becomes. If you have unlocked a new ability, make time to nurture it through meditation or chakra cleansing. If you have prophetic dreams, write them down as you wake to assist in deciphering them and to show the higher realms that you are open to receiving such guidance. Keep a log of the signs and synchronicities you encounter throughout the day. This demonstrates to the divine that you are open and receptive to channeling higher wisdom.

Song: "Good As Hell" by Lizzo

March 6th

Mercury in Aries sextile Pluto in Aquarius

This aspect helps us to feel very optimistic about the new intentions that we are setting in regard to our spiritual connection. We may also feel excited to try some new spiritual practices that we have never tried before, so you may find yourself buying a book on a spiritual topic or wanting to learn more about other religions from across the world, such as Buddhism or Hinduism. Perhaps you want to sign up for a yoga class or buy some crystals to support healing. This is exploratory energy in which you will be open to trying new things, so why don't you add a new magical element to your manifesting intentions? Have fun with it!

Song: "Witchcraft" by Lizzy Jeff

March 7th

First Quarter Moon in Gemini

We have reached the first quarter moon phase, so it is time to make minor tweaks and adjustments. As the moon is positioned in the sign of Gemini, we ask ourselves how to communicate better and connect with the world around us. Gemini rules communication and information, so this energy encourages us to ask ourselves if we have all the necessary information. If we don't, how might we go about obtaining this information? Do we need to ask more questions? Do we know someone who may have the answer to any of the current restrictions that we are facing?

Whenever I think of Gemini, I think of social media and its huge effect on society. What impact does social media have on your daily life? For some of us, social media has become the catalyst for our self-sabotage as we spend hours scrolling or find ourselves in petty disagreements with a perfect stranger across the world because we have a difference of opinion and we are trying to prove a point. Do you need a social media detox? On the other hand, many of us will use social media to leverage our business or reach a wider audience. Social media is not the devil; however, finding the balance between creator and consumer regarding these platforms can be difficult. How can you make social media work for you and not against you?

Gemini is also a very adaptable sign and responds well to change. If you have a Gemini friend, I'm sure you would agree that they become bored quite easily, as they like variety. Embody this Gemini moon energy by asking yourself where you can spice up your life by adding more variety. What can you incorporate into your work routine to feel more engaged in the work that you are producing? Can you expand your diet so you are not bored with the same old meals? Can you explore some new music genres instead of listening to the same tracks you have listened to since the 90s?

Reflection

1. Do I have all the information I need to navigate current challenges, and

78

if not, who can provide valuable insights?

2. What role does social media play in my life, and is it contributing positively or leading to self-sabotage?

3. How can I introduce more variety and excitement into my daily routine, inspired by Gemini's adaptable energy? Are there specific areas in my life, such as work or diet, where I can infuse more diversity and spice things up?

Song: "#SELFIE" by The Chainsmokers

March 9th

Sun in Pisces trine Mars in Cancer

This aspect represents receiving higher wisdom and guidance and acting upon it. This beautiful energy allows us to silence the fears telling us that something doesn't make sense and instead have pure faith in the path shown to us. When we invite the divine into our daily lives, we begin to live in a flow state, silencing the fear of our egoic mind that tries to keep us playing it safe. Making all our decisions from this guided state allows everything to fall into place, presenting us with incredible opportunities to experience and expand.

Song: "AnGel" by Emmy Meli

March 12th

Sun in Pisces semi-sextile Chiron in Aries

With this energy, we can recognize a strong connection between the pain and trauma we have faced in the past and our current reality. Perhaps you push people away due to your past abandonment wounds and have developed an "I'll leave them before they leave me" mentality. Alternatively, it is the other way around, where you cling tightly to relationships and consistently seek validation from others to define your self-worth. If this person doesn't want me, perhaps something is wrong with me. Tracing back the origins of these behaviors allows us to explore them more deeply and recognize how we are participating in our self-sabotage by holding onto wounds from the past. While making these connections, it is a good idea to acknowledge them and how they have kept you safe and then release them into the ethers.

Venus retrograde in Aries semi-square Uranus in Taurus

This aspect brings frustration as we become easily triggered by others and feel the urge to push for outcomes we want within our relationships. It can be very difficult to recognize another's point of view, and we can easily lose our temper. Our egos are loud today, which can create conflict or tension. If you are feeling triggered, try shifting your focus from who triggered you and take the opportunity to tune into your emotions. Ask yourself which part of you feels unsafe. Hold space for the parts of you that are experiencing fear right now. Identifying these pain points helps us recognize that those we are interacting with are also acting from fear. Although it is not our job to diagnose or identify their pain points, we can have more tolerance for their pain.

Mercury in Aries conjunct Venus retrograde in Aries

This is the kind of energy that is likely to warrant a future apology. It can represent explosive communication as we become demanding of others around us. This energy says, "I know you don't like it when I do that, but I'm going to do it anyway." Perhaps you manage to check yourself and think twice before communicating this way; however, you may still be on the receiving end of this energy, making it difficult not to retaliate.

As far as collective energy goes, today is a challenging one. Remember to breathe—the collective energy around us can intensify our feelings, making what we are experiencing seem much worse than it is. I advise you to withdraw from any potential conflict today, as arguments within this energy rarely find a peaceful resolution.

Song: "I Hate Everything About You" by Three Days Grace

March 13th

Mercury in Aries semi-square Uranus in Taurus

There is something you feel passionate about, perhaps a new hobby or project you would like to start, or an opinion you would like to express. Something external is causing some type of disruption, preventing you from expressing yourself in the way you would like, and this can lead to anger and frustration. This energy asks you to choose yourself and not allow yourself to be taken advantage of. Be very mindful of how you express this energy. If you feel anger, frustration, or resentment rising within you, take the time to acknowledge this energy and breathe it out before erupting. It is entirely natural to feel overwhelmed by this energy. This energy also represents wanting to regain control and fight back. What are you allowing to disrupt your peace right now?

Sun in Pisces conjunct Saturn in Pisces

This energy asks us to integrate the lessons we have learned to navigate the current situations we are facing. If we approach people and situations with love, we are likely to receive love and blessings in return. Conversely, if we express ourselves through fear and anger, that energy is likely to hinder us spiritually. We are now asked to choose which version of ourselves we want to embody in this moment to prevent having to learn another lesson or experience more hardship.

Song: "Break Stuff" by Limp Bizkit

March 15th

Full Moon Total Lunar Eclipse in Virgo

I often find the Virgo full moon to be a difficult one to navigate. Virgo's energy is very grounded and practical. It brings up fears surrounding our daily routines like "I need to get this house cleaned up" or "complete this task that I am working on," but with the sun stationed in Pisces, we all feel completely out of balance. At the same time, we process our deeper emotions and release any energetic blockages trapped within our emotional bodies.

This moon will likely make you feel like you are experiencing a hangover for about three days. There is a lot that is going on for us energetically. Virgo also rules physical health, so this release of energy can come up as pain or inflammation within the body, headaches, or nausea. Stay hydrated during this time as you allow your body to purge and release unwanted energy.

You may be highly emotional and sensitive, wondering, "Why am I crying or feeling this way?" The process of energetic release is often an uncomfortable one. It is a deep healing of your mind, body, and spirit. Another thing to be aware of right now is that a Virgo moon brings the energy of service and sacrifice, while the sun in Pisces brings the energy of selflessness and compassion. The blending of these two energies will have you wanting to extend what little energy you do have to those around you. Be mindful of your energy resources and that you are not overexerting yourself.

Reflection

Some suggestions for Virgo full moon rituals are:

1. Use the meticulous energy of Virgo to declutter and organize your space and donate items you no longer need.

2. Focus on health and wellness practices. Cook a nourishing meal or start a new healthy habit like stretching or meditation.

3. Engage in service for others, reflecting Virgo's service-oriented nature. Offer help to someone in need, volunteer, or pay for someone's coffee or groceries.

Sun in Pisces sextile Uranus in Taurus

This is welcomed energy as it helps us to remember that energy is fluid and constantly changing. So, whatever outside influences disrupt you right now, we know that this energy will shift, allowing us more freedom to explore. If you feel as if you are facing a challenge right now, don't try to swim against the current of energy but rather allow things to play out as they will. Any worries and concerns that you have, you can release them through prayer or to the universe. You no longer need to hold onto feelings of discomfort; there is no need to keep your attachments to the outcome. Just release the resistance to change and trust that the universe has your back. There are some days when all we have is our faith, and our connection to the higher realms is strong today.

Song: "Lazy" by X-Press 2

March 16th

Mercury Retrograde in Aries

This Mercury retrograde may have you wanting to tear your hair out at times. It brings the energy of setbacks, miscommunication, and delays. As this particular Mercury retrograde is happening in the sign of Aries, it results from us taking quick action without taking the time to develop a foolproof plan. Regarding our communication, this means blurting something out and then instantly wishing we could take it back. We are likely to all have a serious case of "foot-in-mouth" disease at this time, finding ourselves reacting impulsively to others. This includes sending passionate emails or texts because we feel strongly about something, only to regret it later. It involves throwing ourselves into work projects without doing the appropriate research and having to rectify the situation afterward. This is impulsively deciding to take a road trip without booking your car in for a service first, only to run into car trouble later.

Before taking any action right now, ask yourself if this action needs any preparation or a structured plan to make things run more smoothly. Can you incorporate a backup plan to ensure you don't find yourself stranded in the middle of nowhere or having to apologize for being completely reckless? While there are times when being in the moment and living life without too much forethought pays off, this is not one of those times. If you have something to say, ask yourself what is the best way to deliver this message with love and compassion.

Reflection

1. Have I recently experienced setbacks due to a lack of preparation? What could I have done differently?

2. How can I develop a habit of pausing and thinking before responding, especially in emotionally charged situations?

3. What steps can I take to create more structured plans for my projects and activities?

Song: "Sorry" by Justin Bieber

March 18th

Sun in Pisces conjunct Pisces North Node

This aspect is asking us to have blind faith and trust that everything is working out just as it should. We are being asked to resist the urge to fix or put things right. If any fears are coming up for you right now, silence them by telling your ego, "Shhhh, I am exactly where I need to be." Things may not appear perfect—relationships may feel off balance, our bank account may be in the red—but know that the divine has a plan for you. Do not be afraid to ask for help. Connect through prayer and ask the divine to send you the next steps out of whatever challenge you are currently facing. Trust in Source can be difficult in times of chaos, but this energy asks us to have faith that all is working out just as it should.

This energy represents an unexpected situation popping up that we now have to deal with, likely within the area of our finances. Perhaps you were driving too fast and received a speeding fine in the mail. Maybe an unexpected payment has come out of your account that you did not anticipate, or you have just received word of a rent increase. This energy can make us feel avoidant, so I highly recommend addressing any financial issues swiftly to prevent them from being forgotten and resurfacing as bigger problems in the future.

Song: "Here Comes The Sun" by The Beatles

March 20th

Juno Retrograde in Sagittarius

When Juno moves retrograde, it creates separation within our connections. The direct positioning of this alignment had us searching for a partner with whom we could expand—someone adventurous, motivated, and driven, encouraging us to reach further and embody all that we are destined to be. However, during the retrograde, while we still desire expansion, we are likely to feel that we are better off going it alone, believing that a partner might hinder our progress.

Singles will likely want to remain single and withdraw from forming new connections, creating narratives about how having a partner or someone else to consider only holds them back from expanding and experiencing all they desire.

Those in long-term committed relationships may begin to feel the need for space and a desire to pursue their own interests outside the connection. We are likely to make plans that do not include our partner, or we may begin to feel that our relationship has become stagnant or stale, leading to feelings of restriction and a lack of independence. We crave freedom from our intimate connections and may feel weighed down by having to incorporate our partner into every decision and move we make.

Reflection

1. What specific aspects of my relationship(s) make me feel restricted or hindered?

2. In what ways have I created narratives about being held back by a

partner or potential partner? Are these narratives truly accurate?

3. How can I balance my need for personal growth and expansion with maintaining a healthy relationship?

Sun in Pisces conjunct Neptune in Pisces

This is unfocused and dreamy energy. Some of you may have to read today's energy update three times to let it sink in, or you may have skipped it altogether because you are too busy in a distant land, dreaming about other things. If you find it hard to focus today, I encourage you to dream about an alternate reality or go outside and chase fairies around the garden. Remember to make a wish. As a Pisces, I love allowing my consciousness to wander to Imagination Land or wherever it wants to go. Others may find this energy extremely frustrating because they need to get things done, but I have said it before, and I will repeat it: flow with the energy rather than against it. You only receive more resistance when you try to push through restrictive energy. Instead, find a way to sprinkle more magic into your day.

Song: "Escape" by Rupert Holmes

March 21st

Sun enters Aries

Aries season is about making moves, trying new things until you find something that works, and enjoying sampling all of life's pleasures. We want to experience everything that life has to offer us. We are just going after anything and everything we want and not taking no for an answer or allowing anyone else to tell us that we can't have it. This energy represents seeing something you want and just reaching out and taking it. Aries can be a bit of selfish energy; however, we could all benefit from prioritizing ourselves over others.

In this season, we are in passionate pursuit of our goals, and those goals may be subject to change frequently, so we are likely to become a little sidetracked, although I wouldn't worry. The season to follow this one is Taurus season, and we will have time to be serious and practical then. For now, let's all just be a little reckless and embrace the boundary-pushing teenagers inside of us who are screaming to be expressed. Aries season can be dramatic and intense, but it's never boring. So, embrace the chaos and ever adapting energy and allow the energy to expand your consciousness, encouraging you to embrace your inner badass. Aries' energy encourages us to take risks, and if we fall on our face, we get back up again, running at full speed toward the next challenge until we win. Within Aries energy, we discover an incredible resilience to keep fighting.

Reflection

1. Are there any goals or desires you've hesitated to pursue? How can you channel your inner Aries and go after them with gusto?

2. Think about a recent setback or failure. How can you embody Aries' resilience and bounce back with determination?

3. In what areas of your life do you need to be more reckless and embrace the chaos to discover new possibilities?

Song: "I Want It All" by Queen

March 22nd

Vesta Retrograde in Scorpio

This Vesta retrograde in Scorpio has us delving deep into our unhealed wounds to uncover what lies beneath the surface. We are identifying areas where we still carry guilt or shame and recognizing intrusive thoughts that enter our consciousness. By tracing these thoughts back to their origins, we can better understand them and bring them to the surface to be healed. Many of us may desire to isolate ourselves during this time, becoming defensive and protective over these wounded parts of ourselves. This energy understands that healing only requires finding and understanding the source of our pain. Once these scars are identified, we have shone light upon them so they can no longer exist within the shadows of our subconscious.

As these wounds are triggered, our understanding of them causes them to heal and diminish over time naturally. Our role within this energy is to uncover what has been buried beneath the surface. We must also recognize when to pull back, when we have gone deep enough, and when to come out of isolation and the depth of our emotions for some air. This energy can cause us to get lost within our labyrinth of emotions, determined to find the exit and free ourselves forever.

Remember that healing past traumas takes time; the process should not be rushed. We are not only here to heal but also to experience life and all that it has to offer. It is okay to come up for air now and then.

Reflection

1. What unhealed wounds am I currently aware of, and how do they manifest in my daily life?

2. What feelings of guilt or shame do I still carry, and where do they originate from?

3. What strategies can I use to balance my healing process with living and experiencing life fully?

Venus retrograde in Aries sextile Pluto in Aquarius

Recent energies have left us feeling irritated and somewhat disconnected from the world around us. However, this aspect asks us to embrace the discomfort, recognizing that we often need to become uncomfortable before we can lean into change and find the fire to truly want transformation. This energy asks: How can you channel your current discomfort into something more positive, something that creates change not only within yourself but also within the collective as a whole?

Song: "Scars To Your Beautiful" by Alessia Cara

March 23rd

Last Quarter Moon in Capricorn

This last quarter moon has come at the perfect time. This is the phase of the moon where we dig into our reserves to push through any obstacles or challenges we face. As the moon is currently in the sign of Capricorn, this allows us to be careful and calculated and to assess any potential risks. Capricorns are so thorough in risk assessment and predicting future outcomes that they overprepare for any challenge that comes their way, or, in some cases, they can avoid them altogether. So, we will utilize this energy to ensure that we are safe from potential disasters.

My partner works in the building industry, and each building site has what is called in Australia an Occupational Health and Safety Officer. It is the role of this officer to assess any potential risks within the environment and to address any issues that have the potential to cause future concern. I want you to reflect upon your environment, including work, family, relationships, and any area you feel may be built on an unstable foundation. This exercise requires a hard hat, clipboard, and serious facial expression. Just kidding. We are looking for potential risk factors that may cause a problem in the future. Then, for each potential problem, we will implement one strategy for preventing this problem and one solution if the situation arises. Now, you are more prepared for any challenge over the next few weeks.

Reflection

1. What challenges or obstacles have you noticed recently that require careful consideration?

2. In what areas of your life does an unstable foundation exist? How can you assess and address potential risks in these areas?

3. As you reflect on potential problems and challenges, what strategies can you implement to prevent issues from arising in the first place?

Venus retrograde in Aries quintile Jupiter in Gemini

Sometimes, it's not just okay to be a little selfish—it can be downright empowering! We often become so self-sacrificing that we hesitate to ask for what we truly want and need from others. But today is different. Today, you're encouraged to speak up and boldly pursue what you desire. If you see something you want, don't hold back—reach out and grab it with both hands. Seize the moment and claim what's yours!

Sun in Aries conjunct Venus retrograde in Aries

This energy suggests that you might face some competition in pursuing what you desire or that your wants might conflict with someone else's. So, what will you do? Will you lie down and sacrifice your needs to appease others or keep the peace? Or will you rise to the challenge and fight for what you truly want? The choice is yours.

Sun in Aries quintile Jupiter in Gemini

We all have unique skills, talents, and abilities that make us stand out from the crowd. How can you utilize these gifts to ensure you get what you want? Today is the day to show people what you're made of. If you have hidden talents but don't want to appear showy, now is the time to demonstrate them. This aspect is not only about knowing your strengths but also about boldly sharing them. If you're entering a competitive environment, what makes you stand out? If you have friends in high places who can put in a word for you, don't be afraid to leverage your connections. Shine brightly and let the world see your true potential!

Song: "Stronger" by Kanye West

March 24th

Sun in Aries sextile Pluto in Aquarius

We are all fired up about leaping into the unknown and taking control of our lives. We want to experience all this life offers, seeking adventure and excitement. Our energy feels incredibly expansive, and we will only settle for what we feel we deserve within this energy. We are like a dog with a bone, chasing after whatever sparks a flame deep within our soul. This energy encourages you to hook up with someone sexy you just met, dance in the rain, or chase your dreams. It is an energy of absolute expansion without the resistance and doubts we usually experience.

Song: "Best Day Of My Life" by American Authors

March 25th

Sun in Aries conjunct Mercury retrograde in Aries

This aspect represents a challenge or restriction popping up to slow us down, but we're not letting it bother or distract us from moving forward. The car won't start? No problem; I'll take the bus and enjoy the ride. There was a mix-up with our lunch reservations? Great. We'll find a nearby park and have an impromptu picnic. Is someone upset with us? They'll get over it. We're unstoppable, adapting, and thriving no matter what life throws our way!

Song: "Shake It Off" By Taylor Swift

March 26th

Mercury retrograde in Aries sextile Pluto in Aquarius

Sometimes, when we face setbacks and challenges, and things don't go as planned, it can be a blessing in disguise. These moments force us to come up with a new plan, and often, we find that the new path turns out even better than what we originally envisioned. Any challenge you face today, embrace it as an opportunity to shake things up and step outside your comfort zone. Trust that this will turn out even better than you initially imagined!

Song: "Life is a Highway" by Rascal Flatts

March 27th

Mercury retrograde in Aries quintile Jupiter in Gemini

Today, we are called to tap into a pre-existing skill to get ourselves out of a bind. Throughout our life's journey, we've all acquired a wealth of knowledge, and some of those skills lie dormant, waiting for the right moment. This energy could manifest in various ways: our receptionist may not show up for work, so we need to juggle their responsibilities along with our own. We may get a flat tire and remember how to change it without needing assistance. Or, we might need help from someone with a specific skill, and we know exactly who to call because we've nurtured that relationship and can count on their support.

Mars in Cancer square Chiron in Aries

Be mindful of this energy, as it signals the potential for emotional responses leading to impulsive actions driven by pain. The worst decisions are often made from a place of hurt. It could be something minor, like indulging in comfort food or splurging on an unnecessary purchase, or something more serious, like vandalizing someone's car out of anger. Today, take a moment to check in with your emotional state before making any decisions. Ask yourself: Am I choosing to do this because I'm in an emotionally charged state?

Song: "Hit 'Em Up Style" by Blu Cantrell

March 28th

Venus Retrograde enters Pisces

As Venus retrograde shifts from Aries into Pisces, we face unique challenges in healing our heart space. This transition brings our emotional fears to the forefront, urging us to extend forgiveness and compassion while simultaneously fearing vulnerability. We've endured painful lessons about love and are understandably wary of experiencing that heartache again. Our instinct is to protect our spiritual energy from those who might drain it and to guard our empathy from those who might exploit it.

This placement can feel incredibly uncomfortable, as our deep desire to extend love to others clashes with our hesitation to forgive past transgressions. How can we truly embody the energy of pure love when we're unable to let go of past hurts? This energy creates a confusing mix: on the one hand, we yearn to live in the light of love, while on the other, we're determined not to overextend ourselves to those who have been reckless with our hearts.

Reflection

1. What past experiences have shaped my current fears about extending forgiveness and compassion?

2. In what ways have I overextended myself in the past, and how can I set healthier boundaries now?

3. How can I practice self-compassion while working through my fears of vulnerability?

Venus retrograde in Pisces conjunct Neptune in Pisces

This dreamy, faraway energy has us drifting off into imagination land. What if we give our heart to someone who can't be trusted? What if we forgive someone who wronged us and they do it all over again? What if we choose not to extend love and miss out on a soulmate connection? What if the world were made of marshmallows? What if your pet goldfish is secretly plotting world domination? What if extraterrestrials show up at my door tomorrow and take me back to my home planet, and all this worrying about potential problems was for nothing? Many of the things we worry about never come to pass, but this aspect has us coming up with all kinds of unlikely scenarios.

Today, try to make decisions based on logic rather than fantasy. And if you must worry, at least make it about something actually happening.

Song: "Jar Of Hearts" by Chistina Perri

March 30th

New Moon Solar Eclipse in Aries

Eclipse energy intensifies everything, and this New Moon eclipse will likely make you feel as though you want to jump out of your skin as you become increasingly uncomfortable, feeling that you cannot freely express yourself. This is an energy of wanting to speak your mind and give no fucks about doing so. You have a burning desire to go after what you want and do not wish to feel restricted by how others may be affected.

Eclipse energy can be heavy, and this one brings passion, intensity, and impulsiveness. If you feel irritated by not feeling as though you can express yourself freely, take the time to breathe before erupting. Distance yourself from anyone who may be causing you to feel triggered and explore deeper the passions you keep locked away inside. If there is something you wish you could say, but you know it is not the right time, write it down to help release any emotional expression built up within your energy. If you suffer from anxiety, it is likely to be intensified during this time, so be sure to participate in whatever activities your soul needs to feel safe until the eclipse energy passes. We can release built-up energy in many ways by crying, screaming, or even manic laughter. The method I recommend is through breath. Breathe deeply into your solar plexus chakra, which is located in your stomach, and as you breathe, really push that air out with force, releasing any energetic blockages. Otherwise, search YouTube for a somatic breathing exercise that you can do. These breathwork practices are highly effective in releasing and rebalancing energy.

Reflection

For some new moon manifestation

1. Set Intentions with Passion: Begin by identifying your most passionate desires and goals. Write them down in a concise and assertive manner, reflecting Aries' direct energy. Use strong and affirmative language to express your intentions.

2. Fire Element Meditation: Aries is a Fire sign, so connect with the element of fire in meditation. Light a red or white candle to represent the flame. Focus on the energy and enthusiasm within you, allowing it to burn away any doubts or obstacles.

3. Physical Activity for Empowerment: Channel the dynamic Aries energy into your body, releasing any stagnant energy.

Mercury Retrograde enters Pisces

As Mercury retrogrades backward into the sign of Pisces, we continue to face challenges and setbacks in our communication. Previously, we were dealing with issues due to taking quick action without a structured plan—booking travel plans for the wrong dates, scheduling appointments without checking our calendars, and shooting off texts and emails without considering how they would be received. Now, with Mercury in Pisces, the energy shifts to procrastination and avoidance. We're missing out on the hotel room we wanted because we left booking until the last minute. We're making excuses for missing work deadlines because tasks remain incomplete. Communication is breaking down because we haven't bothered to respond to texts or check our email.

Be mindful of any activities you use to escape from addressing important tasks. This energy will be present for about another week, so try your best to remain focused on the task at hand.

Reflection

1. What are my go-to activities for procrastination, and how can I limit them?

2. How can I create a more effective system for managing my schedule and deadlines?

3. What are some practical strategies to stay focused on important tasks during this challenging period?

Mercury retrograde in Pisces conjunct Neptune in Pisces

This energy might tempt you into indulging in escapism. You may have an important task to complete, but that bottle of wine is calling your name. You might be dreaming up an excuse to knock off work early or thinking about binge-watching your favorite TV series. If you work from home, your bed might be calling for a "little nap." Be aware of the self-destructive patterns and behaviors you use to sabotage yourself.

Sun in Aries semi-square Uranus in Taurus

This is a frustrating energy of wanting to take immediate, impulsive action, but it's not the ideal time. Perhaps you want to book a holiday but have work commitments or business matters to handle. This energy supports making poor decisions that may affect you long-term, so be wary of making any impulsive moves at this time. Don't quit your job because you're having a bad day. Don't remortgage your house because you're desperate for a holiday. Any ideas that are getting you excited right now may require more thought. Every choice we make has consequences; ensure you are not making decisions right now for instant gratification that will have you drowning in consequences later.

Song: "Basket Case" by Greenday

March 31st

Neptune enters Aries

This is a very significant energy shift. Neptune stays transiting a sign for approximately 14 years, and a shift from Pisces- the psychic sign of spirituality and connection to higher realms, into Aries- the sign of self and war, is huge for us as a collective. Neptune represents all things spiritual, imaginative, and the unseen realms, but the downside of Neptune's energy is that it is unknown and vague, which creates confusion and distortion of truth. Neptune asks us to prioritize faith and spirituality, which can leave us with limitless questions as we become seekers of truth. If confused and unsure of what to put our trust in, we can be easily influenced and manipulated by spiritual leaders or those who we feel are spiritually enlightened or can share with us deep spiritual wisdom. Neptune's energy wants us to see the best in everything, which can cause us to become very trusting, leading us to be misled.

Neptune moving into the sign of Aries, will be calling many forward to step into a role of spiritual leadership and challenge the identity of the collective. For those who are not called, we will be going deep into unraveling our spiritual beliefs to find the right guides, spiritual leaders, and mentors to follow. We have spent the last 14 years with Neptune helping us to discover what resonates deeply with us on a spiritual level and expanding our consciousness, so remember the lessons that have been learned. Neptune in Aries will make it easier for us to be swayed. Assess whether the people you are following online or the religions you subscribe to are in energetic alignment for you.

There will be two types of spiritual leaders during this period: those who share messages of separation and those who share messages of unity consciousness. We are already seeing much of this happen. Many tarot readers online share messages referring to "the enemy" and using language like "you are the chosen one," creating separation and division between us and those who come against us. But there are also readers channeling messages of unity, forgiveness, healing ourselves, and extending compassion by praying for those who go against us. Some religions preach their pathway to God as the only way, and conflicts exist between countries with different spiritual belief systems. These conflicts are likely to intensify during this transit. You only need to read through my comments section online to find others with differing belief systems calling me a 'devil worshipper' for using divination practices. With Neptune moving into Aries, the sign of war, we will see more people wanting to fight anyone against their spiritual belief systems.

During this transit, we will see many losing themselves and their identity within these belief systems. We will see many people with a God complex, believing they are superior due to their beliefs. Others who have not done the appropriate healing on themselves will enter spiritual psychosis, having spiritual hallucinations and living in severe paranoia. It will become difficult for us to discern which leaders are channeling higher wisdom and which are struggling with mental health issues. I predict that cult-like behaviors will rise, although these cults will become much more mainstream and less detectable.

To help you better understand this energy, let me give you some examples of what took place during the last time Neptune was in Aries. The most significant was the American Civil War, a major conflict between the Northern and Southern states of America due to differing belief systems regarding the right to keep African Americans in slavery, creating division and separation between North and South, but also black communities versus white communities. Meanwhile, in my part of the world, European settlement in Australia expanded as they forcibly took land from Indigenous Australians, often resulting in violence and massacres. Aboriginal Australians were deeply spiritually connected to the land, and their sacred sites were destroyed to make way for infrastructure and to build agriculture for the European settlers. Assimilation policies forced Indigenous people to integrate into European society, often by removing children from their families and placing them in institutions where they were taught to reject their Indigenous culture and spiritual belief systems.

During this alignment, I ask that you be open to the idea that there are many pathways to God. Your belief systems that work for you may not resonate with another, which is okay. Be vigilant about the people you follow and whether or not they are creating further separation on this planet or assisting collective consciousness by helping us to heal ourselves individually to ultimately raise the collective vibration of the planet. In recent times, many have been called to become spiritual leaders, channelers, and healers. Still, many of those called still need to do the inner work necessary to separate away from ego enough to lead responsibly.

Reflection

1. In what ways have I been influenced by spiritual leaders or figures, and how can I ensure their teachings align with my personal beliefs and values?

2. How can I differentiate between messages of unity and messages of separation in the spiritual content I consume?

3. Am I more prone to trust others unquestioningly in spiritual matters, and how can I develop a more discerning approach?

Song: "People Of The Sun" by Roaman

April Alignments

April 2nd

Venus retrograde in Pisces conjunct Pisces North Node

This energy represents taking a backseat in our relationships, putting in little to no effort, often leading to avoidance. You may have had a spat with someone, and instead of hashing it out, you're feeling completely unbothered, casually blocking them on social media without a second thought. This vibe says, "Why reach out to that friend you haven't heard from in ages? They have not made an effort with you, so we may as well let that connection drift apart."

Have you got a loved one at home in a bad mood? Instead of addressing it or offering a shoulder to lean on, this energy has you thinking, "Salon time! Let's get those nails done because who needs to absorb those bad vibes anyway?" It's the ultimate "I'll deal with it later" attitude, making it easier to put off those tricky conversations for another day—preferably one that never comes.

Song: "Let Her Go" by Passenger

April 5th

First Quarter Moon in Cancer

The first quarter phase of the moon is a time for adjustments and assessments, and with the moon stationed in the nurturing sign of Cancer, our focus shifts to home and family. What does your home environment look like? It may be time to redecorate or declutter to create fresh, positive energy in your living space. How are the relationships with those sharing your home? Is everyone getting along, or is it time for a family meeting to address any bubbling issues?

96

This energy is all about checking in. Ask yourself, is everyone okay? Ensure your significant other is in a good space and has what they need to move forward. Adjust meal schedules to accommodate everyone's needs, book health appointments to keep everyone in tip-top shape, and check in with the kids to ensure they're keeping up with their schoolwork. Offer help with assignments if they're falling behind.

This phase reminds us that nobody gets left behind. It inspires us to make necessary adjustments to ensure everyone at home is comfortable and ready to move forward together.

Reflection

1. What aspects of my home environment bring me the most peace and joy, and which areas feel stagnant or stressful?

2. What are the current dynamics like between family members in my home? Are there any underlying tensions that need to be addressed?

3. How often do I check in with my family about their emotional and mental well-being? What can I do to better support them?

Mercury retrograde in Pisces conjunct Pisces North Node

Have you forgotten something? This energy tells us something needs addressing, yet we're likely to avoid it or keep putting it off. If there's a task you've been procrastinating on or a conversation you're dodging, let me remind you: while Mercury is still in retrograde, delaying it will likely cause more significant problems later. So, put on your adult hat and tackle it now.

Saturn in Pisces sextile Uranus in Taurus

There's a lesson for you to learn today. When we put things off until the last minute or avoid doing what needs to be done because we believe we have plenty of time, we often forget that these issues can intensify. If your car has been making a mysterious clunking noise and you haven't booked it in for a check-up, now is the time to do it. Otherwise, you might wake up one morning to find that your car won't start, presenting further challenges. Similarly, if you've noticed it's time to change the lint filter on your washer or dryer but haven't taken the time, you risk causing further damage to these machines, possibly necessitating costly replacements.

Take a moment to make a quick list of the less significant things that need your attention and get them done now. This proactive approach will help you avoid bigger problems down the road.

Mars in Cancer sextile Uranus in Taurus

This aspect asks us to identify any emotions leaving us feeling unsettled and asks us to consider what these emotions are trying to tell us. It's about taking action to create a safer and more positive space for ourselves and those around us. If you feel your cluttered environment is bringing down your mood, it's time to clear the clutter. If you sense that your teenager's energy is off and suspect they may be going through something challenging, think about how you can address it with them. Perhaps the vibes are low within your work environment—what can you do to lift the energy in the office?

Mars in Cancer trine Saturn in Pisces

This energy allows us to extend love and compassion to others because we can deeply relate to what they are going through. It's the perfect time to invite your neighbor in for a cup of coffee and hold space for them as they unload their built-up emotions or to offer to pay for someone else's groceries because you understand their struggle. Allow yourself to become someone else's earth angel.

Sun in Aries quintile Pluto in Aquarius

"The limit does not exist" is a famous line from 'Mean Girls.' What would you be doing right now if the limit did not exist? This energy allows us the ability to see beyond our limitations. By now, I hope you are beginning to realize that any limits you perceive do not exist; they only exist within your mind and reflect what you think is possible. Once you recognize this, your power and potential become expansive, as you can see that you are the creator of your reality, and everything in your outer reality is just a reflection of what you believe to be true within you. If you believe you are not worthy of unconditional love, you will attract partners who only reciprocate love when you behave in a certain way. If you do not value your time and energy, you will attract people around you demanding your time and energy. There are many examples of people who refused to give in to their limitations, such as any Paralympian ever or those who can think themselves well after receiving a cancer diagnosis. Overcoming the limitations placed upon us by our minds is challenging, but once we break through those blocks, we open up our reality to ultimate potential and opportunity.

Song: "I'll Be There" by Mariah Carey

April 7th

Sun in Aries sextile Jupiter in Gemini

This energy has us buzzing with excitement, ready to dive headfirst into learning something new. It's the perfect time to ask ourselves, "How can we expand our horizons? What can we learn more about?" Maybe it's time to invest in our education or devour books on a fascinating topic. This vibe pushes us to broaden our knowledge. You might find yourself at the library, hungrily searching for books on your latest obsession, signing up for a short course, or even deciding to pursue that bachelor's degree. It's all about embracing the level-up mentality.

Venus retrograde in Pisces trine Mars in Cancer

This energy rewards us for trusting our intuition and feelings about the world around us. Sometimes, we get a gut feeling that something isn't quite right, causing us to hold back or hesitate from extending our love or taking action. This aspect reminds us always to trust that inner voice.

Imagine you had the chance to move into a new home, but something about the property's energy felt off, so you held back from making an offer. Soon after, the perfect property came your way. Or perhaps someone offered an apology that felt insincere, and you wisely withheld your trust, only to discover that they were spreading malicious gossip behind your back days later. This aspect brings confirmation that it's okay to hold back from opportunities when something feels misaligned. Sometimes, hesitation pays off in ways we couldn't foresee.

Song: "Level Up" by Ciara

April 8th

Mercury Direct in Pisces

Mercury retrograde is finally over—thank goodness! We can now celebrate the end of breakdowns in communication and chaos with our gadgets and technology. However, we may still have some messes to clean up or apologies to make for missed deadlines or unclear communication. Here's a reminder of the type of communication we will be returning to, in case you've forgotten the impact of Mercury being in Pisces.

Mercury rules communication and represents how we receive and process information. Mercury does not feel at all comfortable positioned in the sign of Pisces. Pisces' energy is very dreamy and imaginative. You know when you are telling a story and just drift off mid-sentence and then snap back to reality and think, wait, what was I saying? That is this energy. Focusing on important tasks is going to be much harder during this alignment. If you have begun to tap into your intuitive abilities or have begun building a relationship with your spirit team, the connection will be much stronger and your channel much clearer during this time. Your intuition will be strong and hard to ignore, so if something feels off, trust that feeling.

Even for those who don't regularly communicate with higher realms, you may find yourself in a situation where you say something very wise or profound that has a deep healing effect on someone around you and wonder where that came from. We are all tapped into the ethers right now and have the ability to be the channel of divine wisdom even when we don't realize that we are doing it. You will see signs and synchronicities everywhere and consistently see angel numbers so often that it drives you crazy. Questioning your sanity comes part and parcel with Pisces energy.

We are not communicating in the usual way; we are communicating through energy and frequency, so when people speak to us, we may become very emotional or be able to feel what people are saying. It is important to ensure that you have the right kind of people around you right now, as you will have a heightened sensitivity to these energetic frequencies, and those with low energy will begin to affect you. Many people will find themselves heading into a period of isolation during this time as we feel overloaded by everything we pick up within other people's energy.

Our decisions during this time are based on how we feel about a situation rather than what we think about it. The frequency of music will be very healing to us now, and we may find that when we listen to a song, we become quite emotional because the energy of the lyrics deeply resonates within our souls. Rather than thinking I love this song, we are feeling wow. I know what that person was feeling when they wrote that. If you happen to be a songwriter, musician, or creative, you will be doing your best work. Pisces energy is almost poetic as creative inspiration flows right through you. My advice in getting the most out of this energy is to allow your creative juices to flow, even if you do not perceive yourself as a creative person.

Reflection

1. How did Mercury retrograde impact my communication and electronic devices over the past three weeks?

2. Did any issues arise that I need to address or apologize for now that Mercury retrograde is over?

3. What lessons did I learn during this Mercury retrograde about the

importance of clear and timely communication?

Venus retrograde in Pisces conjunct Saturn in Pisces

This energy represents the desire to extend love or forgiveness toward someone while recognizing that it might invite the possibility of being hurt again. You might be considering forgiving someone who isn't sorry or hasn't asked for your forgiveness, making it difficult to move past what has happened. Many people avoid taking accountability for the pain they cause and are not interested in doing the work to heal themselves. This often leaves us to consistently forgive and be the bigger person. However, this aspect asks us to proceed with caution.

If we choose to forgive an unhealed person, we must also maintain boundaries to protect ourselves from being hurt repeatedly. Reflect on what you've learned about dealing with unhealed people in the past. Saturn is asking you: do we need to repeat this lesson?

Song: "Human" Rag'n'Bone Man

April 9th

Venus retrograde in Pisces sextile Uranus in Taurus

This energy brings an external event that forces you out of your comfort zone to address a situation you've been avoiding. Maybe you blocked someone on social media to dodge a conflict, only to run into them face-to-face while out shopping. Or perhaps a troublesome coworker has been causing issues, and you chose not to report it to management, only to be called into the boss's office because they reported you instead. Now, you're forced to defend yourself and resolve the issue.

This aspect will likely have a favorable outcome, so don't panic. Just handle your business instead of taking an avoidant approach. A peaceful resolution is forecast.

Song: "Don't" by Ed Sheeran

April 11th

Mercury in Pisces conjunct Pisces North Node

This energy encourages us to say and do less, often leading us to withdraw from others as we become highly sensitive to their energetic frequencies. It asks us to be the bigger person and avoid conflict. During this time, we may feel the need to isolate ourselves to connect with our higher selves and delve deeply into our emotions, helping us better embody our own energy. It grants us a heightened awareness of others' energetic frequencies, and if you find those frequencies overwhelming, it's perfectly okay to withdraw and rebalance.

Song: "Leave Me Alone" by Pink

April 12th

Mars in Cancer trine Pisces North Node

This energy is a gift, inviting us to lose ourselves in the magic of the moment and grant ourselves permission to do whatever brings us joy. Feel inspired to write a song or share your deepest emotions with someone you love? Now is the perfect time to do it. The great outdoors are calling your name, leading you to wander through a forest and marvel at the natural world. A cherished childhood movie comes to mind, and you decide to watch it again, or you allow yourself to get lost in the pages of a captivating book.

This aspect encourages us to immerse ourselves in the enchantment of life rather than stressing over unfinished tasks and looming deadlines. Embrace the magic and let your heart guide you to experiences that bring pure delight today. Follow that trail of wonder and let yourself be carried away by the joy it brings.

Song: "What A Wonderful World" by Louis Armstrong

April 13th

Full Moon in Libra

Think of Libra energy as Lady Karma dishing out blows and creating balance for any wrongdoings. If you thought you got away with something, now is the time to come clean—or perhaps this energy is affecting someone around you. With this energy, you might hear through the grapevine that a person who wronged you in the past received a heavy dose of karma. It's important to stay balanced as chaos unravels around you. Remember, current events are here to teach you something, even if you're on the negative karma hit list. If someone you love receives negative karma, avoid placing yourself in the crossfire to protect them or soften the blow. Doing so will only prevent them from learning a valuable lesson essential for their soul's growth.

Reflection

1. How do you typically handle situations where imbalances are exposed, or fairness is called into question?

2. Reflect on instances where you've faced consequences for your actions. How did those experiences contribute to your personal growth and understanding?

3. Consider a situation where you might have been tempted to seek revenge or react negatively. How could a more balanced and measured response have influenced the outcome?

Venus Direct in Pisces

Venus retrograde is over, meaning we are less fearful of extending our love energy toward others. Although I have previously discussed this placement, here is a reminder of how this energy affects us collectively.

Venus in Pisces represents the deepest, purest form of love. This energy allows us to see past the flaws of others and find the light within everyone. We recognize that everyone has the potential to heal themselves and find their source of light. This kind of love is pure, romantic, and very forgiving. Within this energy, we are adaptable and change our love frequency to match that of another person. We are willing to sacrifice our selfish needs, wants, and desires to achieve spiritual balance within our connections. In this energy, we believe that if we give out love freely to those around us, others will match that energy, and we will receive pure love from others in return. The problem with this kind of energy is that it can be like wearing rose-colored glasses regarding our connections. We will give people many chances to redeem themselves because we fantasize about what this connection could become. When we sit in an energy of "love has no bounds," we are likely to put aside any boundaries we had in place to protect ourselves.

For singles, we are looking for connections with people who can love with an open heart and those who can match our energy. Be careful at this time, as we are likely to look past red flags and feel that we can heal those who are broken if we just show them what real love looks like. Be wary about forming a love connection with anyone who is recently single and hasn't taken the time to heal from a past relationship because, in this energy, we see many singles searching for a rebound relationship as the broken-hearted are looking for anywhere they can express their love energy. Also, be mindful of the fantasy energy that comes along with this alignment. You may match up with someone on Tinder who lives at a distance, and then 20 minutes later, you are caught up in your head imagining how you will make this connection work long distance, where you will live together, and what your kids will look like.

For those in a relationship, we start to look past our partner's flaws and become more accepting of them; instead, we embrace them and come to appreciate them. We want a deeper kind of love, a love that is a spiritual soul connection. We forgive past discretions and offer a clean slate to connect more deeply with our partner. If our partner tells us they will change, we believe them. Be careful that this does not lead to delusion and that you are not putting aside your boundaries to create a deeper connection with your partner. Giving someone a clean slate is fine, but that doesn't mean we should forget about everything that has transpired throughout our relationship.

Reflection

1. In what ways do I see the potential for spiritual and soulful connections within my current relationships?

2. Am I wearing rose-colored glasses in any of my connections, potentially overlooking red flags or diving into fantasies?

3. How can I ensure that my quest for a deeper, more profound love doesn't lead to compromising my boundaries?

Sun in Aries conjunct Chiron in Aries

This is a dangerous energy because this is an energy of projecting. Although we may not like to admit it, we are all guilty of projecting our pain and traumas onto others. Is the recipient of your outward expression of negative energy really responsible for your reaction, or is your ego pointing to an unhealed wound within you? Pay close attention to your expression of energy toward others at this time. Ask yourself why you are not expressing yourself in a vibration of love. And by that, I don't mean why this person is so annoying, but what within you is affected by this person's expression toward you? Looking at ourselves in this way requires an incredible level of self-awareness. While we can honor our emotions that are coming up, any deep triggers are a red alert to a wound that lies dormant and needs some love and attention.

Song: "All Of Me" by John Legend

April 15th

Sun in Aries semi-sextile Venus in Pisces

This aspect represents aggressively expressing your love toward another. If you have secret, undisclosed feelings for someone, you will likely find yourself expressing them now. This energy embodies feeling a deep love or connection with someone and taking decisive action to show it. Within this energy, there will be absolutely no doubt about our true intentions in our relationships because we will prove our love through our actions rather than just words.

Song: "The One That I Want" by John Travolta and Olivia Newton-John

April 16th

Juno Retrograde enters Scorpio

As Juno retrograde enters Scorpio, we experience a high intensity of sexual energy. However, Juno retrograde can lead us to withdraw from our deep and intimate connections, creating an interesting dynamic. It is crucial to express this sexual energy in healthy ways. You may find yourself getting lost in sexual fantasies and desires or having intimate dreams about someone who is not your partner. A healthy release of this energy could be through masturbation rather than acting on fantasies that could potentially cause problems within your relationship.

Many of us might find ourselves reading a steamy romance novel or being drawn toward watching pornography, both of which are healthy and safe ways to experience this energy. If you are in a committed relationship, consider opening up to your partner about your desires. You may be surprised at what they might be open to exploring together, creating a new level of intimacy and connection.

Reflection

1. What are my deepest sexual fantasies and desires, and how do they align with my current relationship?

2. How comfortable am I with discussing my sexual fantasies and desires with my partner?

3. How can I ensure that my sexual energy is expressed in healthy and respectful ways?

Sun in Aries semi-sextile Uranus in Taurus

Do we need to find more chill within our reactive energy? When things do not work out as planned, most of us can go from zero to 100 quickly and struggle to regulate our emotions. How easily can we separate ourselves from a problem outside our control? Do we instantly become defensive when challenged, or can we receive energies from sources around us without matching that energy frequency?

Sun in Aries semi-sextile Saturn in Pisces

Saturn in Pisces represents the lessons we have learned the hard way. Sun in Aries energy is all about being impulsive and in the moment. This energy reminds us that while we carry the lessons from the past, we do not have to be afraid that those same events will reoccur. We are safe to explore the world without worrying that the worst may happen. Our lessons from the past have taught us to recognize when we are pushing the boundaries too far. We can trust ourselves to avoid repeating the same mistakes. Release any worries about future outcomes and bring your energy back to the present moment and the potential adventures or opportunities within it. Our intuition and internal guidance system will tell us when to slow down.

Song: "S&M" by Rihanna

April 17th

Mercury enters Aries

Mercury is reentering the sign of Aries after its retrograde back into Pisces. We have already experienced this transit, but here is a reminder of what you can expect:

Mercury in Aries encourages us not to think too hard about things before taking action. If you are learning something new, this is the energy of putting down the books and trying to put things into action by getting some hands-on experience. Aries is known as the baby of the zodiac and brings childlike energy, so we are not thinking about consequences right now. We are making decisions based on what will bring us instant gratification. This is a time for making selfish decisions that align with our best interests. This is excellent energy for starting new projects; however, we can become easily bored. If the task at hand becomes repetitive, we may think of something more fun to do. We are easily distracted, and our patience is slim to none. Aries in Mercury does require more discipline because unless we are genuinely passionate about something, we will quickly give up on it. Unfortunately, due to this impulsive energy, we can miss out on stable, long-term opportunities because we seek instant rewards.

Aries is a very energetic and compassionate expression of energy, so this is great communication energy for anyone in a leadership role because we communicate in a way that comes across as enthusiastic, motivational, and inspirational. We have the ability to have a positive effect on the most uninspired people with this energy. The downside to this energy is that we want to express everything with solid opinions and speak our minds passionately, so arguments and disagreements are common occurrences. Aries is the sign of war, so we will unlikely want to back down if our opinions are challenged. We are not afraid of an argument within this energy, and some may even encourage one. In this energy, we are not afraid to say what others are afraid to say, which may lead to offending someone. Many of us will find ourselves having to apologize during this alignment. We do not mean to offend; we are just not giving our thoughts any time to marinate before blurting them out. If you struggle to filter the thoughts from your brain to your mouth, you may struggle most with this alignment. You could be the gentlest communicator and still be affected by this impulsive communication energy. You may even surprise somebody with an angry outburst and shock those around you because they didn't think you had that in you.

Reflection

1. How can I embrace the impulsive energy of Mercury in Aries to inject more passion into my current projects or endeavors?

2. How can I channel Aries's enthusiastic and motivational aspects in my communication to inspire those around me?

3. Are there long-term opportunities I might be overlooking due to my focus on instant rewards, and how can I balance both perspectives?

Sun in Aries semi-sextile Pisces North Node

This energy sparks us to dive headfirst into what brings us joy. Forget lingering in the planning stages—it's time to act! The magic of fast manifestation lies in taking bold steps. The universe meets you with matching energy when you move toward your dreams. Trust that if it's meant for you, the universe has your back every step of the way.

Don't hesitate to call on the divine for support. Got a creative project you're itching to start? Jump in! Ask your spirit team for guidance if you're short on funds or need specific skills. They'll lead you to the following steps, the resources or the right people to propel you forward. Stay open and ready to receive assistance. Remember, you're not alone in this journey—you're co-creating with the universe, and together, the possibilities are endless!

Song: "Last Friday Night" by Katy Perry

April 18th

Mercury in Aries conjunct Neptune in Aries

This energy is a sneaky one. While it empowers us to lead and makes us feel self-assured in our identity, it also subtly introduces an illusion of separation. This aspect requires us to delve deeper into ourselves to identify where our ego lies. For instance, you might encounter someone with a different opinion online and quickly label them an idiot. This energy feels empowering, as it convinces us that we are 'not the same' as those with differing perspectives and that we are right while they are wrong. But is that true?

If someone is living their life in a way you disagree with, is it a reflection of them living the wrong way, or is it just your ego reacting to their behavior being misaligned with your beliefs and programming? What if we allowed people to be who they are without trying to scold them for not meeting our expectations? Embracing this mindset can lead to a more harmonious and accepting view of others.

Jupiter in Gemini sesquiquadrate Pluto in Aquarius

This aspect suggests that we have an opportunity to learn something new and expand our minds today. The beautiful thing about this world is that we all experience life from different perspectives, and when we share our experiences with each other, we are granted the opportunity to expand our consciousness and understanding. However, this aspect also hints that someone else's views may be too out there for you to grasp.

Perhaps we are trying to educate others and share our wisdom, but they feel we need to be more receptive to their ideas. This can create a stubborn energy, where we refuse to accept another's point of view and instead push our own agenda. Embrace the chance to listen and learn from others, even if their perspectives challenge your own.

Song: "You're Wrong" by FOFX
NOTE: This song does not reflect my personal views or belief systems. It is intended to accurately represent current energies.

April 19th

Mars enters Leo

As Mars moves into the sign of Leo, we find ourselves more confident than ever and all fired up to express our creativity. This placement pushes us to express unique parts of ourselves, sharing our gifts, talents, and abilities with the world, saying, "Look what I can do." This placement also comes with a strong determination to show up for ourselves and express our authenticity, so we will no longer be self-sabotaging or making excuses as to why we can't achieve something. Many of us will be hitting the gym, pushing past our limits, or consistently building toward our future. We are producing excellence at an incredible rate and impressing ourselves with our ability to achieve.

This placement gives us main character energy, and we feel as if we are the star of our own movie, with others around us as merely supporting actors. This energy is all about having fun and expressing ourselves, and we will find that others are naturally drawn to our charismatic energy. However, be mindful of becoming too competitive with others around us. Many of us have the tendency to overspend on flashy items at this time or find ourselves seeking more attention or recognition from others. While tapping into our confident leadership energy is great, remember that the only person we have to prove anything to is ourselves, and catch yourself if you find that you are seeking approval or acceptance from others.

Reflection

1. In what ways are you feeling fired up to express your creativity?

2. How are you sharing your gifts, talents, and abilities with the world, and what messages do you want to convey?

3. Consider any tendencies you may have to overspend on flashy items or seek attention and recognition from others. How can you channel your confident leadership energy without relying on external validation?

Song: "Main Character Energy" by Moonlight Scorpio

April 20th

Sun enters Taurus

While we have been flying by the seat of our pants, taking impulsive action, and following our bliss all through Aries season, the beginning of Taurus season is now upon us, which asks us to slow things down and be a little more practical to ground our dreams in reality. After all, we do want our future to be stable, reliable, and built on a solid foundation.

Taurus season will help us assess the practicality and sustainability of everything in our lives and give us the sense to repair any damage we may have caused while being in the reckless energy of Aries. Taurus helps us prioritize the work that needs to be done, and yes, even the tedious tasks we allow to pile up. We are committed to creating positive habits that will help sustain us in the long term and offer us the ability to resist the temptation of behavioral patterns that may be destructive. Taurus season is not all work and no reward; this energy encourages us to reward ourselves for a job well done and celebrate even the small wins and milestones. This season creates the perfect balance of work ethic and self-care, as this sign understands that slow and steady wins the race and recognizes the importance of rest.

Reflection

1. How can I balance the thrill of impulsive actions with a more grounded and steady approach?

2. In what areas do I need to repair any damage caused by recklessness or impulsivity?

3. How can I create positive habits that contribute to long-term stability and success?

4. What practical tasks have I neglected that require my attention during Taurus season?

Mars in Leo trine Neptune in Aries

This aspect has us feeling on top of the world, ready to own the qualities that make us stand out. We are determined to step out of the shadows and boldly show the world what we're made of. This energy declares, "You are a confident, passionate, and creative being with something incredible to offer—so what will you create today?" What actions will you take to make the world stand up and take notice? In which areas of your life can you seize control and step into a leadership role? With this energy, we are determined to show everyone how it's done.

Song: "Humble and Kind" by Tim McGraw

April 21st

Last Quarter Moon in Aquarius

This last quarter moon invites us to explore whether the areas we consider to represent stability in our lives truly reflect an authentic expression of ourselves. Does your current job align with the way you want to show up in the world? Does it provide the space to fulfill the legacy you want to leave behind and the imprint you aim to create for generations to come? Is your home a beautiful representation of who you are, or does your neighborhood lack energetic alignment for you?

When considering our stability, we contemplate what has become our comfort zone. Is your comfort zone still a comfortable place for you, or do you feel the need to explore beyond it? The support of the Sun in Taurus empowers us to make responsible decisions on implementing small steps and strategies for gradual expansion, as well as making prudent choices regarding any outstanding bills, payments, or investments that need attention. This energy prompts us to assess what still makes sense for us and what needs to be shifted and changed to allow us greater freedom of self-expression.

Reflection

1. How does your current job align with the way you want to present yourself to the world, and does it contribute to the legacy you aim to leave?

2. Is your living space a genuine representation of your inner self, and does it resonate with your authentic energy?

3. In terms of stability, does your comfort zone still provide the comfort and freedom you need, or is it time to explore beyond its boundaries?

Sun in Taurus semi-sextile Neptune in Aries

This is an energy of self-improvement, whether it finds you hitting the gym, prioritizing self-care, managing your finances, or listening to a Tony Robbins podcast. While we can't control the world around us, this energy encourages us to focus on what we can control. It's about taking slow, methodical steps in the right direction toward where we want to go.

We recognize that we won't be able to change everything overnight, but by putting in a little work each day, we'll be unrecognizable 12 months from now. This energy isn't about grand gestures; it's about making quiet, behind-the-scenes changes, like cutting out carbs or quitting cigarettes. One day at a time, we'll be dedicated to becoming a better version of ourselves than we were yesterday.

Venus in Pisces sextile Uranus Taurus

This energy inspires us to be the change we want to see in the world, recognizing that the energy we put out is the frequency we will likely receive from others. If others are expecting a reactive response from us, we won't give them the reaction they want or engage in drama. Instead, we will send them love, pray that they see the light, and focus on our own development.

We understand that we can't heal the world by doing the healing work for others; the only healing we are responsible for is the work we do on ourselves. Today, we will embody a frequency of pure love and positive intentions, leading by example rather than trying to change their behaviors.

Mercury in Aries sextile Pluto in Aquarius

This aspect helps us to feel very optimistic about the new intentions that we are setting regarding our spiritual connection. We may also feel excited to try some new spiritual practices that we have never tried before, so you may find yourself buying a book on a spiritual topic or wanting to learn more about other religions from across the world, such as Buddhism or Hinduism. You may want to sign up for a yoga class or buy some crystals to support healing. This is exploratory energy in which you will be open to trying new things, so why don't you add a new magical element to your manifestations? Have fun with it!

Sun in Taurus square Mars in Leo

This energy fills us with inspiration to create and take control of our lives, but it might not yet spark immediate action. It's like hyping yourself up to the max, only to feel like a deflated balloon when it's time to act. Have you ever read a personal development book or listened to hours of motivational podcasts, feeling so pumped up and having countless aha moments, only to finish and let it all fade into the pile of other read motivational books? Or you may feel reluctant to take action or start writing down plans you never actually implement.

To break this cycle, you must act on your inspiration while it's fresh. If you feel the spark starting to wane, commit to doing just one thing—just one thing today—that will set the stage for incredible change in your life tomorrow. Don't let the fire of your motivation die out. Seize the moment, take that first step, and let it propel you forward. Your future self will thank you for the action you take today!

Song: "Fight Song" by Rachel Platten

April 22nd

Saturn in Pisces conjunct Pisces North Node

This aspect guides us toward learning a profound spiritual lesson in resistance versus letting go. How much control can you surrender? If we cling to attachment to outcomes instead of releasing control over situations, this lesson will likely be more painful than it needs to be. Instead of trying to regain control of the wheel and manipulate situations to go in your favor, allow things to unfold as they are meant to. Embrace the flow and trust the process, finding peace in letting go.

Song: "Let It Be" by The Beatles

April 24th

This is an energy of feeling as though we are ready for expansion but being painfully aware of the things that need to be fixed or reexamined. In career or business, this could be wanting to pursue a new career but recognizing that you don't yet have the qualifications required for that role and mapping out the steps it would require you to get there. A higher level of education or skill must be obtained.

You may want to start a business, but you already have outstanding debts, and you recognize that needs to be addressed first so that you can begin your new venture with a clean slate and not have the added pressure of paying off your previous debt. In this case, you may need to temporarily find a job to pay you a stable income and work out a payment plan or consolidate your debts. In love, this could be wanting to take your relationship to the next level by moving in together, joining bank accounts, or getting married. Still, you recognize that underlying issues need to be addressed to achieve a stable foundation for you to build upon.

Song: "Work Bitch" by Britney Spears

April 25th

Venus in Pisces conjunct Pisces North Node

Who are you being asked to be? The divine will likely become loud within this energy, urging you to step into a higher purpose or calling. How can you best embody pure love and extend that energy outward toward the collective? Are you a direct channel to the spirit realm? An energetic healer? Do you have the gift of breathing life into others who are struggling just with your words?

Are you being called to become a guide or mentor, helping others recognize their greatness? Or are you being asked to walk beside them as they heal from their traumas? Embrace this divine calling and allow yourself to be led toward your destined path. The world needs your unique gifts and the light you bring.

Venus in Pisces conjunct Saturn in Pisces

This energy invites us to make deep soul connections with those around us and consider whether those individuals are a vibrational match to our frequency.

Does my partner's energy complement mine? If you are seeing someone new, are you able to connect on a deeper, energetic level, or is this person hot as hell but somewhat shallow and lacking any depth? Does the person you chose to be your life partner appreciate and celebrate your authentic soul expression, or do their eyes glaze over whenever you try to express what is in your heart? Are we allowing space for others to express their desires, and are we ourselves supportive and compassionate friends, lovers, or family members?

Song: "Carry You" by Ruelle

April 26th

Mercury in Aries quintile Jupiter in Gemini

This aspect presents a fantastic opportunity for teaching and learning. If you wish to pursue a course of study or a book that has been calling to you, this energy urges you to stop thinking about it and dive right in. Similarly, if there's a skill you've been wanting to share—whether it's writing a book, creating a course, or starting an online platform to teach others—now is the time to jump right in. This energy reminds us that we don't have to have it all figured out; we can learn and grow along the way.

Sun in Taurus semi-square Jupiter in Gemini

This energy contrasts sharply with the previous one discussed. It may push you to place starting that YouTube channel at the bottom of your to-do list, prioritize other expenses over investing in yourself and your education, or spend another year outlining an online course you'll likely never complete. To navigate this energy, it's crucial to make self-expansion a priority in your schedule. How can you expect others to invest their time, energy, and money into your creation if you can't even invest them into yourself?

Song: "Dare You To Move" by Switchfoot

April 27th

Mars in Leo opposite Pluto in Aquarius

This aspect creates a challenge as we attempt to maintain our confidence but feel the potential of our confidence bubble being burst. We may think the market we wish to tap into is oversaturated, causing us to doubt our ability to make our mark. We may have an innovative product or service we feel the collective isn't ready for. Or we may be afraid that if we put ourselves out there, we won't be well received.

Don't let these fears hold you back from making progress. Remember, no one can deliver a message the way you can, and no one else can create like you do. Share yourself as you feel called to do so. This world needs your unique recipe.

Song: "Not Ready" by Myle

April 28th

New Moon in Taurus

Feel the call to switch up your daily routines as this energy extends an invitation to infuse structure into your life, weaving it seamlessly with your long-term aspirations. Imagine crafting a roadmap for the next five years—where do you envision yourself? This new moon encourages the creation of a detailed plan, outlining the steps needed to propel you toward that future. Even the most spontaneous among us can discover vitality in a well-crafted plan. Amidst these considerations, a question arises: How much energy and resources am I dedicating to my growth and well-being?

Reflection

For some new moon manifesting inspiration

1. Create a Vision Board: Collect images and words representing your goals and desires, especially those related to stability, financial prosperity, and sensual pleasures. Arrange them on a vision board and place it in a prominent location where you can see it regularly.

2. Taurus is associated with growth, so consider planting seeds or a new plant during the new moon. As you plant, infuse your intentions for growth, stability, and abundance into the soil.

3. Financial Planning: Use this time to review and plan your finances. Set specific financial goals for the coming month or even the entire year. Consider creating a budget that aligns with your values and long-term financial stability.

4. Pamper Yourself: Taurus appreciates the finer things in life. Treat yourself to a luxurious bath a massage, or indulge in your favorite meal. As

you do, reflect on your self-worth and how you can bring more pleasure into your life.

Mercury in Aries semi-square Uranus in Taurus

There is something you feel passionate about, a new hobby or project you would like to start, or an opinion you would like to express. Something external is causing some disruption, preventing you from expressing yourself in the way you would like, and this can lead to anger and frustration. This energy asks you to choose yourself and not allow yourself to be taken advantage of. Be very mindful of how you express this energy. If you feel anger, frustration, or resentment rising within you, take the time to acknowledge this energy and breathe it out before erupting. It is entirely natural to feel overwhelmed by this energy. This energy also represents wanting to regain control and fight back. What are you allowing to disrupt your peace right now?

Song: "Plans" by Oh Wonder

May Alignments

May 1st

Venus enters Aries

Venus does not belong in the sign of Aries; it does not feel comfortable there, and our love energy cannot be fully expressed in the way we want to express it. This placement can make for some challenging energy related to our connections and relationships. A full embodiment of love is eternal and long-lasting; however, Aries energy is impulsive, and easily becomes bored. This energy wants to be expressed without worrying about consequences, and here are just a few examples of why this can become a problem. Perhaps you have something in your heart that wants to be expressed, but you know that bringing this topic up will likely cause an argument; we simply do not care about others' feelings right now. Perhaps your love energy wants to be expressed toward someone already committed to someone else; Aries energy is known for being quite competitive and wanting to win at all costs. I am sure I don't need to go into detail about the kind of issue that this can cause. With this energy, we know what we want and will do just about anything to ensure we achieve it. As our passion and desire are at an all-time high, we are likely to experience a higher sex drive at this time. If this becomes a problem, I recommend adding a physical activity to your routine, such as running or other activities.

For singles, Aries energy is assertive, so you are much more likely to initiate contact at this time and go after what or who it is that you want. Aries is a very physical sign, so we are more likely to find ourselves drawn to those we find physically attractive at this time rather than those who are mentally stimulating or have a little more depth. We are also more likely to ignore red flags as we seek more excitement and may see a red flag as a personal challenge. We are easily bored with this energy, so many of us will find ourselves talking to or dating multiple people at once and exploring our options rather than making a deep and meaningful connection with just one person. Anyone who can keep us on our toes by playing hard to get will seem more intriguing to us now, and if

118

we usually do not like to play games, we may find ourselves a little more open to participating in the chase.

For those in a committed relationship, this is an energy of wanting to express our needs and desires openly but without giving much thought to our partner's needs and desires. There is great potential for conflicting energy between the two of you. We are more likely to feel bored, restricted, and stifled within our connections. If this energy comes up for you, I encourage you to find a way to add more excitement or spice things up rather than nitpicking and starting an argument just for excitement or so that you can have passionate makeup sex afterward. This is the perfect opportunity for couples to find ways to turn up the heat or add more passion and excitement to a connection that has become stale.

Reflection

1. How can you best navigate expressing your desires when faced with potential conflict or disagreement in your relationships?

2. Reflect on a past experience where your passion and desire may have led to impulsive actions. How did this impact your relationships, and what lessons did you learn from that experience?

3. How can you incorporate more excitement and passion into your current relationships without creating unnecessary conflict or tension?

Song: "Sorry Not Sorry" by Demi Lovato

May 2nd

Mercury in Aries quintile Pluto in Aquarius

I love this aspect, which allows us to recognize that the desire we have to change and transform ourselves and our lives is half the battle. We no longer listen when someone tells us we can't do something. We know that if we want something bad enough and commit to it, we can have it. This energy has us feeling motivated, enthusiastic and inspired to make significant changes. We feel invincible within this energy.

Sun in Taurus semi-square Pisces North Node

This aspect represents having a looming task that you would prefer to avoid. While the previous energy makes us feel expansive and inspired, inspiration must be followed by action, or it will remain just a dream. Want to develop a product or start a business? Have you put aside a project for a more appropriate time? Now is the appropriate time. Don't let all the excuses you've used up to this point win the battle today.

Uranus in Taurus sextile Pisces North Node

This energy indicates that once you start taking action, your efforts will be met with even more inspiration. Before you know it, you'll find yourself in a creative flow state. This energy might also manifest as meeting the right person to help your inspired idea take flight or having the money and resources you need show up at just the right time. It's a reminder that the universe has your back.

Song: "I Got This" by Kali J & LiTTiE

May 3rd

Venus in Aries conjunct Neptune in Aries

This aspect has the potential to cause some friction within our relationships because it not only indicates having a different point of view than another person but also encourages us to challenge those with differing views. This energy says, "I am right, you are wrong, and you are an idiot if you do not see life the way I see it." It is a very stubborn energy, and interactions with others can quickly escalate. Ask yourself today how you can be more open and receptive to those with different perspectives. Even if your way is right, is enforcing your views worth entering into drama or conflict?

Song: "Stupid Girls" by Pink

May 4th

Sun in Taurus semi-square Saturn in Pisces

This is a difficult energy of wanting to carry forth all of the progress that you have made so far and not wanting to lose momentum but also feeling an overwhelming desire just to take a break or a nap. This season will require us to slow things down but still maintain the necessary amount of effort so we do not lose focus altogether. Imagine you are a bear ready to hibernate for the winter, the only problem being that you are not a bear. You are a human, and as humans, we are expected to produce results and continue to progress forward despite wanting to nap or vacation for months at a time.

Mars in Leo semi-square Jupiter in Gemini

This energy represents being somewhat overconfident. You might feel that you already possess all the skills needed to manifest anything you desire. However, if that were true, you would already have everything you wish to manifest because you would be in energetic alignment with those things. Take some time to consider that you still have much to learn. How can you expand your knowledge and push yourself outside your comfort zone? This energy serves as a reality check, reminding you that there is still work to be done, though it may come with some resistance. Self-awareness is key to overcoming this energy.

Song: "Banana Pancakes" by Jack Johnson

May 5th

First Quarter Moon in Leo

The first-quarter moon phase invites us to look at what is not working and allows us to make some adjustments in areas that could use a little tweaking. With the sun in Taurus and the moon in Leo, this asks how we can bring more life and passion into whatever we are doing. How can we break up the mundane in our lives and make it more fun, inspiring, and juicier? Leo is all about having fun and creating an energetic vibration of embodying main character energy. What can we incorporate into our daily routine that makes us feel pumped up and enthusiastic to tackle any challenge we face throughout our day?

For me, this is often my high-vibe Spotify playlist, which I created for myself based on which songs get me fired up. Also, 30 minutes of yoga helps me get into the zone of prioritizing myself and creating balance within my energy so that I am better able to help and inspire the people that I am here to serve. There are times when I need an extra kick up the butt to get going, and on those days, I will bring out my secret weapon of podcasts by motivational speakers who inspire me to the point that I feel like an absolute rockstar by the time I sit down and begin my work for the day. What is your secret weapon to get you into a state where you are inspired to make a change and stay on your direct path? For some of you, it could be that you are committed to working through this book to help you feel inspired and ready to serve humanity.

Reflection

1. In what ways do you currently infuse fun, inspiration, and vitality into your routine?

2. What creative approaches can you incorporate to make daily tasks more enjoyable and exciting?

3. Identify and share your "secret weapons" for days when you need an extra boost.

Pluto Retrograde in Aquarius

Pluto is known for its destructive nature, bringing about the collapse of anything in our lives that needs transformation. In retrograde, this energy shifts from external transformations and things collapsing around us to internal transformations. This energy entrusts us with the responsibility to transform our outer reality by granting us the ability to choose what needs to be shifted and changed to reflect our inner transformations, however, not before making us feel incredibly uncomfortable. The internal shifts during this alignment will likely make us so uncomfortable that we feel compelled to make outer changes. This is undergoing a deep spiritual transformation and then feeling as though we no longer feel comfortable living in our current reality due to the profound shifts experienced, fostering an intense desire to transform our outer reality to align with the transformations felt within.

Reflection

1. What profound shifts and transformations have I been experiencing internally recently?

2. In what ways does my current external reality feel contradictory to the internal changes I've undergone?

3. What specific aspects of my outer world do I feel compelled to transform to align with my inner evolution?

Song: "Creep" by Radiohead

May 6th

Mercury in Aries sextile Jupiter in Gemini

This energy is like being a young child eagerly putting your hand up in class, or like the movie 'Yes Man' starring Jim Carrey, where you say yes to life and new opportunities. But instead of waiting to be called upon, you stand up and say, "Pick me. I am the right person for the job." This energy is all about self-promotion—why should people listen to you? Why are you so valuable? Why should someone buy your product or service? It's about recognizing your worth and not being afraid to share the value you have to offer. This energy has you playing as the star of the football game rather than sitting on the bench waiting for your opportunity.

Song: "I'm A Star" by Jay Critch

May 7th

Sun in Taurus semi-square Neptune in Aries

You know what you should be doing. Consistency and self-discipline are the keys to pushing through resistance. The decision to show up for yourself is not a one-time event but a choice you make consistently each day. This energy suggests the potential for someone to claim they have a shortcut to all your problems. Be mindful of ads promising to 10x your income quickly or those claiming to have the secret sauce to unlock your potential. If it sounds too good to be true, it probably is.

There are genuine teachers out there who can help you do the work required to manifest your dreams, but you must be discerning about whom you invest in. The best mentors are those who consistently inspire you, possess the qualities you wish to obtain, or deeply resonate with your soul. Before making an investment, sit with it for a while. Ask your spirit team to guide you toward mentors who can take you to the next level rather than falling for a well-crafted sales pitch.

Venus in Aries sextile Pluto retrograde in Aquarius

This is the energy I like to refer to as "the shift." I'm sure you've experienced situations where everything feels stuck and stagnant, your energy is low, and intrusive thoughts keep you from seeing a way out. You decide to give up and stay within your comfort zone. Making a change seems complicated, so instead of trying to change your circumstances, you sit in the void of non-action. This space is okay for a while, but it becomes increasingly uncomfortable over time until you reach rock bottom.

You recognize that you can no longer stay in the discomfort of stagnancy and decide it's time to make a change. You find the inspiration to take action toward changing your circumstances. This space can feel like you've been knocked over the head with your potential or shaken awake. "The shift" can be jolting, but it gives you the passion and desire needed to make a change. You feel empowered and ready to take on any challenge, willing to do whatever it takes. This energy says, "I do not want to live in this reality anymore, and I will do whatever it takes to pull myself out of it."

Mercury in Aries conjunct Chiron in Aries

This is a problematic energy with emotions surfacing that you would rather not address or look at. If something emotional comes up for you, it is easy to forget that you are on a healing journey of becoming your highest version, refusing to give it any of your attention, or lashing out in anger. I usually support looking deeper into your triggers; however, the energy doesn't support that today. You will likely end up feeling triggered and frustrated, so my advice for you today is to breathe and sit with it until you can explore it without feeling overwhelmed by emotions.

Song: "The Power" by Snap

May 8th

Mars in Leo quintile Uranus in Taurus

This energy is a powerful reminder that you have all the tools to overcome any challenge or disruption you face. Does someone think they can outsmart you? Think again—you're smarter. Is life throwing lemons your way? It's time to whip up some lemonade. You've always had the tools in your arsenal, but this aspect propels you into solution mode, bypassing the usual worry and panic when things go awry. You've got an ace up your sleeve; it's just a matter of remembering how to play it. Embrace this energy and tackle your challenges head-on, knowing you're equipped to handle whatever comes your way.

Song: "Watch Me Shine" by Joanna Pacitti

May 9th

Mercury in Aries semi-sextile Pisces North Node

This energy is a powerful reminder that when the divine steps in to assist us or we are presented with an opportunity, we should not be afraid to reach out and take it. If you're still waiting for divine assistance, a lucky break, or a door to open, it might be time to ask yourself if there is already an open door you're too afraid to step through or haven't recognized. Past conditioning might tell you you don't belong on the other side of that door. Sometimes, we have such a clear vision of what we're manifesting that we get in our own way by not recognizing the path laid out before us. Remember, it's not up to us to decide the route, so it may not look how you expected. Embrace any opportunities that come your way now, and metaphorically check your pockets—you already possess the key.

Mercury in Aries semi-sextile Uranus in Taurus

This energy challenges us to embrace destruction and disturbance. It revels in things falling apart because change is far better than stagnation. Welcome disruption—you might even be the one causing it. Your behavior may shock others as you give someone a piece of your mind or challenge another to move out of your way. This energy empowers you to become a bulldozer, clearing out and knocking down any obstacles hindering your progress. Embrace your inner force and forge a path toward your goals with unapologetic determination.

Song: "Take it" by Dom Dolla

May 10th

Mercury in Aries semi-sextile Saturn in Pisces

This energy supports wanting to try something new or getting started on something while also being very aware of our ability to lose focus. This asks us to look deeper into the things that distract us or how we self-sabotage. If we tend to be easily distracted by a new idea or something shiny, that doesn't mean that we shouldn't try something new just to enjoy it. We don't need to become experts in everything that we do. Sometimes, we can just explore something just for the fun of it.

I remember once I became obsessed with watching fire twirling videos; it was so mesmerizing watching people spin their fire staffs and throw them up in the air. I knew I had to try it, so I purchased my fire staff and spent months practicing and learning new tricks. Fire twirling would completely put me in the zone, as all thoughts were released from my mind, and I felt very present in the moment. There was only one problem: I was too afraid to light my staff. I figured that I would probably go up in a ball of flames as although I enjoyed twirling, I am quite uncoordinated and never felt good enough. Eventually, my staff twirling phase passed, and now my fire staff sits in my garage waiting for the day I call on it again. Although I lost my passion for the staff and never got to the point where I was ready to light it on fire, I have no regrets about the energy I put into trying it, dancing around my yard with it, and the power it gave me to express myself. I encourage you to try something new and let go of any attachments to the outcome. Just try it for no other reason than because you want to.

Song: "Dancing Queen" by ABBA

May 11th

Mercury enters Taurus

Mercury enters Taurus in very practical energy, and while it certainly has its place in the world, this energy goes against everything that this book represents. So, this may bring up some challenging aspects in relation to feeling confident in stepping into your full authentic expression and breaking through your resistance. This energy literally screams at you to stay inside your comfort zone and not push yourself. It asks you to take the time to think through your options to ensure that you take the time to make decisions that are right for you. It asks us to choose what is comfortable and always make practical decisions.

I am sure you can see how this energy can hinder your progress to energetic expansion. However, there are aspects of this energy that can help you to become more grounded, and I encourage you to embrace those aspects of this energy. During this period, we will be taking our time to absorb information, so I invite you to work with this energy by considering learning or studying a new skill, enrolling in a course, or reading a book that you feel will help you to step into success by gaining a deeper understanding of a topic you wish to pursue. Reading about marketing, business management, or finances would greatly allow this energy to work for you.

If you have not already, buy a journal and begin writing down all the feelings, breakthroughs, blockages, and emotions coming up for you as you progress through your healing journey. I cannot stress enough how helpful getting your words and thoughts onto paper will be for you at this time. It will allow you to read back, process what you are experiencing, and view your situation from another perspective. As you can separate yourself from what you have written, ask yourself if this were a friend coming to me for advice on this problem, what advice would I offer them?

Reflection

1. Reflect on a time when you felt the urge to stay within your comfort zone and resist daring leaps. What factors contributed to this resistance, and how did you navigate through it?

2. How might learning about marketing, business management, or finances optimize your success?

Song: "Vienna" by Billy Joel

May 12th

Mercury in Taurus semi-sextile Neptune in Aries

This aspect urges us to be discerning about the narratives we hear and the paradigms we subscribe to. Gossip through the grapevine can be colored by the personal views of the storyteller, and media reports may omit details to project a specific narrative. This energy reminds us not to take everything at face value, even from seemingly credible sources. Each of us views events through our unique lens. Trust your inner compass—honor that instinct if it nudges you to seek more information. Do your due diligence before jumping on any bandwagon. Empower yourself by questioning, investigating, and forming an informed perspective.

Song: "American Idiot" by Greenday

May 13th

Full Moon in Scorpio

Full moons represent the peak expression of our emotional energy, and this one occurs within the sign of Scorpio, which is the sign of intensity. Hence, this moon is likely to be a doozy. This energy will have you all up in your feels, and during any full moon, it is always important for us to consider the placement of the Sun, which is currently in Taurus, the sign of long-term commitment and stability. Taurus represents anything in our lives that is stable and long-lasting. The polarizing energy of Scorpio represents the darkness and the shadows, the unseen, if you will.

During a Scorpio full moon, we often find that anything done in the dark will come to light, so we are confronted with painful truths we do not want to see or secrets and hidden motives are exposed. While this energy does feel intense and can feel as if it is here to destroy everything we thought was solid, it is actually here to help us expose anything we have built that is not stable and long-lasting. We see many cheaters exposed during a Scorpio full moon, many friendships falling apart, and even the collapse of businesses. This energy has the potential to bring about the biggest shake-up for you throughout your entire year, and I want to remind you to breathe, as anything unstable within your life is exposed to you by divine orchestration of the universe.

Reflection

1. How do I handle intense emotional situations, and what strategies can I employ to navigate the upcoming cosmic rollercoaster? How can I approach this Scorpio full moon with a growth mindset and resilience rather than fear of disruption?

2. In what areas of my life do I sense instability or lack of long-term commitment, and how can I proactively address these issues?

3. What shadows or hidden motives within myself need acknowledgment and transformation during this transformative lunar phase?

Mars in Leo sesquiquadrate Pisces North Node

This energy can be incredibly frustrating, especially when we know deep down that we are worthy and deserving of more. We've been waiting for the universe to show up, to match the energy we've put out, and to send us our manifestation or golden opportunity. Yet, we find ourselves tired of waiting. Hello, universe, where are you? Are you planning on showing up anytime soon? This energy can make us feel unsupported or even abandoned by our spirit team. It questions whether we must walk this path alone and do everything for ourselves.

Sit with this energy as it arises. Though it is uncomfortable, it is leading you to a breakthrough. The universe has not abandoned you. This pressure is essential to breaking through your limiting belief systems and patterns, allowing you to embody your inner power fully. Embrace this moment as a pivotal step towards your transformation.

Mercury in Taurus square Pluto retrograde in Aquarius

This is a complex energy to navigate, as we strongly desire an internal transformation that is ready to happen within us. However, we still behave in a way that feels safe and comfortable. This energy will make it very scary to align your choices and decisions outside of how you have always done things. It is okay to feel intense resistance to your new version of being; however, I will advise you not to stay there too long. Honor your old self and show gratitude for your journey together. After all, your old version has gotten you to this point in your journey.

Song: "Bad Blood" by Taylor Swift

May 15th

Sun in Taurus semi-sextile Jupiter in Gemini

This energy helps us slow down and take a break from any potential chaos caused by the full moon, offering an opportunity to expand our perspective and reanalyze our position. Suppose you've discovered that your job is unstable. In that case, this energy encourages you to review your employment contract to understand your rights and position better or to search for job listings that put you in a stronger position moving forward. If secrets have been exposed within your relationships, this energy prompts you to gather evidence to ensure you have all the details needed to make informed decisions. This energy asks us, "What have we missed?" and encourages us to review paperwork, finances, old text messages, and more.

Song: "Private Eyes" by Daryl Hall & John Oates

May 16th

Sun in Taurus semi-sextile Chiron in Aries

Today, we are given an opportunity to make a solid investment in ourselves. Our current position on our healing journey and our relationship with money will depend on what this looks like for us. For some, it may involve creating a budget; for others, it could include opening a savings account and committing to putting a certain amount of our income aside to grow that account. We may enroll in a course to further our education or hire a coach to hold us accountable. This could also involve hiring an employee or making other long-term investments, such as purchasing real estate or investing in a business. Whatever this is for you, there is likely to be much resistance in your ability to invest in yourself; however, you are invited to fight through the fear and release yourself from any past conditioning. Silence your ego telling you that you can't or are not worth having more abundance in your future. The decisions that we make right now will set us up for future success.

Mercury in Taurus semi-square Jupiter in Gemini

This energy pulls us into an inner conflict between the desire to expand and the hesitation to step beyond our comfort zone. We envision grand ideas for growth and the steps needed to achieve them, yet we convince ourselves that now isn't the right time. We may need to get our finances in order or complete a previous step before moving forward. While we're unlikely to make decisions that feel unsafe or unstable, we must be mindful of this energy because it can keep us small. That fear and anxiety is your ego speaking. If now isn't the right time to make a move, when will it be? Embrace the discomfort and trust in your ability to handle what comes next.

Sun in Taurus sextile Pisces North Node

This aspect reminds us that we don't have to have it all figured out right now. We don't need to reach a decision or destination today if it feels overwhelming. Sometimes, it's okay to continue making plans and trust in the process. If a decision feels too hasty or uncomfortable, honor that feeling and ask the divine for further guidance on your next steps. This energy encourages us to consider the smallest step we can take that doesn't feel too scary or overwhelming and to take action on that.

Song: "Take It Easy" by Stan Walker

May 17th

Ceres enters Aries

The Ceres asteroid represents how we nurture others and how we wish to be nurtured in return. Positioned in the sign of Aries, this energy can show up aggressively. This energy encourages us to fight on behalf of the ones we love in order to protect them and stand up for them rather than allowing them to fight their own battles. We expect our loved ones to do the same for us in return. We hope they will have our back when challenged by another and defend us if they witness someone talking negatively about us when we are not in the room.

This energy can show up as you fighting for a cause and becoming a warrior or soldier on the front line in order to create change for those who feel oppressed, or you may find yourself fighting a battle on someone else's behalf. This energy says that if you want to cause harm, you must get through me first. This can also show up as encouraging others around us to be independent and stand up for themselves rather than being intimidated. This energy says there is nothing to fear, and if an obstacle is put in front of us, we will not wait for someone else to remove it but rather make our way around it. We are speaking up and showing great courage and strength within this energy and supporting others to do the same. We will not stand by and watch others be bullied, repressed, or belittled. We will do something about it.

Reflection

1. Do you feel your loved ones adequately support and defend you when you're not around? If not, why might that be?

2. Have you ever found yourself fighting for a cause or defending someone else's rights? What motivated you to do so?

3. How can you balance protecting others with encouraging them to stand up for themselves?

Mercury in Taurus semi-square Pisces North Node

This energy represents recognizing that we may have been too passive. Perhaps we chose not to speak up or defend ourselves, and now we are facing the consequences of that decision. We may have taken a few days off work, and now we have to hustle to catch up, or we may have delayed taking action because we were waiting for someone else's contribution. Now, we recognize that we would have been much further ahead if we had just handled the situation ourselves. This energy shows us where we have been slacking off, and, in hindsight, we can now see where we could have given more to a situation.

Mercury in Taurus semi-sextile Venus in Aries

This energy represents developing a strategy before asking for what we need or want from others. For example, if you're going to ask your boss for a raise, first make sure you prove yourself as an asset to the company. If you own your own business and wish to raise the prices of a product or service you offer, this means developing a marketing strategy to ensure your clientele is aware of the value of your service. If you need to ask for more from someone with whom you are in a relationship, your strategy could involve first taking them out for a nice dinner and asking them what more they need from you rather than demanding that they change their behavior. This aspect reminds us not to rush but to be prepared when asking for more from others.

Song: "Can't Hold Us Down" by Christina Aguilera

May 18th

Sun in Taurus semi-square Venus in Aries

This energy embodies frustration, tearing us between remaining passive or diplomatic in a situation and the overwhelming urge to speak out. We may feel that we're likely to explode if we bite our tongue or hold back any longer. One part of us tells us the battle isn't worth it, while another part desperately needs to express itself. This aspect highlights just how uncomfortable passivity can be.

Sun in Taurus conjunct Uranus in Taurus

When you can put consistent action into achieving whatever it is that you want to achieve, the universe responds to evolve that plan or idea, and divine assistance may not be what you expect it to be. Be open to possibilities, and don't let your mind hold you back from what is possible. The thing you want wants you also; as you heal yourself and release any blockages and resistance to it, you become a vibration match for that manifestation. Before you know it, it's yours. You are living your manifestation.

Venus in Aries semi-square Uranus in Taurus

This energy is likely to cause disruption within your relationships and connections. This can be as little as a fiery exchange with a coworker, an upset and unsatisfied customer, or a rude cashier while out shopping. For others, it could be something more intense, such as an argument with a friend, relative, or long-term partner. When this energy is present, it asks us how in control we are of our emotions and how easily we become triggered. It also asks us to consider how we can prevent this from happening again in the future.

Song: "Quiet" by MILCK

May 19th

Mercury in Taurus square Mars in Leo

This energy presents a setback or challenge in taking confident and bold action. You may have an important presentation to give at work, but first, you must prepare and ensure all your PowerPoint slides are in order. Maybe you've finished writing your book and are excited about presenting it to the world, but you must learn to format it correctly before publishing. Or it could be something as simple as having an important event to attend and the perfect outfit but realizing you need to schedule a hair appointment, get a wax, and a spray tan to feel your best. This aspect says, "Hold up, wait a minute—you have a mundane task to complete before stepping into the limelight."

Mercury in Taurus semi-square Saturn in Pisces

Today, as you carefully weigh your options and dig deeper into gathering information before making a decision, you might find an old lesson resurfacing. It's that familiar feeling of caution, a strategy your mind uses to avoid repeating past mistakes. Embrace this moment of reflection, where the echoes of your past meet your present choices. It's an opportunity to uncover a path toward wisdom and growth, using your past experiences to guide you forward. This energy says I have been here before and know what to do.

Jupiter in Gemini sextile Chiron in Aries

This energy encourages us to face challenges head-on, even if they might be painful. We will likely have past triggers exposed within this energy, but those exposed wounds help us rather than hinder us. This can be a painful reminder of where we are or where we have been, empowering us to expand beyond our limitations. When the past or present becomes so uncomfortable that we are determined to shift the energy, we find the strength to do whatever it takes to move beyond it.

Jupiter in Gemini square Pisces North Node

What if you leap off that edge into a new experience, and the universe doesn't catch you? This energy can make us feel as though we are losing faith or struggling to trust that the divine has our back. It can be a lonely feeling to be disconnected from source. Within this energy, we may find ourselves seeking answers from outside ourselves, praying for a sign, or using divination tools to find guidance for the challenges in front of us. We might also find ourselves asking friends or family for advice before making our next move.

Venus in Aries quintile Jupiter in Gemini

This energy has us seeking validation from others. Questions like, "Am I making the right choice?" "Do you think this business idea is good enough?" or "Should I rewrite this chapter?" come to the forefront. While seeking validation might seem like a sign of insecurity, it can be beneficial. Sometimes, we get so caught up in our limiting thoughts that a bit of external validation from a friend can be just the nudge we need. This support can remind us of our strengths, unique talents, and potential. Although we inherently know our capabilities, a little reassurance from others can help reinforce our confidence and perspective.

Pisces North Node semi-sextile Chiron in Aries

This is a beautiful energy of being guided toward your inner truth. Recognizing something within yourself—about who you are, where you have come from, and what you have been through—leads you toward a profound spiritual breakthrough. This energy leaves us with a deeper understanding of our value and the resilience and courage we have shown along our path. It allows us to be forgiving of ourselves and show ourselves more love rather than becoming too critical.

Song: "Pray" by Sam Smith

May 20th

Mars in Leo sesquiquadrate Saturn in Pisces

This energy inspires us to embody main character energy and step into a leadership role in our lives, even though we might painfully remember a past lesson when we did so. Perhaps in the past, when we put ourselves out there, it wasn't well received, causing us to hesitate now.

Recently, I discovered that my daughter is short-sighted and needs glasses. She took the news well and was excited to pick out her new frames, relishing in trying on different pairs and selecting the best options. Although disappointed that she had to wait two weeks for her lenses to be fitted, she excitedly counted down the days until she could pick up her glasses. When the day finally came, she wore them confidently, taking selfies and insisting on video chatting with friends and family to show off her new look.

Today was her first day back at school, and my heart sank as I watched her walk confidently to the school gate, hesitate, and then remove her glasses, putting them in her schoolbag, afraid of what others might think. Is there a past version of you who is a little fearful of becoming the main character in your story?

Mercury in Taurus semi-square Neptune in Aries

This energy encourages us to slow down and see through any illusions that might be causing confusion. Be mindful of what is being projected onto you at this time. Someone may tell you that a project you are working on needs more work or should be done differently. They might be pointing out something in your behavior that needs improvement or insisting they have a better solution to your problem. This can also show up as someone being adamant that you see things from their point of view. To navigate this energy, block out the noise and ask yourself: What do I think? What deeply resonates with me?

Song: "Beautiful" by Christina Aguilera

May 21st

Last Quarter Moon in Aquarius

This last quarter moon invites us to explore whether the areas we consider to represent stability in our lives genuinely reflect an authentic expression of ourselves. Does your current job align with the way you want to show up in the world? Does it provide the space to fulfill the legacy you want to leave behind and the imprint you aim to create for generations to come? Is your home a beautiful representation of who you are, or does your neighborhood lack energetic alignment for you?

When considering our stability, we contemplate what has become our comfort zone. Is your comfort zone still a comfortable place for you, or do you feel the need to explore beyond it? The support of the sun in Taurus empowers us to make responsible decisions on implementing small steps and strategies for gradual expansion, as well as making prudent choices regarding any outstanding bills, payments, or investments that need attention. This energy prompts us to assess what still makes sense for us and what needs to be shifted and changed to allow us greater freedom of self-expression.

Reflection

1. How does your current job align with the way you want to present yourself to the world, and does it contribute to the legacy you aim to leave?

2. Is your living space a genuine representation of your inner self, and does it resonate with your authentic energy?

3. In terms of stability, does your comfort zone still provide the comfort and freedom you need, or is it time to explore beyond its boundaries?

Sun enters Gemini

While we thank Taurus season for reminding us to stay grounded and take a more practical approach to life, it is now time to welcome in the fresh, fun energy of Gemini season, reminding us that it's also important to have a good time. Gemini energy brings a lighthearted and carefree attitude to everything we do; after all, if we are not enjoying the journey, what the hell are we doing here? Have you ever been in a job role or commitment that felt as though it was sucking the life out of you? There will be no room for those things during Gemini season as we spice things up, learn to laugh at ourselves, enjoy parties, social gatherings, and have a good time with friends, loved ones, and coworkers. This energy also inspires us to drop any heavy weight or baggage that keeps us feeling as though we are tied down. Anything that feels heavy has to go during Gemini season, as we are not in the mood to take ourselves too seriously.

Reflection

1. How can you incorporate the playful and carefree attitude of Gemini season into your life? Are there areas where you've been too serious or weighed down by unnecessary burdens?

2. Think about your commitments and responsibilities. Are there any that feel draining or heavy? How can you release or lighten these burdens during Gemini season?

3. Consider the social aspect of Gemini season. How can you infuse more laughter, joy, and fun into your interactions with friends, loved ones, and colleagues?

Sun in Taurus sextile Saturn in Pisces

One of the important aspects to consider when establishing what needs to change and what we are going to do differently is looking at the past and what we have learned about the stability we have obtained. At what time in your past did you feel most stable and secure? What elements do you think contributed to your sense of stability? Likewise, at what time in your life did you feel the least amount of stability and security? What elements do you feel created that experience of instability? We can learn a lot about ourselves by looking at the past. I know it can be uncomfortable, but think of every painful experience from your past as an important lesson to build a free and non-restricted future. What is your past telling you that you need to free yourself from?

Song: "Billionaire" by Travie McCoy

May 22nd

Venus in Aries quintile Pluto retrograde in Aquarius

What we want versus what we need from others are often worlds apart, yet the lines between them can become blurred. This energy represents an inner shift from desiring and needing more to a profound transformation of gratitude for what we already have. What do you need from your relationships today? Is it recognition from others? More understanding? Deeper connection? Better communication from your partner? What if we never receive those things? The realization within this energy can be quite profound as we release our expectations of others and allow them to be as they are without judgment or feeling personally attacked by their behavior. This energy says, "I accept you as you are without trying to change you."

Song: "The Way I Are" by Timberland

May 23rd

Venus in Aries trine Mars in Leo

This energy represents not being afraid to reach out and take what is yours. Be prepared to say thank you today. Many of us have been conditioned to decline gifts or support when presented to us. Have you ever been offered an extravagant gift and instantly thought, "Oh, I couldn't possibly accept that"? Or hosted a party and had a guest offer to help you clean up afterward, but you told them it wasn't necessary? Or had someone apologize to you, and you instantly responded, "There is no need to apologize"? Perhaps receiving compliments makes you extremely uncomfortable. Not today. Today, we will receive all that is available to us. If someone offers you a ride, say thank you. If they offer to pay for dinner, say thank you. If they give you a gift, say thank you. We create a more abundant reality when we are open to receiving from others and recognize when gifts are being offered to us.

There is much misleading information out there, often leading us to seek mentors who can guide us through our confusion. We often forget that our reality is like a choose-your-own-adventure book, with many ways to solve a problem. For example, if you're having issues in your long-term relationship, you might seek out a marriage counselor to help resolve conflicts. However, what are we actually manifesting in this scenario? To get to conflict resolution, we must first have more conflict before finding a resolution.

Alternatively, you could choose a different path to overcome the same problem. You might dive deep into a spiritual practice, such as Buddhism, seeking enlightenment. Along this path, you will learn self-awareness, detachment, compassion, and acceptance, which will first manifest as inner peace within you and then be reflected in your outer reality and relationships. Neither choice is wrong; they simply lead in different directions.

Sometimes, we forget that we have the ability to choose, and it's okay to sample all the flavors. You can take a few lessons from one mentor and a few from another to create the most delicious reality for yourself. This energy encourages us to examine the mentors we have chosen and the influences around us more closely and become aware of how they affect our reality.

Song: "Are You Gonna Go My Way" by Lenny Kravitz

May 24th

Mars in Leo sesquiquadrate Neptune in Aries

We are all living out our own story from our unique perspective. You likely have people in your life who see you as a shining light, representing comfort and stability to them. Others might cast you as the villain in their story because you broke their heart or reflect something within them they don't want to confront. Instead of looking within, they project their pain, anger, and resentment onto you.

It's easy to absorb these role projections and let them shape our identity. But this energy invites us to ask: Who are we in our own story if we remove all projections from others? Someone else's experience of you doesn't have to become part of your reality. It's up to you to decide whether to allow this to happen.

Take this opportunity to design your character and choose your role as the main character in your story. Then, all you have to do is take action in alignment with your character identity, and you become that. For example, if you want to be an author, the moment you release any stories of what others think you are capable of or what you should be and then sit down to write your first paragraph, you instantly become an author.

Mercury in Taurus sextile Pisces North Node

This energy is here to inspire us to do less. You may think, "I can't possibly slow down; I have deadlines to meet and a long list of things to get done." We live in an incredibly fast-paced world where so much can be instantly manifested. Still, instead of appreciating this ability, we live in the illusion that we must move even faster.

Last night, I watched a movie set in an earlier time period. A character had become ill, sent a telegram to the doctor, and waited days for a response to confirm it was okay to travel to see him. They then waited an entire day for a carriage to arrive and collect the ill person before traveling for two days to the doctor for treatment. When they finally reached the doctor, he suggested applying leeches to the skin.

Today, if I had symptoms of a potential medical problem, I could quickly Google my symptoms and, if needed, purchase leeches online or make a doctor's appointment using my phone in seconds.

What if we could remove the illusion of running out of time and the pressure we assign to it and instead embrace the time that we have available?

Mercury in Taurus semi-sextile Chiron in Aries

This energy can make it feel like everything is moving so slowly. I invite you to reflect upon what fears arise when you think about progress taking much longer than you initially anticipated. What if you don't meet the deadlines that you have subconsciously created for yourself? Will all of your efforts have been for nothing, or does the progress that you have made still count and hold value? Any level of progress is a win.

Song: "Slow Low" by Jason Derulo

May 25th

Saturn enters Aries

Saturn is the disciplinarian of the zodiac, the way we learn lessons. For the last 2.5 years, it has been sitting in Pisces, leading us toward profound spiritual lessons and forcing us to make difficult decisions regarding prioritizing our own needs versus sacrificing for others. Now, Saturn moves into Aries, a sign representing impulsiveness, leadership, and instant gratification. Aries reaches out and takes what it wants without overthinking it. If Aries doesn't get what it wants, it either throws a fit or gets bored, abandons the quest, and races toward the next shiny adventure.

Saturn in Aries is not a fun energy to experience. It teaches us to be less impulsive, sternly asks us to slow down, and shows us that hard work, commitment, and discipline will lead us to our desires. During this alignment, we seem to be punished for our impulsiveness or feel stuck, working hard to see little or no reward. This placement says, "Oh, you thought it would be that easy? Think again." We are forced to wait for our blessings, which feels like a punishment, but Saturn is teaching us patience. Many of us will simply give up, feeling like we will never get what we want. We begin to lose enthusiasm and feel stuck in a rut.

Saturn in Aries' lesson is discipline: if you work hard for what you want, you will be rewarded. While this alignment will bring challenges, setbacks, and frustration, there are ways to overcome this energy. The first is not to be afraid of doing things that are hard. Lean into the hard work, roll up your sleeves, and show Saturn what you are made of. Be disciplined, showing up for yourself even when you don't feel like it. When you put everything you have into achieving your manifestations, the victory is much sweeter.

Alternatively, you can release all attachments to the rewards. Do things just for the joy of doing them. Create simply for the pleasure of creating. Heal others because it feels in alignment. If you have an online platform, share yourself and your experiences just because—not for likes, clicks, followers, and views.

Saturn in Aries is like being at a theme park and running directly to your favorite ride, only to discover the line is incredibly long. Recognizing that you'll have to stand in line for hours to ride this ride. Is the reward still worth it? That is up to you to decide. Will you wait in line or prefer to give up and miss out on the opportunity? Is there a way you can enjoy the wait? Can you dance in line or make a new friend in the queue? Perhaps you could watch people passing by and play a game with yourself, trying to guess their zodiac signs just by observing them.

This alignment will be with us for the next 2.5 years, so we might as well learn to embrace the wait.

Reflection

1. How do you typically respond to waiting or delays in your life?

2. What are some ways you can cultivate patience and discipline in your daily routine?

3. What past experiences have taught you the value of persistence and dedication?

4. How can you make the most of waiting periods by finding creative ways to stay engaged and positive?

Mercury in Taurus semi-sextile Jupiter in Gemini

This aspect encourages us to find the step before the step. Before jumping headfirst into a task, have we appropriately researched the most efficient way of doing things? You wouldn't build flat-pack furniture without taking the time to read the instructions first, would you? Well, perhaps you would, although you are much more likely to run into challenges. Before trying to manifest a million dollars or try out a new skill, take some time to find the instruction manual first or learn from someone who knows.

Sun in Gemini trine Pluto retrograde in Aquarius

This is a time for socializing and making connections. You may receive a social invite, receive help from a friend, or spend an hour on the phone catching up and having a great laugh with someone. This energy reminds us of the importance of enjoying the company of others. In our busy lives, it's easy to get caught up in work and personal responsibilities, often neglecting the social interactions that bring joy and fulfillment. Now is the perfect opportunity to reconnect with old friends, strengthen existing relationships, and even form new connections.

Take the time to accept invitations, whether it's a casual coffee date, a dinner party, or a weekend getaway with close companions. These moments of connection are not just about having fun; they also play a crucial role in our emotional well-being. Engaging in meaningful conversations and sharing experiences with others can provide a sense of belonging and reduce feelings of loneliness or isolation.

Additionally, this energy encourages us to be open to the support and assistance those around us offer. If you've been overwhelmed or stressed, don't hesitate to ask your social network for help. Whether it's advice, a helping hand, or just a listening ear, friends and loved ones can offer the support you need to navigate challenges.

Mercury in Taurus conjunct Uranus in Taurus

This energy is an outside force or event coming to shake up your foundation. It's like when you are hosting an event for ten people, and you find that all ten of those people brought a friend, so you now have to find a way to cater to 20 people. Or when you have a hectic day at work, and then you receive a phone call from your child's school informing you that they have vomited everywhere and need to be picked up. These disturbances to our plan or schedule happen occasionally, so it is helpful to avoid becoming too attached to the original plan and learn to be flexible and go with the flow.

Song: "Patience" by Guns N' Roses

May 26th

Mercury enters Gemini

Mercury is at home in the sign of Gemini, and we will experience our minds being incredibly sharp at this time, allowing us to absorb information much quicker. If we are trying to learn a new skill, it may take half the time during this alignment. If you work in a field that involves writing or communication, this alignment will undoubtedly work in your favor, as you can send out twice as many emails, write more songs, or read more books. I recommend reading or listening to a podcast or audiobook at this time, as our minds will be able to retain so much more information than usual and are craving the stimulation of receiving information.

As both Mercury and Gemini rule communication, this is an excellent time for networking or getting to know people on a deeper level. Both of these energies also indicate a certain level of speed, so you will find yourself with more time and energy to accomplish things and get things done. Have you ever had a day when you woke up a little earlier and began working, only to find that you have completed all of your tasks, including all of the housework and vacuumed your car, and when you look at the clock, it is only lunchtime? You think, "How on earth did I manage that?" That is Gemini and Mercury kind of energy, so make the most out of this energy by making a list at the beginning of the day and surprise yourself with the amount of work you can get done.

The downside to this energy is the overthinking that comes with it. We can find ourselves receiving a text from a friend or someone important in our lives, not just taking in what they have communicated but trying to read between the lines. They said this, but did they mean this? Try not to think too far into things as you will drive yourself crazy thinking about possibilities and scenarios that are not even a thing. If you find yourself overthinking, put this energy to good use by cleaning or rearranging something, giving your overactive mind the mental stimulation it needs.

Reflection

1. How can I leverage the sharpness of my mind during alignment to accelerate learning? What topics or skills do I want to delve into through reading, podcasts, or audiobooks during this period to maximize my heightened mental absorption?

2. In what ways can I maximize the benefits of this energy in my professional life, especially if my work involves writing or communication? Considering the potential for increased speed and efficiency, what

tasks or projects can I tackle for increased productivity?

3. How can I avoid falling into the trap of overthinking and reading too much between the lines in my communications with others?

Mercury in Gemini sextile Saturn in Aries

This aspect encourages us to do our research, as there is great potential for learning something valuable. You may find yourself drawn to acquiring a new skill or enrolling in an online course, yet also feeling the urge to jump straight in and learn from experience. This energy reminds us that there is no hurry to get where we need to be. If we take the time to develop our skills, the payoff will be much greater. It's okay to be a beginner.

In a world that often glorifies instant success and rapid achievement, it's important to remember the value of patience and thorough preparation. Embracing the learning process, with all its challenges and setbacks, allows us to build a solid foundation for future endeavors. By immersing ourselves in the intricacies of a new subject or skill, we not only gain knowledge but also develop a deeper understanding and appreciation for the craft.

Song: "Technologic" by Daft Punk

May 27th

New Moon in Gemini

I love a new moon in Gemini. This gives us the opportunity to explore all the things we would like to learn, all the things we would like to experience, and all the ways that we can incorporate more fun and enjoyment into our day-to-day lives. We often think of success regarding stability and finances, but I want you to imagine that you have discovered that you only have 12 months to live. What are all the things that you would like to experience within that time? Put together a bucket list and start prioritizing one of the things on that list. It may be a camping trip with the family or attending a concert by your favorite performer. Perhaps it is attending a festival where you dress up in tribal wear and dance barefoot, or maybe it is traveling to Peru and drinking ayahuasca, having profound shamanic out-of-body experiences. Would you like to travel to India or Europe to experience different cultures or buy a lovely cabin in the woods where you can live out the rest of your time in peace, writing your memoir?

Reflection

1. Create a bucket list. What experiences would you like to include on it?

2. How can you bring elements of your bucket list into your life now, even on a smaller scale?

3. If you were to prioritize one thing from your bucket list, what would it be, and how can you take steps toward making it a reality?

Mercury in Gemini sextile Neptune in Aries

While this aspect encourages us to learn from others and absorb as much information as possible, it also reminds us to do our own research and not accept all information as correct, even if it comes from a credible source. As you are the creator of your reality, and your reality is built upon your belief systems, don't forget to ask yourself questions like: What do I think? Does this resonate with me and how I want my reality to look? Do I need to do my own research on this topic before accepting this information as truth?

Song: " On The Road Again" by Willie Nelson

May 28th

Mars in Leo biquintile Pisces North Node

This aspect brings us a reminder of our strengths. To take leadership over our lives and our direction, it's crucial to recognize the natural skills, talents, and abilities we've been blessed with to help us along our path. Perhaps you were born with natural beauty—there's nothing wrong with using that to your advantage and becoming the face of your brand or business. Maybe you have a keen intellect, allowing you to strategize more efficiently than others. Those with great intelligence and analytical minds often find success in business endeavors. Or perhaps, like me, you have keen intuition, which can be used not only in business but also in navigating relationships and all aspects of life.

Next time you face a challenge, remember to call upon these gifts to help you overcome the obstacle in front of you. They were given to you for a reason. If you have a way with words, write a book or start a podcast. If you're a talented musician, find a way to incorporate musical elements into everything you do. Don't let these skills go to waste.

Sun in Gemini quintile Pisces North Node

It's not only our natural skills that give us an advantage on our journey but also our life experiences and the people we meet along the way. My childhood made me very resilient and streetwise—I'm not easily taken advantage of and always have my wits about me. My previous long-term relationship with someone whom many might consider a computer geek means that if I ever encounter any technological difficulties, I can call on him to solve the problem quickly. My past employment in a management position means I can easily lead a large team and communicate what I need from others. Those early years spent working in the hospitality industry mean I can carry all of my family's dinner plates to the table without making two trips, and I can wash dishes at the speed of light.

This energy asks us to consider where we have come from, what we have learned, and who we know that can help us navigate our next adventure or challenge.

Mercury in Gemini trine Pluto retrograde in Aquarius

This aspect encourages us to shake things up. Our minds are very sharp right now with Mercury in Gemini. How can we utilize this energy to come up with out-of-the-box ideas? This energy also supports reaching out to the collective to expand beyond what you are limited to creating just as one person. Do you know a guy you can collaborate with on a new project, or can you work with the community to come together for some type of fundraiser or common goal? One of the recent ways this energy shows up is by people setting up GoFundMe campaigns to provide relief for people facing tragedy and help relieve some of the financial pressure placed upon them while they heal. This is just one example of this energy in action—finding out-of-the-box ideas to connect with the collective. Sometimes, we are limited by what we are able to achieve ourselves; however, when we come together as a collective, powerful change can happen.

Sun in Gemini quintile Mars in Leo

Sometimes, identifying our strengths can feel like searching for a needle in a haystack. This aspect invites us to reach out and ask around. Don't hesitate to ask a close friend or family member what strengths they admire most about you. Often, being validated by those we love can give us the confidence to embrace our unique abilities.

Another great way to uncover your strengths is to consider what others seek your help with. Do your friends turn to you when they need a solution to a problem, or are you the person they rely on for emotional support, someone who holds space for them while they release their emotions? Are you the

145

cheerleader type who motivates and hypes everyone with an encouraging "You've got this!"? Or perhaps you're the go-to for financial advice.

Understanding our impact on those around us can help us fully embrace our strengths. So, take a moment to reflect on the ways you support and uplift others. Recognize these qualities within yourself and let them shine brightly. Your strengths are your superpowers, and it's time to own them!

Song: "You Learn" by Alanis Morissette

May 29th

Mercury in Gemini quintile Pisces North Node

This energy is about embracing systems that create more efficiency in our lives. It could mean delegating more responsibilities at home to your children, adopting AI technology to help with work, hiring an assistant, a cleaner to mop your floors once a week, or a bookkeeper to handle your business finances. It's about releasing control and allowing space for assistance.

This can also manifest as allowing space for the divine to guide you toward your next steps. If you're facing a challenge and can't outsource it to someone more efficient, you can always outsource it to a higher power, asking to be led toward the solution. Remember, we don't have to have all the answers or solve everything ourselves. Release control and trust in the process.

Song: "Help Me" by Sonny Boy Williamson II

May 30th

Mercury in Gemini semi-square Venus in Aries

This energy represents a clash of opinions regarding productivity and efficiency. You might suggest a more efficient way of managing systems at work, only to have your boss insist on sticking to the current method. You might reorganize things at home, only for your partner to protest that they can't find anything and prefer the old arrangement. This could also manifest as scheduling conflicts for those co-parenting, with each party believing their way is best. Try to find a compromise, balancing your ideas with those of others to create a harmonious and efficient solution.

Mercury in Gemini quintile Mars in Leo

This aspect represents being exceptionally proactive about getting things done. Not only is our mind sharp, allowing us to devise solutions to challenges quickly, but we also have the confidence to take action and implement these strategies. This energy says, "I have a solution; let me show you."

Be aware of the needs and perspectives of those around you. While your proactive approach can be incredibly motivating, it's vital to ensure that you are not overwhelming others or disregarding their input. Collaboration and open communication will help you harness this energy effectively, creating a harmonious and productive environment.

Song: "We Can Work It Out" by The Beatles

May 31st

Sun in Gemini conjunct Mercury in Gemini

This energy is potent for gathering information and finding solutions to your problems. We are open to learning from others and trying different ways of doing things. What can we learn from what others have done, and how can we incorporate these suggestions to benefit our lives? We are not attached to any outcomes right now; we are trying new strategies to allow more freedom within our schedules and finding ways to make things more efficient. In this energy, you may find yourself planning your meals, decluttering, setting up bedtime routines for your children, or redecorating your home for better energy flow.

Jupiter in Gemini biquintile Pluto retrograde in Aquarius

This energy asks you to go beyond what makes you feel comfortable. If you are meal planning, you might incorporate new foods or experiment with different preparation methods. Embrace ingredients from various cultures, try recipes that challenge your culinary skills, or explore healthier alternatives that you've never considered before. This is a perfect time to step out of your culinary comfort zone and broaden your palate.

If you are decluttering your home, you may consider discarding items with sentimental value that no longer serve a purpose. This process can be emotionally challenging, but it also offers a powerful opportunity for growth and renewal, creating space for new experiences and opportunities to enter your life. Consider donating to charity or passing them on to someone who may find new value in them.

If you are redecorating or remodeling, you might shake things up by choosing furniture or decor options you usually wouldn't choose. Step away from your usual style and experiment with bold colors, unconventional designs, or unique materials. Perhaps you've always played it safe with neutral tones and minimalist decor; now is the time to inject some vibrant hues and eclectic pieces into your space.

In your social life, this energy invites you to meet new people and engage in activities that you've previously avoided. Join a club, attend a workshop, or participate in community events that align with your interests but have always seemed intimidating. Or take up a new hobby, learn a new language, or dive into a subject that has always intrigued you but felt too daunting to tackle. By pushing past your limits, you can unlock hidden potentials and achieve a greater sense of fulfillment.

Mercury in Gemini semi-square Chiron in Aries

Sometimes, it feels like the people around us just don't get it. They do not take the time to understand us, and sometimes, it feels like they are set upon misunderstanding us. This is a complex energy to navigate and is likely to have us feeling triggered. I encourage you to delve into these triggers and ask yourself if other people's perceptions of you are any of your business. Do they define you, or are they simply just outside perceptions? The only opinion that matters is your opinion and perception of yourself. Do not allow yourself to become bogged down by other people's projections.

Venus in Aries semi-sextile Pisces North Node

This energy shows up as unwanted assistance but asks that we remain open to possibility. Someone might offer you a perspective you didn't ask for, but instead of reacting negatively, try to listen. There could be nuggets of wisdom within this alternate perspective. Someone might show you a better way of doing things, which may initially be irritating, but allowing others space to share their knowledge, experiences, and perspectives can greatly help us expand. This aspect questions how open we can be when we already have a plan or goal in mind. The divine sends us assistance in mysterious ways. What if you could not receive the assistance you've been praying for because you were too busy maintaining control to notice? Imagine waking each day with the expectation that someone will cross your path with the assistance or information that you need. That would naturally increase your ability to learn and grow.

Song: "A Spoonful Of Sugar" by Julie Andrews

June Alignments

June 1st

Mercury in Gemini quintile Saturn in Aries

This energy serves as a gentle reminder that we should not take on too many tasks at once and that quality work takes time. In our fast-paced world, it can be tempting to juggle multiple responsibilities simultaneously, aiming to accomplish as much as possible in the shortest amount of time. However, this often compromises the quality of our work and can leave us feeling overstimulated and overwhelmed. If you find yourself in this situation, it's crucial to recognize the signs of overextension. Pushing yourself too hard can result in burnout, which not only affects your productivity but also your overall well-being.

To prevent this, ensure that you allow yourself appropriate rest and downtime. Taking regular breaks and giving yourself permission to step back can recharge your energy will improve your focus when you return to your tasks. This energy emphasizes the importance of pacing yourself and managing your workload effectively. It's about finding a balance between achieving your goals and maintaining your mental and physical health.

Sun in Gemini semi-square Chiron in Aries

As we are inspired to live our best lives and find joy in every moment, we will likely want to ignore any pain or triggers presenting themselves to us now. The excitement of pursuing our passions and basking in the beauty of the present can often overshadow the deeper issues lurking beneath the surface. It's natural to want to focus on the positive, but it's important to acknowledge that our unresolved emotions and triggers still need attention. We are becoming good at turning a positive into a negative without exploring the root of the issue, which can lead to a buildup of unresolved emotions over time.

I don't want to spoil your fun today, so if any issues present themselves that have you feeling triggered, write them down so that you can revisit them later.

This way, you can fully enjoy the moment without the weight of unresolved feelings dragging you down. Take note of what causes you discomfort or irritation, and set aside time to reflect on these triggers when you're in a more grounded state of mind.

Song: "Sunshine" by One Republic

June 2nd

Mercury in Gemini quintile Neptune in Pisces

You will likely receive guidance through songs and music or thoughts and inspirations. We have much mental energy present, so the universe will use communication and technology to get through to you rather than tapping into your emotional energy or receiving downloads through meditation. Pay attention to any information you come across, books you are drawn to reading, or any inspirational messages you receive to guide you toward your next steps. If you experience something odd, such as a donkey crossing the road on your commute to work, google it. What is the spiritual meaning of a donkey crossing your path? Use the resources you have available to connect with your spirit team.

Jupiter in Gemini semi-sextile Uranus in Taurus

Have you heard the saying, "It's not what you know but who you know"? This aspect creates an opportunity that may seem unexpected at first glance, but it results from the energy you've put into expanding your network. Your boss might recommend you for a higher position, a friend could nominate you for an award, or someone might suggest just the right person to help you overcome your current obstacle.

Venus in Aries conjunct Chiron in Aries

This energy can be dangerous because we act from a place of emotion. If you find yourself in a situation where you are overwhelmed with feelings of love and gratitude, then you are going to want to express that deep level of emotion and show others that you sincerely appreciate them. The problem arises when we express ourselves from a place of pain or fear. This causes us to lash out in anger or resentment if we have emotions hidden beneath the surface that we have not addressed. Tune into your emotions as they come up and ask yourself whether you are reacting from a space of love or fear. Fear is an emotion that feels icky and creates a negative sensation within your body, such

150

as anxiety, stress, or worry. If the emotion feels positive, such as joy, gratitude, and forgiveness, that is the frequency of love.

Song: "With A Little Help From My Friends" by Joe Cocker

June 3rd

First Quarter Moon in Virgo

What is working? What isn't? This energy focuses on the small details rather than the big goals. Does your current environment support the goal that you are working towards? Have you made time in your schedule for everything you would like to accomplish? Are you doing enough or slacking off and needing more discipline? What about your health? Are you eating well and taking care of your body? Could you benefit from exercise in the mornings to get your blood pumping? How much sleep are you getting? This energy allows us to identify any area in our lives that may set us up for failure. Virgo energy brings our focus to our daily routines, and the Sun in Gemini allows us the flexibility to switch up and change anything that is not working to create an environment for us to thrive.

Reflection

1. Have I structured my daily schedule to accommodate the tasks and activities essential for my success? How can I adapt and change my routine to foster an environment where I can thrive?

2. Am I maintaining the discipline required to achieve my objectives, or am I experiencing a lapse in motivation?

3. How am I prioritizing my health, including nutrition, exercise, and sleep, to support overall well-being?

Sun in Gemini quintile Saturn in Aries

This energy is likely to make you want to have a little fun. You may prank a work colleague to bring laughter and excitement into the workplace or plan a night out with your friends. However, this energy also carries with it the lessons from the past regarding being too impulsive and reminds us not to take things too far. There is a fine line between having a laugh with a coworker and workplace bullying and harassment. Similarly, a night out with friends can quickly become a boozy night filled with regrets.

This energy encourages us to remember that having fun with structure and limits can still be enjoyable and is better than facing grave consequences for not learning lessons from the past. So go ahead and enjoy yourself, but remember the importance of balance and moderation.

Song: "GYM" by Mindstarx

June 4th

Mercury in Gemini sesquiquadrate Pluto retrograde in Aquarius

This aspect indicates an annoyance or disturbance that can throw you off your game. With all of the Gemini energy about, we find ourselves surrounded by people who want to communicate their opinions, feelings, and unsolicited advice. You cannot control the communication of others; you can only control your reaction to what has been said. You get to choose how much of another person's words you want to absorb and whether or not you wish to take outside projections on as part of your story. You know who you are, your heart, and your intentions. Someone else's opinion is just that—their opinion.

Song: "Shut Up" by Simple Plan

June 5th

Sun in Gemini quintile Neptune in Pisces

This energy is fun, imaginative, and playful. How can we bring more playfulness into our day? When did you last dance in the rain or sit out toasting marshmallows under the stars? Think of your reality like your blank canvas, put on your art smock, and let life get a little messy. Don't be afraid to color outside the lines. What can you do that is outside of your usual routine or structure and brings color and playfulness back into your life?

Venus in Aries semi-sextile Uranus in Taurus

This is the recognition that you cannot control any other person. People in this life will let you down at times; there will be times when they show you less consistency and have habits and defense mechanisms to protect themselves from pain. The only thing within your control is how you react to these situations when they come up. Are the behaviors of others something that you can work with, and do you have the ability to unconditionally love and support them even when they are projecting their shadows and unhealed trauma upon you? Or is how they express these shadows a deal-breaker for you, and do they interfere with your ability to heal yourself? In other words, can we heal together, or is the toxicity of this connection becoming too much to bear?

Venus in Aries sextile Jupiter in Gemini

This energy represents getting what you need from those around you. If your boss isn't taking you seriously about that raise, you can easily find work elsewhere at another company. If your partner dismisses your feelings, you have a friend who will hold space for your emotions and frustrations. And if the guy you've been talking to on dating apps isn't giving you the attention you desire, remember that there are plenty more fish in the sea. This energy reminds us that we can still get what we want; we may just have to expand our net.

Song: "Worth It" by Able Heart

June 6th

Mercury in Gemini sextile Mars in Leo

This energy feels like a flood of inspiration streaming through. Ideas flow abundantly, and not only do we have the creative sparks, but we also possess the energy and motivation to follow through with action. There is excellent potential to achieve greatness within this energy, and you may surprise yourself as you take charge of your life with newfound confidence.

You are waking up feeling a surge of excitement and clarity, knowing exactly what steps to take to bring your dreams to fruition. Projects that once seemed daunting now feel like exhilarating challenges waiting to be conquered. You find yourself tackling tasks with purpose and enthusiasm, making rapid progress, and achieving results that exceed your expectations.

This is a time to embrace your inner leader and step boldly into roles and responsibilities you might have previously shied away from. The universe is aligning to support your endeavors, and opportunities that once seemed out of reach are now within your grasp. As you ride this wave of inspiration, you'll notice a ripple effect in all areas of your life, from your career to your relationships.

Mercury in Gemini square Pisces North Node

This aspect can bring confusion as you have an inspired idea but hesitate to take action, leading to overthinking. Your inner dialogue might be saying, "Maybe I should wait for this other opportunity to come through first," or

"Perhaps I should wait for a sign from the universe." We often forget that when we are in a state of awareness, receiving inspiration, and feeling motivated to take action on something that feels aligned, that is what being in divine alignment feels like. Don't overthink it; just do it!

Yes, source speaks to us through signs, synchronicities, and songs on the radio, but inspired ideas are also how God works through us. When you feel that spark of inspiration, that's your green light. That's the universe nudging you forward, saying, "Go ahead, this is your moment."

Song: "Can't Hold Us" by Macklemore & Ryan Lewis

June 7th

Venus enters Taurus

Venus is at home in the sign of Taurus, and so this alignment is sensual and inspires us to explore the depths of love and commitment. This placement calls into question just how loyal the people and connections within our lives are. Are they committed to a relationship that is long-term and stable? Are the people around us trustworthy, and do we feel safe allowing them to take up space within our hearts? In our friendships, we are looking for connections that are low maintenance and want to feel secure, knowing that if we reach out to a friend in our time of need, they will be there to support us and hold space for us, regardless of how long it has been since the last time we connected. We do not want conditional types of love or friendships; we seek love and connection built upon a firm foundation.

We want connections that provide us with a sense of safety and security, like a partner or friend offering us a warm hug, making us feel intense comfort as we melt into them. Another important thing to mention about Venus in Taurus is the energy of luxury that wants to be expressed. This time is about appreciating life's finer things, such as your favorite meal or a luxurious bubble bath with candles and bath oils. What tends to happen during this placement is that we easily find ourselves spending more money to achieve that luxurious feeling. We are eating out more and spending more money on designer-label clothing or home decor to create more ambiance within our homes, so this is just a warning to watch your bank balance. I'm not saying that you cannot enjoy having beautiful things and experiences, but spend responsibly so that you don't find yourself regretting the decisions made now in the future.

For singles, if you are in the market for love right now, being influenced by this energy will likely attract you to a partner who feels stable and secure to you. Someone who has a stable job or is resourceful in being able to take care of themselves and who has their own resources to contribute to a connection. We will not be footing the bill for every dinner with this energy present. If we get a sense of instability, such as someone still in a situationship with their ex, we are heading for the nearest exit. We are protecting ourselves from any situations that seem a little shaky. We are also taking our time to get to know a person before committing rather than jumping into a whirlwind romance with the wrong person. If we are going to open up and be completely vulnerable with a person, we will first want to be sure that this is the right kind of person to do so with. We are open to starting something new but more likely to be attracted to those demonstrating long-term potential.

Those of us in committed relationships question whether our person is someone we can trust. Are they loyal? Are they committed, or are they showing signs of inconsistency? Are they committed to making things work, or are they inconsistent in the energy they give to our connection? We are questioning the longevity of our relationships and if any issues need to be resolved to create more stability within our connection. Can our partner provide stability and safety for us? I don't mean just financially but in all areas. Do they make us feel as though we are the only one for them, or do we feel we constantly have to compete for their attention? This energy makes us feel like we want to nurture and take care of our significant other, but are we receiving the same level of commitment in return? The downside of this energy, which is important to explore, is whether we are staying in a situation that is not good for us due to our sense of loyalty and commitment to another. A healthy relationship is one in which your love energy is reciprocated, and sometimes, we can find ourselves hopelessly devoted to someone not worthy of our love.

Reflection

1. In your friendships, do you feel a sense of security and assurance that your friends will stand by you in times of need, regardless of the time elapsed since your last interaction?

2. Reflect on your spending habits during this period. Are you indulging in the finer things responsibly, or is this a time to reassess your financial decisions to avoid future regrets?

3. How do you perceive the loyalty, commitment, and consistency of your connections? Are there areas that need attention to enhance stability?

Mars in Leo quincunx Pisces North Node

This energy empowers us to take control of situations that may initially feel stagnant or challenging. We won't wait for that cutie to ask us out—we're ready to make the first move. We won't sit around waiting to be recognized by our boss; instead, we'll show them what we're capable of. We won't be passive in a conflict; we will demonstrate our strength if we feel misrepresented. We won't wait for loved ones who remain disloyal and noncommittal to change their behavior; we're moving on without them.

This aspect identifies areas of your life where you need to take more leadership and hands you the captain's hat. It says, "Right, I am steering this ship from now on," rather than being a passenger heading in someone else's direction. Embrace this energy to take decisive action, assert your needs, and carve out the path that aligns with your true self.

This is the time to harness your inner strength and leadership qualities. Don't hesitate to take charge, whether in your personal life, career, or relationships. The universe aligns with your assertiveness, ready to support you as you steer your life toward your desired destination. Seize this moment to lead your journey and watch as doors open and opportunities arise, leading you to a more fulfilling and empowered life.

Mercury in Gemini sextile Chiron in Aries

This beautiful energy allows us to communicate deeply from our heart space. To utilize this energy, think back to the most challenging battles you have fought in your lifetime. Now, separate yourself from it and imagine your closest friend facing that challenge. How would you handle the situation? What advice would you give to your friend? What actions would you take to ensure your friend felt safe, loved, and nurtured through that struggle? Write a heartfelt letter to your friend detailing everything you want to say or do to support them. Once you have completed your letter, cross out your friend's name, address that letter to yourself, and read it back. If you are feeling up to it, repeat the process addressing your current challenge.

Venus in Taurus semi-sextile Saturn in Aries

This aspect reminds us that the deepest connections do not happen overnight. They are built on a foundation of trust, mutual respect, and understanding, which take time to develop and strengthen. Rushing into decisions, whether they are about reconciliation, new relationships, or fixing long-term commitments, often leads to overlooked issues and unresolved feelings.

When someone has broken our trust, the path to rebuilding should be gradual. Trust is earned through consistent actions over time. Allowing space for this process enables genuine change and healing to occur rather than a superficial quick fix.

In new relationships, starting as friends lays a solid foundation. Friendship allows you to see another person's true character and intentions. It helps you determine if they align with your values and if they are genuinely interested in a deeper connection beyond physical attraction.

If your long-term relationship seems to be falling apart, rather than slamming the door shut, allow the person to whom you have committed so much time to rectify the situation. Relationships are complex and require ongoing effort from both parties. Considering options like counseling can provide a neutral space to address problems and work toward a resolution.

This aspect emphasizes the importance of patience and the value of time in nurturing and evaluating relationships. It encourages you to slow down, observe, and allow people to demonstrate their intentions and commitment through their actions. Trust the process, and give relationships the time they need to reveal their true potential.

Song: "Still The One" by Shania Twain

June 8th

Mercury in Gemini biquintile Pluto retrograde in Aquarius

This energy represents awareness of a part of you that has yet to be expressed. We all know that we have the potential to achieve a lot of things; however, some of those things are difficult to visualize becoming part of our reality. This energy is like an internal whisper saying, "I wish I had the courage to express this part of myself." What are you keeping beneath the surface? What are you not saying? This is a recognition of your untapped potential.

Song: "Courage to Change" by Sia

June 9th

Mercury enters Cancer

With Mercury shifting into the sign of Cancer, we are all highly intuitive and able to feel the deep emotions behind what people say. So, we are using our intuitive gifts to support our communication. Our communication style during this time is quite nurturing as we become excellent listeners and hold space for people to express their emotions or whatever is on their hearts and minds. As people speak, we can connect emotionally to what others are saying, and likewise, our words have a healing effect on others. A simple conversation with a friend or loved one feels like a deep therapy session as we allow people to go deeper with us and meet them with empathy and compassion.

Another thing that we also tend to experience during this alignment is thoughts and memories of the past as we attempt to process our emotions. This may be you delving deep into healing your childhood trauma, or this could show up as having obsessive thoughts about an ex or an old friend who did you wrong. The downside to this energy is that what people say and how they actually feel do not always line up, so we may become easily triggered if those communicating with us seem insincere. Decisions we make now will be based on how we feel about a situation rather than the information we receive, so we may find ourselves defending a friend or loved one even if we know they are wrong. Ensure you are not sacrificing your better judgment due to deep love for another.

Reflection

1. How can I leverage my heightened intuition during this alignment to enhance my communication with others?

2. In what ways can I nurture my listening skills and hold space for people to express their emotions more effectively?

3. Am I currently addressing any childhood trauma? Do memories or thoughts of the past arise during moments of emotional processing, and how can I use them for healing?

Mars in Leo biquintile Saturn in Aries

This energy suggests that you might be facing a situation where you've invested so much energy without seeing any results or change that you're ready to give up. When we encounter obstacles that seem insurmountable, it's easy to feel defeated and question the value of our efforts. This energy can make us feel like we're fighting a losing battle, where no matter how hard we try, we can't make progress. It's natural to feel frustration and fatigue in these moments.

The challenges we face are often mirrors reflecting back areas of growth that we need to address. We can uncover valuable insights by stepping back and asking what lesson is hidden within the struggle. Consider what the situation is teaching you about patience, resilience, and perseverance. Is there a pattern in your approach that needs to be adjusted? Are there aspects of the situation you have control over and others that you need to release? Sometimes, the lesson is about letting go of the need for immediate results and trusting the process.

Venus in Taurus semi-sextile Neptune in Aries

How teachable are you? If you are reading this book, it is fair to assume that you have embraced a journey of self-growth and spirituality and have much to teach those around you. However, it is very easy for us to develop a spiritual ego and dismiss others around us as "asleep" or "unhealed." Consider that every relationship you encounter is not merely a spiritual assignment for you but a connection where both parties have something to learn from each other. Ensure your ego is not creating stories about you being more enlightened or "woke" than another. Allow the teachings from others to be absorbed. Just as you are the teacher, you are also the student. Being teachable also means being receptive to feedback and criticism. It requires courage to look at oneself honestly and acknowledge areas where growth is needed.

Mercury in Gemini semi-sextile Uranus in Taurus

Is there anything around us that is feeling unstable? Our living environment? Our bank account? Our relationship? How can we utilize all of the current mental energy to find solutions to these problems? For me, I have found solutions to many problems by reading books. One of my biggest challenges in adulthood is keeping my home organized, as I tend to accumulate things. Also, being an overachiever when it comes to business projects, I overextend myself. Two books changed everything for me: "The Clutter Connection" by Cassandra Aarssen and "The Life-Changing Magic of Tidying Up" by Marie Kondo.

We all struggle with things and don't always have the answers or solutions. However, I have learned that if I don't have the answer, someone else will. I just need to find it. Could you benefit from learning more about investing or budgeting from an expert? Reading a book written by a marriage or relationship expert can help you navigate challenges within your relationships. We don't need to solve every problem on our own. There is a plethora of resources available to help us.

Mercury in Gemini conjunct Jupiter in Gemini

What area of your life could you use more knowledge? This energy supports researching, finding, and absorbing the information you need. When my spirit team told me I was to write this book, I did not know the first thing about writing. Since I began, I have had to learn about writing, publishing, editing software, book cover design, and so many other things that I have spent hours researching to bring this book to fruition. We live in a world where all kinds of information are readily available to you at any time, and that is pretty cool. If we existed at another time, we would be so much more limited by the information available. Make the most of this energy and absorb all you can from people and available resources.

Sun in Gemini sesquiquadrate Pluto retrograde in Aquarius

This energy suggests that something within you is ready to transform and change. This aspect brings about profound revelations regarding our identity, purpose, and the roles we play. The labels and titles we assign ourselves throughout our lives give us a sense of identity and fuel our ego. This aspect asks us to reexamine some of those labels that have formed our identity. Which of them do we cling to and why? Each of these roles contributes to how we see ourselves and how we believe others see us. They can provide a sense of belonging, accomplishment, and direction. However, they can also become limiting if we hold onto them too tightly or allow them to define us too rigidly.

Song: "Shadow Work" by Kromestar, Katja

June 10th

Pallas Retrograde in Aquarius

When Pallas entered Aquarius, many of us felt pulled toward a cause or experienced a deep calling to stand for something and create change in the world. We began finding causes we could get behind and fighting for the underdog. Some of us started voicing our views on controversial or political topics, finding charities to donate our time and resources to, helping people find their voices, or adopting animals from shelters. We started thinking deeply about the difference we could make in the world as individuals and what we could do to change humanity.

Now that Pallas is turning retrograde, this placement brings us to question internally whether what we are fighting for still resonates with us and challenges whether our belief systems have changed. Perhaps we became involved with a church, club, or community organization only to discover that their views do not align with ours. We may have discovered more information about a political candidate we were backing and now wish to withdraw our support. We could have been openly speaking out about a controversial topic, which has opened up a dialogue. Now, our perspective is beginning to shift as we become open-minded to a different point of view. Perhaps a charity we have been supporting is not distributing funds or assistance in a way we feel is best. Maybe we chose to become vegan and now recognize that veganism no longer aligns with how we wish to live our lives. Or it could be that the band we worshipped since our teenage years still brings back good memories, but the music and lyrics no longer align with the person we have become.

This aspect questions what we stand for and allows us to see that changing our minds about what still resonates with us is okay. It invites us to reassess our commitments and make adjustments where necessary, ensuring that our actions and beliefs are in harmony with our evolving selves.

Reflection

1. Are your current actions and affiliations in alignment with your core values and beliefs?

2. How comfortable are you with changing your mind about a cause or belief you once held firmly?

160

3. How can you ensure that your actions and beliefs remain authentic to your evolving self?

Jupiter enters Cancer

Jupiter, the planet of expansion and luck, offers us the potential to grow and create more opportunities based on its zodiac placement. As it shifts into Cancer, the sign of emotions, nurturing, comfort, home, and family, our focus turns to the closest bonds and connections around us. Many of us will begin to focus on our intimate relationships and consider the next steps. Is it time to tell someone we have feelings for them? Is it time to progress from dating to being official? We could join our assets and move in together or consider buying our forever home. Is an engagement or marriage on the cards, or is it time to start building a family?

This alignment also prompts us to spend more time and energy on those we consider family. We might blow off a party or event to spend the evening eating popcorn and having a movie night with the kids. We might plan family adventures such as camping trips or events that bring together all extended family members for great food and belly laughs.

This alignment asks us how we can better nurture the relationships around us. Can we update the children's bedrooms to create a safer space for them at home? Do we need to reduce our work hours to dedicate more time to our children? Do they need more emotional support? Can we spend more one-on-one time with them so they open up to us, or should we enroll them in therapy? Can we show more interest in their passions and support them in their hobbies?

What are we doing to make our partner feel nurtured? Are we making time to take them out on dates? Are we speaking their love language? Can we show more appreciation to them by cooking their favorite meals? Are we meeting all their emotional needs? Some of us at this time will consider what we can do to heal and nurture others. Can we help others through their emotional trauma or extend ourselves to a friend going through a breakup or difficult transition? Can we pop an extra serving of dinner over to our elderly neighbor?

However, there is a downside to this energy. We become incredibly empathetic and emotionally vulnerable, and unfortunately, some people may take advantage of our kindness. This energy tells us that everyone is redeemable and deserves second chances, but what if they require multiple chances and mistake consistent forgiveness for weakness? This energy can open us up to energy vampires or make us too comfortable in unhealthy family dynamics or volatile relationships. While this energy encourages us to bring down our walls, extend ourselves outward, and sometimes be the bigger person, we should not eliminate our personal boundaries.

Reflection

1. Is it time for me to consider merging my life more closely with someone else, such as moving in together or planning a future together?

2. How can I prioritize and nurture my family relationships more effectively?

3. How can I balance supporting others while maintaining my own emotional well-being?

Mercury in Cancer square Saturn in Aries

Much emotional energy is circulating right now, and those around us can easily influence or affect our energetic field. If people around you seem moody and you begin feeling the same, it can be difficult to differentiate which energy is yours and which belongs to them. This energy will have you weeping your little heart out after hearing an emotional song or watching a sad movie. Take some time to breathe and assess whether these emotional responses are triggering a wound within you or whether it is your current sensitivity to your environment.

Venus in Taurus square Pluto retrograde in Aquarius

This aspect can be a difficult one to face as it calls our relationships with others into question. Are we on the same page or have completely different views? As we have both grown and evolved as humans, have we grown further apart? Can this situation be rectified, or have we become too set in our new ways of being? This aspect highlights the contrast between deciding who we are and how that fits in with our connections with others who have been consistent in our lives.

Mercury in Cancer square Neptune in Aries

This energy says, "Nope, I do not resonate with that." Perhaps you cannot find common ground with someone you care deeply about, or someone is attempting to sway you to their way of thinking. Maybe someone is trying to sell you something, but what they are saying doesn't align with the energy you're feeling from them. Perhaps someone you follow for guidance is trying too hard to convince you to take a particular action, making you feel they have an ulterior motive. If something feels off, it probably is. Trust your intuition.

Mars in Leo biquintile Neptune in Aries

This aspect encourages you to blaze your own trail and take action in alignment with what deeply resonates with you, even if that means upsetting another in the process. It's about embracing your authentic self and staying true to your inner compass, regardless of external pressures or expectations. Sometimes, the path you need to take will diverge from what others believe or want for you, and that's okay. We can be open to alternate points of view without adopting them as our own. This journey requires courage and self-assurance, reminding us that it's possible to respect and understand differing opinions while firmly standing our ground.

Song: "Can't Stop Me Now" by The Next Step

June 11th

Mars in Leo trine Chiron in Aries

This aspect serves as a potent reminder that despite all the trials and tribulations we've endured and the emotional wounds we carry, we have arrived at this moment stronger than ever. Every day we've faced, every obstacle we've overcome, has shaped us into resilient, tenacious individuals. Now, we stand at a crossroads and must decide: will we let our scars define us, or will we embrace the incredible strength and resilience that have brought us here?

Remember, it's not the scars that define you, but the courage and determination with which you wear them. You are stronger than you know and more capable than you ever imagined. Stand tall, face your challenges with confidence, and know that you are equipped to conquer anything that comes your way. Your story is one of resilience, strength, and unwavering spirit. Embrace it, and let it guide you to even greater heights.

Mercury in Cancer quincunx Pluto retrograde in Aquarius

This energy suggests that we want to avoid our feelings by either distracting ourselves from them or projecting them onto others around us. This can be an energy of feeling sorry for ourselves or choosing the role of a victim. Allowing this energy to creep in will keep you stagnant and unable to move forward, as it has us believing that we have no control over our lives. Ask yourself what emotions are keeping you stuck right now. Are you unable to forgive someone? Are you still waiting for an apology from the past? Are you praying and wishing that someone will receive karmic justice for what they have done to you? Are you waiting for some sort of closure or compensation? Your pain is not going to be cured by something or someone outside of you. It is our responsibility to heal ourselves and free ourselves from cycles of the past.

Song: "Survivor" by Destiny's Child

June 12th

Full Moon in Sagittarius

This full moon, in the sign of Sagittarius, encourages us to look at any relationships or connections that may feel restrictive and prompts us to do something about it. The Sun is positioned in the sign of Gemini, so we will likely want to talk about and express our feelings to those around us. The full moon in Sagittarius often brings to our attention anything that has been said or done in the dark, and when such things are exposed, we will want to face these issues head-on. If someone has been talking about you behind your back or lying to you, it will likely be exposed during this full moon.

This energy makes us want to stand up for ourselves and defend our honor rather than look the other way. This moon is all about exposing honesty, and we are sharing how we feel, so be careful with this energy because just as things are being exposed around you, any underlying feelings of bitterness and resentment that you have regarding people around you are also likely to come to the surface. Be mindful of who you are talking to at this time because if you are gossiping about someone else, it is likely to be exposed at this time. Many conflicts arise within this energy as friendships and relationships are put to the test.

Reflection

1. Are my current connections stimulating and matching my vibe, or do I need to seek out new faces and explore deeper connections?

2. Have any harsh truths been exposed during the Sagittarius full moon? Are there any discussions that I need to confront or address?

Mercury in Cancer sextile Venus in Taurus

This is a beautiful energy of experiencing love without the need for words. It encourages us to say less and observe more. What are the true intentions of those around you? We can discover the answer to this question just by observing their actions and gestures.

For instance, my partner often does things that annoy me, but that's normal after many years together. However, he knows me so well and speaks my love language fluently. Knowing how much I struggle during the winter, he wakes up earlier than I do to ensure my mornings are as comfortable as possible. He takes the time to remove the icicles from my car, turns on the heating, and checks the cupboards to ensure I have everything I need to make lunches for the children.

This energy also helps us identify those around us with negative intentions. It makes us keenly aware of those who say they love us but fail to show it through their actions. In this space of silent observation, we can discern true intentions and separate genuine love from mere words.

Pay attention to the small gestures, the quiet acts of kindness, and the consistent efforts that speak volumes. This energy teaches us that actions often reveal more about a person's intentions than their words ever could.

Song: "Best Of Your Intentions" by Roy Joseph

June 13th

Mercury in Cancer quintile Chiron in Aries

This aspect helps us recognize that our pain can be a gift to fuel our creativity and creation. The best songs ever written are produced when the artist is experiencing deep emotional pain. The most popular movies are those that tug on our heartstrings, and the best-selling books are written by authors who are not afraid to be vulnerable and peel back the layers of the most intense emotional pain they have ever experienced. Many of us who have experienced the most pain become healers, whether we are healing others through our words, energy, or art. How can you turn your pain into something beautiful?

Song: "Vincent" by Don McLean

June 14th

Sun in Gemini square Pisces North Node

Some days, we wake up feeling blessed and abundant, effortlessly seeing the beauty and opportunities around us. On other days, finding those blessings is like searching for a needle in a haystack. This aspect can have us focusing on the burdens in our lives that prevent us from having more fun. However, this doesn't mean the blessings aren't there; it just means we need to take a moment to acknowledge them. Even amidst the struggle, there is always something to be grateful for. By shifting our perspective, we can uncover the hidden gems and appreciate the abundance that surrounds us, even on challenging days.

Venus in Taurus semi-square Pisces North Node

This aspect may make us feel like we need more from others. We long for our friends to check in more often, our romantic partners to show a deeper level of commitment, and our family to have our back when needed. The struggle within this energy is that it encourages us to take a step back and wait for others to meet the expectations we've placed upon them. However, the reality is that we don't have to wait. We can pick up the phone and call a friend we haven't heard from. We can plan a date to rekindle a distant connection, and we can invite our family over for dinner to strengthen our bonds. By flipping the script and giving more to our connections rather than waiting for others to act, we may be surprised at how our energy is reciprocated. Taking the initiative can lead to deeper, more fulfilling relationships and a greater sense of connection and support.

Song: "Grateful" by Callmestevieray

June 15th

Vesta Direct in Scorpio

Vesta has been retrograde, causing us to keep our dreams, wishes, and desires to ourselves as we assess what is safe to share and what to keep private. This period has made us somewhat untrusting of those around us. However, now that Vesta is stationed directly, we can stop worrying so much about others' intentions and delve deeper into our own. What purpose are we here to serve, and how do we align ourselves with this purpose? Vesta in Scorpio propels us to passionately and intensely align our lives with this purpose.

Having identified our roles within the collective, we are now dedicated to researching and understanding the intricacies of this calling, striving to fulfill our true potential. Those of us who were just beginning our spiritual journey or dipping our toes in the healing waters are diving even deeper into personal transformation, demonstrating a solid commitment to our path. We are firm in severing connections, situations, or themes that do not align with our purpose. Scorpio's intensity and Vesta's deep fire propel us to investigate why we arrived at this moment in time and commit ourselves to the path of our highest timeline without distraction or interference. This period marks a time of profound personal transformation and dedication to our true calling, allowing us to step into our roles with clarity and conviction.

Reflection

1. What do you believe is your true purpose in this life? How can you better align your daily actions with this purpose?

2. Reflect on your current intentions. Are they in alignment with your highest self and true potential? How can you ensure your actions consistently reflect these intentions?

3. In what ways can you deepen your commitment to your spiritual path and personal transformation? What distractions or interferences must be eliminated to stay true to your highest timeline?

Song: "Breakaway" by Kelly Clarkson

June 16th

Mars in Leo square Uranus in Taurus

This aspect represents a moment where your confidence might take a hit. You may have applied for a role or position, feeling certain it was yours, only to receive a call saying you were unsuccessful. You might produce what you believe is your best work, only to have it critiqued by a customer or your boss. As a content creator, you might post something you're sure will go viral, only to receive minimal engagement or even negativity from your audience.

These experiences challenge you to maintain your confidence and resilience in the face of setbacks. Don't let these moments define you or hold you back. Keep creating, producing, and putting yourself out there. Whether it feels like a leap or a stumble, each step is still progress. Remember, the most significant successes often come after the biggest challenges. Learn from every experience, and keep moving forward with optimism and determination. Perseverance is the key to success.

Jupiter in Cancer square Saturn in Aries

This aspect represents feeling restricted in matters related to home and family. You may wish to relocate, but external circumstances suggest it's not the right time. Maybe you have to postpone the family camping trip due to illness or a bad weather forecast. You might want to take the children to a carnival, but your finances aren't great.

However, in these moments of restriction, there is an opportunity to culti-vate creativity and resilience. Try to make the best of your situation. If you can't move right now, consider small changes at home that can bring a fresh feel. Plan a fun indoor adventure or a movie night with camping-themed snacks if the camping trip is postponed. If the carnival is out of reach, create a mini carnival at home with games and treats.

Focusing on what you can do rather than what you can't will help you find joy and connection in the present moment, turning challenges into memorable experiences for you and your family.

Song: "Ironic" by Alanis Morissette

June 17th

Mercury in Cancer semi-square Uranus in Taurus

This energy reflects having little to no control over your environment. It might manifest as a subtle feeling that something is off or escalate to feeling like a victim of your current circumstances. Remind yourself that you are the creator of your own reality to shift out of this disempowering energy. If you believe you lack control or see yourself as a victim, that perception will manifest in your reality.

Manifestation starts with the thoughts and beliefs held in the subconscious mind. Reprogramming these thoughts can be challenging, but visualizing step-ping through a portal is an effective technique I use. Imagine you are in a portal of lack, worry, and strife. Now, visualize yourself walking out of this portal and into another—one of ultimate potential where anything is possible. Fully immerse yourself in this experience. As you leave the first portal, notice how it feels to leave behind negative thoughts. As you enter the second portal, focus on the sensation of stepping into an energetic frequency that opens you up to infinite possibilities.

By consciously making this shift in your mind, you can begin to transform your reality. Remember, your thoughts and beliefs shape your world. Embrace the power you have to create a life filled with potential and positivity.

Mercury in Cancer semi-square Mars in Leo

If you were to fully own your personal power and step into your most authentic self, how would that impact those closest to you? Imagine becoming the CEO of your life. Would this mean spending less time with family and loved ones? Would you find yourself more absorbed in work, possibly needing to put your children in care? Could it lead to falling out with close friends due to an energetic misalignment? Could others view you differently?

This aspect creates a conflict between striving to become your best self, following your ambitions, and wanting to be available for those you love and wish to strengthen bonds with. Balancing personal growth and maintaining close relationships is a delicate dance. We are asked to consider how stepping into your power affects your time, energy, and relationships.

Song: "Making The Bed" by Olivia Rodrigo

June 18th

Mars enters Virgo

Mars, the planet of action, is moving into Virgo, the helpful sign of the problem-solver. This brings a potent energy of fixing everything in our lives, starting with ourselves. As Virgo also rules health, many of us will find ourselves highly dedicated to better eating habits and fitness routines. Virgo encourages us to strive for perfection, making us very goal-oriented. Every action we take during this alignment has a purpose. We're no longer accepting our own excuses.

However, we must remember that perfection is not a realistic goal. We don't need to be overly critical of ourselves. So, before you start counting every calorie, lifting more weights than is comfortable, or depriving yourself of nutrients for a health cleanse or detox, remember that balance and moderation are the keys to making lasting changes.

This energy affects our health, mind, and environment. You may find yourself on a self-development journey or fixating on a project such as decluttering or redecorating your home. We're identifying anything we can improve or make better and following up by rolling up our sleeves and fixing it.

Problems can arise when we overextend ourselves to others, trying to fix their issues which they may not feel need fixing. Mars is also the planet of war and conflict, so it's important to mention how this can affect our interactions with others. In conflict, this energy will identify everything wrong with the other person as we criticize flaws and point out how they can improve. Often, it's not what you say but how you say it that causes problems. Try to remove the judgmental, critical tone from your words, and unless you're willing to help find a solution, there's no need to point out the flaws in others.

The best way to navigate this energy is to stay in your lane and focus on helping to heal and improve yourself rather than identifying and trying to fix everyone else's problems. If someone wants your help, they will ask for it, and then you can work together to motivate and inspire each other.

This energy can also greatly assist us in business as we can easily identify problems and quickly rectify them with appropriate solutions. Those in the business of helping others, such as healers, coaches, counselors, nurses, and doctors, will thrive within this energy.

Reflection

1. How can I balance my drive for self-improvement with self-compassion and avoid being overly critical of myself?

2. What specific areas of my life, both personal and professional, can I identify for improvement, and how can I take purposeful action towards them?

3. How can I recognize when I am overextending myself to fix others' problems, and what boundaries can I set to focus more on self-healing?

Sun in Gemini sextile Chiron in Aries

This aspect encourages us to treat ourselves. Give your soul exactly what it is that you need today. What were you lacking as a child? Perhaps you never received any kind of praise or recognition. If that is the case, it is time for you to stand in front of the mirror and recognize yourself. Gas yourself up with positive affirmations. Some of us were not even provided with basic needs as children. If this is you, brush your teeth, wash your hair, and cook yourself up the most amazing meal. If you grew up in poverty, buy yourself something nice. You are so worthy of whatever you were lacking as a child. Nurture the child version of yourself who is so deserving of love and attention.

Sun in Gemini semi-square Venus in Taurus

This energy represents becoming bored with our current connections and yearning for something more exciting. Perhaps you and your partner always do the same thing on weekends, and you long for the two of you to get away and have an adventure. You may find yourself listening to a friend or family member talk about the same topic repeatedly, wishing for a change. Be bold, take the reins, and be the first to invite more excitement into your connections. This energy says, "I love you and am here for you, but can we have more fun?"

Song: "Fix It" by Lady Blackbird

June 19th

Last Quarter Moon in Pisces

Wait, what was I doing? This is the part of the lunar cycle where we are supposed to be finishing things off or making final adjustments to anything that we are trying to manifest, but Pisces energy has us all distracted and unfocused. We are much more likely to binge-watch Netflix, read a book, or take a nap in this energy. So, ask yourself what needs to be done right now and then reward yourself with those things. Indulge in self-sabotaging behaviors only after your tasks are complete.

Reflection

1. Reflect on a time when distractions hindered your progress. What strategies can you employ to stay focused and on track during similar phases?

2. What are the most common self-sabotaging behaviors you tend to indulge in when feeling distracted or unfocused?

3. How can you strike a balance between indulging in leisure activities, like binge-watching or reading, and ensuring that essential tasks are completed first?

Sun in Gemini biquintile Pluto retrograde in Aquarius

We are quick to distract ourselves by participating in things that will give us instant gratification. We don't want to look deeply at ourselves and take responsibility for our situations and choices, which have kept us trapped and restricted. But if you allow yourself to go there, a deep inner transformation will begin to take place. We cannot heal and shift what we do not recognize. While Pluto continues retrograding through Aquarius, we are constantly presented with opportunities for deep self-reflection and transformation. Still, we have to be willing to go there and accept accountability for the choices that have led us to where we are.

Jupiter in Cancer square Neptune in Aries

Do not allow anyone else to dictate how you live your life. In today's world, we all have a platform to share our opinions, and we're constantly bombarded with information about what is deemed appropriate. This can create unnecessary doubt and hesitation. You may wish to move house, but the collective fear of rising house prices makes you rethink your decision. You might want to start a family, but worry about bringing children into a world fraught with challenges. You may wish to marry someone you love deeply, but alarming divorce statistics make you anxious.

It's okay to live your life in a way that goes against familial pressures or societal norms. Live for today, and trust your inner guidance rather than seeking a road map from external sources. Your path is uniquely yours, and your decisions should reflect your true desires and values, not the fears and expectations of others.

Song: "Self Sabotage" by Abe Parker

June 20th

Mars in Virgo quincunx Saturn in Aries

This energy brings its fair share of frustration, as we are eager to solve a problem proactively, yet immediate action isn't possible, or it requires more time than anticipated. You might have decided to take on a second job, but finding an appropriate position is proving to be a challenge. You could feel inspired to begin a new career only to discover that obtaining the necessary qualifications will take three years. Perhaps you have identified the perfect person to help solve a problem, but upon calling to set up a meeting, you find they are out of town for a while.

This energy combines the clarity of having the answer to a problem and the enthusiasm to act upon it, but it demands incredible patience and persistence to implement your plan. It's a lesson in balancing urgency with patience and determination with endurance. The key is to stay focused on your goal, maintain your enthusiasm, and trust that the time and effort you invest now will pay off in the long run.

Song: "Wait In Line" by James Bay

June 21st

Sun enters Cancer

Cancer season is upon us, inviting us to delve deep into our emotional state and feel all the feels. Our home space is becoming our main priority as we nurture ourselves and our relationships with the people closest to us. We find ourselves highly sensitive and emotional during this season as we internally process our emotions and spend more time in the comfort of our own homes rather than experiencing the social butterfly energy we had throughout Gemini season. This season is about creating a nurturing home environment for us to feel safe in, deepening our relationships by talking about our feelings and emotions, prioritizing our self-care, allowing space for ourselves to delve deep into our fears and emotions, and allowing ourselves some grace. At the same time, we experience moodiness and fluctuations in energy.

I like to think of Cancer season as the great purge. It can be heavy and emotional; however, if you allow yourself to process whatever deep emotions want to come up, by the end of this season, you will be feeling freer and lighter than ever. An important thing to remember during this season is not to rush through the process. Feel what you need to feel, explore what you need to explore, release what you need to release, and cry when you need to cry. Think of yourself during this season as a mother nurturing a baby, only instead of a real baby; your deep emotions are the baby, your inner child is the baby, and your past version is the baby. Allow yourself to hold space for the version of yourself that still carries pain.

Reflection

1. Think about the concept of the "great purge" during Cancer season. What emotions or experiences are you hesitant to confront, and how might allowing yourself to process them contribute to a sense of freedom and lightness?

2. Consider the advice to not rush through the process during Cancer season. How comfortable are you with sitting with your emotions and allowing them to unfold naturally, and what benefits might come from this approach?

3. Can you embody the role of a nurturing caregiver to your own emotions, inner child, and past experiences during this time? Explore the idea of holding space for the version of yourself that still carries pain. What practices or rituals can you incorporate to create a safe and

supportive space for emotional healing?

Sun in Gemini semi-sextile Uranus in Taurus

There are many things in this life that we cannot control, like the rising cost of living or natural disasters, but we can control how much we allow these things to rent space in our minds. There have been times when I had no money in my bank account and was presented with the choice to fall to pieces or make the most out of the resources I had available to me. I remember one time when my partner and I were both ill and unable to work and broke. I went to the kitchen and found flour, sugar, milk, and butter. I almost had enough ingredients to whip up some homemade pancakes, so I knocked on my neighbor's door and asked if she could spare some eggs. We made pancakes for dinner. I felt like such a failure as a parent, and my son turned to me and said, "Mom, this is the best dinner ever." My point is you do not need to waste your mental energy focused on things you cannot control but rather recognize the abilities and resources you have to create potential for yourself.

Mars in Virgo quincunx Neptune in Aries

My dad used to always say, "There's more than one way to skin a cat," meaning that there was always another way to go about things if our current method was presenting a challenge. My dad was a country boy who grew up on a farm, and as a result, he was incredibly resourceful. He always seemed to know exactly what to do in every situation, although his ideas and solutions were often unconventional and would upset the people around him. But that didn't matter much to him as long as he got the job done.

One memory that sticks out to me is when my dog had become very old and ill and then was attacked by another dog. She was not going to survive the attack. Rather than take the dog to the vet to be euthanized like a 'normal' person, my dad channeled his inner country boy and took care of it himself. We were all horrified and traumatized by what he had just done, but he just shrugged his shoulders and said, "The dog was going to die anyway." In his mind, he had not only solved the problem but also saved himself from an expensive vet bill.

This energy asks us to be a little more resourceful when facing current challenges and not worry so much about the appropriate thing to do that spares everyone else's feelings. Although this is an extreme example, and I do not at all suggest that you resort to harming animals, sometimes you just have to do what needs to be done, even if it may cause upset to someone else.

Song: "Right Now" by Resource

June 22nd

Mercury in Cancer trine Pisces North Node

This aspect supercharges our intuition to its highest potential. Today, trust those gut feelings and inner whispers—the divine is sending you powerful re-inforcements. It's the perfect moment to meditate, still your mind, and connect deeply with your inner guidance. Engage in spiritual practices like divination if you're called. Embrace this opportunity to open yourself up fully, allowing the universe to reveal the next steps on your soul's journey.

Song: "Rescue" by Lauren Daigle

June 23rd

Venus in Taurus semi-square Saturn in Aries

Building trust within connections takes time, especially in relationships where trust has been broken or inconsistency has been shown. Sometimes, our connections can fall apart in what seems like an instant, but when wounds have been exposed, regaining a person's trust takes time. This aspect reminds us not to be too trusting of those around us, and to put the required effort into our relationships. Apologies are great, but it takes demonstrating changed behavior for a person to feel safe again.

You may find yourself frustrated that someone cannot move past a disagreement, or you yourself may not be hasty to forgive and forget. Wounds that cut deeply need more than a band-aid to heal them. This energy reminds us to slow down in healing our connections and give all parties the time they need to recover.

Mars in Virgo sextile Jupiter in Cancer

When you embark on a journey of self-improvement, whether adopting healthier habits, practicing mindfulness, or pursuing personal growth, you become a beacon of positive change. Your actions and attitude create a ripple effect, encouraging others to reflect on their lives and make positive changes. Remember, leading by example is one of the most powerful ways to inspire those around you. So, embrace your own journey to self-improvement, and watch how your transformation encourages others to follow suit.

Sun in Cancer square Saturn in Aries

Cancer season asks us to allow any unprocessed emotions to bubble up and come to the surface to be healed. Although we may want to push them down and avoid being an emotional wreck, this period encourages us to confront the pain and trauma we carry from the past. We may want to move forward rather than dwell on the past, but this aspect will cause those emotions to continue bubbling up until they are acknowledged.

This energy often manifests as feelings of sadness, depression, anger, and mood swings. The sooner we acknowledge and address our pain, the sooner we can release these emotions and return to feeling more like ourselves. Embracing this process allows us to heal and ultimately move forward with a lighter heart and a clearer mind. Remember, healing is not linear, and giving yourself the space to feel and process your emotions is a crucial step toward genuine well-being.

Venus in Taurus semi-square Neptune in Aries

This energy makes us want to ignore inconsistencies within our connections. A problem may need to be addressed within a relationship, or you may be growing distrust of those around you. However, this energy says, "I don't want to deal with that right now." Sometimes, we wait for others to show up more consistently for us or for another's behavior to change, but unless we address underlying issues, others often do not know what we expect from them or that there is a problem at all.

Over time, these minor issues grow into much bigger problems until we eventually explode with anger over something that could have been quickly addressed or rectified at the first display of the behavior. If you are waiting for someone to change their behavior or show you more consistency, ask yourself if you have clearly communicated your needs and expectations. Have you asked for more from them? Addressing issues early on can prevent them from escalating and help foster healthier, more transparent connections.

Song: "Total Eclipse Of The Heart" by Bonnie Tyler

June 24th

Mars in Virgo quincunx Pluto retrograde in Aquarius

This aspect leaves room for a substantial transformational internal shift. Initially, this energy can make us feel disconnected from others or our environment, powerless to change it. Efforts to bring about change may seem in vain. However, this energy also opens up a doorway to turn our focus inward, creating an internal shift that is then reflected in our outer reality. Remember, things are only an issue if we perceive them to be.

This internal shift can dismantle belief systems we have held as truths for a long time. Our reality transforms as we let go of outdated perceptions and embrace new perspectives. The key lies in understanding that our internal landscape shapes our external experiences. This is a time to challenge our long-held beliefs, question their validity, and make room for new, empowering thoughts that align with our desired reality. Embrace this period of introspection and transformation, and watch as your outer world begins to reflect the changes you make within.

Sun in Cancer square Neptune in Aries

This energy asks us to take stock of the constant stream of energetic influences within our lives and identify how they contribute to our overall vibration. Do you surround yourself with positive people, or is your group of friends overwhelmingly negative? What about the content you consume? I've always loved to watch true crime documentaries, but I know that consuming this type of content has a negative effect on my vibration. What about the influencers you follow? Does the content you consume leave you feeling motivated and inspired, or does it leave you feeling low?

Consider making conscious choices to surround yourself with positive influences. Seek out content that inspires and motivates you. Engage with people who uplift and support you. By curating a more positive, energetic environment, you can elevate your vibration and create a more fulfilling and joyful life. Remember, you have the power to choose what influences you allow into your life, so choose wisely and prioritize your well-being.

Venus in Taurus semi-square Jupiter in Cancer

This aspect has us eager to move forward and take the next steps within our connections. We might make a relationship exclusive, pick out engagement rings, move in together, or expand our family. This energy encourages us to ensure that all parties are on the same page and not rush into things too quickly. The strongest relationships are those built together, where both partners show consistency and commitment rather than one person driving the progress while the other is just along for the ride.

Take the time to have meaningful conversations about your future together. Are your goals and visions aligned? Are you both ready for the next step? It's essential to build a foundation of mutual understanding and shared aspirations. This aspect reminds us that a relationship thrives on balanced effort and mutual respect.

Song: "Man In The Mirror" by Michael Jackson

June 25th

Jupiter in Cancer quincunx Pluto retrograde in Aquarius

This aspect presents as a disturbance within our home or space of safety. Perhaps we experience a disagreement with a family member, or our neighbors' behaviors drive us crazy. We may have received a rent increase notification or have to make repairs within the home. This energy again asks us to explore what can be transformed within us to solve the problem. Can we shift our belief systems? Are we placing too many expectations on family members or neighbors because they are not behaving in a way we deem appropriate? Can we remove ourselves from feeling as if we have fallen victim to a rent increase or a repair bill and recognize that it is natural for rent prices to increase over time and for old appliances to break down and need to be replaced eventually? Shifting our perception of our reality allows us to move from a victim mentality to a space of empowerment.

Mercury in Cancer square Chiron in Aries

Our emotions are all over the place right now. Do you know how they say never to shop on an empty stomach? Here is another tip for you: never make a decision in an emotionally charged state. This aspect indicates that all decisions we make right now are based on how we feel, so with energy like this, we will often see many arguments and relationship breakups. Also, I want to encourage you to watch your words right now as Mercury in Cancer brings us the ability to hurt people with our words. It is as if we know exactly what to say to trigger someone's emotions. If you are about to say something hurtful, ask yourself if you are speaking from your heart space or reacting from your pain.

Sun in Cancer quincunx Pluto retrograde in Aquarius

This energy is heavy, and everyone who has begun a journey of healing themselves or experienced a spiritual awakening will be able to relate to feeling this way. This is when we tell ourselves that healing all this emotional stuff is too hard, and can't we go back in time and choose to stay asleep? Like The Matrix movie, we chose this path, taking the red pill to expand our consciousness and begin powerfully healing ourselves. But now, we are starting to feel like the Matrix was not so bad after all. This entire journey becomes difficult at times when we feel like we have little control over anything. Still, when we experience this type of energy, we are headed towards a major breakthrough in consciousness, so don't give up.

It can be difficult to feel as though you are making any progress in life when you are emotionally charged. If you are holding unprocessed emotions, allow them to come up for release. If you struggle to shift back into expansive energy and your breathing feels shallow and your chest tight, I highly recommend trying some somatic breathing techniques to shift any emotional energy stored within your body. Examples can be found on YouTube.

Go easy on yourself today. Ensure you drink plenty of water and nourish your body with healthy eating, giving yourself what you need to feel comfortable. Remember, self-care is not a luxury but a necessity, especially when navigating through emotionally turbulent times. Prioritize your well-being and take the time to listen to your body and its needs. You are doing your best, and it's okay to slow down and take care of yourself.

Song: "Lost Boy" by Ruth B

June 26th

New Moon in Cancer

This new moon in Cancer brings about all the feels, asking us to look at what could be changed to better support our emotional needs. What is most important to us, and what do we want to nurture? Are our emotional needs being met, and what do we need in order to feel like we are being nurtured? Is it more love and support from our family? Perhaps, for you, it is taking better care of your health and body or eating better.

What emotions are coming up for you right now? Take the time to honor those emotions—the loud ones, the niggling ones that come up from time to time, and even the mostly silent ones that just seem to whisper to you during your times of stillness. If you can, try to make some time to allow peace and stillness; this can help allow you the space to hear them. Meditation, yoga, walking, or simply lying on the grass looking up at the clouds can help you identify any emotions you have that may be calling out for your attention. What is your intuition whispering to you right now about your next steps? What does your body need? Now is a beautiful time for you to connect and become familiar with yourself. Are there people around you right now that leave you tired or drained? Become aware of which energies affect you, even if those effects are subtle.

Reflection

1. In what aspects of my life can I make changes to better support my emotional needs?

2. What relationships or situations currently contribute positively to my emotional well-being?

3. What practices or habits can contribute to better health, both physically and emotionally?

Song: "7 Years" by Lukas Graham

June 27th

Mercury enters Leo

Mercury in Leo is my favorite energy for communicating. When we communicate during this time, we bring the energy and vibe with confidence and enjoyment. Our storytelling is captivating and exudes confidence, wit, and entertainment. This is the energy of posting social media content and then watching it back repeatedly, thinking to yourself, "Damn, I'm hilarious." We are playful and have fun in all that we do. If you have a passion project, now is an excellent time to present it to the world because others will resonate with that passion. The confidence we have in our thoughts and beliefs is unshakable. We vibe and feel ourselves, embracing self-expression, and we have no time for anyone bringing negative energy our way or letting down the vibes.

If we receive hate during this time, we don't pay it any mind. When experiencing this empowered and confident energy, it's not uncommon for others to try to bring us down, wanting us to return to their level. How we respond to this energy is where our true power lies. Instead of reacting to negative energy, take notes. Who are these people triggered by you living your best life and being in your high-vibing energy? Are these your people? Allow these individuals to expose themselves while you shine bright and radiate your energy.

Reflection

1. In what ways do you consciously bring positive energy to your interactions, and how does it influence the dynamics of communication?

2. Consider your response to negative energy during times of empower-

ment and confidence. How do you typically handle hate or negativity, and what strategies do you use to maintain your positive vibes? How can you maintain authenticity and positive energy, regardless of external influences?

3. Think about your social circle and how they react to your high-vibing energy. Have you experienced others attempting to bring you down? How did you respond, and what did you learn from those situations?

Mercury in Cancer sextile Uranus in Taurus

You will find that as we take some time away from the obstacles we face, the energy will shift and begin to calm down. Sometimes, we just need to disengage and allow everything to calm down and work itself out. Sometimes, we can get so used to overcoming challenges that we cannot recognize when we are going against the flow of energy, and we begin to flow against the current. After some self-care and pampering of our mind, body, and spirit, we are more inspired to walk away from any conflict or drama.

Sun in Cancer sextile Mars in Virgo

This aspect allows us to identify what is most important to us and take decisive action toward that. If we deeply love someone but our relationship is in tatters, we can work toward rebuilding it. If our children are struggling to keep up in school, we can rectify the situation by prioritizing their progress or hiring a tutor. This energy inspires us to roll up our sleeves and improve the areas in our lives that require the most attention, prioritizing them with renewed focus and determination.

This is a powerful time for transformation and proactive efforts. It's about recognizing where our attention is needed most and diving in with commitment and purpose. The energy supports us in taking meaningful steps to enhance and repair our connections, goals, and responsibilities.

Venus in Taurus sextile Pisces North Node

This aspect asks us to surrender to the flow of the universe. If we try too hard to push through resistance, we often create more resistance for ourselves. Instead, invite the divine to help you with your current challenges. If you cannot find an immediate solution to a problem, ask that one be shown to you. If you are constantly overthinking a problem and getting caught up in worry and anxiety, release your struggles to God and just breathe. Commit yourself to a spiritual practice to feel more connected, rather than just seeking divine assistance when you require a savior. This way, when you face a challenge, you will feel safe knowing that the divine has your back.

Embracing this energy means trusting in the timing and wisdom of the universe. Sometimes, our most significant breakthroughs come from moments of stillness and surrender, rather than from relentless pushing and striving. By cultivating a daily spiritual practice—whether it be meditation, prayer, journaling, or simply spending time in nature—we build a strong foundation of faith and connection. This consistent practice reassures us that we are not alone and that divine guidance is always available, not just in times of crisis but as a constant presence in our lives.

Song: "I Surrender" by Hillsong

June 28th

Mercury in Leo trine Saturn in Aries

Persistence will be your greatest ally today. This energy will have you springing out of bed, giving yourself a little pep talk, and facing the day with unwavering determination. Picture yourself as a personal trainer, both for yourself and those around you, cheering everyone on with a spirited, "You've got this! One more rep, let's go!" Push yourself to go the extra mile, inspire those around you, and create an environment where everyone feels empowered to achieve their best. Whether tackling a difficult project, supporting a friend, or hitting a new personal best at the gym, your persistence and positive energy will lead to success.

Song: "Push It" by Salt-N-Pepa

June 29th

Mercury in Leo trine Neptune in Aries

This aspect calls us to step into our power and embrace leadership in our lives. It's time to take charge and let the world see what you're capable of. This energy rewards those willing to confidently share their unique gifts and talents. Whether you're launching a new product or service, teaching on a public platform, or taking the lead on a project at work, this is your moment to shine. Don't shy away from the spotlight—this is your time to be loud and proud of who you are and what you bring to the table. The universe is encouraging you to embrace being the center of attention and to celebrate your strengths.

Song: "Ghetto Supastar" by Pras, Ol'Dirty Bastard and Mya

June 30th

Mercury in Leo opposite Pluto retrograde in Aquarius

Even when we're achieving great things, it's easy to feel like we're not doing enough or that we don't deserve the recognition we're receiving. That small, insecure voice inside us that whispers, "You're an imposter," can be loud and persistent. It tells us we're just faking it until we make it. But here's the thing: so what if we are? Many of us put on a brave face and pretend to be confident, waiting for that moment when we're finally "ready." But what happens when we arrive at our destination? When others start recognizing our efforts and accomplishments?

This aspect encourages us to step out of the outdated mindset of constantly striving to become something more and instead acknowledge what we have already become. It's time to recognize the incredible roles we've stepped into and the successes we've achieved. The truth is, many of us never feel completely worthy, unable to see ourselves through the eyes of others who admire us. But today, try to silence that inner critic telling you there's still more work to do. Embrace the part of you that has already made it, the version of yourself that has grown, evolved, and accomplished so much. You deserve to stand on that platform and own your success. Celebrate the journey you've taken, and let yourself fully appreciate the person you've become.

Song: "Started From The Bottom" by Drake

July Alignments

July 1st

Sun in Cancer quintile Chiron in Aries

By this stage, you may be starting to realize that exploring your deeper emotions has its benefits. Allowing space for these energies to resurface and recognizing them frees up our heart space to make peace with them. We are showing compassion for ourselves, and as a result, the pain seems to diminish, and the things that used to trigger us now have less of an effect on us. As we allow trapped emotions to show themselves, they will diminish over time, allowing us to live in peace rather than consistently identifying ourselves with our past traumas.

Mercury in Leo semi-sextile Jupiter in Cancer

This energy encourages us to reach out and uplift those closest to us. It's a time when we naturally find ourselves offering support, inspiration, and motivation to the people we care about. You might find yourself encouraging your children, celebrating their achievements, or helping them overcome a challenge if they're struggling. Your partner might be the one needing a boost, and you're there to remind them of their strengths, expressing your faith in their ability to succeed. This energy is all about building each other up, spreading positivity, and creating an atmosphere of mutual support and encouragement within your relationships. It's a time to be the cheerleader for those you love, knowing that your belief in them can make all the difference.

Song: "Scars To Your Beautiful" by Alessia Cara

July 2nd

Venus in Taurus semi-sextile Chiron in Aries

When we delve deep into our own stories that we have created for ourselves to protect us from our trauma, it offers us a little window into how we may be sabotaging the relationships around us. It also allows us to see how the other people we are connecting with protect themselves from us. This allows us to sit down and become vulnerable with the people in our lives, explaining why we behave in the way we do and sharing with them what we are committed to changing within ourselves. It also involves holding a compassionate space for them to explore their defense strategies, understanding why they exist, and how they may commit to changing their behaviors to allow us to become closer to them.

Mercury in Leo sesquiquadrate Pisces North Node

This aspect is like a beacon, illuminating the path toward the person you're destined to become. You might feel inspired to start a podcast, become a coach, launch a YouTube channel, or open a healing practice. Whatever direction you're being drawn toward, know it's because you already possess the skills, talents, and abilities needed to step into that role. It's natural to feel hesitant, especially if you've built a successful career in another field, but remember—your past experiences have been preparing you for this moment. The skills you've gained are transferable, and they've been leading you to this point in your journey. You don't need to be an expert right away; you'll learn and grow as you go. Think of this as an exciting adventure, not a final destination. Embrace the journey with curiosity and enthusiasm, knowing that each step forward is a step toward fulfilling your true potential.

Song: "Live Your Life" by T.I.

July 3rd

First Quarter Moon in Libra

This first-quarter moon allows us to examine our relationships in greater detail and asks us what we can do to create more harmony and balance in our relationships moving forward. Can we forgive those who have wronged us? Is there any chance of reconciliation, or do compromises need to be made in our connections? What are we willing to sacrifice to create happiness for those we care most deeply about, and what would we need to see from the other party to ensure that the connection is equal, fair, and balanced for everyone involved? This energy asks us to consider where we could see more effort from others and not be afraid to ask for it, and where we ourselves could bring more to the table. Be honest with yourself; are you somewhat selfish with your energy, or are you too self-sacrificing, ignoring your own needs to please another?

Reflection

1. Reflect on past conflicts or challenges in your relationships. How open are you to forgiveness, and what steps can you take to foster healing and harmony in those relationships?

2. What aspects of your own needs and desires are you willing to compromise, and where do you draw the line to ensure your well-being?

3. Consider the role of honest communication in your relationships. Are there aspects where open dialogue could lead to better understanding and mutual growth?

Song: "I Won't Give Up" by Jason Mraz

July 4th

Mars in Virgo biquintile Pluto retrograde in Aquarius

This energy is all about stepping into your power and becoming the best version of yourself. It's the kind of energy that makes you take a hard look at where you can make more effort and improve. You might find yourself diving into inspirational podcasts or stocking up on self-development books. This is the moment when you're ready to toss those cigarettes, pour the liquor down the sink, and hit the gym with newfound determination. You're realizing that the key to transforming your outer reality starts with transforming yourself.

Song: "Be Better" by Diz and the Fam

July 5th

Venus enters Gemini

Our relationships and connections are coming into focus with a particular emphasis on our friendships. We want people around us who can stimulate us and match our vibe. We are more likely to connect with new people at this time as we become curious about others and want to learn more about them. If any connections have become stagnant or boring, we will likely withdraw from those people right now as we want to be around people we can just be silly with and who bring out our inner child. This is a very playful energy, and if you have children, you may find yourself more likely to play dress-ups, build forts, or play Legos. For those who don't, you may still want to do these things by hosting a costume party, camping with a tent instead of a fort, or planning a romantic evening where you and your partner stay in and build Legos.

For singles, we are more likely to have more than one person we are talking to and enjoy flirting right now or getting to know someone rather than rushing things or getting too deep with the people around us. We are keeping it casual when it comes to dating, allowing us to try out different experiences. We seek those who can mentally stimulate us by having interesting conversations or making us laugh. We are also more likely to want to go on fun adventure dates rather than Netflix and chill as we assess whether the person we are connecting with can match our vibe. Also, we are more likely to flirt with a sexy stranger at a party or initiate a conversation with our cute neighbor as we recognize that new connections can be found anywhere rather than just on dating apps. We are much more spontaneous when dating and meeting new people.

For those in a committed relationship, it will become very obvious if that relationship has become stale as we attempt to find ways to spice things up. We may be more likely to flirt with our partners, send them a sexy text while they are at work, or purchase tools to spice things up in the bedroom. Venus in Gemini is sexy, flirty, and fun, so why not use this opportunity to reignite the flame between you and your partner? Plan fun dates with your partner or stay in and watch a comedy and play board games for a laugh as you connect with the inner child within you.

Reflection

1. Reflecting on the potential withdrawal from stagnant connections, consider: Are there relationships in my life that feel dull or uninspiring, and how can I bring more playfulness and silliness into those connections?

2. For those in committed relationships, prompted by Venus in Gemini, ask yourself: In what ways can I spice up my relationship, introduce more playfulness, and reignite the passion with my partner?

3. Reflecting on the pursuit of spontaneity in making new connections, ask yourself: Am I open to meeting new people in unexpected places, and how can I foster spontaneity in my social interactions?

Neptune Retrograde in Aries

When we hear the word "retrograde," we often think of chaos, destruction, and setbacks. However, Neptune's movement in retrograde can be a truly positive force in our lives. Neptune in Aries has pushed us to dig deep into our beliefs and question the belief systems that surround us. With Neptune in retrograde, we are granted the clarity to see through illusions, enabling us to align with beliefs that resonate with us.

During this period, you might find yourself questioning long-held affiliations. Perhaps the church you've been attending feels more like a business venture than a spiritual refuge, prompting you to seek a more genuine path. Maybe an influencer you've admired for years no longer aligns with your values, and you decide to unfollow them. This retrograde is a time when the masks worn by those in positions of power or influence begin to slip, revealing their true nature. We might witness public figures—celebrities, influencers, even government officials—fall from grace as their true selves come to light.

Neptune's retrograde brings a much-needed reality check, urging us to see things as they truly are. It's a time to discover our own personal truth and stand firmly in it. This energy encourages us to disconnect from the illusions we've clung to and become more grounded and realistic in the belief systems we choose to embrace.

Reflection

1. What belief systems have I been holding onto that may no longer resonate with my true self?

2. Are there any affiliations or influences in my life that I need to reassess or let go of?

3. In what ways have I allowed external authorities or influencers to shape my beliefs, and how can I reclaim my power in defining my values?

Venus in Taurus conjunct Uranus in Taurus

You may require more support in making decisions. For example, you may be a stay-at-home mom who wants to return to the workforce, but this would require help from those around you. Can your partner change their work schedule to work in collaboration with yours? Do you have friends or family that can help with children and get them to and from school? Remember to reach out to your support network with any issues you may be facing right now; that is why we call them our support network.

Song: "Bad Boy For Life" by Diddy

July 7th

Venus in Gemini sextile Saturn in Aries

Take the opportunity to have a little fun with someone that you love. Go on a date to an amusement park or surround yourself with children inspiring you to play and have imaginary adventures. Sometimes it begins to feel as though the universe has placed on us a time-out while we wait for something exciting to happen or for our dreams and manifestations to pick up speed. Rather than waiting, allow playfulness to enter your reality now. Take a friend out for ice cream with extra sprinkles or dance with a lover in the rain.

Venus in Gemini sextile Neptune retrograde in Aries

This energy highlights the reality that conflicting views are inevitable within our connections. It could be that those you love have chosen a path of materialism while you are more focused on healing and inner reflection. They might support a different football team, hold religious beliefs that clash with your own, or even have political views that starkly contrast yours. Perhaps they hold homophobic opinions while you are a strong ally of the LGBTQ+ community. But does this mean you can't enjoy their company? Absolutely not.

Just because someone's belief systems conflict with your own doesn't mean you can't come together, share a laugh, and create lasting memories. We are all entitled to our perspectives; these beliefs are just one small piece of what makes up who we are. Instead of focusing on what divides you, why not bond over what you share? You might find that the common ground between you is far more significant than the differences that separate you. Embrace the diversity of thought within your connections, and allow these differences to deepen your understanding and appreciation of one another.

Sun in Cancer semi-square Uranus in Taurus

The outside world can begin to feel overwhelming as we shift our focus to that which we can control. Today, we may be creating a safe and welcoming space within our home, taking better care of our bodies, or spending time with our children. We appreciate the little things without feeling pressured to do or be more. Uranus in Taurus may cause an outside distraction; however, you get to choose how much energy you extend toward it and whether or not you allow your energy to be pulled away from what is most important to you.

Venus in Gemini quintile Pisces North Node

This energy carries a wave of nostalgia, returning us to the simple joys we cherished as children. You might stumble upon a movie you once adored and feel compelled to share the experience with your children, bringing the magic of your past into their present. Perhaps a song plays on the radio that once guided you through the turbulence of your teenage years, or you find yourself revisiting an old hobby that used to fill your days with excitement.

This is an invitation to weave the playfulness and joy of your childhood into your current life. How can these cherished interests find a place in your work, family, or even your business? Can you blend your youth's creativity and freedom with adulthood's responsibilities and routines? Embrace this energy as an opportunity to reignite passions that may have dimmed over the years and let them infuse your present with a renewed sense of wonder and enjoyment.

Song: "Daydream" by Lily Meola

July 8th

Uranus enters Gemini

Uranus, known as the great disruptor of the zodiac, thrives on challenging the status quo, shaking up stagnant systems, and initiating profound transformation. As Uranus makes its slow, deliberate shift from Taurus into Gemini, we're about to experience one of the most significant astrological transits of 2025. This shift is less focused on individual upheaval and more on collective transformation.

For the past seven years, Uranus in Taurus has relentlessly shaken up our foundations, especially in areas related to the Earth, business, and finances. We've witnessed drastic economic changes, financial pressures mounting for many, small businesses collapsing, and large corporations consolidating more power. As Uranus prepares to leave Taurus, some financial relief may be on the horizon, but the planet's disruptive influence is set to target new domains as it moves into Gemini.

Gemini, the sign of communication, intellect, and community, will be the new playground for Uranus's transformative energy. First and foremost, we can expect dramatic changes in how we communicate. The systems we rely on—phones, the internet, and social media—will be vulnerable to disruption, with a likely increase in hacking and other cybersecurity threats.

Gemini's influence on the community suggests a revival of collective engagement. The isolation many have felt since the COVID-19 pandemic will begin to dissipate as we seek innovative ways to reconnect with our communities. This could manifest as a rise in new social media platforms emphasizing genuine connection over the influencer-follower dynamic dominating current apps. We may see a return to the community-focused aspects of platforms like Facebook but with new players offering alternatives that prioritize real engagement over endless ads.

Education, another Gemini-ruled domain, will also see significant upheaval. The traditional education system may undergo a radical transformation, with more learning taking place online and becoming less structured, potentially integrating AI tools to personalize and enhance the learning experience. Gemini's adaptability will help us collectively embrace these changes, becoming more flexible in our approaches to work, education, and life.

In our work lives, Gemini's love for freedom could inspire many to break away from the conventional 9-to-5 grind. We may see a shift towards creating multiple income streams, working less, and enjoying life more. This period will likely spur incredible innovations that make life easier, the kind that we'll wonder how we ever lived without.

Historically, Uranus in Gemini has been associated with themes of social justice, misinformation, and conflict, particularly in the United States. The last three occurrences of Uranus in Gemini coincided with the American Revolutionary War, the Civil War, and World War II. While these conflicts have specific astrological ties to the geographical location of the United States, they also highlight the potent link between communication and conflict during these times.

Each period saw significant communication advancements: newspapers in the Revolutionary War, the telegraph during the Civil War, and radio and film during World War II. Now, with the advent of smartphones and instant access to information, we all have the power to shape the narrative. But with this power comes the responsibility to discern truth from manipulation. As Uranus in Gemini disrupts our communication channels, it's crucial to remain vigilant and critically evaluate the information we consume.

During this transit, the ability to distinguish reality from illusion will be more critical than ever. Whether misinformation comes from official sources or the general public, staying grounded in truth and exercising discernment will be essential. Uranus in Gemini is here to remind us that while change and disruption are inevitable, our ability to adapt and find clarity amidst chaos will be our greatest strength.

Reflection

1. Am I prepared for the shifts that Uranus in Gemini may bring regarding my personal and professional life? How can I proactively position myself to thrive during these changes?

2. What innovative ideas or projects have I been contemplating, and how can I bring them to life in this dynamic and transformative period?

3. How do I discern between accurate and manipulated information in today's media-saturated world? What practices can I adopt to ensure I'm consuming and sharing truthful content?

Venus in Gemini trine Pluto retrograde in Aquarius

You may find your friendship circle expanding and changing as you open up to new connections and engage more with groups, clubs, or online communities. Meeting new people and forming new connections can be scary, but with Venus in Gemini, we are more open to finding a common interest with others. As our connections expand, we expand with them, finding people more aligned with our energy.

Mars in Virgo sesquiquadrate Chiron in Aries

This aspect is likely to bring up some fears and limiting beliefs when taking action toward a solution. You might find yourself thinking, "I feel lonely and want to put myself back out into the dating scene, but I'm afraid I'll get my heart broken again," or "I know I need to start prioritizing my health, and I would join a gym, but I'm scared of being judged by others for my body, just like I was when I was younger." The frustrating part of this energy is that you've already identified the solution to your problem—the only thing standing in your way is the fear rooted in past traumas and conditioning.

This energy challenges you to confront those fears head-on. It's an invitation to recognize that the past doesn't have to dictate your present or future. The limiting beliefs that once served as protective mechanisms are outdated and only holding you back from the growth and happiness you deserve. By acknowledging these fears and gently pushing through them, you open the door to the healing and progress waiting on the other side.

Song: "Video Killed The Radio Star" by The Buggles

July 9th

Mercury in Leo quintile Uranus in Gemini

This aspect invites a burst of creativity and spontaneity, pushing us to break away from the ordinary and embrace the unconventional. It's a time to let your imagination run wild and think outside the box in a way that grabs attention and leaves a lasting impression. Suppose you're faced with a task like giving a presentation at work. Instead of delivering the usual slides, you might consider turning it into an entertaining musical number or a skit that keeps your audience engaged and excited.

For those with a public platform or content creators, this energy might inspire you to step out of your usual niche and try something bold and unexpected to boost engagement. It's about embracing the theatrical and tapping into that inner performer. Whether through humor, drama, or a creative twist, this aspect encourages you to have fun with it and not be afraid to be a little extra. The key is to enjoy the process and let your personality shine through in whatever you do.

Song: "Bohemian Rhapsody" by Queen

July 11th

Full Moon in Capricorn

This full moon will bring our attention back to our long-term goals. Think back to your goals for 2025 at the beginning of the year. Are we still making progress toward achieving them? At the beginning of the year, we were so inspired to achieve great things; however, life happens, and by this stage of the year, we have recognized that there are other things we need to prioritize, such as home and family. How can we prioritize the day-to-day tasks while also making time to put energy toward our big dreams and desires? Where do we need more balance between these two things?

It's Cancer season, and with the sun in Cancer, we are adjusting to do what feels comfortable. We prioritize our health, home, family, and children, ensuring that we are paying attention to everything that needs our attention and not becoming burnt out by being too goal-focused. What do we need to do in our home, and what can we do for our body to best support our long-term goals? Incorporating self-care and balance into our routine will ensure we can maintain consistency longer. It is time for us to recommit to ourselves at a pace that is more comfortable for us. This energy can make us feel uninspired and defeated as if we should be further ahead by now. When these types of thoughts come up, I want you to go back and look at where you came from at the beginning of the year and what challenges and obstacles you faced that were not part of your original plan. Celebrate yourself for where you are now, allow yourself some grace, and vow that you will prioritize your mind, body, and spirit moving forward.

Reflection

1. Looking back on your goals for 2025 at the beginning of the year, what were the key aspirations and ambitions you set for yourself? How have these goals evolved or remained consistent over the course of the year?

2. Considering the unforeseen challenges and changes that life may have presented, what adjustments or shifts have you made in your priorities?

3. Recognizing that life can sometimes lead us away from our initial plans, how do you navigate feelings of being uninspired or defeated? What strategies can you employ to stay focused and recommit to your goals at a pace that feels comfortable for you?

Venus in Gemini semi-sextile Jupiter in Cancer

This aspect invites us to infuse joy and playfulness into our family relationships by reconnecting with the experiences that once brought us closer together. It asks us to think about the activities that made us feel cherished and loved as children and find ways to recreate those moments now. Maybe it's time to gather the family and recreate an old photo, capturing the passage of time while reliving those memories. Or perhaps you can bring all the cousins together for a game you used to play as kids, this time with an adult twist, bringing laughter and nostalgia to the forefront.

You might consider revisiting childhood adventures with your own children, sharing the magic of those experiences across generations. Whether organizing a camping trip, planning a barbecue, or simply gathering the extended family for a day of fun, this energy encourages us to blend the past with the present. Reexperiencing the moments that once made us feel special can strengthen our family bonds and create new memories that honor the love and connection we've always shared.

Song: "We Are Family" by Sister Sledge

July 12th

Juno Direct in Scorpio

As Juno retrograde enters Scorpio, the intensity of our intimate relationships reaches new heights. This is a time when we are driven to go the extra mile to demonstrate our deep commitment and loyalty to those we love. The energy of this placement amplifies intimacy, not just in terms of heightened sexual energy but also through profound, soul-baring conversations. We want to know every facet of our partner's emotions to understand their deepest wounds from past relationships and childhood traumas. We're willing to open ourselves up and embrace vulnerability, and we desire for our partner to feel equally safe sharing their own vulnerabilities.

Scorpio's influence brings a black-and-white, all-or-nothing approach to our relationships. We think long-term about our connections during this time, asking ourselves if our current partner is genuinely marriage material. Even if the relationship is relatively new, we're considering if this person could be a lifetime partner. However, this energy also brings a strong sense of unforgiveness. Should our trust be betrayed during this period, the chances of reconciliation are slim, as the intensity of Scorpio can turn a scorned lover into one who is resolute in their decision to walk away. This alignment often leads to intense breakups when loyalty is called into question.

Reflection

1. What steps can I take to ensure my partner feels safe and supported in expressing their vulnerabilities with me?

2. Am I ready to consider the potential for a lifetime partnership, and what qualities am I looking for in a partner to ensure that?

3. Am I willing to explore and address the emotional wounds of both myself and my partner?

Mercury in Leo biquintile Pisces North Node

This aspect immerses us in a flow of divine guidance, signs, and synchronicities, nudging us to take more control over our lives and confidently step into leadership roles. You might notice that the songs on the radio are all about empowerment or find yourself repeatedly encountering inspirational quotes that seem perfectly timed to set your day up for success. Pay close attention to the books that come your way, the advice from friends, or opportunities for higher learning and motivation. The divine's encouragement may be subtle, but if you stay open and receptive, you'll be guided toward the following steps to help you reach your full potential. Embrace these signs as they are the universe's way of aligning you with your purpose and path.

Sun in Cancer trine Pisces North Node

If you've been dealing with challenges at home, such as disagreements among family members or appliances breaking down, there's no need to worry—this aspect brings a wave of help and assistance your way. You might notice your children suddenly getting along and working together harmoniously, finding common ground more easily. A neighbor might offer to mow your lawn, easing some of your stress, or a friend might connect you with someone who can repair your broken appliance at an affordable price. This energy encourages you to step back, do less, and allow the support you need to come to you. Trust that help is on the way.

Song: "Bleeding Love" by Leona Lewis

July 14th

Saturn Retrograde in Aries

As Saturn moves into retrograde through Aries, we are being called to revisit lessons we've encountered in the past. Since Saturn first entered Aries, we've been navigating setbacks, learning patience, and understanding the value of discipline and commitment. We've seen firsthand how great rewards are born from great effort. But now, with Saturn in retrograde, it's as if the universe is asking, "Did you learn that lesson, or do we need to go through it again?"

This retrograde period might tempt us with opportunities that seem too good to be true—quick fixes, get-rich-quick schemes, and shortcuts that promise fast success. However, these temptations come with consequences. Saturn retrograde is notorious for testing our resolve and integrity. It's a time when we may be tempted to cut corners, but doing so could lead to setbacks that undo the progress we've made.

It's crucial to carry forward the lessons we've already learned to navigate this energy. Remember the importance of consistency, effort, and the slow, steady climb toward success. Avoid the lure of instant gratification and remain committed to the disciplined path that Saturn has already shown, which leads to real, lasting rewards. If we don't, we may repeat old patterns and face setbacks that could have been avoided. Stay mindful, stay disciplined, and trust in the process.

Reflection

1. In what areas of my life am I tempted to take shortcuts, and what might the consequences be if I do?

2. How have discipline and commitment shaped my past successes, and how can I apply those principles now?

3. What can I do to ensure I am learning and growing from these repeated lessons rather than falling into old patterns?

Song: "T-Shirt" by Runaway June

July 16th

Venus in Gemini semi-square Chiron in Aries

Gemini energy is fun and flirty but lacks depth. Are we avoiding letting people in deeper or keeping loved ones at arm's length? If we have many connections around us that seem superficial or surface-level, why is that? It is important to remember that the connections around us often reflect the energy and effort we put into them. While a relationship takes two, our partner will likely reflect the energy we extend toward them.

Song: "Surface Level Love" by Jessika Allegra

July 17th

Venus in Gemini quintile Saturn retrograde in Aries

Relationships don't always have to be about overcoming obstacles or delving into deep emotional issues. They can be lighthearted, fun, and filled with joy. This aspect brings an opportunity to make someone smile, share a laugh with a friend, or simply enjoy the presence of a loved one. Even when things feel heavy, we can focus on the lighter side and find happiness in the simple pleasure of being together. This energy encourages us to ask ourselves: How can we lighten the mood?

Song: "Good Times" by CHIC

July 18th

Last Quarter Moon in Aries

This last quarter moon phase can be a difficult one, as the sun in Cancer is bringing up all kinds of emotions, and with the Aries moon influence, this can make us somewhat reactive and wanting to challenge those around us. If we feel misunderstood or attacked by those we love, we will want to fight and defend ourselves. We may find it difficult to let things go or to calm down before becoming defensive or reactive. This energy tells us that if someone starts something right now, we are going to finish it. We do not want others to think that they can continue to manipulate our emotions and have an overwhelming urge to stand our ground to prevent others from being able to walk over us in future situations. We are setting firm boundaries in this energy, but be mindful of the energy you use to enforce them, as sometimes the message can become lost when we act in aggression or reactiveness. If we want others to hear us, we must remain calm because if we don't, the recipient will likely match that energy, which can become an argument.

Reflection

1. How do you typically respond when you feel misunderstood or attacked by loved ones, especially during emotionally charged phases?

2. Reflect on a recent situation where you found it challenging to let go or calm down before becoming defensive or reactive. What triggered this response, and how could you have approached it differently?

3. Consider the urge to stand your ground and set firm boundaries during this energy. How can you balance assertiveness with mindful communication to ensure your message is effectively conveyed?

Venus in Gemini quintile Neptune retrograde in Aries

It's natural to have differing views and philosophies from those we love, but this aspect encourages us to focus on the common ground we share rather than the differences that separate us. By concentrating on the connections and mutual interests, we can strengthen our relationships and build a sense of unity, even when our perspectives diverge. This energy invites us to celebrate what brings us together and to nurture the bonds that keep us connected despite our individual beliefs and opinions.

Saturn retrograde in Aries conjunct Neptune retrograde in Aries

Be mindful of offering unsolicited advice to others who are not actively seeking your guidance. When we've overcome our challenges, it's natural to want to share what we've learned with those we see struggling. However, it's essential to recognize where people are in their own journey. If someone deeply identifies as a victim of their circumstances, they may not be ready or open to hearing solutions. As healers or those who feel called to serve, it's easy to jump at the chance to help others, but sometimes our wisdom may be disregarded. Remember, if someone truly wants your guidance, they will ask for it. Be discerning when and how you offer your support to ensure it's received as intended.

Mars in Virgo sesquiquadrate Pluto retrograde in Aquarius

This energy can be particularly frustrating as it sharpens our ability to see solutions to collective problems yet also magnifies the challenge of implementing them. For example, large supermarket chains dominate the market, consistently raising prices on essential items and making it difficult for the average family to make ends meet each week. A straightforward solution might be to rally the community to boycott these major supermarkets, forcing them to lower their prices to more reasonable levels. This aspect emphasizes the moment when frustration with a problem reaches a tipping point, compelling us to take bold action to create change. The energy drives us to stop talking about the issue and start doing something about it, galvanizing others to join us in the fight for a better, fairer outcome.

Song: "The Fighter" by Gym Class Heroes

July 19th

Mercury Retrograde in Leo

As Mercury retrograde moves back into the sign of Leo, we are starting to see those minor setbacks and annoyances that we have been facing have less effect on our day-to-day routines and begin to affect the areas where we are trying to make significant changes and areas where we are starting to create growth. You may have started a business, and sales have been relatively steady, but you may see sales or clients decline during this time, causing you to wonder whether this was a good choice for you. If you have begun to expand your reach on an online platform, you may see a halt or decline in followers. You may have stepped outside of your comfort zone and received negative feedback from others, or a product or service you have launched has been a complete flop.

The current disturbances encourage us to throw in the towel and give up. Our ego may seem very loud right now, telling us, "See, I told you that wouldn't work out; you should have listened to me and stayed inside your comfort zone." We cannot allow these setbacks to knock our confidence or make us give up. Although this energy can feel overwhelming, we have come too far to give up on ourselves now. So, we are going to dust ourselves off and keep pushing. We are building resilience.

Reflection

1. How do you typically respond to setbacks in your endeavors, and what strategies can you employ to maintain motivation and perseverance?

2. How do you handle criticism, and what can you learn from these experiences to improve and adapt in the future?

3. Exploring the influence of the ego during setbacks, how can you distinguish between constructive self-reflection and the ego's attempts to discourage you? What affirmations or practices can you implement to stay resilient in the face of self-doubt?

Mercury retrograde in Leo sextile Venus in Gemini

This energy is about embracing the support around us, allowing others to lift us up rather than feeling weighed down by the challenges we face. It's like when you experience a moment of humiliation, and someone reassures you, saying, "One day, you'll look back and laugh at this." This aspect invites us to bypass the victim mentality and jump straight to laughter and lightheartedness. Whether you're seeking support for yourself or offering it to a loved one, this energy encourages you to find the humor and silver lining and create a space filled with love and laughter. It's about lifting each other up, seeing the brighter side of things, and turning challenges into opportunities for joy and connection.

Song: "They Don't Like Me" by Cryptic Wisdom

July 20th

Sun in Cancer square Chiron in Aries

This energy is deeply sensitive, and it's okay to feel overwhelmed or emotional today—you're not alone in this. It's a day when your heartstrings might be pulled in multiple directions, wanting to extend compassion and understanding to those you care about while also recognizing the need to protect your own energy. It's a balancing act between being there for others and honoring your own feelings, insecurities, and emotional needs. Remember, it's okay to take a step back and care for yourself even as you support those around you.

Jupiter in Cancer quintile Chiron in Aries

This energy can be challenging to navigate as it brings deep emotional wounds to the surface and invites us to explore our ancestral traumas. You may find yourself triggered by a parent or even by your own behaviors, which are rooted in childhood wounds. As these deep-seated scars emerge, it's important to welcome them, as doing so is a crucial step toward transforming your reality. By facing and healing these traumas, you allow yourself to break free from toxic cycles of behavior, paving the way for future generations to live free from these burdens.

Song: "Family Portrait" by Pink

July 21st

Venus in Gemini sesquiquadrate Pluto retrograde in Aquarius

This aspect creates irritation or frustration within your relationships or connections. You might feel like the people around you are holding you back or not aligning with your goals and desires. This energy creates a tension where it seems like you and your loved ones are moving in different directions, leading to a natural urge to distance yourself or pull back from some of these connections for the time being.

Mars in Virgo opposite Pisces North Node

This energy can be particularly frustrating as we strive to improve and heal ourselves, often feeling a lack of support from those around us. A spiritual journey frequently thrusts us into periods of isolation and deep introspection, making it feel like a solitary expedition into the depths of our souls. In moments like these, we yearn for someone to hold our hand, to guide us through the darkness. While the divine often offers assistance and holds our hand through much of the journey, there are times when it feels as though God lets go, leaving us to find our own way through the struggle—much like a parent encouraging a child to learn a new skill. "I'm going to let go now; you're on your own, kid." This can leave us feeling disconnected and unsupported by the universe, as if we are navigating the challenges alone.

Song: "Isolation" by Jeff Beck & Johnny Depp

July 22nd

Venus in Gemini square Pisces North Node

Current placements have us feeling a strong pull toward a higher purpose and a deeper connection to the Divine. This aspect invites us to reflect on how we can integrate the lessons we've learned about our path and purpose into our relationships. For example, if you've been drawn toward spiritual practices like yoga and meditation, consider how you can share these practices with your friends and family. If you've embraced a philosophy such as Buddhism, consider how to apply its teachings to your current relationships. If you follow an organized religion like Christianity, ask yourself what you've learned about being a good Christian and how to embody those values in your interactions with others.

This aspect challenges us to use the wisdom and insights we've gained on our spiritual journey to enrich our connections with those we care about. It encourages us to share our light, love, and creativity, deepening our relationships and bringing more harmony and understanding into our lives.

Song: "Teach Me How To Dougie" by Cali Swag District

July 23rd

Sun enters Leo

We have just been through the great purge of Cancer season, which brought to the surface our hidden emotions, fears, and insecurities that needed addressing. It was a difficult time for us; however, on the other side, we have a deeper understanding of ourselves and more confidence in who we are and how we want to express ourselves. We have compassion for all we have experienced and overcome throughout our journey and recognize our strength and resilience. Now that Leo season is here, we are embodying our warrior spirit and owning our power. We feel prepared to face any challenge that comes our way, confident in our abilities, and know that we can express ourselves authentically without worrying about judgment from others. We know who we are and are ready to show the world, so everyone best be prepared for the empowered version of us.

Reflection

1. What lessons have you learned about your strength and resilience during the recent emotional purge, and how do these insights shape your perception of your capabilities?

2. How do you envision expressing yourself authentically? What aspects of your identity are you more confident sharing with the world?

3. In what ways do you anticipate showing the world the empowered version of yourself during this season, and what aspects of your authentic self are you most excited to share?

Song: "Shout Out To My Ex" by Little Mix

July 24th

Sun in Leo sextile Uranus in Gemini

This energy encourages us to explore innovative ways to communicate our message to the world. In a landscape dominated by social media platforms and rapidly evolving AI technology, how can we harness these tools to reach a broader audience? Perhaps it's time to market ourselves on a new platform or to embrace today's technology to enhance our communication methods.

I recently consulted with a client who had an incredible story to share about overcoming harrowing challenges. However, due to her life struggles, she lacked the basic writing and publishing skills many of us take for granted. Despite this, she possessed a remarkable storytelling ability. Recognizing this, I introduced her to the voice-to-text capabilities on her computer, allowing her to verbally narrate her story, which was then transcribed into text.

I also guided her in using AI technology to correct any miscommunicated text and structure her sentences and introduced her to Grammarly to refine her grammar and punctuation. While she'll still need to hire an editor, she now has her story almost ready for publication. It's truly remarkable that someone illiterate can publish a book in today's world.

So, how can you leverage the resources available today to improve your communication? Whether it's embracing AI tools, learning new platforms, or refining your messaging strategy, the opportunities are vast and ever-expanding. This is a call to innovate, adapt, and use the tools at our disposal to amplify our voices and stories like never before.

Venus in Gemini square Mars in Virgo

This aspect inspires us to reach out and offer a helping hand, eagerly finding solutions to other people's problems. However, it's important to be mindful not to overstep boundaries. What you perceive as a problem might not be an issue for someone else, and while your intentions are purely to help, sometimes it's best to focus on applying your solutions to your own challenges instead. This aspect encourages self-awareness, asking us to discern when it's appropriate to step in and assist, and when it's wiser to stay in our own lane.

Mars in Virgo biquintile Chiron in Aries

This is a refreshing and empowering energy, as we start to tap into our resourcefulness to overcome long-standing limitations. We recognize that the patterns and behaviors ingrained in us since childhood can be changed. We can unlearn unhealthy habits, develop better strategies to manage anxiety and seek therapy to heal past traumas. If we've never experienced healthy relationship dynamics, we can educate ourselves by reading books and seeking guidance on how to cultivate them. This energy brings a sense of hope and possibility, reminding us that we have the power to rewrite our narratives and create a healthier, more fulfilling life.

Song: "Better" by The Screaming Jets

July 25th

New Moon in Leo

I love a new moon in Leo, and this energy becomes extra potent with the Sun also in Leo. It allows us to envision ourselves as the main character in our own story, fully embracing that main character energy. Leo's energy is fun, vibrant, and energetic, akin to being the star of our own movie. So, let's imagine embodying that main character energy – the self-obsessed version of ourselves, not the one focused on people-pleasing or putting others' needs before our own. This version of us is carefree, living in the moment, expressing ourselves with passion and excitement.

Reflection

Draw yourself, embracing this main character energy. Bonus points if you're sporting a totally extra outfit. Get creative, give yourself the hair you desire, and add any tattoos you want. Think of it as if you're creating yourself as a sim or video game character, full of charisma and extra flair. Now, considering that you are your story's main character, let's set some intentions for this upcoming lunar cycle, wording them as if they have already happened. Set your intentions now.

Sun in Leo trine Saturn retrograde in Aries

This aspect invites us to reflect on the lessons we've learned from playing it small throughout our lives. What opportunities did we miss because we lacked the confidence to seize them? Were there moments when we chose not to put ourselves forward in a competition, even though we knew we had the skills to succeed? This energy isn't about dwelling on missed chances or regrets; instead, it serves as a powerful reminder to step into the spotlight now. It encourages us to embrace our potential, take center stage, and finally permit ourselves to shine.

Sun in Leo trine Neptune retrograde Aries

This energy encourages us to examine our belief systems that may limit us from taking control of our lives. Do we think it's selfish to prioritize our dreams above all else? Do our spiritual beliefs hold us back because we feel that a higher power will take care of everything for us? What about the tarot reader or spiritual guide we follow online who constantly assures us that our blessings are just around the corner? As a tarot reader with public platforms, I can tell you that offering such optimistic messages brings success and high engagement—but remember, energy fluctuates. While it's beneficial to have faith in something greater, these beliefs can sometimes stop us from fully stepping into our power by making us passive participants in our lives.

Song: "Permission To Shine" by Bachelor Girl

July 26th

Sun in Leo opposite Pluto retrograde in Aquarius

This aspect invites us to dive deep into self-examination, encouraging us to explore our place within the collective and the roles we aspire to. It asks us to consider how we perceive power and those who wield it. What makes someone powerful in your eyes? Is it those with a large Instagram following and, therefore, broader influence? Do you believe that wealth equates to power? And based on these beliefs, where do you see yourself in the grand scheme of things?

This energy challenges us to question what we need to transform to feel more powerful. Is it our belief systems that need to shift, or is it a matter of aligning our choices and actions with those beliefs? Are we giving our power away by admiring others who appear to have more influence, or can we reclaim our power by redefining what true power means to us?

Mars in Virgo quintile Jupiter in Cancer

This energy asks us what we can do to better nurture those around us. What values and qualities do we want to instill in our children? Since children learn by example and experience, how can we create a more nurturing environment and align our actions with our values within the home? How can we create a safe space for our partner to ensure their needs are met? Do they need more support and encouragement from us? Do they crave more intimacy or connection?

Song: "Money And Power" by CASHYEP

July 27th

Mercury retrograde in Leo biquintile Pisces North Node

This energy suggests a hidden blessing within what seems like a challenge or obstacle. Recently, I lent my car to a friend over the weekend, and as I began driving my children to school on Monday morning across town, the fuel light came on. This upset me because my friend had left the car with no fuel. To make matters worse, I realized I had forgotten my wallet and had no money to fill the tank. Finding a solution to this problem delayed me by 30 minutes. I finally managed to get my children to school and drove back home. As I arrived,

I received a phone call from the school informing me that my daughter had forgotten her lunchbox, so I had to make the trip again. Annoyed and frustrated that I was now over an hour late for work, I dropped off the lunchbox and hurried back to my car. Right beside where my car was parked, a woman was crying. At that moment, I realized why I had faced so many delays—I was meant to be there at that moment to help this woman. Sometimes, what appears to be a setback is actually a hidden blessing. See if you can identify the hidden blessings in any challenges you face today.

Mercury retrograde in Leo quintile Uranus in Gemini

Similar to the previous energy, a disturbance or miscommunication can lead to an unexpected blessing. I struggle through the winter period. I am a solar-powered being who can't operate at total capacity when the sky is grey. I use the wintertime to hibernate from the world and work diligently on my projects, such as this book. Last week, I woke to find bright sunlight streaming through the blinds—a beautiful sunny day mid-winter. I wished I could go outside and play, but I stick to a strict schedule during winter to ensure I remain productive while battling the winter blues.

When I opened my computer to begin writing, I faced every challenge imaginable. Web pages wouldn't load, and my computer was unresponsive. After further investigation, I discovered that my laptop needed some serious updates. The updates were estimated to take about two hours. Usually, this would send me into a spin, but on this particular day, it meant two hours of yoga in the sunshine, which I so desperately needed to revitalize my energy.

Sometimes, the universe throws us off our planned course to give us exactly what we need, even if it's not what we initially wanted.

Sun in Leo sesquiquadrate Pisces North Node

Sometimes, the very thing we need is the realization that we possess the strength to push through the struggle. While it can be anxiety-provoking when things don't go according to plan, choosing to face challenges head-on and overcoming them can significantly boost our confidence. When we unlock the solution ourselves, it empowers us, transforming obstacles into stepping stones rather than allowing challenges to break us down. Each time we navigate a hurdle, we reaffirm our resilience, reminding ourselves that we are more capable than we often give ourselves credit for.

Song: "Detour" by Bis

July 28th

Venus in Gemini biquintile Pluto retrograde in Aquarius

This energy fosters a profound internal breakthrough, particularly concerning your identity and what you bring to the world. As we peel back the layers of our being, we gain the ability to see ourselves through the eyes of others, leading to a newfound appreciation for who we are. This process allows us to recognize our unique strengths, talents, and the impact we have on those around us. It's a moment of self-discovery where we embrace our true selves, shedding old insecurities and stepping into our full potential with renewed confidence.

Song: "Breakthrough" by Adam Hicks

July 29th

Mercury retrograde in Leo semi-square Venus in Gemini

This energy brings attention to a potential issue or miscommunication between you and someone else. It might show up as someone being critical of you or misinterpreting your words. This can lead to bruised egos or feelings of upset, but remember that other people's words and opinions only hold as much power as you allow them to. Take a moment to evaluate whether this issue truly deserves your energy—could it simply be a case of miscommunication or misunderstanding? Then, consider how much weight this should carry in terms of your self-worth. Will you let it linger, or will you choose to shake it off and move forward?

Venus in Gemini sextile Chiron in Aries

This energy asks how you can work with others today to support your healing. What are other people's projections of you, and do you wish to take ownership of someone else's projections, or can you simply recognize the healing journey of another? How can you create a supportive environment for the people around you to explore themselves without sacrificing your own frequency?

Mercury retrograde in Leo semi-sextile Jupiter in Cancer

This aspect challenges us to go beyond our comfort zones by asking if we can nurture and support someone, even when they are being difficult. Can you hold space for another's emotions or perspective, even when you feel their views aren't valid? Can you back down in a disagreement and agree to disagree without feeling the need to be right? Can you still express love to someone who's getting on your last nerve? And, perhaps most challenging of all, can you apologize for your role in a conflict, even when the other person refuses to take any accountability? This energy encourages us to embody a frequency of love, even when it's the last thing we feel like doing.

Song: "I Hate U, I Love U" by Gnash

July 31st

Chiron Retrograde in Aries

Chiron is the planet helping us heal those deep emotional wounds we have been carrying around, some of which have been with us since childhood. In my opinion, Chiron in the sign of Aries is favorable because this accelerates our healing process and allows us to face our wounds and shadows head-on. At times, it can feel a little aggressive, but many of us have been on an incredible soul-healing journey since 2018, and that is due to this alignment.

What is happening now is that Chiron is in retrograde, meaning that it has begun moving backward through Aries, which means that some of the healing work we have done is returning. We may find ourselves triggered by old emotional wounds. We may find ourselves thinking, "Damn, why am I feeling this way again?" We are facing old wounds and trauma that we thought we had worked through already. Our old triggers are being placed in front of us just to see how we respond.

Check in with yourself when these things come up, asking yourself if you are really done with this healing or if there is something within you related to this wound that could use a little more attention. Think of this retrograde as if you had a significant wound. You nurtured the wound, kept it covered and clean, and it has healed nicely. Now, just the scar remains. It looks good on the surface, but the fresh skin is sometimes sensitive to the touch. Imagine you are out in the sun, and you can feel the sun's rays having a negative effect on the wound, realizing that perhaps there is more that you could have done to protect this particular wound, and maybe it was not as healed as you thought. That is what this energy feels like. This retrograde will be here until the end of the year, and it may feel like we are going backward a bit in our healing journey, but think of it as if we may have skipped a step and the universe is trying to make us aware. A quick tip: the missed step is often true forgiveness, whether it be for others or forgiving ourselves.

Reflection

1. Do you still carry deep emotional wounds from childhood? If so, what are they?

2. Reflecting on the soul-healing journey since 2018, what transformative experiences or insights have you gained through Chiron's alignment in Aries?

3. When faced with the recurrence of old wounds and trauma, how can you check in with yourself to determine if there are unresolved aspects requiring additional attention?

Venus enters Cancer

As Venus shifts into the sign of Cancer, we feel our emotions much more deeply. Do we feel safe, loved, and nurtured, and how can we express our love energy to create a safe space for those we love? How can we nurture those we love to develop a sense of comfort and safety? We are also likely to focus on our homes and how to make our environment more comfortable. This can be a challenging alignment as we shift focus to what is weighing heavily on our hearts, and the fluctuation of our emotions can make us feel up one minute and down the next. This is a particularly challenging alignment for air signs as they are asked to get out of their heads and into their heart space.

For singles, this can be a lonely time for those still searching for love as we become more aware of people around us who have found their person and have deep, intimate emotional bonds. We begin to ask ourselves when it will be our time to experience love on a deeper level. We may also find ourselves looking back on memories of relationships that we have had in the past and reminiscing on old times. While dating, we are searching for connections that have some depth to them and those willing to tell us how they feel and share the lessons they have been through. We are not afraid to allow someone to get vulnerable with us. We are searching for someone loyal and stable who could potentially be our forever person, so we are less likely to want a casual fling. We will not tolerate those who ignore our texts or phone calls or go ghost on us. We are ready to nurture others around us, but only those who are considerate of our own emotions and energy.

For those in long-term relationships, this Venus in Cancer alignment can feel like a rollercoaster of emotional mood swings. We want to create more depth and emotional intimacy within our relationship. We want to feel as though we are safe and protected and like our partner has our back. We would go to the ends of the earth to protect those we love, and we expect that same energy in return. We are likely to be highly triggered by our partners if they behave dismissively or make us feel unappreciated. We want to feel free to be able to express our emotional needs. We are willing to sacrifice for love but need reciprocity from our significant other.

Reflection

1. In what ways can I express my love energy to create a safe space for those I care about?

2. How do I navigate the challenges of fluctuating emotions, especially when they impact my mood and decision-making?

3. How can I maintain healthy boundaries while still expressing deep empathy and compassion in my connections?

Mercury retrograde in Leo semi-square Mars in Virgo

There's a lot of emotional energy swirling around right now. When these emotions turn negative, they can range from mildly uncomfortable to deeply painful. In those moments of pain, our instinctive response is often to project that pain outward, blaming someone else for what we're feeling. However, it takes a deeper self-awareness to recognize that when an emotional trigger surfaces, it's an opportunity to lean into that pain and heal it rather than avoid it. If you find yourself reacting emotionally to someone else, it's often because a part of you believes there's some truth in their harsh words or that their actions toward you make you feel unworthy. Take the time to go deep and uncover the true source of your pain.

Song: "Emotion" by Destiny's Child

August Alignments

August 1st

Venus in Cancer semi-sextile Uranus in Gemini

This energy hints at an unexpected surprise in our relationships. You might receive a text from someone you never expected to hear from, an unexpected apology, or even run into your best friend from school whom you haven't seen in a decade. This could also manifest as a surprise pregnancy announcement. The critical question is: Are you excited to hear from this person, or does it stir up mixed emotions? Can you maintain a balanced energy and avoid becoming reactive if the surprise isn't entirely welcome? This aspect presents a unique opportunity for love, connection, reconciliation, or setting things right. How open are you to embracing what comes your way?

Sun in Leo conjunct Mercury retrograde in Leo

This aspect is like playing a game of chess with the universe. The universe applies a little more pressure by making its move, and you respond with checkmate. While the universe has recently sent you setback after setback, you have gained more strength and self-confidence along the way with each challenge. Does the universe really think that it can defeat you now? Not a chance. This is like two very powerful energies in a battle to see who the victor will be; only your opponent has faced off against you so many times that it has created a warrior. Every time you have been challenged, you have overcome the challenge. This time will not be any different. No challenge has taken you out yet.

Song: "Centerfold" by The J. Geils Band

August 2nd

First Quarter Moon in Scorpio

We have been looking deeply at the connections around us, attempting to identify any areas that need improvement, and recognizing relationships that do not support us in expressing ourselves the way we want to. With the first-quarter moon in Scorpio, we are turning the microscope back on ourselves, delving deeper into why we behave the way we do. We ask ourselves profound questions: Why do I self-sabotage in love, career, finances, or any other area where I consistently set myself up for failure?

We also question why we have yet to act upon our inspirations. Why have I not started my own business? Why have I not ended a relationship I know is not good for me? Why have I not taken more control and responsibility over my finances? This moon is helping us identify where we still have blocks and areas in which we still don't quite believe we are capable. Can you imagine how different your life would be if you acted upon it every time you had a soul realization or inspiration rather than creating excuses for why you can't or weaving stories around why this is not the right time? We are identifying the tricks our ego uses to sabotage us from pushing past our perceived limitations.

Reflection

1. What fears or doubts have prevented you from pursuing your entrepreneurial goals or ending unhealthy relationships, and how can you address these obstacles?

2. Reflect on a specific instance where your ego may have sabotaged you from pushing past perceived limitations. How can you recognize and counteract these ego-driven tendencies in the future?

3. Reflect on past instances where you may have created stories around why it's not the right time to pursue certain goals. How can you reframe these narratives to empower yourself and take meaningful action?

Venus in Cancer square Saturn retrograde in Aries

This energy can be incredibly frustrating, especially when we go out of our way to help or nurture others, only to feel like our efforts go unnoticed or unappreciated. It can feel like we're surrounded by ungrateful people—but don't let that dim your light. Just because others don't recognize your kindness doesn't make it any less valuable. Their inability to see your warmth likely comes from being too wrapped up in their own darkness to appreciate the blessings around them. And let's be honest—we've all been there. Don't let someone else's shadows become your own. Keep shining.

Venus in Cancer square Neptune retrograde in Aries

This aspect brings challenging energy into our closest relationships, highlighting differences in perspectives. You and your partner might have contrasting views on parenting, or your ideas about intimacy in a relationship differ entirely. You could find yourself at odds politically or, even more difficult, ethically. Maybe you don't support a family member struggling with addiction or engaging in petty crime because you believe those things are wrong.

This energy urges us to remain open and receptive to differing perspectives, even when it's uncomfortable. It challenges us to ask: Can we try to understand, even if the other person is unwavering in their beliefs and unwilling to listen? Can we engage in active listening with someone whose views—perhaps even racist or homophobic—are deeply troubling without immediately interjecting to tell them they're wrong?

By asking deeper questions and truly listening, we may not change our opinions, and that's okay. But in the process, we might learn something that shifts our consciousness and transforms the way we see the world.

Song: "Sabotage" by Bebe Rexha

August 3rd

Venus in Cancer quincunx Pluto retrograde in Aquarius

Consider the role you have played in your relationships. Do you need to ask someone for forgiveness, or do you need to forgive yourself? Did you choose not to listen to your intuition or ignore the red flags? Did you have walls too high for another person to penetrate, or did you participate in self-destructive behaviors? This aspect is about taking accountability and responsibility for our feelings and actions. We will feel major resistance to taking accountability because our ego wants to protect itself. Still, if there is anything that you are feeling any kind of guilt or shame about, I suggest you journal about it to release it from your energy and tell yourself, "I am sorry, I love you, and I forgive you." Then I suggest you burn it afterward because we do not want to leave our innermost confessions lying around for just anyone to find.

Mars in Virgo quincunx Chiron retrograde in Aries

This energy brings a heightened awareness of past mistakes and a desire to make things right—whether you hurt someone you love, stayed in a relationship too long, or missed an opportunity when it was within reach. While it's possible to offer apologies, whether to others or ourselves, we can't change the past, and dwelling on it won't help. Instead, this energy encourages us to release the shame and guilt we've been carrying and focus on moving forward.

You may feel the urge to fix what went wrong, but remember: the lessons belong in the past. What truly matters is how you show the world—and yourself—what you've learned. While you can't time travel and undo those mistakes, you *can* fix them in the present by demonstrating your growth and embodying the person you wish to become. So, can you fix the past? Yes—but it starts right now.

Song: "I Fucked Up Again" by Big B

August 4th

Uranus in Gemini quintile Pisces North Node

This energy is all about making life easier, so be open to new ways of doing things! It presents opportunities to lighten your load, whether it's someone offering to help with a task on your to-do list or embracing technology, like AI, to draft an email in half the time. The key here is not to resist because you like the old way of doing things.

As an avid reader, I spent years with my nose in a physical book, cherishing the feel of holding one in my hands. When ebooks started to take over, I resisted for ages, until I finally gave in—and wow, what a game changer! Not only do I save money on physical books, but my carbon footprint is smaller, and I can whip out my phone to read anytime, anywhere. Waiting in line became my pleasure. Then came audiobooks. Again, I was hesitant, but once I embraced them, they became a blessing too. Now, I can pop in my headphones and listen while doing housework or driving—multitasking has never been easier.

What can you embrace today that could simplify your life? Whether it's technology, help from others, or a new way of doing things, lean into this energy and allow it to make things easier for you!

Song: "New Technology"- Radio Edit by Azael

August 5th

Sun in Leo semi-sextile Jupiter in Cancer

This is actually a great energy for all of us as a collective, and it's highly contagious. This aspect radiates good vibes and positive energy, making us feel incredibly optimistic as if anything is possible. Due to the contagious nature of this energy, you may find yourself rolling on the floor laughing with family members, dancing around the house, or singing at the top of your lungs—and hearing the neighbor join in! Your mission today is to spread this positive contagion as far as possible. And if you wake up in a bad mood, find someone who's already "infected"—it won't take long before you're vibing high along with the rest of us!

Sun in Leo biquintile Pisces North Node

This aspect beautifully complements the previous one, as we begin to find blessings in every moment and our worries start to fade. When we allow ourselves to do less and simply let our energy flow into the present, we often end up achieving more. There's no need to strive for perfection in this energy because we recognize that perfection is already who we are.

Song: "Gratitude" by Londrelle

August 6th

Sun in Leo quintile Uranus in Gemini

This aspect is all about having confidence in your unique abilities. Even if thousands of others have already created something similar to what you want to bring into the world, remember—*no one* can do it quite like you. This energy encourages you to push the boundaries and present yourself or your ideas in a way you may not have felt brave enough to do before. It's about recognizing your talents and running with them, full steam ahead.

Even in a crowded space, there's room for your personal twist. This energy is about seizing that realization—embrace what you do best, no matter how many others are doing it too, and confidently put your spin on it. The world needs *your* version.

When we're feeling a little low on confidence, it's perfectly okay to ask for some validation from those we love. If you're working on a creative project or thinking about expanding into something new but feeling hesitant, reach out to your closest friends or family. After all, they know you best and can remind you of just how much of a badass you really are. Deep down, you already know it, but sometimes a little boost from the people who believe in you is exactly what you need. There's no shame in seeking that reminder!

Song: "Unique" by Lenka

August 7th

Mars enters Libra

Mars in Libra is an interesting mix because Mars is the planet of action, aggression, and confrontation, while Libra represents balance, fairness, and diplomacy. These two energies don't naturally align, so what we get is an internal conflict between wanting to take bold action and the desire to keep the peace at all costs. Right now, you might find yourself going out of your way to avoid confrontation—even when it's staring you in the face.

Under this energy, we're more likely to shy away from actions that could upset others. For example, you might pass up a job promotion because you feel someone else deserves it more, or you might struggle to say no when people ask for favors, even if they're overstepping your boundaries. While avoiding conflict can be beneficial—like choosing to walk away from unnecessary drama—it can also backfire if people start seeing you as too passive, leaving you open to being taken advantage of.

This people-pleasing energy can also lead to seeking outside advice before making tough decisions. The tricky part is you must be careful about who you confide in. Venting to a friend about someone could easily be misconstrued as gossip, which might make the situation even worse.

Since this is collective energy, it could also manifest in you hearing that someone's been talking behind your back. More likely, though, they're just seeking advice on how to handle the situation, trying to figure out a peaceful strategy before approaching you. In the end, this people-pleaser vibe has us all walking on eggshells, avoiding important conversations, and procrastinating on resolving issues that need to be addressed.

Reflection

1. In what areas of my life am I sacrificing my needs or desires to avoid

upsetting others?

2. How do I typically respond when someone oversteps my boundaries, and how might I better assert myself in these situations?

3. Do I seek validation or advice from others before making decisions, and if so, why?

4. How can I distinguish between seeking guidance and engaging in gossip when discussing conflicts with friends or loved ones?

Song: "I Don't Want to Fight" by The Last Slice

August 8th

Sun in Leo semi-square Mars in Libra

This energy has us fiercely determined not to let anyone or anything distract or negatively affect our vibe. It's the energy of "Nope, not today." A bill arrives in the mailbox? We're not opening that today. A call comes in from someone who loves to vent their frustrations? Sorry, voicemail can handle that one. That co-worker who always has a stick up their ass? We're giving them a wide berth today. Our peace is the top priority in this energy, and we're not letting anything disturb it!

Venus in Cancer quintile Chiron retrograde in Aries

This energy signals the resurfacing of a past trigger related to how we were nurtured. Maybe someone at work makes a casual comment about how many cookies you ate in the lunchroom, and it brings up memories of food being restricted by your parents. Or perhaps you witness a child being yelled at or walking around with holes in their shoes, triggering something deep inside you. You might even experience someone ghosting you, reopening an old abandonment wound from childhood.

With Chiron currently in retrograde, we're consistently being asked: *Have I truly healed this?* Whatever the trigger may be, remember it's reflecting something within you. There's no need to assume your co-worker was fat-shaming you or to lash out at a parent for their approach to parenting. Instead, sit with the emotion, acknowledge it, and nurture yourself through it.

Song: "Show Up" by Aiza

August 9th

Sun in Leo sesquiquadrate Saturn retrograde in Aries

This energy can be frustrating—it gives you the confidence to take action, expand your horizons, or step into leadership of your life, but you're met with resistance. There's an obstacle in the way, whether it's securing funds for a new venture or waiting for a legal document to be approved. Whatever the challenge, trying to stubbornly push through is unlikely to help. This energy is a waiting game. Instead of banging your head against the wall, ask yourself if there's something else you can focus on in the meantime to work with this energy. Patience is key here.

Mars in Libra trine Uranus in Gemini

This aspect is all about the idea that less is more. You know the saying, "A watched pot never boils"? Well, today, we're getting rewarded for something we've been avoiding. It's like putting off house maintenance because you couldn't afford to hire someone, only to have a friendly neighbor over for coffee who casually offers, "Want me to fix that for you while I'm here?" Or maybe you've been procrastinating on editing your novel, only to discover a computer program that does it all for you. Imagine all that unnecessary effort you saved!

This energy is the best—who doesn't love being rewarded for being a little lazy?

Mars in Libra opposite Saturn retrograde in Aries

This energy shows up as avoidance—whether you're dodging a conversation or someone else is dodging you. Either way, patience is going to be required. It might manifest as a rescheduled appointment, someone ghosting or blocking you, or even giving the silent treatment. The message here is clear: now is simply not the time for direct confrontation or resolution.

Song: "I Don't Fuck With You" by Big Sean, E-40

August 10th

Full Moon in Aquarius

This moon brings out our inner rebel who wants to break all the rules and be unapologetic about it. With the sun in Leo, we already have the influence of loud, energetic, warrior-type energy. We are already feeling main character energy and being a little extra. We want to be seen, heard, and well-received. This moon is like saying, "Forget being well-received; this is who I am, this is what I stand for, and my unpopular opinion is (insert unpopular opinion here)." We don't care about what is expected of us. We don't care about what behaviors would be seen as appropriate, and we do not care about the potential consequences of our actions. We are showing up as our true, authentic selves, and if someone is triggered and offended by that, oh well. This moon will have us breaking all of the rules placed upon us by society, and it feels completely liberating. However, I will warn you too much of a good thing can have repercussions, so have fun, enjoy yourself, and try not to get arrested.

Reflection

1. How comfortable am I with expressing my true, authentic self, regardless of societal expectations?

2. In what ways can I balance the desire for liberation with a mindful consideration of potential consequences?

3. What unpopular opinions or aspects of my identity am I ready to unapologetically embrace and share with the world?

Sun in Leo sesquiquadrate Neptune retrograde in Aries

This energy comes from being so frustrated and irritated by someone else's poor leadership that it pushes you to step up and take action. Maybe you see someone spreading false information online, so you decide to share the facts. Or management is creating a toxic environment at work, and you decide it's time to take the issue to HR. This energy is about standing up and saying, "If you're not going to lead from a place of love and integrity, then step aside." It's about stepping into your own power to make things right.

Mars in Libra opposite Neptune retrograde in Aries

Following the previous energy, stepping into your power is likely to ruffle some feathers. However, this energy isn't about engaging in conflict or arguing. It's about calmly stepping up and leading by example. If someone can't handle their role properly, you're here to show them how it's done—not to belittle them, but to demonstrate a better way. This energy is about promoting improvement, not making anyone feel less capable, but inspiring a shift towards something more effective and positive.

Song: "Show You How It's Done" by JF

August 11th

Mars in Libra trine Pluto retrograde in Aquarius

This can be a challenging aspect to navigate as it asks us to closely examine our own passive behavior. Do you find yourself sacrificing your needs and desires to keep others happy? Do you assert your boundaries when necessary? And what if someone repeatedly disregards those boundaries—what consequences, if any, would follow? Do you avoid difficult conversations to steer clear of conflict? Do you ghost or block people without explanation when their energy feels misaligned, or do you feel it's your responsibility to always be the peacekeeper, the "bigger person"?

These questions prompt an inner transformation, pushing us to reflect on our behavior and identify what, if anything, needs to shift. Only by doing this can we create a more balanced outer reality.

Sun in Leo quincunx Pisces North Node

This challenging aspect calls on us to find the delicate balance between being too forceful and too passive. Sometimes, we may miss out on great opportunities because we step aside and let someone else go first. Likewise, while avoiding or blocking isn't the best way to handle conflict, neither is charging in with aggression—so where's the middle ground? This energy encourages us to reflect on our lives and ask: Where can we assert ourselves without being overbearing? How can we seize opportunities without crossing into selfishness?

There are no wrong answers here—only opportunities for personal growth and a chance to embrace a new way of being. It's about finding that sweet spot between standing firm in your power and staying considerate of those around you.

Song: "Not Backing Down" by Blanca

August 12th

Mercury direct in Leo

Mercury retrograde is finally behind us, and now it's time to feel the momentum pick up! We're stepping back into a flow where there's less resistance, especially in areas where we've been working to expand and make our mark. Our ability to communicate with clarity, confidence, and conviction is back, and we're ready to share our passions and visions with the world.

We're no longer holding back! If you've been facing setbacks—whether it's criticism, slow business, or a dip in followers—that energy shifts *now*. We're showing up anyway, pouring our passion and purpose into everything we do, even if it feels like no one's paying attention. We know what we're here to do, and while it's great when others resonate with us, what truly matters is spreading our vibrant energy as far and wide as possible.

If haters come out of the woodwork, we don't flinch. When we're shining this brightly, it's inevitable that some will try to pull us down to their level. Our power lies in how we respond. Instead of getting caught up in negativity, pay attention. Who's triggered by your high-vibe energy and your refusal to dim your light? Are these people aligned with your journey?

Let them reveal themselves while you keep glowing and radiating your energy. You're unstoppable, and now is the time to shine brighter than ever!

Reflection

1. Where have I felt resistance in my life recently, and how am I now ready to overcome it and step into my full potential?

2. How can I communicate my passions and ideas with more confidence and conviction, regardless of external feedback?

3. What motivates me to continue sharing my creativity and energy, even if I feel like no one is listening?

Ceres Retrograde in Aries

Ceres in Aries has had us fiercely nurturing others, ready to defend those we love and stand up for causes we believe in. We've been warriors for justice, fighting for fairness on behalf of others. But now, with Ceres in retrograde, the energy shifts, and it's time to ask ourselves: *Who's out here fighting for us?* Are we pouring too much of our energy into others, while neglecting to stand up for ourselves? Do we fight just as fiercely for our own well-being?

This retrograde encourages us to use our voice when we feel mistreated. If we aren't being nurtured properly, it's time to let others know. No more staying quiet and shouldering the burden alone. This period may also stir up old wounds, reminding us of the times in childhood when we weren't nurtured in the ways we needed. But now, we have the power to heal by giving ourselves what we lacked.

Did you miss out on hearing words of encouragement as a child? Now's your chance—speak affirmations to yourself every day, reminding yourself of your worth. Did you grow up without access to nice things? Treat yourself to something special, knowing you deserve abundance. Were your accomplishments overlooked? It's time to celebrate *you*. Throw yourself a party, reward yourself with a weekend getaway—recognize your successes and show yourself the love you've been missing.

This energy is a call to nurture yourself with the same intensity and passion you've given to others. You are worthy of that love, that care, and that recognition. It's time to rise up and stand tall for yourself—just as you would for anyone you deeply love.

Reflection

1. In what ways have I been fiercely fighting for others, and how can I begin to fight just as hard for myself?

2. Who in my life actively supports and nurtures me, and am I surrounded by people who fight for my well-being?

3. How can I celebrate my achievements and ensure that I recognize and reward myself for the progress I've made?

Saturn retrograde in Aries sextile Uranus in Gemini

This aspect is a powerful reminder that hard work and patience will pay off. We're starting to see proof that taking our time with a project leads to success, or that creating distance from those who negatively affect our energy allows them to come back with the right attitude—if they want to be received positively. Maybe you've been waiting for a contract to come through, and finally, it's happening. Or perhaps you were passed over for a promotion, only for an even better opportunity to appear.

This energy encourages us to trust the process, showing us that instant gratification isn't always the answer. What once felt like a frustrating delay now reveals itself as a hidden blessing in disguise.

Song: "The Climb" by Miley Cyrus

August 13th

Venus in Cancer conjunct Jupiter in Cancer

This aspect is likely to encourage us to take extra time to nurture those around us—or to allow ourselves to be nurtured. You might find yourself checking in on your elderly parents, ensuring they have everything they need, or spending more time snuggling up on the couch with loved ones. Whether it's prioritizing time to help your children learn a new skill or making a special dinner to ensure everyone feels satisfied, home and family take center stage.

Work projects may take a backseat during this energy as we focus on deepening our connections and savoring quality time with the people who matter most.

Song: "Family Man" by Fleetwood Mac

August 14th

Venus in Cancer semi-square Uranus in Gemini

This energy is interesting, as it highlights the growing sense of disconnection we feel in an increasingly connected world. You might notice it at the dinner table, where your teenagers are glued to their phones instead of engaging in conversation. Or maybe you share exciting news on social media, hoping someone will call to celebrate with you, but instead, you're met with nothing more than heart reactions and thumbs up.

It can also show up in more personal moments—like trying to have a meaningful conversation with someone you love, only to be interrupted by the constant stream of bells, whistles, and notifications pulling attention elsewhere. Somehow, in a world where we are more connected than ever, we feel more disconnected than ever before. This energy invites us to reflect on how we can connect with those around us more meaningfully.

Song: "Disconnected" by Anna Clendening

August 15th

Mercury in Leo sextile Mars in Libra

This energy is about sprinkling our pixie dust of optimism wherever we go. When we encounter someone feeling down, we have the magic to lift them back up with our good vibes and infectious positivity. Within this energy, our charisma shines, giving us the power to breathe life into those around us. We inspire others with our ideas and remind them of their worth, reigniting the fire within them. Plus, we can easily navigate conflicts—who wants to argue with someone radiating such good energy? This is a time to spread joy, inspire others, and be the uplifting presence everyone needs.

Song: "Here Comes The Sun" by The Beatles

August 16th

Uranus in Gemini quintile Pisces North Node

This aspect represents a blessing that comes through technology. It often shows up as a nudge of divine guidance, like stumbling upon a meme that speaks directly to what you're going through or seeing an online tarot reading that resonates deeply, giving you clarity on your next steps. Maybe you've been asking for guidance, and suddenly, you hear a song on the radio that feels like it's speaking to you directly as if the message is coming straight from the ethers into your ears.

Pay attention to those warm, tingling sensations—goosebumps, hairs standing on end, or "spirit tingles." These are confirmations that the message you're receiving is indeed from a higher source. Stay open to the ways the universe is speaking to you through technology.

Venus in Cancer trine Pisces North Node

Allow yourself to be nurtured today. This energy might show up as a friendly hug from a friend or an unexpected offer to buy you lunch. Remember, God is expressed through each and every one of us—we're all earth angels, wandering this world seeking opportunities to shine our light upon others. Today might be a gentle test of how open you are to receiving care from those around you. Instead of telling someone their help isn't necessary or feeling like you owe them something in return, try simply saying, "Thank you," and allow yourself to receive the kindness wholeheartedly.

Song: "Manifesting Magic" by Samantha Leah

August 17th

Last Quarter Moon in Taurus

This is when we give ourselves a pat on the back and the credit and recognition we deserve for powerfully healing ourselves. We have reached the Last Quarter Moon in Taurus, so here is what I need you to do today— are you ready? Absolutely nothing. You have come a long way in your healing journey, and I will need you to take the time to recognize your hard work today. Let it be a long, hot bath if you must do anything today. This is a reflective energy, but in the sign of Taurus, we are all about our comfort and slowing things down. We are indulging by sleeping in, having a pajama day, eating whatever we want, indulging in the little things such as our favorite hot beverage, listening to some slow, mellow music, reading a book, doing some yoga or stretching, or simply taking a nap. Whatever feels indulgent to you, that is what you should do. I don't care what you do as long as you acknowledge your progress. You don't have to make a grand gesture to yourself, but I recommend buying some flowers or giving yourself a slight pat on the back. We deserve it. This energy will be present for the next couple of days, so enjoy it by doing less.

Song: "Lumiere" by Emily Sage

August 18th

Sun in Leo biquintile Saturn retrograde in Aries

This energy suggests being recognized for a special talent or ability you possess, bringing validation from someone else. It could be as simple as a compliment on your fashion choices that boosts your confidence, praise from your boss for a job well done, or a family member appreciating how you nurture those you love. No matter where the recognition comes from, there are two ways to receive it: with gratitude or negativity. You could choose to feel blessed for the acknowledgment, or you might respond with frustration, thinking, "I've always worked hard—why are you only noticing now?" or even the passive-aggressive "Finally, I'm getting some recognition."

Instead, be thankful for the acknowledgment, no matter how long it took to arrive. Focus on the positive energy that comes with being seen for your efforts.

Song: "Recognition" by Curtis Clacey

August 19th

Mercury in Leo sextile Mars in Libra

This is a beautiful energy of finding someone who inspires you to finally take action on something you've been hesitant to dive into. It might show up as teaming up with someone who keeps you accountable and motivates you to keep pushing toward your goals. It could be hiring a mentor, listening to a motivational podcast, or simply taking inspiration from those around you. This energy is about receiving that extra spark to reignite the fire within you that may have dimmed. The inspiration could come from a piece of art that moves you, or some wise words of encouragement from a friend. Whatever the source, this energy brings a fresh wave of motivation to get back on track.

Sun in Leo biquintile Neptune retrograde in Aries

Just as others can inspire us, we can also be put off by the way some people approach things. This aspect represents encountering someone in a leadership position whose methods feel counterproductive or misaligned with your values. But even this can reignite your fire—to do it better. It's like when someone tells you how to make more money, and you immediately know their way won't work for you, so it motivates you to find a different path. Or maybe a loved one is skeptical about your business succeeding, which only pushes you to prove them wrong. Sometimes, instead of arguing or resisting, the best response is to show a better way through your actions. This energy drives you to rise above and lead with your own vision.

Song: "Inspiration" by E.N Young

August 20th

Sun in Leo trine Chiron retrograde in Aries

This energy suggests that an emotional situation or trigger you are currently facing is something you have already dealt with before. Therefore, you already have the solution. Perhaps your confidence in your current direction has been knocked, or a traumatic situation or event presents a challenge. This energy suggests that you already have the solution to the problem because you have previously learned this lesson, allowing you to move forward with confidence.

Song: "Selling The Drama" by Live

August 23rd

Sun enters Virgo

Virgo season is all about finding your flow. Virgo energy calls into question our daily habits and asks whether our current schedule supports us or if changes need to be made. Our work life comes into focus as we address whether our chosen career path supports and allows for the freedom of expression of our soul. We ask ourselves what we need to do to make our day run more smoothly and whether our health needs prioritizing at this time. Are we getting enough sleep? Are we too stressed or burdened by too much responsibility? Do we need to incorporate a stricter routine to support our health and fitness goals?

The support of Virgo energy allows us to find new ways to become more efficient and organized as we consistently ask ourselves, "What would make today run more smoothly?" Once we have more control over our daily routine and can introduce consistency to that routine, we find ourselves having more time to tackle other things on our to-do list that we may have ignored for too long. Virgo season brings us the hyperfocus to get things done, from home maintenance, car maintenance, decluttering, cleaning out the wardrobes, meal planning, health appointments, work projects, and organizing every aspect of our lives. We are taking accountability for our habits that may be holding us back and creating new ones that will better support us on our path to success.

Reflection

1. In what ways can I evaluate my daily habits to ensure they align with my goals and overall well-being during Virgo season?

2. How does my current career path contribute to my sense of soul expression, and are there changes I need to consider?

3. How can I prioritize my health and fitness goals more effectively, and do I need to implement a stricter routine?

4. What areas of my life, such as home maintenance, decluttering, or work projects, have I been neglecting that Virgo season encourages me to address?

Mercury in Leo biquintile Pisces North Node

This aspect highlights the effortless impact our energy has on those around us. Without even trying, we leave a positive imprint on others, and the confirmation often comes subtly. It might be someone saying, "You're so inspiring," or "Thank you, you've helped me become more optimistic." Or it could show up in the form of laughter as your lightheartedness lifts the room's energy.

Tune into the responses you receive when you smile at a stranger or encourage a child by asking about a new skill they're learning. Every moment, we leave an energetic mark on those we interact with, often without even realizing it. Try to become more aware of how your energy brings healing and joy to others and recognize that your presence truly is a gift in any environment.

Past traumas may surface today, making it easier for you to feel triggered. Perhaps you see a spoiled child, and it stirs up memories of growing up in poverty. Maybe an aggressive teen cusses you out, bringing you back to the days when you were punished harshly for speaking out of turn. Or you witness someone wasting food, reminding you of the times you were forced to finish every last vegetable on your plate.

You may even encounter someone whose behavior feels disrespectful, leading you to conclude they weren't "raised right." And maybe they weren't—perhaps they grew up without proper guidance or were raised by absent or struggling parents. But the truth is, that's not the point. What you're seeing is a reflection of something within yourself. The ideas you hold about what's proper or appropriate are shaped by your own life experiences.

This aspect invites you to heal your own wounds rather than project your frustrations onto the world when others don't align with the values you were conditioned—or even forced—to adopt. It's a powerful moment for inner reflection and release, allowing you to let go of judgments that stem from past conditioning.

Song: "Routines In The Night" by Twenty One Pilots

August 24th

New Moon in Virgo

In the popular movie "Miss Congeniality" starring Sandra Bullock, she plays an FBI agent thrust undercover into a beauty pageant. However, she falls short of beauty pageant standards, leading her to enlist the help of a pageant coach named Victor Melling. His role is to refine and transform her to meet the criteria of a beauty queen. Though the task seems challenging, he utilizes various resources to achieve a favorable outcome. Similarly, the New Moon in Virgo encourages us to adopt the role of Victor Melling in our own lives. We must assess what is working, identify areas that need refinement, and determine the resources required for improvement. Questions like, "What do I want my home, bank balance, and relationships to look like?" should guide our intentions for this new lunar cycle.

Reflection

1. What aspects of my life are currently working well, and where do I need

improvement?

2. In what areas do I feel the need for refinement or transformation?

3. What resources, whether internal or external, do I have at my disposal to facilitate positive changes?

Sun in Virgo quincunx Saturn retrograde in Aries

This aspect signals an obstacle standing in the way of your productivity and efficiency. Maybe you were eager to work out, but an injury is forcing you to wait until your body heals before you can hit the gym. Or perhaps you had a detailed plan to tackle housework, only for a loved one to drop by unexpectedly, leaving you to entertain them before getting back to your to-do list.

This energy is all about committing to a routine but learning that sometimes, life has other plans. It's a lesson in patience and adaptability, reminding us that while we may be dedicated to our goals, we can't always control the timing or circumstances.

Mercury in Leo quintile Uranus in Gemini

This aspect highlights connecting with someone who perfectly matches your vibe. You might stumble upon a new creator online, and their energy resonates so deeply that you hit 'follow' immediately because you just *need* more of that vibe in your life. Or maybe you meet someone who shares your love for books, and they inspire you to think, "Where have you been all my life?"

It could even be swiping right on a dating app and diving into the most riveting conversation with someone who truly *gets* you. As you banter back and forth through texts, they consistently bring a smile to your face that lasts all day.

Remember, when we admire others, they reflect our energy. The qualities you see and love in someone else are also present within you. You're bringing the vibe, too—it sometimes just takes the reflection of another to help you see it more clearly.

Jupiter in Cancer semi-square Uranus in Gemini

This aspect can be pretty frustrating as you may find yourself struggling to explain something, only to be met with misunderstanding. This energy can show up in various ways—maybe you're trying to help your child with their homework, but they just can't grasp the way you're explaining it. Or perhaps you have an interaction with someone where a language barrier makes communication difficult. Most frustrating of all, though, is when you're speaking the same language but still experience a breakdown in communication—it's as if the person is determined to misunderstand or twist your words instead of simply absorbing what you're trying to convey.

This energy challenges us to stay patient and adaptable. Instead of getting caught up in frustration, try to explore alternative ways to communicate and bridge the gap. Seek a deeper understanding of one another and find new approaches to connecting and being heard.

Song: "Perfection" by Guy Sebastion

August 25th

Sun in Virgo square Uranus in Gemini

This aspect may first appear as a disruption to your daily routine, but it ultimately forces you to find a more efficient solution. For example, you might be someone who relies on carrying your appointment book everywhere, but if your planner gets destroyed and you lose access to all your appointments, it could push you toward downloading a scheduling app. Now, you can access your calendar anytime, anywhere, without worrying about forgetting or damaging your planner again.

Or perhaps you've been using an outdated phone that's running frustratingly slow, and you've been resistant to upgrading. Today, your phone might finally give up, leaving you no choice but to invest in a newer model. Suddenly, you're able to enjoy faster speeds, better features, and more efficient task management.

This energy urges us to adapt and embrace the upgrades and innovations available to us. Resisting change will only slow you down while leaning into it can significantly improve your efficiency.

Sun in Virgo semi-square Jupiter in Cancer

This aspect encourages us to be more mindful of where we're exerting our energy and to find ways to create a balance that aligns with our priorities. If you have a family, you might decide to introduce "no devices after dinner" as a way to ensure you're spending quality time together and creating meaningful memories. Maybe you'll start turning down overtime at work to dedicate more time to loved ones, or perhaps you'll need to establish boundaries with family or friends so you can focus on bringing a personal project to life.

This energy also invites us to explore more efficient ways to be productive while involving those we care about. If your partner feels neglected because you spend too much time at the gym, perhaps you can set up a home gym and work out together. The key question here is: *How can we create more balance that works for everyone?* This aspect is all about finding solutions that foster harmony in both our personal and productive lives.

Sun in Virgo quincunx Neptune retrograde in Aries

This energy says, "My way is better". Perhaps your nutritionist has given you an eating plan, but you instinctively feel the need to tweak it for better results. Or maybe you're learning a new instrument, but you discover a more effective technique that works for you, different from what your music teacher advised. You could even be in an online course, and something the instructor says sparks a fresh stream of ideas about how you could approach the subject in a better way.

This can also happen on a spiritual level—perhaps a leader you've been following shares something that no longer resonates with your personal truth. The key here is not to criticize or judge another person's methods, even if your ego wants to. Instead, recognize that while someone in an authoritative or leadership role may lead you in one direction, there comes a time when you're called to step into your own leadership. Whether that means going your own way or guiding others down a new path, this energy invites you to trust your instincts. If you believe you can do it better, then step up and do so.

Sun in Virgo quincunx Pluto retrograde in Aquarius

This aspect may encourage us to make drastic changes. However, old habits die hard, so transforming our entire lives overnight is not a realistic expectation. Despite the desire for a productivity superpower, creating new habits takes time, and the temptation to revert to old patterns will be present. It can feel like a struggle between the version of yourself you aspire to be and the one you previously identified with. It's crucial to remember that it's okay to be somewhere in between; there's no need to take things to extremes. If you've identified with hoarding and struggling to throw anything away, you won't suddenly become a minimalist without a speck of dust in your home overnight. Allow yourself to exist somewhere in between and extend some grace to yourself in this process.

Song: "Efficiency" by Dorothy Shay The Park Avenue Hill Billie

August 26th

Venus enters Leo

As Venus enters Leo, we are all beginning to feel very confident in what we have to offer other people. We will likely put a lot more energy into ourselves and how we look, seeking connections and relationships that can match our energy. With the right person, we are willing to go all in and truly express how we feel about those we care about, putting energy and attention into those who are worthy of it. Due to us exerting much of our love energy outward, it will become noticeable when others are not reciprocating the same energy in return. We want to feel we are a priority and that others are proud to have us as their friend or lover. We will not be kept a secret; we want others to make it clear that they are rolling with us.

For singles, we are likely to put more effort into our appearance right now to appeal to the opposite sex. I know that does not sound very deep or spiritual, but that is the effect of Leo's energy on us. If we are interested in someone or have hidden feelings, we will let them know, as Leo has us feeling confident enough to shoot our shot. We are searching for a partner who is confident in themselves and doesn't require constant reassurance from us; however, not too confident. We will be quickly turned off if we feel a potential love interest has their attention elsewhere. We want to be the king or queen of someone's world, not the side piece. We are very attracted to those with a more playful energy that can make us laugh, and as our sex drive is heightened at this time, we need someone who can get our motor running.

Those of us in relationships need to know that our partner appreciates us, and we want to feel as though we are a main priority. We are more willing to extend our love energy at this time as we attempt to make our partner feel special and appreciated. Sexual energy is heightened, so we can expect to have more intimate moments and put more energy into our appearance to appeal to our partner. We feel bold in the bedroom; many of us will send flirty texts throughout the day while our partner is at work. We will also find other ways to spice things up, such as making time for dates and doing activities together that remind us of when we fell in love. We may find ourselves thinking of new ways to show our partner we appreciate them. If our partner is not interested in reciprocating our energy or responding to our efforts, then this is likely to be the cause of major arguments at this time. We know our worth and what we have to offer, so lord help anyone making us feel we should settle for less.

Reflection

1. Consider the qualities you seek in a partner, especially during this period of heightened self-confidence. How do these qualities align with your values and what you want in a relationship?

2. Explore your feelings about being a priority in relationships. How does it make you feel when you sense that others are not reciprocating the same level of energy and commitment?

3. Explore your efforts to make your partner feel special and appreciated. What creative or thoughtful gestures have you employed?

Mercury in Leo sesquiquadrate Saturn retrograde in Aries

This energy urges us to push harder against any obstacles that arise today. If we're challenged by someone, backing down won't feel like an option. This often follows the realization that things aren't progressing as quickly as we'd like, stirring up feelings of frustration and determination. It can manifest as a fiery resolve—if this obstacle won't move, then we'll make it move. This is the kind of energy that fuels perseverance and refuses to accept limitations.

Venus in Leo quintile Mars in Libra

This energy brings love, forgiveness, and understanding, making collaborating and connecting with others easier today. It's a shift from conflict, with the realization that fighting only drains our energy. Instead, we're inspired to focus on the positive qualities in those around us—even in people we may have considered adversaries. This aspect reminds us that everyone has good within them, and it encourages us to seek out and appreciate those qualities, fostering a more harmonious environment.

Mercury in Leo sesquiquadrate Neptune retrograde in Aries

This energy is an intriguing one, but it comes with caution. It reveals a different side to someone that they don't typically show to the world. You might interact with a celebrity who is adored by many, only to discover they're actually rude and dismissive to anyone they don't deem important. Or perhaps you have a friend on social media who constantly flaunts the "Instagram-perfect" version of their relationship, while you know their marriage is far from ideal. Maybe you hear rumors about a spiritual leader involved in a scandal that contradicts the values they preach.

The challenge here is: what do we do with this new insight? Do we spread it as gossip or expose it on social media? Do we confront the person about their inconsistencies? Or, is it better to simply choose how much of their public persona we engage with, freeing ourselves from the emotional hold that their inauthenticity may have over us? This energy asks us to consider how we handle seeing behind the mask, and whether it's our role to act on it or to quietly detach.

Venus in Leo trine Saturn retrograde in Aries

This beautiful energy encourages us to lead with love, making sure we express it deeply so that those we care about feel nurtured and valued. Whether it's telling a friend how much they mean to us, planning a special date for our partner, or simply cuddling on the couch with our children, this energy invites us to pour love into every interaction. It also reminds us that the more we share our love openly, the more it will be reflected back to us, creating a cycle of warmth and connection.

Mercury in Leo semi-sextile Jupiter in Cancer

If you've read The 5 Love Languages by Gary Chapman, you'll recognize that one of those love languages is words of affirmation—and this aspect is the perfect embodiment of that energy. Today, we're encouraged to offer loving and encouraging words to those around us. Whether it's telling someone who's always there for you, "I appreciate you," or letting a loved one know, "I couldn't do this without you," the power of affirmation is profound. Even something as simple as, "I love your new outfit," can brighten someone's day. Hand out compliments today like they're going out of fashion, and watch how much positivity you create!

Song: "My Life Would Suck Without You" by Kelly Clarkson

August 27th

Venus in Leo sextile Uranus in Gemini

This absolutely beautiful energy highlights the discovery of new ways to express love to those we care about. Maybe you notice how offering someone encouragement towards their dreams makes their face light up and warmth radiates from them—so you do more of that. It's about finding the key to someone's heart and using it to unlock deeper, hidden pieces of who they are.

Take time to discover the love languages of the people in your life and learn to speak them fluently. And remember, these love languages might not be limited to the traditional five from Gary Chapman's *The 5 Love Languages*. For example, my husband's love language is food! Understanding how people uniquely feel loved can open up more meaningful connections and make your relationships flourish.

Venus in Leo trine Neptune retrograde in Aries

This energy serves as a reminder not to let others influence your personal relationships. You've likely heard the saying, "Three's a crowd," and when it comes to relationships, it's spot on—relationships are between two people. It's important to protect the connection you have with someone, free from outside interference. If I argue with my partner, I don't need someone else dictating how I should feel afterward or what consequences he should face for hurting me. Similarly, if my sibling has a falling out with my mother, I shouldn't be pressured to cut off my relationship with her or allow it to be influenced.

This also applies to public figures or people we admire. If a celebrity, like Ellen DeGeneres or P. Diddy, falls from grace, we are entitled to form our own opinions without being swayed by others. Staying true to how *you* feel may not always be the popular choice, but it allows you to remain authentic.

Mercury in Leo quincunx Pisces North Node

We're not always going to see eye to eye with those around us, and others may not understand why someone inspires us or why we hold certain relationships close. Your family may not approve of the person you love, and your friends may not get why you maintain a relationship with someone they consider their nemesis—but that's okay. You don't need to constantly explain or justify your choices. Let others feel how they feel, without trying to change their minds.

If they disagree, let them. If they voice an opposing opinion, let them. In return, ask for the same respect. Request that they allow you to live your life on your terms, trusting in your decisions without feeling the need to constantly defend them.

Song: "Let Them" by Queen Humble

August 28th

Venus in Leo opposite Pluto retrograde in Aquarius

This energy can initially bring up feelings of being overlooked, as if you're not a priority in someone else's life or not receiving the praise and appreciation you deserve. But beneath that frustration lies a deeper realization: Why are we prioritizing relationships where we don't feel valued? If we're seeking validation from others for our hard work or efforts, it's time to stop placing our worth in the hands of people who don't truly matter.

Instead, turn inward and ask the one person whose opinion holds real weight—*yourself.* Are you proud of the person you're becoming? Can you recognize your own progress and celebrate your accomplishments, even if no one else does? This energy encourages self-reflection and empowers us to validate ourselves, without relying on external approval.

Song: "Proud Of Myself" by Lil Xxel

August 29th

This energy is likely to make us pull back from connections where we feel underappreciated or unsupported. It's the kind of energy that says, "I haven't heard from a friend in months—I'm not going to be the one to reach out again." Or, "I'm done bending over backward for my partner without any acknowledgment of my efforts." It might even have you rethinking your efforts with a problematic relationship, like a passive-aggressive mother-in-law.

This vibe is about doing *less* for those who aren't giving anything back, and instead, focusing your energy on the relationships that feel reciprocal. It's about preserving your time and emotional investment for those who truly value you, allowing you to give more to the connections that matter most.

Uranus in Gemini sextile Neptune retrograde in Aries

Building on the previous energy of "do less," this energy encourages us to stand firm in who we are and not let others' lack of effort taint our own. If you're the kind of person who smiles and extends kindness, even to a passive-aggressive mother-in-law who harbors animosity, then keep being that person. Her animosity is *her* problem—don't make it yours.

Similarly, if you're the friend who always reaches out, checks in, and makes plans, don't stop because someone else isn't matching your energy. Every friendship circle has that one person who holds it all together, and if you find joy in playing that role, then don't let others' lack of effort harden your heart. Stay true to who you are, even when others fall short because your kindness and consistency are your strengths—not weaknesses.

Song: "Don't Change" by INXS

August 31st

Mercury in Leo biquintile Saturn retrograde in Aries

"Practice makes perfect" is the theme of this energy, reminding us that perfecting a skill may take more time than we initially expected. Maybe you're eager to start a new project but realize you need to learn the necessary skills first, or you want to create social media content but feel too nervous to get in front of the camera. The good news is, all of these skills can be learned.

In a world where instant gratification reigns, it's easy to forget that mastery takes time. Any skill that doesn't come naturally can be developed through patience, persistence, and repetition. This energy encourages us to embrace the journey and trust that with consistent effort, we'll get there.

Sun in Virgo biquintile Pluto retrograde in Aquarius

This aspect calls us to turn our awareness inward and reflect on the role we might be playing in things not going as planned. It's easy to see ourselves as victims when things are difficult, but it takes real courage to look at ourselves honestly. Even if you feel you aren't at fault for your challenges, ask yourself: *What could I be doing differently to make this process smoother?*

Are you being disciplined in carving out time to learn new skills? Are you minimizing distractions around you? Do you need extra support, like a tutor or mentor? Are you fully using the resources available to you, or are you holding yourself back with a negative mindset?

This energy encourages us to take responsibility for our own growth. It reminds us that making changes—whether in our mindset, approach, or habits—can pave the way for real progress.

Mercury in Leo biquintile Neptune retrograde in Aries

This energy invites us to do things differently and break free from the illusion that success has to look a certain way. It's about redefining success on your terms, tuning out the noise, and setting your own goalposts. If success for you means being able to sit still and focus on studying for 30 minutes a day, then don't let anyone else's idea of success sway you.

Let's be honest—so much of the "success" we see around us is an illusion anyway. Just this morning, I watched a video titled "My Morning Routine for Success," and this woman woke up with her hair in a perfect high ponytail and a full face of makeup. Also, she *woke up* with the camera rolling...impressive, right? I mean, if I could apply makeup and slick back the perfect ponytail while I sleep, I'd save time and probably be extra successful too.

I won't go into all the fake inconsistencies, but let's just say the shifting sun and her eyeliner were dead giveaways that this "morning routine" took at least two days to film. This energy is here to help us break through the illusions about what success is supposed to look like and reconnect with what it means for *us*.

For me, on days when my illness flares up, success simply means getting out of bed and into the shower. And that's *enough*.

Song: "Ways To Go" by Alec Benjamin

September Alignments

September 1st

First Quarter Moon in Sagittarius

During this time, we begin feeling a lot of pressure. We are stressed and over-burdened with responsibilities. During this first-quarter moon, I advise taking a break from it all. Sagittarius energy is all about freedom, travel, adventure, and expansion. So go for a walk, embark on an adventure, or just have some fun. Do whatever feels adventurous to you. Change your hair, plan a night out, and take some time away from whatever you are working on or whatever in your life is causing you the most stress. Sagittarius is also a planet of luck; we must remember that while creating our reality, we are not alone; we are co-creating with the universe or God. If you can honestly say that you have been showing up for yourself and working hard to create your new reality, don't forget that the universe will match that energy. That is literally how manifestation works. If you are putting in all the work, then it's okay to take a break for a few days and give the universe a chance to match your energy.

You may find that the problem you are facing right now will magically work itself out. That is divine intervention. The trick to allowing that is to disconnect from the perceived problem entirely and hand it over to the universe. If you are constantly thinking about it, you are emitting that frequency and manifesting the problem to still exist in your reality. It is a complex law to master, but if you can master it, it really does work. If you are having a night out, stay present and throw yourself into the experience. Once you hand a problem over to the universe, that is it. It's not your problem anymore. Trust that the universe has it covered and focus on something else, preferably something positive. So go and enjoy yourself; what are you waiting for?

Reflection

1. How can I incorporate elements of freedom, travel, adventure, and expansion into my routine?

2. What actions can I take to disconnect from my current stressors and hand them over to the universe, trusting in divine intervention?

3. What steps can I take to stay present and fully immerse myself in enjoyable experiences, particularly when taking a break from my usual responsibilities?

Mercury in Leo trine Chiron retrograde in Aries

This is a very powerful aspect. When we have faced our own shadow and dedicated ourselves to overcoming the pain of our past, we are blessed with the opportunity to heal others around us who may be facing similar struggles. The universe will guide us toward our purpose, asking us to step up and lead others to provide healing and support to the collective. This energy makes our path seem much clearer, as we are blessed with lucky opportunities and gifts from the divine for following our path, which aligns with what we came here to do.

Song: "The Wanderer" by Dion

September 2nd

Saturn Retrograde enters Pisces

Saturn's retrograde has been in Aries, teaching us harsh lessons in impatience and reminding us that only hard work and dedication bring us closer to our manifestations. Now, while still in retrograde, Saturn is shifting back into Pisces, and the energy here is quite different.

Saturn retrograde in Pisces isn't the most ideal alignment. It can make us feel like we're going backward, repeating old lessons. Saturn in Pisces embodies all the profound wisdom and spiritual lessons we've learned throughout our journey—those tough challenges where we had to pull ourselves out of the depths. In retrograde, it's like the universe is checking in to see if we've genuinely learned those lessons or if we're at risk of falling back into old habits.

This energy can be tricky and tempting. Remember the vices or toxic cycles that took you forever to break? Be prepared to feel the pull of those temptations again—whether it's an ex reappearing, old bad habits creeping back in, or familiar patterns resurfacing. It might feel like the universe is testing you, and in truth, it is. The universe is inviting you to make the same mistakes, but you've already learned the lessons.

The key here? Don't fall into the trap. You've come too far to go back now. Trust the wisdom you've gained, and stay grounded in your growth.

Reflection

1. What significant challenges have you faced, and how have they contributed to your growth and understanding?

2. What vices or bad habits have you successfully overcome, and how might they resurface during Saturn's retrograde?

3. What specific situations or decisions from your past do you think the universe is urging you to reevaluate, and what can you do differently this time?

Mars in Libra sesquiquadrate Uranus in Gemini

This energy is downright irritating. It pushes us to have uncomfortable conversations we'd rather avoid or to apologize when we feel totally justified in our actions. It whispers, "Be the bigger person" or "Keep the peace," even though internally, we might feel anything but peaceful—a raging sea of emotions brewing underneath.

It's the kind of energy that feels like being a small child forced to team up with your bully for a class project. It may take every ounce of strength you have to "play nicely," but once you push through the animosity, the sense of liberation that follows is undeniable. Overcoming the tension, even when it's the last thing you want to do, can feel unexpectedly freeing.

Song: "Self Sabotage" by Ruelle

September 3rd

Mercury enters Virgo

This is one of my favorite alignments of the entire year—Mercury in Virgo. There's no better sign for Mercury to transit through, especially when it comes to getting things done. Virgo is all about precision, detail, and efficiency, and when Mercury, the planet of communication and intellect, moves into this sign, it ignites a period of hyper-productivity and focus. Suddenly, we find ourselves powering through work and projects like never before. Our ability to multitask feels almost superhuman, and the clarity and sharpness of our minds allow us to tackle tasks we've been procrastinating on for ages.

During this time, you'll likely find yourself making health appointments, finally setting up that dentist visit or wellness checkup you've been putting off. Creating schedules and setting plans for every area of your life—from work to fitness to personal goals—will feel not only easy but enjoyable. We'll be chipping away at to-do lists that once felt overwhelming, and the best part? It'll all seem somewhat effortless. The alignment between our mental clarity and practical execution will be seamless, and we'll be impressing ourselves with how sharp, organized, and on top of everything we are.

Expect to feel an increased sense of satisfaction as you work through details with a level of precision that may have eluded you before. Whether it's clearing out clutter, sending out important emails, or even tackling complex projects, Mercury in Virgo gifts us with an almost supercharged ability to get things done—quickly, efficiently, and thoroughly. This energy makes us feel like we've hit our stride, and we can finally see the fruits of our labor starting to pay off.

Reflection

1. What specific tasks or projects have I been procrastinating on, and how can I now approach them with clarity and focus?

2. In what ways can I bring more organization and structure to areas of my life that feel chaotic or overwhelming?

3. How can I use this heightened mental sharpness to set meaningful goals for my health, well-being, and overall life balance?

Mercury in Leo quincunx Saturn retrograde in Pisces

This is a difficult aspect, feeling like you have come too far in building up your confidence and self-worth to go backward and allow others the chance to throw you off your game. This energy reminds us of the lessons we have learned in the past and asks us not to forget them. Only you can decide if another is worthy of your energy moving forward or if you are happy to close out the cycle and move forward without them.

Song: "Yackety Yak" by The Coasters

September 4th

Mercury in Virgo quincunx Neptune retrograde in Aries

This energy can bring frustration, as we find ourselves highly productive and efficient, yet someone else insists their way is best. Maybe it's your boss wanting you to complete a project in a specific, outdated way, even though you've come up with a more streamlined solution. But they insist you stick to the old method. Or perhaps your partner offers to help fold and put away the laundry, and while you appreciate the gesture, they've folded the towels wrong and completely disrupted your closet system, leaving you frustrated knowing you'll have to reorganize everything later.

It's that aggravating feeling of knowing you have a more efficient way of handling things—if only they'd listen! This energy challenges us to balance our desire for productivity with the patience needed when others just don't see things the way we do.

Mercury in Virgo square Uranus in Gemini

This energy encourages us to embrace innovative technology to boost our productivity. But where might you be resisting modern advancements? Are you hesitating to upgrade your phone, even though it's slow, simply because the old one still works? Are you sticking to a paper diary for scheduling when a digital planner could streamline your day? Are you washing dishes by hand when installing a dishwasher could cut your cleanup time in half?

Perhaps you're reluctant to use social media, despite knowing it's the most effective way to reach a wider audience and skyrocket your business sales. While seeing where others resist change is easy, it's harder to recognize it within ourselves. We often have personal reasons or excuses—whether it's avoiding the self-checkout or refusing to try online grocery delivery.

So ask yourself: *Where are you resisting change?* What modern tools or technologies could you be embracing to make your life more efficient?

Mercury in Virgo quincunx Pluto retrograde in Aquarius

This energy is likely to have us throwing ourselves into daily tasks rather than dealing with whatever is happening within our relationships. I don't know about you, but I am very efficient at cleaning and getting things done when there is a deep emotional wound that I am attempting to avoid. If being productive brings you a sense of comfort, then by all means, indulge in your work and day-to-day tasks. Clearing out and organizing wardrobes and scrubbing floorboards can lift your mood as you gain a sense of accomplishment and great pride when the task is complete. It is important to remember that those negative feelings and emotions will still be there waiting for you when you are done with your task.

Jupiter in Cancer trine Pisces North Node

This energy brings an opportunity for help, allowing you to do less work. Maybe your partner steps in to assist with a household chore, your boss provides better tools to make your job easier, or your child surprises you with a robot vacuum that cleans the floors while you check off other tasks—or better yet, sit back and relax.

This aspect reminds us to be open to receiving help, however it shows up. Instead of resisting or feeling guilty about the support, embrace it and say "thank you." When we remain open and grateful, we create space for more blessings and assistance to flow into our lives.

Sun in Virgo sesquiquadrate Chiron retrograde in Aries

We're becoming more aware of the things that trigger us throughout the day and seeking solutions to reduce or eliminate them. This might mean being more vocal about our triggers so others are less likely to push our buttons. Alternatively, we may realize that we fall back into old habits when we're overtired, and the solution is to prioritize getting enough rest to stay balanced and in control. Identifying these patterns helps us create a more peaceful, productive environment.

Mercury in Virgo semi-square Mars in Libra

This aspect represents doing something you'd rather not do. Maybe you don't want to stay late and work overtime, but it's your turn, so you do it to keep the peace with your coworkers. Or perhaps you work from home, and a family member drops by unannounced, fully aware you're busy, but instead of turning them away, you invite them in to avoid any conflict. This energy is all about sacrifice—sacrificing your time or energy to maintain harmony in your relationships and environment.

Song: "Anything You Can Do, I Can Do Better" by Irving Berlin & Ethel Merman

September 5th

There is so much to do and so little time—this energy is all about prioritization. Are you getting lost in your to-do list and neglecting time with family and friends? Or are you spending so many hours at work that your housework is falling behind? It can be tough to balance everything that demands your attention. This is the moment to reevaluate your priorities, as it's easy to fall into the trap of making success and achievement your main focus while neglecting the people you love and care for.

Take a step back, assess your work-life balance, and ask yourself what needs to shift for a healthier and more fulfilling balance between your personal and professional life.

Mars in Libra quincunx Pisces North Node

One thing that should never top our priority list is engaging in conflict with others. This energy encourages us to take a more passive approach to negativity that could pull us away from what truly matters. If your mother-in-law makes a passive-aggressive comment, let it go. If someone cuts you off in traffic, wish them patience and hope they get home safely. Dealing with negative comments online? Block, delete, and move on without allowing the distractions to take up space.

Any negativity you're facing from others requires you to assess whether the conflict is worth your time or just a distraction from something far more important. Stay focused on what truly matters and let the small stuff slide.

Venus in Leo biquintile Pisces North Node

A powerful way to overcome negativity from others is to pause and truly appreciate the people who support you. Surround yourself with those who uplift and encourage you. While not everyone will recognize your talents, there are people who do. Lean into the comfort and positivity they provide, and let their encouragement remind you of your worth. Embrace the light they see in you, and allow it to shine even brighter in the face of negativity.

Mars in Libra square Jupiter in Cancer

This energy is all about leaning on those who are there to support and hold you up. If you've had a disagreement with your partner, it's reaching out to your mom or a close friend for validation and emotional support. Rough day at work? This is coming home and allowing your partner to massage the tension out of your neck. This aspect reminds us that we can face and overcome any challenge with love and support from friends and family. It's a gentle reminder that we don't have to carry our burdens alone.

Song: "I Don't Wanna Fight No More" by Will Moseley

September 6th

Venus in Leo quintile Uranus in Gemini

This energy encourages us to speak from the heart, expressing our deepest emotions to those we care about. Whether it's reminding loved ones how much we appreciate their support or sharing feelings with someone who may have hurt us, now is the time to let it all out. Interestingly, this energy suggests that these heartfelt messages may be better delivered through indirect means, like sending flowers with a card that says "I appreciate you," shooting a heartfelt text that reveals your innermost feelings or commenting encouraging words on a friend's social media post.

You might even slide into someone's DM's and confess a long-standing crush. This energy is all about the bravery to express our emotions, giving voice to the things we'd typically leave unsaid. It's a time for emotional honesty.

Song: "How I Really Feel" by G. Pace

September 7th

Uranus Retrograde in Gemini

The alignment of Uranus in Gemini has been urging us to embrace the rapid changes happening around us, particularly in the realms of technology, communication, and connection. Whether adapting to new digital tools, navigating evolving social platforms, or reshaping how we interact with others, this energy pushes us to be open to innovation and transformation. But when Uranus turns retrograde, the energy shifts—not only are we encouraged to embrace change, but we're also called to *become* the change.

This means becoming more proactive in how we approach shifts in our world. For example, instead of just adapting to new technology, you could take a coding or data analysis course to understand and contribute to the innovations shaping our future. Communication could be as simple as learning a new language or stepping out of your comfort zone to improve public speaking skills, using these new skills to foster deeper connections.

On a personal level, this energy invites us to reassess how we contribute to progress in our relationships and communities. Instead of resisting changes in the way people communicate—like the shift toward remote work or online gatherings—you can become a leader in these spaces, creating new ways for people to connect and collaborate.

In short, Uranus retrograde in Gemini calls on us to not only accept the transformations around us but to actively shape them. Whether by improving our skills, advocating for innovation, or taking leadership in new spaces, this is the time to align ourselves with the forward momentum and *be* the change we wish to see in the world.

Reflection

1. In what areas of my life have I been resisting change, particularly in terms of technology, communication, or connection?

2. How can I shift from simply accepting change to actively participating in it? What steps can I take to contribute to progress in my community or industry?

3. What new skills or knowledge can I acquire to better adapt to and influence the innovations happening around me?

Sun in Virgo semi-sextile Venus in Leo

This energy offers a beautiful opportunity to express our love through thoughtful actions. Maybe you notice a post announcing that your partner's favorite band is coming to town, and without hesitation, you grab tickets because you know how much a date to this concert would mean to them. It's that moment of inspiration where you think, *"You know who would absolutely love this?"*

Or, perhaps you have a friend who's unwell and in the hospital. You offer to pick up a few essentials from their apartment, but you take it a step further while you're there. Knowing they've been struggling due to their health, you tidy up their space, easing a burden they might not have had the energy to express. This energy is all about those small, meaningful gestures that show how deeply we care.

Mercury in Virgo biquintile Pluto retrograde in Aquarius

I love this aspect because it represents the powerful moment when we realize we can achieve or change something we once believed was out of reach. Initially, this revelation can feel uncomfortable, as it forces us to confront all the limitations we've placed on ourselves. Thoughts like, "I'm never going to be able to pull this off" or "I'm a total imposter" might bubble up. But instead of resisting these feelings, we should welcome them.

By facing this inner resistance head-on, we begin the process of breaking through it. Through this courage to confront our doubts and fears, we move from "I can't" to "I am limitless." Embracing this discomfort is what ultimately propels us forward, unlocking possibilities we never thought were within our grasp.

Venus in Leo sesquiquadrate Saturn retrograde in Pisces

This is an energy of giving people second chances and allowing them to show us that they are worthy of us; however, there is a little niggling feeling in the back of our minds telling us that we may be going against our better judgment. While we are willing to forgive in this energy, forgetting past indiscretions is much more difficult. Are you willing to offer others a clean slate, or could you not endure the pain of being let down again? If you are considering giving someone around you another chance to prove themselves to you, I suggest taking things slowly to ensure you do not get swept up in your feelings and ignore any red flags in repeated behavior. While others' intentions are most likely pure at this time, it is not always easy for people to follow through with new patterns of behavior.

Song: "Aloha Ke Akua" by Nahko And Medicine For The People

September 8th

Total Lunar Eclipse in Pisces

This moon will likely have us feeling very out of sorts as if we can't be bothered doing much of anything. While the Sun is in Virgo, providing an outward expression of energy to create a reality reflecting the version of ourselves we wish to express, this full moon draws us inward. We find ourselves in a back-and-forth between the desire to work hard for a new reality and holding ourselves accountable and the inclination to hide away and hibernate. Despite the desire to be productive, feelings of unworthiness may surface, leading to self-sabotage and procrastination.

This moon will likely take us deep into our feelings; Pisces' energy is intense, especially with the added lunar eclipse. Tears may flow for seemingly no reason, and it is a time for deep reflection. If you feel like resting, sleeping, or binge-watching a television program, honor that urge. There might be a tendency to seek distractions to avoid feeling emotions, so it's essential to steer clear of destructive behaviors like drugs or excessive alcohol consumption.

The psychic energy is potent during this time, heightening our intuitive abilities. Empaths may experience increased stress or anxiety, not every emotion felt being their own. Healers might feel strange buzzing sensations in their bodies, particularly in their hands. Mediums may notice shadows in the corners of their eyes or feel a presence around them. For seers, prophetic dreams or visions may unfold.

Whatever you experience during this time that feels otherworldly or strange, don't be alarmed. As you heal spiritually, your body will be attuned to higher frequencies, part of the process of creating a deeper relationship with the divine. We all possess these abilities; we just need to learn to tap into them. Meditation is highly recommended at this time to connect deeper with the divine. If you feel comfortable, get out a deck of oracle or tarot cards to make the most of this energy. The universe wants to send you guidance if you are open to receiving it.

Reflection

1. What emotions and deep reflections are surfacing during this intense Piscean energy, and how am I processing them in a healthy way?

2. How do I recognize and cope with the desire to self-sabotage or procrastinate, especially when faced with challenging emotions?

3. How am I navigating the heightened psychic energy during this time, and what experiences or sensations am I noticing within myself?

4. How am I distinguishing between my own emotions and those I may be absorbing from others, and what self-care practices can support me in managing increased anxiety?

Venus in Leo sesquiquadrate Neptune retrograde in Aries

What is love? This energy brings us to a profound awareness of those around us who are spreading messages of fear. You might notice agendas of division and fear in the news or media, or see someone with influence veering down a dark path. This can provoke anxiety or unease, but there's an antidote to this fear—the absence of love—and that is to spread more love.

Instead of fighting or pushing against those who are in a lower vibration, send them love. Uplift them and offer compassion for those who have seemingly lost their way. It's easy to get lost in the darkness, but finding our way out is much easier when someone with a compassionate heart shines their light and gently leads us toward it. By spreading love and understanding rather than engaging in conflict, we elevate ourselves and those who need it most.

Song: "Shine" by Fia

249

September 9th

Mercury in Virgo sesquiquadrate Chiron retrograde in Aries

Just because you haven't managed to do something successfully in the past does not mean you will never succeed. If you are using this book as a companion for your self-growth, then you are learning much about yourself and your limitations. Some of us procrastinate, leaving everything until the last minute, while others have difficulty managing our time. For some, it is an issue with saying no when we know we do not have the time and energy to extend toward others. We are learning about these limitations that have become our behavioral patterns. We have taken the time to identify them, and we have been taking accountability for them. We are growing and expanding to meet our ultimate potential. So, the next time we attempt a great accomplishment, we are prepared to push through our resistance.

Sun in Virgo sesquiquadrate Pluto retrograde in Aquarius

This aspect encourages us to set up our day in a way that guarantees success. For many, this begins with prioritizing health. It's about recognizing that fueling our bodies with the right foods provides more energy, setting the tone for a productive day. By dedicating time to exercise, we build strength, reduce stress, and improve our focus. Incorporating meditation or a spiritual practice allows us to approach the world with kindness and patience, making us less reactive to challenges that come our way.

This energy is about identifying the small, intentional steps that lead to the most significant transformations. When we start the day with purpose—nurturing our mind, body, and spirit—we lay the foundation for a day when success feels inevitable.

Song: "Wait I Can Do That Better" by Ditto

September 10th

Venus in Leo quincunx Pisces North Node

This energy encourages us to redirect our focus away from those who are not making us a priority or making an effort to understand us. It's a call to stop investing our time and emotional energy into relationships that feel one-sided, and instead, channel that energy toward people and situations that genuinely value us.

For example, you may find yourself constantly reaching out to a friend who rarely initiates contact or seems indifferent to your efforts. Instead of continuing to chase their attention, this energy encourages you to step back and let them come to you if they choose to. If you're in a romantic relationship where your partner isn't making the same effort to nurture the bond, it might be time to pause and evaluate if you're being valued the way you deserve.

In a work setting, perhaps you've been going above and beyond, yet your contributions are overlooked or unappreciated. This energy reminds you to stop overextending yourself for those who don't see or acknowledge your worth.

Ultimately, this energy is about conserving your energy and setting healthy boundaries with those who aren't reciprocating, allowing you to prioritize yourself and invest in relationships that offer mutual respect and understanding.

Song: "Do Less" by Apollow

September 11th

Sun in Virgo opposite Pisces North Node

This energy reminds us not to force things. If you're juggling a mountain of tasks but your body is crying out for rest, permit yourself to take that break. When you're struggling to find a solution to a problem, sometimes the best thing you can do is let it go—stop chasing the answer, and allow it to come to you naturally. If you're dedicated to a new workout routine but feeling worn out, listen to your body. Ignoring its signals could lead to injury, so prioritize recovery.

This energy is all about being guided by your higher self, your intuition, and the subtle cues your body gives you. When we become too laser-focused on our goals, we can lose touch with that inner compass that helps guide us. By slowing down, tuning in, and allowing yourself to be led by what feels right, you open up space for solutions, healing, and progress to flow naturally. Trust the process, and let your inner wisdom guide the way.

Venus in Leo semi-sextile Jupiter in Cancer

Connection with loved ones may be the missing piece in your life right now. This energy encourages us to prioritize this, whether calling a relative to check in on their wellbeing, preparing your family's favorite meal, or taking the kids out for ice cream. It's about stepping back from the busyness of everyday life and making time for meaningful interactions.

Retreat from the chaos and plan a moment for connection, whatever that looks like for you. Whether it's a cozy movie night, a heart-to-heart chat, or simply sitting in the presence of a loved one, these moments have the power to soothe the soul and leave you feeling more grounded and connected.

Song: "Spending Time With You" by Janet Jackson

September 12th

Mercury in Virgo sesquiquadrate Pluto retrograde in Aquarius

This energy pushes us to dedicate ourselves to self-improvement. Whether that's signing up for a gym membership, buying personal development books, enrolling in a new course, or adding something to our daily routine that we believe will make us more productive and balanced, we may find ourselves reassessing our goals, looking at the habits we want to break, and focusing on new strategies for personal growth. This energy doesn't just motivate us to make surface-level changes but rather encourages us to dive deeper into the areas of our lives that need more structure and discipline. It's about developing habits that align with the person we want to become, whether that's through fitness, mental growth, or learning new skills that will serve us in the long run. It's a time of laying the groundwork for a more productive, efficient, and ultimately fulfilled version of ourselves.

Mercury in Virgo opposite Pisces North Node

This aspect is excellent for overcoming challenges, as it allows us to easily find solutions to any obstacles we may be facing. Instead of forcing our way through problems with sheer determination, this energy encourages us to take a step back, assess the situation, and approach it with practicality. It's about carefully evaluating the "mountains" that may be obstructing our path, and instead of bulldozing through, we're inspired to make a thoughtful plan and take it one step at a time.

This energy supports a straightforward, methodical approach, giving us the patience to break down more considerable challenges into manageable tasks. Whether it's a professional hurdle or a personal setback, we feel more empowered to tackle problems without becoming overwhelmed. It's a reminder that sometimes the best way to achieve what we want isn't through brute force but through careful strategy, persistence, and thoughtful action.

Song: "I've Got A Plan" by My Friend The Chocolate Cake

September 13th

Sun in Virgo sextile Jupiter in Cancer

This aspect often inspires us to reorganize our homes to create better structure and flow in our living spaces. You might find yourself clearing out clutter, finally tackling those overstuffed closets or drawers, and creating a sense of order. It's also a great time to create meal plans so you're not wasting time each day wondering what's for dinner—helping you feel more prepared and efficient.

You may even feel the urge to move furniture around or add new elements, like plants, to create a sense of balance and positive energy flow, aligning with feng shui principles. Whether rearranging a room for better functionality or adding touches that bring a sense of peace and harmony, this energy pushes us to make our home a sanctuary that supports productivity and well-being.

Sun in Virgo biquintile Chiron retrograde in Aries

This reflective energy asks us to divert our attention from whatever is happening around us. We need to call back our energy and ask ourselves what emotions are surfacing within us that cause a sense of insecurity and instability. We are urged to identify if we are still experiencing feelings of lack or unworthiness due to a past wound that requires attention. Honor any feelings or fears arising now and allow them to surface rather than burying them deep down.

Mercury in Virgo sextile Jupiter in Cancer

This aspect provides us with the support we need to embrace and implement new changes. Whether it's your partner helping you rearrange furniture and declutter, making it a shared effort, or your child offering to lend a hand with cooking dinner or redecorating a room, this energy emphasizes the power of teamwork. It's a reminder that changes are more effective and enjoyable when everyone works together to make them happen. Collaboration not only lightens the load but also strengthens the bonds between us as we navigate these transitions together.

Mercury in Virgo biquintile Chiron retrograde in Aries

This energy encourages us to dive into a new project, learn a new skill, or take on a fresh hobby. Life can get busy, but making time to learn something like playing the piano or picking up a new language can give us a sense of continuous growth and progress. It's about expanding our horizons, challenging ourselves, and keeping our minds active. This energy asks us to pause and contemplate: *Where can I grow? What can I create?* It invites us to explore new avenues that enrich our lives and keep us feeling inspired and forward-moving.

Song: "Get Busy" by Sean Paul

September 14th

Vesta enters Sagittarius

Vesta moving into Sagittarius can stir feelings of confinement and restlessness, creating an overwhelming desire to do more, have more, and experience more. This energy fuels a longing for freedom, adventure, and the thrill of testing our limits. We want to explore new horizons, take risks, and immerse ourselves in the unknown, pushing boundaries to experience all that life has to offer.

During this time, we might find ourselves making bold, even risky, moves—like selling our home to buy a van and travel the world, or investing everything we have into a new business venture. There's a deep urge to break free from routine, explore new places, and embrace different cultures. This energy calls us to become wandering nomads, untethered from responsibilities, constantly seeking the next adventure.

It may lead us to question the structures we've built and tempt us to walk away from conventional commitments in favor of personal exploration. The excitement of this energy invites us to embrace life fully and take chances, as we crave experiences that challenge the boundaries of what we thought possible.

Reflection

1. In what areas of my life do I currently feel confined or restricted, and how can I create more freedom for myself?

2. What bold or adventurous steps am I yearning to take, and what is holding me back from pursuing them?

3. How can I balance the desire for risk and adventure with my existing responsibilities and commitments?

Sun in Virgo conjunct Mercury in Virgo

This aspect is all about planning our next adventure. Whether it's taking a deep dive into your work schedule to carve out time for a new project, reviewing your finances to find ways to save for that dream vacation, or, if the resources are already available, creating an exciting itinerary for your next trip, this energy encourages thoughtful preparation. It's a time for assessing where we stand and putting plans in place to ensure that the next big adventure—whether it's travel, a creative endeavor, or a personal goal—is not just a dream but something we can actively work toward.

Mars in Libra biquintile Pisces North Node

This energy encourages us to surrender to what is. It invites us to take a step back and honestly acknowledge our current circumstances, embracing our life stage rather than feeling confined or limited by it. Instead of resisting where we are, we're asked to find appreciation for the present moment—recognizing that every phase, no matter how challenging or uncertain, holds value and lessons. This energy teaches us that acceptance leads to peace, and by appreciating our journey as it unfolds, we open ourselves up to growth and possibilities.

Venus in Leo biquintile Saturn retrograde in Pisces

We are very aware of what we have to offer to others around us. Often, it is difficult to see ourselves through the eyes of another, so this can bring up feelings of unworthiness. However, during Cancer season, we learned to love and accept ourselves, so now we expect that others will love and accept us in the same way. We are not wasting time on relationships and connections that constantly challenge us. We recognize the kind of love we are worthy of and are not willing to settle for anything less. We are even thankful for the harsh lessons in love, as they have helped us recognize what we don't want. We have so much love to give, and we need supportive connections that will reciprocate that energy.

Song: "Brand New" by Ben Rector

September 15th

Last Quarter Moon in Gemini

The last quarter moon in the sign of Gemini is calling us to wrap things up. If anything has been left unsaid or if you have been avoiding having a difficult conversation with a lover, family member, friend, or coworker, now is a good time to do that because if we don't and if we leave things unspoken, that either turns into built-up resentment over time or confusion for either you or another person. Suppose you removed your energy from another person but did not communicate the reasons why; that will come back to cause problems later. If someone has upset you, but you didn't say anything or set any kind of boundary, they are likely to repeat that same behavior, and next time, you may not have the patience to ignore it and respond in anger. If you do that, it will seem unwarranted; to the other person, it seemingly came out of nowhere, and you will end up looking like a crazy person.

This is also a great time to push through any work that needs to be completed. Geminis are good at leaving everything until the last minute and then getting a lot done in a short time, although they can get shiny object syndrome, so they tend to get distracted pretty easily. Eliminate as many distractions as possible, turn your phone off, and stop scrolling on socials. This is a productive time to finish things up so that we can shift our focus onto new manifestations when the new moon phase comes.

Reflection

1. Are there any unsaid or unresolved matters that need to be addressed between me and others?

2. Have I been avoiding difficult conversations with loved ones? If so, what steps can I take to initiate those conversations now?

3. Am I communicating my boundaries clearly to prevent future misunderstandings and conflicts?

Song: "All I Have" by Jennifer Lopez

September 16th

Venus in Leo biquintile Neptune retrograde in Aries

This aspect may initially feel challenging, as it highlights the absence of love we perceive in the world around us. However, it ultimately serves as an inspiration to create change by sprinkling our own unique "love dust" on our environment. Instead of feeling helpless or overwhelmed by the state of things, we are reminded that if we want to see a difference, it begins with us. By leading with love and kindness in our daily interactions, we become the catalysts for the change we seek. This energy empowers us to take responsibility for shaping a more compassionate world, one small act at a time.

Mars in Libra biquintile Uranus retrograde in Gemini

This beautiful energy calls us to become the peace in spaces filled with turmoil. You may naturally step into the role of mediator, helping to resolve conflicts between friends or family members. Alternatively, this energy might inspire you to volunteer in your community, offering support to those less fortunate, or taking on leadership roles to create meaningful change. It's an energy of calm, compassion, and action, encouraging us to be the anchor of stability in chaotic environments, spreading harmony wherever we go.

Mercury in Virgo semi-sextile Venus in Leo

This energy inspires us to seek new ways to express our love and appreciation for those around us. It could be as simple as leaving a heartfelt note for your partner before they head off to work, surprising a friend with a small gift that reminds you of them, or planning a thoughtful date or outing that shows someone how much you care. Maybe it's offering a listening ear to someone who's been struggling or going out of your way to help a colleague who's overwhelmed with their workload. Whether through small gestures or grand acts, this energy encourages us to be creative and intentional in showing our love, and making others feel seen, valued, and appreciated.

Mercury in Virgo semi-sextile Mars in Libra

This is an interesting energy where we feel compelled to step in and create solutions for problems that may not directly concern us, all with positive and loving intentions. For instance, you might find yourself helping a colleague resolve an issue at work, even though it's not technically part of your job, simply because you want to support them. Or perhaps you notice a friend struggling with something personal, and without being asked, you offer thoughtful advice or assistance to help lighten their load. You may even volunteer to organize a neighborhood cleanup or assist a family member with a project they've been putting off, purely because you want to make a difference. This energy drives us to be problem-solvers, motivated by a genuine desire to help and improve the lives of those around us.

Venus in Leo sextile Mars in Libra

This energy encourages us to collaborate with individuals we may typically find challenging to work with, promoting a spirit of cooperation and understanding. For example, you might be paired with a colleague whose approach clashes with yours, yet this energy pushes you to find common ground and achieve a shared goal. Or, perhaps you're working on a family project, and you usually butt heads with a sibling over different ideas, but now you're more open to compromise and cooperation. It could even show up in community settings where you're teaming up with someone you don't see eye to eye with, but together, you're able to create something meaningful. This energy challenges us to set aside differences for the greater good, fostering growth and productive outcomes through teamwork.

Song: "One Love" by Bob Marley

September 17th

Mercury in Virgo quincunx Chiron retrograde in Aries

This energy is all about mastering our mindset. If we focus on the lack, of restrictions, and pain within our lives, we will receive more of that within our reality. Many of our limitations are due to our becoming fixated on the negative experiences within our lives. If we identify as broke and lonely, we experience more financial struggles and do not open ourselves up to forming new relationships. Try rewriting the narrative surrounding the area of your life where you experience the most lack or limitation. For example, rather than thinking we are broke and financially struggling, change the narrative to "I am inspired, committed, and empowered to create more financial stability within my life." Instead of feeling lonely, affirm, "I am self-sufficient and independent, yet open to creating deeper relationships with those who are a vibrational match to my energy."

Venus in Leo trine Chiron retrograde in Aries

In terms of our relationship energy, if we do not force things to work with others, issues tend to resolve themselves. When our energy is entangled in triggers and emotions, it can be helpful to withdraw until the energy settles down and we become less reactive to others. This is an excellent time to reflect on whether we can find common ground with others or ask ourselves if it would be better for everyone if we just went our separate ways.

Mars in Libra opposite Chiron retrograde in Aries

This aspect shows up as avoidance. It's the feeling of "I don't want to deal with that right now" or "I'd rather not talk about it." You might ignore calls, avoid difficult conversations, or even ghost someone altogether. But the real question isn't just *what* you're avoiding—it's *why* you're avoiding it. This is where the opportunity for introspection comes in. Are you dodging a conflict or uncomfortable situation, or are you avoiding your own emotions? Is it fear of being vulnerable or appearing weak that's causing you to retreat? This energy invites you to look deeper and understand the root of the avoidance, offering a chance to confront the underlying fears and emotions that are holding you back.

Song: "I So Hate Consequences" by Relient K

September 18th

Mercury in Virgo opposite Saturn retrograde in Pisces

Deadlines are looming upon us, but our bodies are telling us that we need a break. Tune into your body and ask what it needs at this time. For some, it is a nutritious meal or even comfort food. For others, we may play music to soothe our souls while internal transformation occurs. And for others, we may feel as though we have energy trapped within us that needs to be released. If this is you, watch a sad movie that you know will trigger a good cry and release of energy. Alternatively, you can look up somatic breathing exercises on YouTube, as these are very effective in releasing trapped emotions.

Song: "Exhausted" by Lxst

September 19th

Mercury enters Libra

Get ready to be involved in some excellent communication. This is a very harmonious placement where our exchanges with others seem very pleasant. This is a time when underlying relationship issues are often resolved because we are all more open to equal and balanced communication. The influence of Libra in Mercury means that we are all very open and willing to listen, compromise, and find equal ground when the goal is to create more harmony with others. This can be a slow process because Mercury represents information and communication. Libra is all about having all the facts before making any decisions, so this slows down communication significantly. So, this is like saying, "I hear and receive what you are saying, but I am going to need some time to think about what we can do moving forward," or if there are uncertainties about any holes in communication, we are fact-checking that information before resuming communication. As I said, communication is pleasant but can also be painstakingly slow, particularly if you communicate via text or email. This is like sending a heartfelt text message and then waiting three days for a response. The trick to navigating this energy is allowing yourself and others the time needed to process feelings and emotions. Any impatience during this time is unlikely to be well received.

Reflection

1. How do you typically handle unresolved issues in your relationships? How might adopting a more balanced and harmonious communication approach contribute to resolution?

2. Consider a time when communication felt pleasant and slow, requiring careful consideration. How did this influence the depth and quality of the exchange, and how might you apply similar principles to future communications?

3. Reflect on a recent communication challenge in your life. Do you feel slowing down and having patience and understanding could improve the outcome?

Venus in Leo quincunx Saturn retrograde in Pisces

This energy makes relationships difficult. Perhaps you and another person are struggling to understand each other right now. This energy makes it very difficult to relate to and understand someone else's struggle or find common ground with another. With this energy, things often seem worse than they actually are. What feels like irreconcilable differences usually has a solution; however, we are having difficulty working with others. Taking some space from others to process your emotions is highly advised.

Sun in Virgo quincunx Chiron retrograde in Aries

This energy signifies a feeling of inadequacy, which can manifest in various ways. You might feel like you are not the right person for a job or task that you have been presented with. Some of us may be striving for perfection that seems unattainable. At the same time, others might be critical of their appearance or criticize themselves for feeling a particular way or being too emotional. Imposter syndrome may creep in, making us feel completely out of our depth. It's crucial to remember that you are perfect just the way you are. Even when faced with your shadows and limitations, you are a perfect human having a healing experience. Cut yourself some slack and allow these thoughts to float by.

Mercury in Libra opposite Neptune retrograde in Aries

This aspect brings an interesting dynamic, where you find yourself saying, "I hear you, I understand your perspective, but I definitely don't agree—my way is best." It's the kind of energy where, even though you've listened and can empathize with someone's viewpoint, you remain firm in your own stance. For example, during a team meeting, a colleague might propose a solution to a problem, and while you can see their reasoning, you're convinced your approach will be more effective. In a relationship, your partner might want to handle a situation one way, but despite understanding their reasoning, you feel strongly that your method is better suited. This energy highlights the balance between respecting others' opinions while staying confident in your own convictions, even when that means holding your ground.

Song: "Maybe I Need More Time" by Kim Taylor

September 20th

Venus enters Virgo

Venus entering the sign of Virgo is entering dangerous territory. Venus, the planet of love and harmony, is moving into Virgo, a sign known for its practical, analytical, and sometimes helpful nature. This energy prompts us to put every one of our relationships under a microscope, questioning what we can find wrong within our connections. While it helps clear out any unresolved issues within our connections, it also brings forth nitpicky energy. If you have a personality flaw, someone will likely point that out to you during this time. If this happens, I suggest sitting with it for a while, assessing whether it's something you feel the need to improve or if it's something others will have to learn to get used to. We are all spotting red flags in everyone right now, which isn't necessarily bad if we have understanding and genuine harmony, balance, and reciprocity in mind. The problem arises when we want to fix others.

For those of us who are single and dating, you will likely be hypercritical of any new potential interest you meet. This energy involves being on a date, noticing a little dirt under the fingernails, and not wanting to see that person again because of it, or developing an online connection and interpreting slight deviations from the norm as red flags or inconsistencies. Try to be less critical and open to giving new connections a chance.

If you are in a long-term committed relationship, you may find that the two of you are hypercritical of each other at this time. Try to rein it in if you feel the urge to tell your partner everything that is wrong with them. If there are underlying cracks within the foundation of your relationship or unresolved issues, now is a great time to address them and come up with solutions. Virgo's energy is constructive and seeks to fix everything by finding practical solutions to a problem. If you genuinely want to improve your connections by learning to communicate better, spending more quality time with your partner, or seeking counseling, this energy will support that. However, if you are trying to fix your partner by creating a diet plan for them, restricting their alcohol consumption, or suggesting they alter their behavior in any way, that is not a good use of this energy and will likely lead to resentments between the two of you to be resolved and healed in the future.

Reflection

1. How might being hypercritical of potential interests hinder the development of meaningful connections, and how can you cultivate a more open-minded approach?

2. How might heightened criticism during this time affect the dynamics of your relationships, and what strategies can be employed to prevent unnecessary conflict?

3. What personal insights arise about your own tendencies in relationships and areas for potential growth in handling criticism and addressing issues?

Mercury in Libra trine Uranus retrograde in Gemini

This aspect encourages us to embrace modern technology as a tool for effective communication. Whether it's sending a quick voice message through a messaging app instead of a lengthy email, hopping on a video call to have a more personal conversation, or using social media to reach out to someone we haven't spoken to in a while, technology opens up new ways to connect. For instance, if you're working on a project with a colleague in another time zone, utilizing collaboration platforms like Zoom makes communication smoother and more efficient. Even in personal relationships, using technology like Face-Time or WhatsApp can help bridge the gap when in-person conversations aren't possible. This energy is about leveraging technology to foster clearer, quicker, and more meaningful communication.

Mercury in Libra trine Pluto retrograde in Aquarius

This energy helps us recognize where we can improve and where we may have fallen short, especially by encouraging effective listening. For example, in a work setting, if a colleague expresses frustration about a project, instead of immediately defending yourself, you take the time to listen carefully, gaining insight into their perspective and understanding how you might approach things differently in the future. In personal relationships, this energy might show up when a friend or partner shares how your actions have impacted them. By listening openly, you not only grasp their feelings more deeply but also see where you can adjust your behavior to strengthen the relationship.

Through active and empathetic listening, we gain a clearer understanding of others' perspectives, helping us to grow and improve our connections.

Uranus retrograde in Gemini trine Pluto retrograde in Aquarius

This energy arrives like an epiphany, prompting us to wonder why we hadn't realized certain truths sooner. It makes us question how we've been stuck in old patterns and conditioning for so long. It's the kind of moment where suddenly, something clicks, and we begin to see that the way we've been approaching things—whether in our work, relationships, or personal growth—has been limiting us. We might ask ourselves, *Why didn't I see this before? Why was I holding onto that old belief or habit for so long?* This energy encourages us to break free from outdated thinking and embrace a new, more enlightened way of doing things. It's a powerful reminder that growth comes when we're open to questioning our past and evolving beyond it.

Mercury in Libra quintile Jupiter in Cancer

Now that we've experienced a personal breakthrough, this aspect brings an exciting energy as we begin applying what we've learned to all areas of our lives, especially our home life and personal relationships. There's a renewed sense of purpose in wanting to break old cycles, whether it's letting go of outdated habits or patterns of communication that no longer serve us. We feel inspired to lead by example, showing our family and future generations that growth and change are possible. It's not just about bettering ourselves but about creating a more harmonious, loving environment for those around us, setting a solid foundation for those who come after us to thrive.

Song: "Do Better" by Stormzy

September 21st

Venus in Virgo quincunx Neptune retrograde in Aries

This aspect encourages us to step up and take charge when we feel we can handle a situation better than the person currently in control. It's a challenging energy, often making compromise difficult as we're convinced our way is the most effective. For example, you might find yourself frustrated with a team leader at work who isn't managing a project efficiently, and despite their authority, you feel compelled to take the reins. Or perhaps in a family setting, you might feel that a sibling isn't handling a family issue appropriately, and you step in, convinced that your approach will yield better results. While this energy fuels confidence, it can also create tension if not managed carefully, as it leaves little room for collaboration or shared responsibility. The key is finding balance—asserting leadership where needed but also remaining open to dialogue and cooperation.

Mars in Libra quincunx Saturn retrograde in Pisces

This aspect calls for us to check our ego at the door and resist falling back into toxic cycles of behavior, especially with those we struggle to see eye to eye with. If it feels like you're being pulled onto a familiar merry-go-round of conflict, it's Saturn testing you—asking whether you've truly learned the lesson or if you're destined to go another round. The key here is recognizing the patterns, choosing a different, more mature response, and breaking free from the repetitive cycles that no longer serve you. It's a reminder that growth often means leaving the ego behind and choosing peace over pride.

Venus in Virgo square Uranus retrograde in Gemini

This aspect brings the challenging feeling of being responsible for teaching others how to "act right." We might feel inspired to create change in our relationships by pointing out where others can improve, often with good intentions. However, it's easy to get caught up in focusing on others' growth and lose sight of the person we are truly here to heal—ourselves. So, let me ask you: *How can you improve?* This energy invites us to turn inward, recognizing that change in our outer reality starts within. Instead of getting distracted by others' shortcomings, we are called to reflect on our own behaviors, patterns, and areas for growth.

Venus in Virgo quincunx Pluto retrograde Aquarius

This aspect brings us to a deeper level of self-awareness and self-realization, helping us understand that we are capable of being more adaptable and flexible. It shines a light on the fact that, while we may strive for perfection, we are not flawless—and that's okay. This realization encourages us to embrace growth and be open to change, recognizing that there's always room for improvement. By accepting our imperfections, we free ourselves from rigid expectations and become more fluid in how we approach challenges and relationships, allowing for more personal and emotional growth.

Song: "So Annoying" by Mae Muller

September 22nd

New Moon Eclipse in Virgo

In the popular movie "Miss Congeniality" starring Sandra Bullock, she plays an FBI agent thrust undercover into a beauty pageant. However, she falls short of beauty pageant standards, leading her to enlist the help of a pageant coach named Victor Melling. His role is to refine and transform her to meet the criteria of a beauty queen. Though the task seems challenging, he utilizes various resources to achieve a favorable outcome. Similarly, the New Moon in Virgo encourages us to adopt the role of Victor Melling in our own lives. We must assess what is working, identify areas that need refinement, and determine the resources required for improvement. Questions like, "What do I want my home, bank balance, and relationships to look like?" should guide our intentions for this new lunar cycle.

Reflection

1. What aspects of my life are currently working well, and where do I need improvement?

2. In what areas do I feel the need for refinement or transformation?

3. What resources, whether internal or external, do I have at my disposal to facilitate positive changes?

Sun in Virgo opposite Saturn retrograde in Pisces

Be careful about how much attention you give to feeling like a victim. We have done so much work on ourselves to empower ourselves, but the current energy can have us feeling helpless and as if we are not in control. What is happening in the news or around us may be pulling our attention away from our daily routine, which has the ability to set us back significantly. This energy will only have as much power as you allow it to. So, if you are feeling overwhelmed and victimized by circumstances, rein it in and try to transmute your energy to one of empowerment.

Song: "I Guess, I'll Leave" by Kiahna-Jade

September 23rd

Mars enters Scorpio

Mars feels right at home in Scorpio; this energy is about decisive, obsessive focus. We become laser-focused on manifesting our desires, pouring 100% of our energy into everything we do. We move in silence during this time, keeping things private and low-key. This isn't a period for broadcasting our goals or dreams, as the more people know, the more potential there is for negativity or outside opinions tainting our vision. Instead, we say less and produce more, fully committed to our ambitions while protecting them from external interference. The approach here is simple: go all in and keep your mouth shut.

The keyword for this energy is *intensity*. It's an all-or-nothing vibe, extending even into our relationships. Loyalty becomes a considerable theme—if someone betrays our trust, the reaction will be swift and harsh. Vengeance looms large within this energy. If they go low, we'll go lower, as betrayal is taken very seriously under this influence.

On top of that, sexual energy is heightened, making intimacy feel intense and consuming. Everything, from passion to loyalty and revenge, is amplified. With Mars in Scorpio, we are driven, powerful, and unapologetically focused on what matters most.

Reflection

1. How can I protect my goals and dreams by maintaining privacy and focus during this time?

2. In what areas of my life am I giving less than 100%, and how can I change that to commit to my manifestations fully?

3. What does loyalty mean to me in my relationships, and how do I handle feelings of betrayal?

Sun enters Libra

Libra season is here, and this means shifting our focus from the details and structures of our lives to the relationships and connections within our lives. Navigating Libra season in terms of our inner healing can be challenging because relationships involve the energy of other people besides just us. During this season, we will be asked to step outside ourselves and consider how our actions may affect those around us. We'll also be weighing our relationships, asking ourselves if the connections around us are supportive or if they are holding us back from embodying our authenticity. We desire loving and supportive connections even when we are not showing them our best energy. We seek forgiving and nurturing connections even in times of misalignment and difficulty.

Libra season prompts us to give others the same grace in return. We will be delving deep to create more balance in our friendships, family dynamics, business partnerships, and intimate relationships. Empowering ourselves to make fair and balanced decisions when it comes to the people in our lives, regardless of how tough some of those decisions may be. There may be some connections we choose to close the door on at this time to protect our energy, or there may be connections where we feel the need for stronger boundaries. This season can be emotional, but much healing, reconciliation, negotiation, and understanding are available to us if we lean into the energy of Libra season.

Reflection

1. How can I assess the impact of my actions on those around me during this Libra season?

2. In what areas of my life can I empower myself to make fair and balanced decisions, even if they are challenging?

3. Am I willing to embrace healing, reconciliation, negotiation, and understanding in my relationships?

Uranus retrograde in Gemini quintile Pisces North Node

This energy suggests that communication or technology disruptions work in your favor. Instead of feeling frustrated, consider that these obstacles are happening *for* you, not *to* you. For example, you might miss a call from your boss, only to later find out that all the computer systems at work had crashed, forcing everyone to do things manually—something that would have been a nightmare for you. Still, you were blissfully unaware and unaffected by it. Or perhaps your family members got into a heated argument in a very public social media thread, but you missed the drama due to being distracted or unavailable at the time. In hindsight, it was a blessing as you avoided getting caught up in the mess.

Whatever breakdowns or disruptions occur today, take a moment to say thank you. You're being guided away from something that could have brought more stress or complications.

Song: "Intensity" by Sub Era

September 24th

Mars in Scorpio quincunx Neptune retrograde in Aries

This aspect represents having a firm, unwavering belief about something and feeling compelled to go all in to defend it. When you feel strongly about your perspective, you're willing to stand your ground, no matter what. For example, if you firmly believe in a particular approach to a work project, you won't hesitate to argue your case, even if it means challenging your boss or colleagues. In personal relationships, you might feel passionate about a political or social issue and find yourself going to great lengths to prove your point, even if it leads to heated discussions with family or friends. This energy makes compromising difficult, as you're fully committed to standing by your convictions and ensuring others understand your perspective.

Sun in Libra opposite Neptune retrograde in Aries

This energy can be challenging to navigate because it brings a strong sense of being uncompromising with others. You may feel so certain of your beliefs or opinions that you're willing to create conflict to prove you're right and others are wrong. For instance, in a disagreement with a friend, you might dig in your heels, refusing to see their side of the argument because you're determined to "win" the debate. Or at work, you may clash with colleagues, unwilling to adapt your approach even when collaboration is necessary because you're convinced your way is the best. This energy makes it challenging to find middle ground, often leading to unnecessary tension and friction in relationships.

Sun in Libra semi-sextile Mars in Scorpio

This energy suggests a shift in our approach, where we can finally put aside our strong convictions to find understanding or compromise with others. We recognize that openness to someone else's perspective might lead to better outcomes. For example, in a work meeting, you may realize that blending your ideas with a colleague's input creates a stronger solution than either of you had individually. Or, in a personal disagreement, you find yourself willing to listen to your partner's side, recognizing that compromise could bring more harmony to the relationship. This energy shows that cooperation and flexibility often lead to more successful and fulfilling results than standing firm in our beliefs alone.

Sun in Libra trine Uranus retrograde in Gemini

This aspect encourages us to share our vision with others, reminding us that collaboration can significantly lighten the load. When we work with others on a project, not only does it reduce the burden, but their fresh perspectives may offer insights we've overlooked. This energy invites us to embrace the input of others, recognizing that they might bring creative solutions or ideas we hadn't considered. Instead of dismissing suggestions too quickly, we're encouraged to remain open to new possibilities, understanding that teamwork can enhance the overall outcome and help us achieve our goals more effectively.

Song: "Let's Work Together" by Canned Heat

September 25th

Sun in Libra trine Pluto retrograde in Aquarius

This energy offers a chance for forgiveness, reconciliation, or a deeper understanding in our relationships, but it also challenges us to reflect on who we want to be in this moment. Just because an opportunity to make things right or take the high road presents itself doesn't automatically mean we're ready or willing to act on it. The question becomes: *Who do you want to be?* Is being the bigger person more important, or are there boundaries you need to maintain? This energy asks us to weigh our choices carefully, guiding us to align our actions with what matters most to us in the long term.

Mars in Scorpio quincunx Uranus retrograde in Gemini

This energy suggests facing a challenge head-on but refusing to give up, instead finding a different way to approach the problem. Enormous obstacles may feel like small hurdles under this influence. You might realize, "So I can't climb this mountain, but I can go around it," even if it means being set back a few weeks or working twice as hard. The key message here is resilience—no goal is off-limits, and no challenge will defeat us. We adapt, adjust, and persevere, knowing that while the path may change, our determination remains steadfast.

Mars in Scorpio square Pluto retrograde in Aquarius

This aspect suggests an overwhelming intensity toward manifesting your goals, where you become so consumed by the pursuit that you completely lose yourself in the process. The path ahead becomes an obsession, and you pour everything you have into it, with failure simply not being an option. For instance, you might be working on a new business venture and working 16-hour days, neglecting social relationships and self-care because success feels like the only outcome that matters. Or you could be pursuing a personal fitness goal, pushing yourself beyond limits, and so focused on the end result that you lose sight of the balance in your life. In this energy, the drive for achievement is so strong that you may not even recognize yourself, as everything else takes a backseat to your determination.

Venus in Virgo semi-square Jupiter in Cancer

This energy is one to be mindful of, as those around you may become critical of your newfound intensity toward manifesting your goals. Perhaps loved ones are complaining that you're spending too much time at work or neglecting their needs, feeling overlooked in your pursuit of success. Your laser focus on becoming all you can be may create conflict or tension in your relationships. However, this energy also makes it likely that you'll want to ignore these complaints, viewing them as distractions from your path. The challenge here is balancing your drive with maintaining healthy connections, even as others' negativity or concerns may feel like obstacles to your progress.

Song: "No Distractions" by R-Kap

September 26th

Venus in Virgo biquintile Pluto retrograde in Aquarius

This energy reminds us that how others perceive and relate to us stems from how much we value ourselves. When we find authentic love, appreciation, and acceptance for ourselves, we will reflect more of that energy from our connections. If we doubt ourselves and our abilities, that will be felt within our energetic field, and others will share that same experience of us. When we truly embrace our flaws and what makes us unique, others will love and accept those things about us. This can become like a superpower as we are able to ask ourselves, "What within me is reflecting this perception outside of me to be reflected back at me?"

Song: "Reflection" by Christina Aguilera

September 27th

Sun in Libra quintile Jupiter in Cancer

This energy suggests finding a solution or compromise with those we love deeply. It's about recognizing the importance of balance and making sure that while you're focused on a demanding project, the people who matter most to you don't feel neglected. For example, you might agree that once this work project is complete, you'll take your family on a vacation, fully unplugged and free from distractions. Or, you could set a boundary by turning off your devices at a specific time each evening to spend quality time with your loved ones. The goal is to create a sense of balance so your family or close relationships feel nurtured and prioritized, even amidst your ambitions. This energy encourages compromise to ensure that both your goals and your relationships flourish.

Mars in Scorpio sesquiquadrate Pisces North Node

This energy suggests a deep reluctance to slow down or ease up, even though you're fully aware that maintaining the same level of intensity is becoming unsustainable. There's an internal struggle between knowing you need to take a break and the fear that doing so might cause you to lose focus or momentum. It's the mindset of, *"I know I need to rest, but what if slowing down means I won't achieve my goals as quickly?"* This energy pushes you to keep going, even when every sign points to the need for balance, making it difficult to permit yourself to pause without feeling like you're losing ground.

Song: "Be The One" by Dua Lipa

September 28th

Mercury in Libra sesquiquadrate Uranus retrograde in Gemini

This energy reflects the feeling of understanding the need for change yet not being entirely happy about it. It's like when you know you must adjust your approach, but the motivation comes more from a sense of guilt than a genuine desire to shift. For example, you may recognize that you've been working too much and neglecting your family, so you agree to spend more time with them, but deep down, you're not thrilled about stepping back from your projects. Or maybe you've realized that your intense focus on a goal has affected your health, and though you reluctantly agree to scale back and rest,

271

part of you resents the disruption in your momentum. This energy is about making necessary changes, but not without a sense of internal resistance or frustration.

Song: "I Don't Want To Be" by Gavin DeGraw

September 29th

Mars in Scorpio biquintile Saturn retrograde in Pisces

This is an intense energy of realizing that you may be allowing others to influence your actions and decisions. Are you staying true to yourself, or are you altering your behavior to please someone else? Perhaps you're holding back, limiting your potential to avoid being seen as "too much"—too loud, too intense, too ambitious. This energy pushes you to ask, *Who are you, really?* How much of your authentic self is being restricted by your environment or the people around you? It's a call to break free from external pressures and reconnect unapologetically with the fullest expression of who you are.

Venus in Virgo sesquiquadrate Chiron retrograde Aries

Some critical energy is circulating, stirring up old wounds of not feeling enough. Perhaps someone in your environment is being overly critical, triggering those feelings of inadequacy. Or maybe it's you who is wishing someone else would change their behavior to better align with what feels suitable for your world. Either way, this aspect offers a powerful opportunity for self-reflection. It's a moment to pause and consider how external judgments—or your own expectations of others—impact your sense of worth and balance. Rather than focusing on others, the energy invites you to look inward and address the parts of yourself that still need healing and acceptance.

Mercury in Libra quincunx Pisces North Node

This energy can feel frustrating, as if no matter how hard you try, you just can't get through to the another person. You speak the same language, yet they seem determined to misunderstand you. Finding common ground feels impossible, and it may leave you wanting to withdraw from conversations altogether, thinking it's not worth the effort to explain your point of view. As you retreat into isolation, distancing yourself from the situation, I want you to reflect: *Were you truly listening to them?* Were you genuinely trying to understand their perspective, or were you solely focused on making your point? This energy calls for deeper self-awareness and a more mindful approach to future communication.

Song: "Shut Up" by Black Eyed Peas

September 30th

First Quarter Moon in Capricorn

This is "go big or go home" energy, with the First Quarter Moon in Capricorn representing determination, practicality, and commitment. It provides the push to recommit ourselves to whatever requires focus and attention. Currently, the sun is in Libra, suggesting a real commitment to healing relationships for many. However, some may choose to divert their attention from complex relationship healing by immersing themselves in work or a passion project to sidestep the chaos. This alignment encourages us to refocus our energy where we believe it is most needed.

For those familiar with the game Mario Kart, a racing game often played during family game nights, there's a strategic move at the beginning where timing is crucial. A well-timed start gives a supercharged moment, propelling the player to the front. If the timing is off, a false start occurs, and the player shifts into a focused and determined energy to catch up and win the race. This is the energy we're experiencing now—regardless of the initial start or setbacks, we are refocusing our energy to overcome challenges.

Reflection

1. In what areas of my life do I currently feel the need to recommit my focus and attention?

2. Can I relate the "go big or go home" energy to a personal experience or situation where I needed to refocus and overcome setbacks?

3. What specific goals or areas of my life do I want to "win the race" in, and how can I apply a laser focus and determination to achieve them?

Song: "You're The Best" by Joe "Bean" Esposito

October Alignments

October 2nd

Juno enters Sagittarius

Juno is not a planet, but as an asteroid, it holds major significance when it comes to love and deeper connections. When Juno makes a move, our relationships and intimate bonds feel the shift. During this alignment, we're not just open to being challenged in our relationships—we actively welcome it. We're drawn to partners who challenge our minds, beliefs, and perspectives, but who are also open-minded themselves. We want someone who has their own opinions yet isn't stuck in them. This is a time where we grow together by pushing each other to see things from new angles and experiencing fresh perspectives.

This energy craves deep conversations and a genuine curiosity about how our partner sees the world. We want to know what shaped their outlook, what they've been through, and how that influences their beliefs. Right now, people who can teach us something are incredibly attractive—we want to know what books they read, the people they admire, and their sources of inspiration. The routine and mundane won't cut it; we're itching for adventure, for spontaneity. This is the energy of booking a last-minute trip or trying out that brand-new restaurant instead of the usual pizza and movie night.

In fact, this alignment thrives on the unpredictable—a spontaneous road trip with no destination in mind, simply saying, *let's get lost together*. We need a partner who can adapt, who won't feel threatened when we suddenly change plans or decide to embark on a solo adventure. This energy doesn't want to be confined by relationship expectations or routines. If we need time alone, we want those around us to respect that without questioning our motives. This period is about embracing freedom, exploration, and growth—together or apart.

Reflection

1. How open am I to being challenged in my relationships, and how do I respond when my beliefs are questioned?

2. Am I willing to step out of my comfort zone with my partner and try new things, or do I tend to fall into routine?

3. How do I balance the need for togetherness with the need for independence in my relationships?

Mercury in Libra square Jupiter in Cancer

This aspect encourages us to foster a more harmonious environment within our homes and family relationships. If conflict or tension arises, this energy helps us gain clarity on others' perspectives and find ways to resolve issues peacefully. We are more understanding, open to compromise, and willing to put in the effort needed to create a balanced and supportive atmosphere. This energy invites us to prioritize peace and connection, seeking solutions that benefit everyone involved to maintain harmony in our closest relationships.

Mars in Scorpio biquintile Neptune retrograde in Aries

This aspect brings an intense drive where everything we do is given 100 percent. If we lack the skills to complete a task, we'll find the quickest way to learn—whether that's binge-watching YouTube tutorials or seeking out advice. If we don't have the tools needed, we'll exhaust every resource and all of our energy to acquire them. And if someone else is handling something in a way we don't feel is up to par, this energy doesn't hesitate to say, *"Move outta my way, I'll show you how it's done."* It's an all-or-nothing energy that thrives on mastering the situation and taking control when things aren't going as planned.

Song: "Jumpin', Jumpin'" by Destiny's Child

October 3rd

Venus in Virgo sesquiquadrate Pluto retrograde in Aquarius

When you have consistently been keeping yourself small to accommodate other people, and then you decide to choose yourself and empower yourself, other people around you may not like it. This energy is likely to present as tension within your relationships. Others may not realize that if they choose to challenge you, they are now challenging a new empowered version of you, not the people-pleasing version, and you will do everything in your power to protect yourself and your energy.

Mercury in Libra biquintile Pisces North Node

This is the energy of doing less and conserving our energy. We're giving others the space to show us who they are, without forcing or pushing for control. Instead of fighting or arguing, this energy invites us into a state of peace and calm, where we can listen to others with true intent, without being triggered or feeling the need to interject with our own perspective. It's a state of inner strength and serenity, where nothing can disrupt our peace. This energy says, *"I am unshakable,"* and allows us to remain grounded and centered, no matter what is happening around us.

Song: "Irreplaceable" by Beyonce

October 4th

Mercury in Libra biquintile Uranus retrograde in Gemini

This energy leans toward indirect communication, giving us the space to think carefully before we respond. We prefer taking our time to craft thoughtful, well-articulated emails or long text messages, ensuring that we express ourselves with precision. This energy says, *"I want to get this exactly right,"* so we are more likely to pause and reflect on our feelings before sharing them. Some of us may even turn to writing letters, appreciating the slower, more intentional process of communication. This energy encourages careful expression, allowing us to convey our emotions and thoughts with clarity and depth.

Mercury in Libra opposite Chiron retrograde in Aries

While the behaviors of others may still trigger us, we also recognize that any negative emotions arising within us point toward a wound that still needs addressing. Consequently, we tend to be more forgiving of others when they are having a bad day or reacting negatively to us, acknowledging our imperfections and ongoing healing. We are all individuals with wounds from the past, carrying the scars of our experiences, and some wounds may run deeper than others. This energy presents an opportunity for us to view others as mirrors reflecting our pain back to us. We are fundamentally the same, all carrying our unique burdens. Those who violate others and act selfishly often do so as a coping mechanism to avoid confronting their pain, making them some of the most deeply wounded among us.

Song: "Letter" by Meg Mac

October 5th

Pallas Direct in Aquarius

Pallas has been in retrograde bringing us to question internally whether what we are fighting for still resonates with us and challenges whether our belief systems have changed. Now that Pallas is direct again, many of us will feel pulled toward a cause or feel a deep calling to stand for something. We may find ourselves wanting to fight for the underdog, such as combating homelessness, helping young people find a voice, or feeling compelled to take in an animal from a shelter. We are radical thinkers right now, finding innovative solutions to old problems, sometimes using unorthodox methods and always wanting to push the envelope a little further.

In this energy, if a problem exists, we will likely want to fix it ourselves rather than pay a professional. For example, if your washing machine breaks, rather than calling a repairman, you might search YouTube videos, watch a professional disassemble it, and learn to check all the filters before diving in and getting your hands dirty. This placement says, "Stand back, I've got this." If we can't fix it the usual way, we may devise some MacGyver-style contraption to solve the problem.

Many legal matters come up during this placement. Generally, more people are likely to sue each other during this alignment, and our reckless behavior can sometimes see us facing charges for things like vandalism or hacking. We might even find ourselves arrested after a not-so-peaceful protest or for defying authority. So, if you find a cause to get behind, keep this in mind.

Reflection

1. How have I expressed my own individuality and unique voice in the past?

2. What causes or issues am I most passionate about, and why?

3. How do I handle conflict or resistance when my ideas or values are challenged?

Venus in Virgo opposite Pisces North Node

This energy can be challenging as it amplifies our ability to easily spot the faults and areas where others need improvement. However, instead of offering help or support, we may adopt a "not my problem" attitude, feeling detached from any responsibility to help others heal or grow. The mindset here leans toward *"sort yourself out,"* which can come across as judgmental without offering anything constructive. It's a tough energy that may highlight weaknesses in others, but without the compassion or willingness to lend a hand, making it important to remain mindful of how we communicate and interact with those around us.

Mercury in Libra quincunx Saturn retrograde in Pisces

This energy suggests a sense of frustration, reflecting the desire to make the right choices without sacrificing oneself or falling into familiar patterns that could perpetuate karmic cycles. Saturn's influence emphasizes the importance of drawing on past experiences to navigate present challenges. Despite potential doubts about trusting others, the focus shifts towards trusting oneself to make decisions aligned with personal needs and boundaries. This period calls for a balance between acknowledging past lessons and cultivating self-trust in decision-making.

Song: "Killing In The Name" by Rage Against The Machine

October 6th

Venus in Virgo biquintile Chiron retrograde in Aries

This energy encourages us to embrace our flaws, own them, and celebrate them. We have learned a lot about ourselves through relationships with others and are probably well aware of the traits and behaviors that can trigger others. Does that mean we should conform to a mold that would make other people comfortable? Hell no! If you are someone who becomes highly emotional, it is probably because you have experienced great pain in your past. If you are loud and a little chaotic, it is probably because you have experienced needing to be heard in a chaotic environment or upbringing. If you can become reactive and combative, it is probably because you have always felt as if you have had to fight your whole life. Your past wounds and experiences do not make you broken; they make you unique and have helped define the person that you have become. We are not ashamed of who we are. We embrace it.

October 7th

Mercury enters Scorpio

Mercury in Scorpio always creates an interesting dynamic because we all become very secretive, highly intuitive, and somewhat suspicious. This alignment feels like we are all in a game of Cluedo, trying to solve a murder mystery. So, if there is anything that we have been hiding—be it secret lovers, health conditions, job opportunities, or passion projects that we have been keeping under wraps—it may just be exposed during this time. Everyone around us behaves like an investigator, and they are super suspicious. While usually, we can get away with keeping some things to ourselves, we may find ourselves being interrogated, and it seems like people around us are a little too all up in our business. This works both ways, so if someone around us is keeping something from us, we will feel it intuitively. We are much more perceptive than usual. We feel a need to get to the bottom of what it is that they are hiding. We are all putting on our private investigator hats and will not stop until we have answers.

This energy doesn't just apply to the people around us but also to any topic that we do not have answers to. We may find ourselves getting deep into the occult, using or watching tarot for insight and answers, watching true crime documentaries, or documentaries of any kind. If we want to publish a book but don't know how we will figure it out with this energy present. This kind of investigation is a much better use of our time and energy. Uncovering truths about what everyone else is hiding around us, while satisfying, can lead to further problems within our relationships, and we may just find out something we do not want to hear. Most of the secrets people are hiding are none of our business, and if they are our business, we will find out. These secrets will eventually expose themselves; what is done in the dark will always come to light. Use this energy very wisely and to your advantage rather than getting caught up in something that you have no business being caught up in.

Reflection

1. What secrets or hidden aspects of myself have I been reluctant to share with others?

2. How do I feel about the idea of others uncovering my secrets or hidden truths?

3. How can I respect the boundaries of others while still seeking the truth

279

or understanding in my relationships?

Full Moon in Aries

This full moon empowers us to reflect on our ambitions and true desires. We can vividly envision the reality of our manifestations, feeling them with all our senses. However, with the sun in Libra, challenges arise regarding our focus on personal goals, requiring us to consider fairness to others. For example, the desire to move across the country conflicts with familial needs, seeking promotion may impact a longer-tenured coworker, starting a business creates obligations to a current boss, and returning to work after having children raises concerns about our children's well-being. Shifting perspective involves questioning whether family dependencies are genuine or codependent, considering external assistance for incapable family members, evaluating coworker qualifications for a promotion, and understanding that pursuing personal goals can contribute to providing for our children's stability. While sacrifices may be necessary, our needs should be balanced with the needs of others, acknowledging that everyone's well-being matters.

Reflection

1. In considering ambitions and desires, what specific goals or manifestations are currently at the forefront of your mind?

2. How vividly can you envision the reality of achieving those goals? Can you visualize, feel, taste, and smell the success you are striving for?

3. Are there any potential codependency situations playing out, are you sacrificing your pursuit of personal goals for the needs of another?

Uranus retrograde in Gemini quintile Pisces North Node

This aspect encourages us to embrace innovative technology and let it handle much of the work for us. In today's world, many tasks that used to take hours can now be automated, allowing us to focus on more important matters. For instance, scheduling appointments can be handled by apps like Calendly, which eliminates the back-and-forth of finding a meeting time. Housework can be streamlined with smart home devices, such as robot vacuums or automated lighting systems, saving both time and effort. Even business processes, like social media management or customer service, can be automated using tools like Hootsuite or AI chatbots. This energy pushes us to explore how technology can simplify our lives, freeing up time and energy for creative pursuits or personal growth.

Mercury in Scorpio quincunx Neptune retrograde in Aries

This energy brings heightened suspicion, particularly toward those in leadership roles, making us question their motives and intentions. We may start to doubt whether a boss or manager truly has the team's best interests at heart or wonder if a politician's promises are just empty words meant to serve their own agenda. For example, in the workplace, we might find ourselves second-guessing the decisions of a supervisor, thinking they may be acting out of self-interest rather than for the good of the team. In personal relationships, this could manifest as feeling uncertain about a friend or family member's true intentions, causing us to read too deeply into their actions or words. This energy pushes us to critically evaluate those in power and reconsider whether their leadership aligns with our values and expectations.

Song: "Suspicious Minds" by Elvis Presley

October 8th

Mercury in Scorpio quincunx Uranus retrograde in Gemini

This energy is incredibly intense and can drive us to take drastic, sometimes questionable, measures to uncover the truth. It's the kind of energy that might push someone to hack into private accounts, read through someone's messages, or even install spy software or a tracker on their phone. While the urge to uncover hidden information can feel overwhelming, it's important to remain mindful and not get carried away with this need for control. Crossing boundaries in the name of seeking the truth can lead to significant consequences, so it's essential to pause and reflect on whether these actions are worth the potential damage they might cause to trust and relationships.

Mercury in Scorpio square Pluto retrograde in Aquarius

This aspect is a challenging one to navigate, as it forces us to question whether our drive to uncover the truth is healthy or if it's crossing into the territory of obsession. Are our suspicions valid, or are we simply being paranoid? This energy invites us to turn the magnifying glass inward, encouraging self-reflection rather than constantly scrutinizing those around us. It pushes us to consider our own motives—are we truly seeking clarity, or are we feeding into an unhealthy need for control? By examining our intentions, we can determine whether we are acting out of genuine concern or letting fear and insecurity take the lead.

Song: "Stay Paranoid" by Lul Sis

October 9th

Venus in Virgo sextile Jupiter in Cancer

This is a great aspect that allows us to easily identify potential problems within the home and family dynamics. It encourages us to work together with loved ones to find practical solutions. For example, you might notice tension building between family members over shared household responsibilities. Instead of letting it simmer, this energy helps you to sit down with everyone, discuss the issue, and come up with a fair chore schedule that works for all. In a work setting, you may spot inefficiencies in team communication, and rather than blaming or ignoring the problem, you collaborate with colleagues to create a streamlined process. This energy is all about finding harmony by addressing problems early and working together to improve them.

Mercury in Scorpio sesquiquadrate Pisces North Node

This energy suggests discovering information that may initially cause anxiety or irritation, but instead of reacting impulsively, you choose to let it play out. Rather than rushing to solve the issue or confront someone, you might decide that the information you've received doesn't require immediate action. Instead, it serves as an eye-opener, revealing the truth of what's really going on. It could be that this knowledge helps you gain clarity or prepares you for something in the future. Sometimes, this energy encourages us to simply observe and gather insight, recognizing that not everything demands a quick response—some things are best understood with time.

Mercury in Scorpio biquintile Saturn retrograde in Pisces

Be mindful of falling into a past cycle within this energy. It suggests that you may start to recognize the familiar signs—you've been here before. Perhaps a situation feels like déjà vu, or you're noticing red flags that mirror those from a past relationship or experience. Trust what you know. This energy asks you to avoid repeating old patterns, especially when you already carry the wisdom from those previous lessons. You have the ability to rely on that hard-earned knowledge to guide you down a safer, more conscious path, ensuring you don't repeat the same mistakes. Stay alert to the signs and make choices based on your growth.

Sun in Libra sesquiquadrate Uranus retrograde in Gemini

This energy embodies the mindset of, *"I'm not going to be the one to make the first move or apologize. Why should I always have to be the bigger person?"* It reflects a resistance to taking the lead in resolving conflicts, especially when you feel like you've always been the one to extend the olive branch. For example, if you're in a disagreement with a friend or partner and feel like you've always been the one to apologize or compromise, this energy has you standing your ground, waiting for them to make the first move. Or perhaps at work, you've been the one to smooth over tensions between colleagues, but now you're ready to let someone else step up. This energy challenges the notion of always having to be the one to mend fences, encouraging you to let others take responsibility for their actions.

Song: "Complicated" by Avril Lavigne

October 10th

Venus in Virgo quincunx Chiron retrograde in Aries

This energy will likely have us projecting our pain and insecurities onto others, making it challenging to find common ground with loved ones. If you notice that those you love are projecting onto you, try to recognize that they are dealing with their own pain and insecurity. Show patience and compassion. If you find yourself projecting, turn inward and ask what is happening within you that is causing anger, pain, or resentment toward another person. What past experiences are triggering these emotions? Taking some time alone to evaluate your emotions might be a good idea during this period.

Mars in Scorpio sesquiquadrate Saturn retrograde in Pisces

This energy suggests that our patience is being thoroughly tested, and we may be prone to making rash decisions as a result. Rather than waiting for things to unfold naturally, we feel an overwhelming urge to take control and force things to happen. It's like the frustration of being stuck in the same spot finally boils over, and we break free of the chains holding us back—ready to make bold moves. However, this impatience can lead to impulsive choices, often driven by anger or insecurity about where we are in life. It's important to be cautious, as acting hastily can result in mistakes or falling into temptation. Before making any big decisions today, ask yourself, *Will I still think this is a good idea tomorrow?* This energy will tempt us to do things we wouldn't normally consider, so it's crucial to pause and reflect before making any significant moves.

Song: "Breakaway" by Kelly Clarkson

October 11th

Mercury in Scorpio biquintile Neptune retrograde in Aries

This energy is one where your obsessive thoughts and sharp investigative skills actually pay off, revealing what isn't being executed properly and where improvements can be made. It's like noticing flaws in a project at work that everyone else missed, and instead of just pointing fingers, you step up to take the lead and fix the issues. This energy inspires us to stop focusing on where others are falling short and instead recognize our own potential to make things better. For example, you might notice inefficiencies in a group task and, rather than complaining, you take charge, implement a new system, and end up elevating the whole team's performance. It's about turning criticism into action and realizing that you have the skills to lead and improve the situation.

Sun in Libra quincunx Pisces North Node

While the previous energy encouraged us to take on a leadership role, this energy suggests that opportunity for collaboration may be on the horizon, and not everyone will be on board with all your ideas. There may be resistance, especially when it comes to allowing others to have input or finding compromise to work nicely with others. However, it's important to check your ego and ask yourself if you could benefit from someone else's help. Just because they haven't done a great job in the past doesn't mean they aren't now inspired to step up and contribute more effectively. By embracing collaboration and being open to others' ideas, you may find that working together produces even better results than going it alone.

Song: "My Band" by D12

October 12th

Venus in Virgo opposite Saturn retrograde in Pisces

This aspect represents a challenge in relationships or connections that we have already faced in the past. This allows us to handle the situation differently. If you ghosted someone from the past, perhaps you have come back into contact to reconcile, or if you argued with someone in the past, now you have the opportunity to forgive them. Perhaps someone tried to gently enforce a boundary with you, and you refused to respect that boundary, so now they feel they need to be more forceful in their approach. You are faced with a difficult decision here, whether you choose the same path you chose in the past or opt for a different outcome. I cannot tell you what the correct decision is or what the consequences will be, so choose carefully. I encourage you to meditate, connect with your spirit team and intuition, and ask for help and assistance in making the best decision. If this feels like a test, that is because it is.

Song: "Make It Right" by Jonas Brothers

October 14th

Last Quarter Moon in Cancer

If you are moody, overly sensitive, emotional, and a little unstable, you are not alone. A last-quarter moon in Cancer will certainly do that to us. If there are any emotions that we have left hidden beneath the surface, they are likely to be feeling very exposed and vulnerable right now. This is the energy of feeling like we are fine and then quickly realizing that we are definitely not fine. This energy can fluctuate from feeling emotional in one moment because we are so incredibly grateful for our family or loved ones that we are overcome with emotions of gratitude to the next moment feeling completely unsupported and as if we are in the depths of emotional despair, feeling as though we are potentially on the verge of having a nervous breakdown.

Many of us will feel like we want to avoid watching sad movies or consuming emotional content during energy shifts like this, but I actually recommend it. I advise adding a box of tissues to the shopping list and letting those tears flow. Release that energy, even if you don't quite understand where it is coming from. Also, we can expect to see others having a similar experience, so while scrolling through social media, we will likely come across creators just pouring their little hearts out, sobbing and ugly crying. We are having a great emotional purge right now, so just allow those feelings and emotions to come up and be released. Also, we can expect a call from a loved one pouring out their emotions at this time. I encourage you to support each other through this energy. Luckily, it will only be potent for a couple of days.

Reflection

1. What emotions have I been suppressing or avoiding that might be surfacing during this energy shift?

2. What activities or practices bring me emotional comfort and relief

during challenging times, and can I incorporate them into my routine now?

3. What lessons or insights might be hidden within the depths of my emotions during this period of vulnerability?

Venus enters Libra

We are all beginning to feel very connected and harmonious right now as Venus is returning home to the sign of Libra. This is where Libra is comfortable and does her best work. Venus wants us to connect, create harmony, get along, and play nicely with others. Libra brings balance, reciprocity, fairness, and equality. This is a great time for romance and making deeper connections. It is an energy of putting aside selfish desires to better connect with those around us. It is being willing to sacrifice our own desires not because we feel we have to but because we want to. This is a time when we leave the house and we see a lot of couples holding hands and connecting on a more intimate level. This is a great time for dating if you are single or taking your relationship to the next level if you are already in a connection.

For those of us who are single, we generally feel a little giddy, romantic, or sexy during this time. This energy can feel a little like falling in love, and this doesn't have to be just romantic connections but even exploring new friendships. Putting yourself out there, meeting new people, and then finding a new friend you vibe with. It may feel like you have known them forever, and you are thinking, wow, where have you been all of my life? It's fun; it's carefree and floaty. We are dating with long-term potential in mind and assessing how others fit into our long-term plans. If we don't see any long-term potential with a connection, we will likely just enjoy it for what it is. Perhaps our values do not align completely, but we are still open to fleeting romance and enjoying the company of another.

For those of us in long-term relationships, we are finding ways to make it work, trying to work through any existing issues. We are very open-hearted as we approach our connections with forgiveness and reconciliation in mind. Within this energy, we choose to pick our battles with our partner and recognize that a minor disagreement does not affect how much we love our partner and their significant role in our lives. We are likely to feel more loved right now as we prioritize quality time with our partner, sit closer together on the sofa, or spend more time in bed in the morning, embraced by a cuddle. We are willing to put more energy into making our partner happy if that energy is reciprocated.

I would like to remind you to stay true to your values at this time. It can be easy in this energy to give in to other people's needs, wants, and desires because we want to connect and make others happy, but this can sometimes come at our own expense. The South Node, also in Libra, supports us not giving in to our people-pleasing tendencies, so the urge to sacrifice ourselves for what others need won't be too strong, but if you are a person who tends to sacrifice your own needs for others, be very aware of what you are sacrificing at this time.

Reflection

1. How can I prioritize my needs and values while still fostering meaningful connections with others?

2. What long-term potential do I see in my current romantic or platonic connections, and how does it align with my personal goals?

3. How can I navigate romantic or social situations with an open heart, focusing on forgiveness and reconciliation, especially if there are existing issues?

Pluto Direct in Aquarius

Pluto has been in retrograde in Aquarius but now moves back direct while we have already covered this alignment here is an alignment of what you can expect. Pluto intensifies and transforms collective energy. Pluto moving into the sign of Aquarius is a 20-year-long transit, and we will all experience this energy playing out all around us. It will be all over the news and affect our lifestyle. This energy dismantles any corruption of power from those in a position of authority and creates more equality, putting more power in the hands of the people. We will experience protests, rebellion, and revolutionary behavior as we demand a shift of power from those abusing their power over the collective. This energy will be loud as we experience the collective fight for freedom and human rights. Government structures will be dismantled as we head toward a human revolution.

We will also see many advancements in technology; we have already seen the development of AI, and we are all becoming accustomed to being served by robots at the supermarket checkout. This is only the beginning of advancements in technology, including medical advancements, space enhancements allowing us to discover more about life beyond this planet, environmental advancements, and other innovative humanitarian advancements. This transit will be present until 2044, and there will be resistance to this energy from those in leadership roles, so it will be a trying time for all of us. This energy will bring about a global transformation which the world has never seen. During this transit, I advise you to voice what you feel passionately about and join forces with others who deeply resonate with your purpose and what you feel you have been called to do. Be the change you want to see in the world, but also learn to withdraw from any global issues that may be causing you to get caught up in cycles of fear. Be mindful of the agenda of your news sources and connect within to see through any illusions being projected onto you.

Reflection

1. In what ways can you contribute to the collective fight for freedom and human rights?

2. What causes or issues are you most passionate about, and how can you actively be the change you want to see in the world?

3. How do you balance staying informed about global issues without getting caught up in cycles of fear?

Venus in Virgo semi-square Mars in Scorpio

This energy suggests that something is not working as it relates to a current goal or manifestation, yet there is a strong resistance to acknowledging and accepting the obstacle. It's as if we can see the problem, but we refuse to confront it, hoping that pushing through will somehow fix everything. For example, you may be working tirelessly on a project, but instead of recognizing that a lack of resources or time is holding you back, you keep pushing forward without adjusting your strategy. Or, perhaps you're manifesting a relationship, but the person you're focused on isn't reciprocating, and instead of accepting this, you hold on tightly, ignoring the signs that it's time to let go. This aspect asks us to step back and honestly assess where resistance is blocking progress, so we can adjust our approach rather than forcing something that isn't aligned.

Venus in Libra opposite Neptune retrograde in Aries

This is a challenging energy that asks the critical question: who will take the lead in our relationships? If you've been avoiding a family member, lover, or friend, or resisting spending time with them, the question becomes, *who will be the first to step up and make the effort to rebuild understanding?* One of you has to take the first step if there's ever going to be a chance for reconciliation. There's no right or wrong answer here, but it's a perfect time to reflect on whether your ego might be standing in the way of healing the relationship. Are you waiting for the other person to make the first move, or are you willing to bridge the gap yourself? This energy encourages us to explore what's truly holding us back.

Song: "Breathe Me" by Sia

October 15th

Mars in Scorpio sesquiquadrate Neptune retrograde in Aries

This energy encourages us to use our negative emotions as fuel to create meaningful change in our reality. Often, we tolerate situations until they become unbearable, and it's only in those moments of frustration or anger that we are pushed to take action. For example, you may stay in an unfulfilling job for years, but once the stress and dissatisfaction reach a boiling point, it finally motivates you to look for a new opportunity or start your own business. Similarly, in relationships, you might tolerate poor treatment until the pain becomes too much to bear, prompting you to set boundaries or walk away. This energy transforms those negative emotions into powerful catalysts for change, pushing us to stop waiting and start creating the life we truly want.

Venus in Libra trine Uranus retrograde in Gemini

This energy encourages us to think outside the box and develop innovative ideas to foster better teamwork and understanding within our relationships. Instead of relying on the same old patterns of communication, we might explore new ways to connect, like setting up regular "check-in" meetings with a partner or family member to discuss feelings and goals openly. For example, introduce a shared hobby, like cooking together or taking a dance class, to strengthen bonds and create a fun, collaborative environment. In a work setting, organizing a team-building retreat or setting up collaborative brainstorming sessions can help break down barriers and create a more cohesive unit. This energy pushes us to be creative in how we approach relationships, finding new ways to build trust and unity.

Mercury in Scorpio sesquiquadrate Saturn retrograde in Pisces

This energy can be deceptive, tempting us with something we once desired. An old flame or opportunity may reappear from the past, stirring feelings that once felt significant. However, it's essential to be mindful of accepting what no longer serves you just because it was something you once put all your energy into manifesting. What you wanted in the past may not align with who you are now. Ask yourself, *Is this manifestation still in harmony with my current path, or is it merely a distraction?* This is a moment to evaluate whether what's resurfacing truly supports your growth or pulls you away from where you're meant to go.

Venus in Libra trine Pluto in Aquarius

This aspect represents an opportunity to come together and collaborate with someone, but it raises an important question: at what cost? In order to work closely with another person, you may need to compromise or sacrifice some of your boundaries. Perhaps this means letting go of complete control over a project or allowing someone to have more input in an area where you usually stand firm. Only you can decide if the collaboration is worth the potential cost of bending your limits. It's a delicate balance between teamwork and self-preservation, and this energy asks you to carefully weigh whether you're willing to make that trade-off.

Song: "Boulevard Of Broken Dreams" by Green Day

October 17th

Sun in Libra biquintile Pisces North Node

This aspect highlights the ability to accept others for who they are and where they are in their journey. It's easy to get caught up in our expectations or illusions of how we think others should behave, often projecting our standards onto them. However, this energy encourages us to embrace a more accepting and understanding approach. For example, if a friend is not as ambitious or driven as we think they should be, instead of judging them, this energy teaches us to respect that they are on their own path and timeline. Similarly, if a family member struggles with personal growth or makes decisions we disagree with, we are reminded that everyone evolves at their own pace. This energy invites us to release control, stop trying to change others, and instead offer empathy and support, understanding that everyone's journey is unique.

Song: "We're All In This Together" by Ben Lee

October 18th

Mercury in Scorpio sesquiquadrate Neptune retrograde in Aries

This energy brings a sense of suspicion, causing us to question the actions and motives of those around us. We find ourselves scrutinizing the true intentions of the people we allow to influence our decisions. Are they using their influence responsibly or abusing the power they hold over us? In this energy, we begin to challenge whether the people we often elevate and admire genuinely deserve such admiration. Are they guiding us in a positive direction, or manipulating us for personal gain? This energy invites us to take a step back and critically assess whom we place on pedestals and whether they are serving our best interests or merely advancing their agendas.

Sun in Libra square Jupiter in Cancer

This energy suggests tension brewing in our closest connections, whether it's a family drama, conflict between children, or an argument with your significant other. You can feel the tension in the air, and it's clear that something needs to shift. The question is, how will you respond? Will you fuel the conflict by engaging in the drama or letting your emotions take over? Will you encourage compromise and step in as a mediator, helping to resolve the situation? Or will you choose to stay out of it entirely, letting others handle the problem on their own? This energy presents a choice; how you handle it can determine whether the tension escalates or dissipates.

Sun in Libra biquintile Uranus retrograde in Gemini

This energy suggests that we hold the power to change things within our reality. It encourages us to avoid disturbances by taking the time to truly understand the root of the problem, rather than reacting impulsively. This requires us to step back and try to see all points of view, not just our own. By broadening our perspective, we can find solutions that create harmony instead of further conflict. Whether it's a misunderstanding in a relationship, tension at work, or inner frustration, this energy reminds us that change starts with us and our willingness to consider different perspectives.

Sun in Libra opposite Chiron retrograde in Aries

The relationships and connections that we have with others are designed to mirror back to us our past wounds and trauma, which are still to be healed. Ever wonder why you are playing out the same abandonment scenario over and over again or why you are constantly seeking validation from others? It is because that wound within you is yet to be healed. For those of us who have trouble enforcing boundaries and saying no, we don't generally have just one needy friend; this pattern tends to play out within many of the connections around us as we continue to sacrifice ourselves for others. Some of us tend to sabotage our relationships and push others away from us out of fear of getting hurt. Look at the relationship cycles in your life and ask yourself what the patterns are. Once we find the pattern, we can easily identify the core wound and change our behavior to create more harmony in our relationships moving forward.

Song: "Stay" by Rihanna

October 19th

Mars in Scorpio trine Pisces North Node

I love this energy because it suggests a gift, luck, support, or blessing coming our way with seemingly little effort. It serves as a reminder that our manifestation game is strong, and sometimes the universe rewards us in unexpected ways. For example, you might receive an unexpected bonus at work or an opportunity that aligns perfectly with what you've been hoping for, even though you didn't actively chase it. Maybe you randomly run into someone who offers you the exact help or advice you need at just the right moment. This energy highlights that sometimes when we are aligned and focused on our intentions, the universe steps in to deliver without needing to struggle or overexert ourselves. It's a gentle nudge from the universe, showing us that our manifestations are being heard and supported.

Venus in Libra quintile Jupiter in Cancer

Following the previous energy of an unexpected blessing, this aspect gives us the chance to prioritize home and family. It might mean taking the family out for dinner to celebrate a new opportunity or success, or perhaps a colleague's assistance at work allows you to leave early and spend more time with loved ones. This energy encourages us to shift focus away from the hustle and enjoy the little moments with those who matter most. Whether planning a fun family outing or simply relaxing at home together, it's a reminder to celebrate and nurture the bonds we share with those closest to us.

Song: "The Best Day" by Taylor Swift

October 20th

Mercury in Scorpio trine Pisces North Node

This energy encourages us to tune into the subtle cues from the universe, guiding us toward alignment with our higher path. Often, this energy shows up as an intuitive nudge—a gut feeling or a series of coincidences that seem too perfect to ignore. Perhaps you overhear a conversation that speaks directly to a question you've been pondering, or you notice repeating symbols that point you toward a particular choice. Today is a day to remain open, listen closely, and trust in the signs around you. Follow where they lead, knowing the universe is gently pushing you in the direction meant for you.

Sun in Libra quincunx Saturn retrograde in Pisces

This energy suggests we are attempting to find balance within our connections, but challenges may arise due to differing life experiences. Misunderstandings might persist, and if someone seems determined to misinterpret you, trying to shift their perception within this energy is likely to fail. Taking some space away from them could be beneficial, allowing you to explore common ground in other areas or accept that having differing opinions is okay.

Uranus retrograde in Gemini quintile Pisces North Node

This energy reminds us that sometimes less is more, especially when solving a problem or resolving conflict. Instead of trying to over-explain, justify, or control a situation, stepping back and allowing space can be the most effective approach. For example, during an argument with a partner or friend, rather than continuing to talk in circles or trying to convince them of your point, pausing and giving both sides time to cool down can lead to greater understanding. In a work situation, rather than micromanaging a project or task, delegating and trusting others to handle their responsibilities can lead to a smoother outcome. This energy encourages us to remember that silence and restraint can often do more to diffuse tension than forceful action ever could.

Song: "Say Less" by John Michael Howell

October 21st

Mercury in Scorpio conjunct Mars in Scorpio

It's time to put on our detective caps, but instead of rushing into interrogation mode, this energy encourages us to step back and observe all the evidence before taking action. Sometimes, in our eagerness to get to the truth, we can overlook crucial details. By sitting back, observing, and piecing everything together, we may uncover something we initially missed. Whether in a conversation with a loved one, a situation at work, or a personal dilemma, taking a moment to quietly assess the bigger picture can lead to the clarity we need before making our next move.

Mercury in Scorpio quintile Pluto in Aquarius

This energy represents a strong sense of self-assurance and standing up for your rights. It's about confidently owning your truth and not allowing others to manipulate or gaslight you into doubting yourself. You know what you know; within this energy, you have the facts and "receipts" to back it up. Whether in a personal relationship, at work, or in any situation where you're challenged, this energy empowers you to stand firm and not be swayed by others' attempts to twist the narrative. You are grounded in your truth; no one can take that away from you.

Mars in Scorpio quintile Pluto in Aquarius

Sometimes, our obsession with finding out information can be a gift rather than a hindrance. It puts us in a much stronger position when it comes to backing up our argument. The extra effort we put into researching, gathering facts, or investigating details allows us to be more informed and prepared, giving us the upper hand in a debate or discussion. For instance, when faced with a disagreement at work or in a personal relationship, having the facts ready can allow you to assert your point more effectively. In this energy, knowledge becomes power, and our deep dive into information becomes the key to standing firm in our truth.

Song: "Every Breath You Take" by The Police

October 22nd

New Moon in Libra

The New Moon is the perfect time for setting intentions and manifesting what we desire in our lives. With this particular New Moon falling in the sign of Libra, the focus is on relationships and connections. It's a time to reflect on how we want our relationships to evolve and what steps we can take to create more harmony, love, and balance.

Start by asking yourself: *How do I want my relationships to look moving forward?* Consider what practical actions you can implement to achieve this vision. For example, if you're in a partnership, maybe it's time to plan a regular date night to prioritize your connection. Are there ways you could learn your partner's love language better or engage in deeper conversations about each other's needs? This is a chance to recalibrate your bond and align with long-term goals.

The same goes for friendships—can you make more effort to check in and be present? Are there relationships that have become difficult and need firmer boundaries? This energy also encourages you to consider whether it's time to distance yourself from toxic connections to maintain your peace and well-being.

Libra's energy also inspires future planning in relationships. Now is the ideal time for those long-term conversations—discussing marriage, how many children you'd like to have, or moving in together. It's about deepening connections or manifesting new ones. If you're seeking new relationships, think about what kind of partner you desire and what your non-negotiables are. Are you open to socializing more to invite new friendships into your life?

One key theme that comes up with this New Moon is compromise. Libra is about balance and harmony, so ask yourself: *Where can I be more flexible to manifest the best outcomes?* Perhaps you need to be more understanding with those you love, or maybe it's time to budge regarding legal matters or contracts. Flexibility can lead to more peaceful resolutions, and as the saying goes, you catch more flies with honey than with vinegar.

Reflection

1. How do I envision my relationships evolving in the future? What specific steps can I take to manifest these changes?

2. Are there conversations I've been avoiding in my relationships that need to happen? What's stopping me from addressing these important topics?

3. Are there relationships in my life that have become toxic or draining? How can I assert firmer boundaries to protect my emotional well-being?

Song: "Let's Call The Whole Thing Off" by Ella Fitzgerald & Louis Armstrong

October 23rd

Sun enters Scorpio

Scorpio is the sign of profound transformation, so it is no surprise that Scorpio season can be the most uncomfortable of all. All that no longer serves us begins to fall away as we transition into a higher form of consciousness and adjust to our new frequency. Scorpio season is messy but in the most beautiful way. We use this season to go deeper and darker into our shadows, which makes for the most significant transformations. If you are reading this book, you intend to heal yourself in a way that supports you in living a life that is more aligned with your soul and feels more authentic to you. There is no dipping your toe into the healing pond during Scorpio season; we are turning the dial to 100. Tears and fears will emerge as we plunge deep into our darkness to release our resistance. Life may start to feel like a rollercoaster you wish you could get off of, but I promise you it will all be worth it in the end.

Anything that is misaligned or no longer serving us will likely be put to a complete end during this season, and if we cling to what is trying to leave our life, we will likely get caught up in the crossfire. This season is all about release and surrender. This season may have us down on our knees, praying for some relief from our pain as we surrender ourselves to the divine. The trick to navigating Scorpio season is to remain in a state of flow. If it doesn't flow, we let it go. Allow the divine to move through you as we release any fear and attachment to outcomes, connections, structures, and belief systems that no longer serve us.

Reflection

1. What aspects of my life no longer serve my highest good and must be released during this Scorpio season?

2. How comfortable am I with delving into my shadows and embracing the discomfort that comes with deep transformation?

3. How can I surrender myself to the divine and trust the process of releasing fear and attachment?

4. Are there specific structures, belief systems, or connections in my life that I'm clinging to, even though they are trying to leave?

Neptune Retrograde enters Pisces

A Neptune retrograde allows us to see things for what they truly are, stripping away the illusions we may have been living under. This energy can feel like a painful reality check, as it's like removing the rose-colored glasses and coming face-to-face with the truth. However, this clarity serves as an inspiration to stop merely dreaming and start actively turning our aspirations into reality. Neptune retrograde encourages us to disconnect from the fantasies and delusions we may have created for ourselves, allowing us to become much more grounded and realistic in our decisions and actions. It's a time of facing the truth and making conscious, practical moves toward genuine progress, even if the initial clarity feels uncomfortable.

Reflection

1. Have you ever experienced a situation where removing "rose-colored glasses" felt like a painful reality check, and what lessons did you draw from that experience?

2. Reflect on instances in your life where illusions or delusions influenced your decisions. How might you incorporate a more grounded and realistic approach in such situations?

Sun in Libra quincunx Neptune retrograde in Pisces

When we communicate to others that we need more from them and challenge their efforts, we are likely to see a side of them that we don't like. This is a time to go within and search for answers on whether or not you are able to grow with the people around you or whether the differences between you are irreconcilable. Many connections break down with this type of energy present; separations take place, and emotional reactions are likely.

Song: "Not For Me" by Sarah Proctor

October 24th

Sun in Scorpio quincunx Uranus retrograde in Gemini

This energy brings a painful realization of the need to release attachments to relationships or desires that simply aren't working out. It's about acknowledging that, despite all the effort, time, and energy you've poured into trying to make something work, there comes a point when you have to ask yourself: *Is it worth continuing to exhaust my resources?* This moment of clarity, while challenging, is essential for growth. It forces us to face the truth that some things are not meant to be, and it's time to let go. The energy calls for introspection and tough decisions, but ultimately, it frees us from the burden of forcing situations that aren't serving our highest good.

Jupiter in Cancer square Chiron retrograde in Aries

This energy will likely expose a deep wound tied to something we still carry from childhood. If you're feeling pain or discomfort in your current reality, this energy encourages you to reflect deeply on past experiences or traumas that continue to make this wound tender in the present. It's a powerful moment for introspection, inviting you to uncover how unresolved childhood experiences may still be influencing your emotions, reactions, or relationships today. By bringing these wounds into your awareness, you can heal and release them rather than allowing them to unconsciously shape your present. This energy invites you to nurture your inner child and move toward emotional freedom.

Song: "Hurt" by Johnny Cash

October 25th

Sun in Scorpio square Pluto in Aquarius

This energy calls for a profound level of self-awareness, urging us to take a deeper look at our role in the conflicts in our lives. It invites us to examine whether we've been expressing our opinions constructively or if we've crossed into aggression. There's a fine line between standing up for what we believe is right and letting our ego lead the way in a negative direction. While we are not responsible for how others perceive us, we are responsible for managing our triggers and keeping our ego in check when it becomes inflamed. This energy is about recognizing that true strength comes from self-control and understanding, not from overpowering others.

Mercury in Scorpio quincunx Chiron retrograde in Aries

In order to embrace forgiveness, we must first delve back into the pain and emotions of the past and address what went wrong. This energy is here to help us do just that. We are justified in feeling how we feel and must honor our emotions. If someone has hurt us, they should be made aware of our experience to ensure that they are clear on our boundaries and the types of behavior that we will not tolerate in the future. There is likely to be some deep communication happening within this energy as we not only express our own emotions but also hold a safe space for others to express their emotions to us so that we can gain a deeper understanding of their experience.

Mercury in Scorpio trine Jupiter in Cancer

This aspect suggests the comforting presence of support from a friend or loved one. Whether it's someone to confide in, vent your frustrations to, or simply someone who lifts your spirits and provides a healthy distraction, this energy highlights the importance of leaning on those we trust. In moments when you're feeling low or overwhelmed, this connection offers a safe space to release your emotions, feel understood, and be reminded that you are not alone. It's a reminder that sometimes, a compassionate ear or a fun distraction from someone you love is exactly what you need to pull you out of a low vibration.

Song: "No More Drama" by Mary J Blige

October 26th

Sun in Scorpio biquintile Saturn retrograde in Pisces

Does it feel like a test? Like you've been thrown back onto the merry-go-round of life, facing the same karmic cycle you thought you were ready to close out? If so, you hold the key to breaking free, but perhaps you've been looking in the wrong place. If you're waiting for someone to come save you, it's time to accept that they won't. You're the one who has to save yourself. And if you're hoping for someone else to change their behavior, it's likely they won't. It starts with *you*, my love. The real question is: *What do I need to change within myself to stop this cycle from pulling me back in?* The answers are within, and only through self-reflection and transformation can you break free for good.

Sun in Scorpio sesquiquadrate Pisces North Node

While you may have identified what needs to change, this aspect brings resistance to actually confronting the truth and taking active steps toward transformation. The energy feels like a constant delay—*"I'll start tomorrow,"* or *"When this certain thing happens, then I'll change."* It encourages excuses and rationalizations for why now isn't the right time. You know deep down what needs to be done, but this energy tempts you to put it off, creating a cycle of avoidance and procrastination. It's a tricky space to navigate, as the desire for change is present, but the will to act on it feels distant.

Mercury in Scorpio trine Saturn retrograde in Pisces

This aspect indicates us discovering something that we may have previously missed. Hindsight is 20/20, and we often find when something is revealed to us, we look back and recognize that the signs were there all along. Perhaps we ignored some red flags or the signs sent to us by the universe. This is the energy of putting all of the pieces together and recognizing that we have been guided toward the answers all along.

Song: "I'd Do Anything For Love" by Meat Loaf

October 27th

This energy encourages us to take the initiative in our relationships and connections, even when it feels uncomfortable. Have an issue with a coworker? This is the time to set up a meeting and address it directly. Is there tension with someone close to you? This energy nudges you to reach out and say, *"We need to talk."* Maybe you've been waiting for an apology, but this energy pushes you to be the first to offer one, even if it comes with a sense of reluctance or anxiety. You may feel hesitant, but deep down, you know that taking the first step is the key to healing and moving forward. It's about pushing through the discomfort to create better understanding and connection.

Song: "How To Save A Life" by The Fray

October 28th

Venus in Libra quincunx Pisces North Node

This energy asks us to recognize when we've done all we can in a relationship and to accept that we sometimes won't see eye to eye with someone. There are moments when differences become irreconcilable, and no amount of effort will bridge the gap. Relationships take two committed people; if neither share the same goals or willingness to meet halfway, it can feel like banging your head against a brick wall. If you've exhausted your energy trying to make things work but the other person won't meet you in the middle, it might be time to accept that you've done enough and it's okay to stop trying.

Mars in Scorpio quincunx Chiron retrograde in Aries

This energy will likely stir up intense emotions, leaving us feeling vulnerable and raw. It can come on suddenly, overwhelming us with feelings that are often expressed negatively, such as anger, hostility, or anxiety. The potency of this energy makes it easy for emotions to spiral out of control if we're not mindful. It's important to stay grounded and resist the urge to let these heightened emotions take over. Instead, take a step back, breathe, and try to process your feelings before reacting so you don't allow your emotions to run away with you.

Song: "You Oughta Know" by Alanis Morissette

October 29th

Mars in Scorpio trine Jupiter in Cancer

There are some very intense energies swirling around right now, and this energy brings a reminder to channel that intensity in the right direction. Instead of getting caught up in frustrations or obsessing over what isn't going right, focus your energy on nurturing the relationships that support you. Get intense about the things that lift you up—whether it's a new project you're working on, formulating creative ideas, or pouring passion into something positive in your life. Channel this powerful energy into the blessings you already have, and watch how it transforms your reality in meaningful ways.

Sun in Scorpio biquintile Neptune retrograde in Pisces

This aspect asks us to look deeper within ourselves and investigate the parts of ourselves that we keep suppressed. This is a nostalgic energy of looking back at the past and connecting with the dreams, wishes, and desires we once held dear to us. What interests and hobbies have we had since childhood? What did we dream our life would be like? What do we wish we had more time for? When we are children, we dream differently; we can imagine ourselves living a fairytale life without limitations. Connect with the fairytale adventure that you were once able to believe in so strongly, and ask yourself how you can reconnect with that and harness some of that magic to manifest in your current reality.

   Song: "Till I Collapse" by Eminem

October 30th

Mercury enters Sagittarius

As Mercury enters Sagittarius, a shift occurs in the way we express ourselves. If you've been living life as a delicate wallflower, being mindful of manners, and avoiding rocking the boat, that is about to change. This energy particularly benefits those with a platform, bringing enthusiasm and animation to communication. While it may come off as extra at times, it's ultimately fun. This energy allows us to communicate passionately, and people respond positively. We have the ability to speak life into others, making a significant impact with our words. Think of us as motivational speakers, not just offering encouragement but also urging people to stop making excuses, get up, and make a move. The delivery might be blunt and forceful, inspired by Sagittarius' truth-telling nature, but it can inspire significant change by holding others accountable. Sagittarius energy rejects small talk and negativity, focusing on good vibes only. Confronting negativity, we are ready to call out those who refuse to take accountability for their circumstances. It's a season of brutal honesty, bringing forth authenticity rarely seen. This alignment may reveal true feelings, and navigating this transit might be a challenge for those easily offended. Remember, others' opinions are just that—opinions, holding only the power we allow them to have over us.

Reflection

1. Reflect on a moment when someone spoke to you with passion and enthusiasm. How did it impact you, and how might you incorporate a similar approach in your communication style?

2. Consider the concept of being a motivational speaker who encourages action rather than just offering reassurance. How can you embrace a more direct and forceful communication style to inspire change in yourself and others?

3. In what areas of your life could you benefit from a season of brutal honesty, fostering authenticity and a deeper understanding of yourself and others?

First Quarter Moon in Aquarius

This is a time for thinking outside the box and making necessary adjustments. With the Sun in Scorpio, our primary focus is delving deeper into ourselves and transforming into the person we want to be. We are making friends with our shadows, our past, our darkness, and the wounds we carry. We are asking ourselves what we truly desire, and this First Quarter Moon in Aquarius is asking us why we don't have it yet. We are calling ourselves out on the behaviors holding us back and taking more accountability for our financial situation, our failed relationships, or the areas where we have made less-than-stellar efforts.

During this time, we will be cutting out anything that no longer serves us and getting more serious about bringing in things that are in higher alignment. Some of us will be giving up unhealthy habits and hitting the gym. Others will dissociate from people who drain our energy and immerse themselves in new communities that align with our energetic frequency. Some who are addicted to social media will stop being mere consumers and instead become creators, sharing their energy and wisdom with the wider collective. There is a heightened level of intensity to the commitments we are making to ourselves at this time.

Reflection

1. What manifestations have you yet to be able to achieve? What steps can you take to align closer with your desires?

2. Are there any destructive or self-sabotaging behaviors you are calling yourself out on and taking accountability for?

3. In what ways are you actively cutting out elements in your life that no longer serve you, and how dedicated are you to creating positive changes in your life?

Mercury in Scorpio trine Neptune retrograde in Pisces

We will likely feel aligned and supported by the divine during this time. I recognize that this is a painful time of inner transformation, but if you are able to go deeper and darker into your own shadow, the divine will be there to support you. Ask for assistance to be guided toward your deeper core wounds that need to be released from your energy field, and allow yourself to feel supported by God, the divine, your guides, ancestors, angels, and loved ones in the spirit world who are helping you in your healing journey.

Mercury in Scorpio biquintile Chiron retrograde in Aries

Pay attention to any negative emotions coming up for you at this time. You may feel an urge to suppress them, thinking that your recent transformation has disconnected you from your past pain. However, that is often not the case at all. If you are feeling triggered right now, take the time to feel into those emotions. Allow your triggers to guide you as you delve even deeper into the core wounds of your soul. There may be a pain point that you have missed and needs to be addressed.

Mars in Scorpio trine Saturn retrograde in Pisces

Temptation is swirling, and it's important to be mindful of slipping back into negative thought patterns or limiting belief systems. Behaviors you've worked hard to overcome, like anger or numbing emotional pain through substances or other unhealthy outlets, may resurface. While temptation may be knocking at the door, this aspect grants us the awareness to recognize it for what it is. Use this awareness to stand firm and not fall back into old habits or lower your frequency just to soothe the ego. Stay grounded, and remember the progress you've made.

Mercury in Sagittarius opposite Uranus retrograde in Gemini

This energy is all about honesty—brutal honesty, even. If directed at others, it can easily hurt feelings because, as they say, the truth hurts. Another way this energy manifests is by picking apart our faults. While self-awareness is essential for growth and healing, it's equally important to nurture ourselves through the process. Being too hard on yourself can lead to unnecessary self-criticism. The key here is balance: recognizing areas for improvement while offering yourself compassion and understanding along the way.

Song: "Truth Hurts" by Lizzo

October 31st

Mercury in Sagittarius sextile Pluto in Aquarius

Today, we're bringing all the positive vibes and inspiring energy to those around us. You might find yourself uplifting an entire group, motivating your coworkers during a challenging project, giving your friends a much-needed pep talk, or even hopping onto social media to sprinkle some positivity to your followers. Maybe you'll share an encouraging quote or story that resonates deeply with others or take the time to leave supportive comments on friends' posts. This energy is contagious, and by spreading good vibes, you inspire others to do the same, creating a ripple effect of encouragement and optimism.

Song: "Don't Worry Be Happy" by Bobby McFerrin

November Alignments

November 2nd

Venus in Libra biquintile Pisces North Node

This energy is about allowing space in your connections, giving others the room required to process emotions or reflect after a conflict. Sometimes, it's important to recognize that not everything requires immediate resolution. This might mean stepping back and letting a work colleague or family member cool off after a disagreement or simply enjoying some alone time without feeling pressured to address issues right away. Allowing this breathing space creates a healthier dynamic where both parties can return with a clearer perspective, ready to move forward when the time is right.

Song: "Breathe" by Blu Cantrell & Sean Paul

November 3rd

Venus in Libra opposite Chiron retrograde in Aries

Everyone that is put on our life path is here to teach us something about ourselves. Some relationships and connections are incredibly positive, lifting us up and cheering us on. Others offer guidance and wisdom, like a wise sage who has lived many lifetimes. Some are supportive, offering a shoulder to cry on or a comforting hug when life becomes overwhelming. And then those connections which trigger us beyond what we think we can tolerate, feeling karmic in nature. Even those connections we may label as toxic or karmic are still here to teach us something—perhaps about self-love, creating firm boundaries, patience, resilience, or pushing us to behave in ways misaligned with our character. Many of these connections are just here for a season.

This aspect may have us feeling at odds with other connections around us. If someone is triggering you right now, ask yourself what category they fall into and what role they play in your life, and consider the lessons you have learned from them throughout your journey together. Is this someone you feel is worthy of keeping around?

Venus in Libra biquintile Uranus retrograde in Gemini

This energy encourages us to reach out to our network and strengthen our connections. It invites us to reflect on whether an apology or reconciliation needs to be initiated. Is there a difficult conversation we've been avoiding, or a friendship we've neglected due to being too busy? Now is the time to mend those bridges, nurture those relationships, and address any unresolved issues. Reaching out can bring healing and clarity, creating stronger bonds and more harmonious connections with those around us.

Sun in Scorpio sesquiquadrate Saturn retrograde in Pisces

This is an interesting aspect that teaches us not to rely on anything external for our happiness. It encourages us to release anything that may be keeping us bound, whether it's an addiction, negative thought patterns, or a person we know isn't good for us. This energy presents a challenge by bringing temptation to the surface, asking us to reflect: What is stronger—our inner strength and resilience or our need for external fulfillment? It's an invitation to break free from these dependencies and trust that true happiness comes from within, empowering us to make healthier choices for our well-being.

Venus in Libra square Jupiter in Cancer

We've been experiencing some problematic energy surrounding our relationships lately, often giving too much time and attention to those we consistently struggle to get along with. This is a reminder to shift our focus toward the people who nurture us and bring positivity into our lives. Instead of engaging in conflicts or getting caught up in other people's drama, this energy encourages us to show appreciation for those who truly support us. It might inspire gestures like buying flowers for your mum, simply to brighten her day and express gratitude. It's about investing our energy in the relationships that truly matter.

Song: "Jar Of Hearts" by Christina Perri

November 4th

Venus in Libra quincunx Saturn retrograde in Pisces

Our relationships and connections are causing us some concern right now, and we are being asked not to forget the lessons we have learned in love in the past. The divine does not want us to repeat the same mistakes over and over again within our connections, which keeps us trapped in karmic cycles. Before becoming reactive to the people around us, we are asked to take a break away from anyone who is causing us anxiety. Take some time to gather your thoughts and consider what your history with this person has taught you before you make permanent decisions going forward.

Mars in Scorpio trine Neptune retrograde in Pisces

This is a challenging aspect that represents seeing through illusions. Sometimes, we can become so focused or obsessed with manifesting a particular outcome that we ignore the red flags or signs telling us that the path we're on may not be the right one. We create our own delusions, convincing ourselves to keep pushing forward, but this energy feels like a reality check or awakening. While it may be painful or we may resist the truth being revealed, it's truly a gift. This moment allows us to re-route and avoid continuing down a path—or pursuing a person—that isn't aligned with our highest good. In the end, it's an opportunity to realign with what serves us best.

Song: "Don't Speak" by No Doubt

November 5th

Mars enters Sagittarius

Mars, the planet of action, conflict, and war, residing in the sign of Sagittarius, creates an intense and passionate energy. During this alignment, we are setting big goals, and no dream seems too grand or unrealistic. We become visionaries; if we correctly channel this energy, the seemingly impossible can become possible. Sagittarius brings a need for adventure and expansion, fueling us with a desire to live life with purpose. Many of us may feel inspired to enroll in higher learning, explore new philosophies, or travel, driven by an insatiable thirst for knowledge and experience.

However, this restless energy can also lead to impatience. Boredom with routines may settle in, making us feel stagnant and causing us to crave something more. This pursuit of "something more" can convince us that the grass is always greener elsewhere, leaving us feeling unsettled in our current reality and struggling to find meaning.

When it comes to conflict, Mars in Sagittarius ignites a passionate need to express ourselves. We may become volatile with a short fuse if we feel restricted during this time. Thankfully, this fiery energy is like a firecracker—explosive but quick to burn out, allowing us to return to a good vibe after the initial burst. Our attacks are likely to come in the form of witty or sarcastic remarks, delivered spontaneously. We're not interested in dragging out drama, as we quickly move on. However, a word of caution: Sagittarius thrives on brutal honesty, and while we might drop truth bombs casually, they can cut deeper than intended. Our words have the potential to cause unintended wounds, especially when they hit too close to home.

Sagittarius is also the sign of freedom, and one of the most empowering aspects of this energy is our resistance to being controlled. If someone tells us to do something, we're more likely to do the opposite, simply to prove that no one dictates our actions or controls our lives. This rebellious streak allows us to reclaim our autonomy and embrace the freedom to live on our own terms.

Reflection

1. What are the big, visionary goals that I've been hesitant to pursue, and how can I channel this passionate energy into making them a reality?

2. In what areas of my life am I feeling restless or stagnant, and how can I incorporate more adventure or purpose into my daily routine?

3. Have I been brutally honest with others or myself in a way that may have caused unnecessary wounds? How can I be more mindful of the impact my words have on those around me?

Mars in Sagittarius biquintile Chiron retrograde in Aries

This aspect is likely to stir up feelings of restriction, whether it's the sense that we lack freedom in our relationships, feel limited in our ability to grow within the workplace, or don't have the resources to escape an environment that leaves us feeling trapped. It's important to remember that the only limits that exist are the ones we perceive to be true. There's always another way to bring about the change we desire, to find a path that excites and inspires us again. However, our past conditioning may be especially loud today, whispering doubts and telling us that pursuing the adventure we crave won't lead to success. Now is the time to challenge those limiting beliefs and open ourselves up to new possibilities.

Mars in Sagittarius opposite Uranus retrograde in Gemini

This energy has us feeling limited by technology, leaving us with a sense of frustration and uncertainty. We may want to publish a book but don't know where to start. Perhaps we have an amazing business idea but are unsure of how to market it. Or we might be trying to build a social media following but feel lost on how to go viral or make a lasting impact. This energy whispers, "I want to be bigger, but I feel so small," tricking us into believing there's no room for us to expand in these spaces. However, this is merely a perception, not a reality. The tools we need to grow are out there, and this is a reminder to be open to learning, seeking advice, and finding creative ways to break through the barriers technology may present.

Song: "Can't Hold Us Down" by Christina Aguilera

November 6th

Full Moon in Taurus

Full Moons are an intense time of heightened emotions, adding to the mix that this particular full moon is happening during Scorpio season, a season of intensity. It is not uncommon for us to be experiencing feelings of uncertainty. This moon will highlight anything in your life that seems unstable, particularly in the realm of resources and finances. Many of us will have anxiety over access to resources or our limited funds in the bank. Bill increases may be stressing us out, or not having enough money to cover our basic needs may leave us feeling hopeless. The energetic frequency of this moon makes it very difficult for us to find solutions to these problems because the issue seems to intensify. This moon may leave us feeling depressed or as if we have little control over our resources. If you find yourself in a low frequency during this time, take some time to do an activity you love. Watch a comedy to cheer yourself up, enjoy gardening, or engage in whatever activity helps lift your spirit.

Reflection

1. What aspects of my life feel unstable or uncertain, especially regarding resources and finances?

2. How is the rising cost of living affecting my overall well-being, and what strategies can I employ to navigate this stress?

3. What mindset shifts or approaches can help me navigate intensified

problems and find practical solutions?

Song: "I Need A Dollar" by Aloe Blacc

November 7th

Venus enters Scorpio

Venus in Scorpio can be a very challenging alignment as it prompts us to question all of our connections. During this time, we seek trust and loyalty from others, determined to identify who is genuinely supportive and who may have hidden agendas. We put our connections to the test, questioning the authenticity of those around us. It's crucial not to get too entangled in the potential toxicity of this energy. For example, if we're questioning a friendship where we feel like we are always the initiator of contact, it's not productive to play games by intentionally refraining from reaching out to see if the other person reciprocates. This energy can lead to self-sabotage as trust issues peak and walls go up, requiring everyone around us to prove their worthiness. It's important to reflect on whether we're engaging in these behaviors and avoiding expressing our true feelings due to a fear of vulnerability. Are we resisting sharing our emotions out of concern that they may not be reciprocated?

For those who are single, there's a reluctance to let down our guard when establishing new connections. Background checks, digging into pasts, and playing hard-to-get are common tactics. However, it's advised to refrain from engaging in these games if genuine interest exists. Express feelings honestly and avoid unnecessary complexities.

In long-term committed relationships, there might be a tendency to bring up past issues to create distance or test loyalty. While this energy can be toxic, it gives us a sense of security when a partner chooses love, even in challenging moments. For those who have broken negative relationship patterns, there may be a push for deeper emotional exploration, asking partners to express their true feelings about the relationship and other connections. This alignment demands depth, and surface-level responses won't suffice.

Reflection

1. How do I test my connections' trust and loyalty, and is this serving my relationships positively?

2. In what ways am I playing games or engaging in self-sabotage due to trust issues and a fear of vulnerability?

3. Am I resisting expressing my true feelings to others out of concern that they may not be reciprocated, and how does this impact my relationships?

Mars in Sagittarius sextile Pluto in Aquarius

This aspect gives us an overwhelming urge to stand up for ourselves in any area where we feel restricted or confined. Whether it's a loved one imposing limits on us or a person in a position of authority holding us back, we're ready to speak our truth. However, if you're aiming your frustrations at someone in power, be mindful of the potential consequences that could arise from acting impulsively. This energy also has an element of solidarity, so you may find yourself with an ally by your side. Two voices are louder than one, and much can be accomplished when standing together, especially when confronting authority. It's time to weigh the risks but also embrace the power of unity and self-assertion.

Venus in Libra quincunx Neptune retrograde in Pisces

This energy can bring about a sense of loneliness or the feeling that no one understands our experience. The path to healing can be a very lonely one at times, and that does not mean that we are physically alone. We are often surrounded by people with good intentions; however, this is the feeling of having no one we can truly resonate with on a deep level. Perhaps we feel energetically disconnected from our partner, friends, or family. We may feel unsupported, but remember that there is always an outside source with which we can connect and develop a relationship that will help guide us through these challenges. We can connect to Source for support in many ways, whether through prayer, divination, or meditation. Allow yourself to reach out to divine support and ask them to send you signs to let you know you are supported.

Sun in Scorpio sesquiquadrate Neptune retrograde in Pisces

This energy can represent becoming obsessed with a dream or desire. Having a dream is not negative; however, we need to practice manifesting with practicality. This involves consistent actions aligning with that desire, rather than obsessively praying, wishing, hoping, and dreaming about it. Give it everything you've got to strive toward it, and you will be rewarded for your efforts.

Venus in Scorpio quincunx Uranus retrograde in Gemini

Be mindful of trying to catch people out within this energy. This aspect can make us feel highly suspicious of those around us, encouraging us to go to great lengths to prove our suspicions right. You may find yourself engaging in gossip, trying to uncover what others are up to, or gathering dirt on those who raise your suspicions. You might even comb through old messages or communications in search of clues. If you're feeling uneasy about someone, take a moment to ask yourself: are your suspicions valid, or are you letting paranoia get the better of you? It's important to remember that when we focus on finding problems, we often create them. We are co-creators of our own reality, and if we dedicate too much energy to looking for issues, that's exactly what we'll manifest. Stay balanced, and be careful not to let suspicion cloud your judgment.

Song: "Mr Brightside" by The Killers

November 8th

Uranus Retrograde enters Taurus

Uranus is innovative and responsible for all the cool and unique advancements we see around us, such as selfie filters, cryptocurrency, and Teslas. It also comes in with a bang and has a breakthrough type of energy. It has been sitting in Taurus since 2018; Taurus is the sign of earthly matters, material things, money, and resources. That's why we have seen so many advancements in this area over the last few years. When it moves retrograde, it creates more of an internal shift rather than an external one, which is breakthrough energy. It comes through as more of a sudden realization or epiphany.

This affects us as individuals, as we do not feel limited by what once appeared to be obstacles. "I can move and afford to buy this if I just do this." "This way of doing things is not working for me, but I hadn't considered this opportunity." This is like having a belief system that says, "I will never own my own home in this economy," and then realizing that this is not off-limits to us. We are taking more accountability with this energy, recognizing that if we make this change, we will have the resources to achieve what we desire. While in the sign of Taurus, this energy may be somewhat subtle but very powerful. Taurus and Uranus are both slow-moving, so this is not a drastic change, but the epiphany or realization is likely to feel sudden or drastic. To help support this energy, I highly recommend reading any books on investments or finances. This energy helps us release any old conditioning associated with the resources available to us and allows us access financial abundance.

Reflection

1. How can you reconsider your limitations and take more accountability for creating positive changes?

2. Have you identified any old conditioning or limiting beliefs regarding money and resources that you are ready to release and overcome?

3. What action can you take right now to secure more financial stability for yourself?

Pluto in Aquarius semi-square Pisces North Node

This energy encourages us to pull back from the constant bombardment of political, collective, and global issues that can easily consume our minds and energy. As I write this, news about Sean 'Diddy' Combs' charges is everywhere, and I can't escape it. Every time I open social media, I'm met with whistleblowers sharing their truth or speculation about who might be next on the celebrity hit list to face charges or testify. While it's important to support justice and hear victims' voices, there's a point where all this chaos can become overwhelming. It's not just in the news; it's invaded my personal life too—my husband has opinions, my children are talking about it, and even my friends bring it up. This energy serves as a reminder to check in with ourselves and ask: when is it time to disengage from the drama? While these issues may be important, be mindful not to let them consume you entirely. Finding a balance between being informed and preserving your peace is critical.

Venus in Scorpio sesquiquadrate Pisces North Node

This energy encourages us to suppress our feelings for the time being. If someone is irritating or annoying us, we're more likely to hold back, keeping our emotions under wraps rather than confronting them head-on. In our connections, we may be saying and doing less, allowing situations to unfold naturally while we quietly observe. By doing so, we're gathering more evidence and insight into what's happening rather than prematurely jumping to conclusions or escalating tensions. This is a time of patience, where restraint may prevent unnecessary conflict.

Venus in Scorpio biquintile Saturn retrograde in Pisces

This energy serves as a reminder of the power of moving in silence. There are times when it's best not to reveal too much about our projects or intentions, allowing us to work without external pressure or interference. For instance, if you're starting a new business or developing a creative project, keeping your plans under wraps prevents others from imposing their doubts, opinions, or even envy on your work. Moving in silence can also help you stay focused, avoiding the distractions that come with oversharing. Additionally, revealing your success only when you've accomplished your goals can have a more significant impact. Whether it's personal growth, career moves, or financial goals, keeping your progress private gives you the freedom to navigate challenges without the added pressure of others watching your every move.

Venus in Scorpio square Pluto in Aquarius

This energy is likely to have us uncover some deceit or hidden information around us. You may find yourself stumbling upon a message or overhearing a conversation that reveals something previously concealed. For example, perhaps a colleague has been making moves behind the scenes, and you come across an email thread that uncovers their true intentions. Or, in a relationship, you might notice minor inconsistencies that lead you to discover a hidden truth. This energy pushes us to pay closer attention to the subtle clues in our environment, allowing us to piece together information we might have missed. Whether it's a hidden agenda, a financial discrepancy, or even a friend not being entirely honest, this energy urges us to dig deeper and uncover what's really going on.

Song: "Luxurious" by Gwen Stefani

November 9th

Sun in Scorpio trine Pisces North Node

This is a liberating energy of releasing expectations about how we thought things were going to go or turn out. Initially, it may be painful to let go of things we once held dear or belief systems we have clung to for so long, but this discomfort is often replaced by a profound sense of surrender. By releasing control, we allow ourselves to fall back into flow with our divine path, trusting that what is meant for us will unfold naturally. Instead of resisting or forcing outcomes, we are left full of faith, feeling more connected to the universe, and guided by a higher purpose. This energy invites us to trust the process, knowing that what lies ahead is precisely what we need, even if it differs from what we originally envisioned.

Song: "The Shore" by Matt McClure

November 10th

Mercury Retrograde in Sagittarius

We are all pretty familiar with Mercury retrograde and its ability to derail our plans and set us back. Be prepared for rescheduling, miscommunications, and cancellations. Now, we must put an extra couple of table settings for the event we are hosting because someone's plans fell through, or we must cancel altogether because no one bothered to RSVP. We haven't found the perfect gift because they were sold out online, so we must travel to 5 stores to find it. This is the energy of setbacks and minor inconveniences.

As Mercury is in the sign of Sagittarius, the chaos we will be experiencing now will restrict us from having more fun. We may find that our travel plans are delayed, we have trouble securing tickets for a concert or event we plan to attend, or our electronics, such as televisions, phones, or wifi may be having meltdowns. As many of us are already getting into the holiday spirit and generally busy with events, end-of-year parties, Christmas shopping, and everything else that comes along at this time of year, we will be, in a sense, too distracted to be distracted by this Mercury retrograde. While we will feel the frustration, it won't take us long to refocus and get back on track. Nevertheless, we can expect some disruption during this alignment. While frustrating, we are still in very high spirits, so we will quickly go from frustration and anxiety to being able to laugh about what is happening and transmute any negative energy into positivity.

Reflection

1. Are there any specific plans or events in your life that you anticipate may be affected by the current Mercury retrograde in Sagittarius? If so, create a backup plan.

2. How can you maintain a positive and resilient mindset despite potential disruptions caused by Mercury retrograde?

3. Do you employ specific strategies or practices to stay focused and centered during chaotic times?

Venus in Scorpio semi-sextile Mars in Sagittarius

This energy brings about a perfect opportunity to learn from those around us but more subtly and stealthily than usual. It's not about asking a bunch of questions or seeking advice outright, but rather learning through quiet observation. For example, you might find yourself gaining inspiration from your favorite creator, paying close attention to how they move, how they build their brand, or the choices they make, all without them even knowing they're being observed. This kind of "stealth mode" learning allows you to absorb valuable insights and strategies without directly engaging, making it a more intuitive and personal experience.

Song: "Ironic" by Alanis Morissette

November 12th

Jupiter Retrograde in Cancer

A Jupiter retrograde asks us to reflect upon where we can expand. Due to this retrograde falling in the sign of Cancer this energy encourages us to assess where we can expand by offering more care and support to those around us. It's a moment to ask ourselves how we can better nurture both our environment and relationships.

Can we offer more to our friends by making time for a coffee or a quick phone call to check their emotional well-being? Within the work environment, are we in a position to mentor a trainee or help a colleague by reviewing their project? This retrograde pulls us toward spending more time at home, focusing on our partners, children, and pets to ensure they're not feeling neglected. We might find ourselves creating a more nurturing space by renovating or making the home environment more welcoming, whether organizing a play area for the kids or building a space for our pets to enjoy.

Additionally, this energy highlights the need to nurture ourselves. Are we taking care of our bodies by examining our diets or increasing our water intake? Are we setting aside time for things that rejuvenate our souls, like stretching in the mornings, taking a relaxing bubble bath, or simply sitting in the sunshine with a good book?

The key to this energy is the gentle exploration of how we can offer more nurturing to others and ourselves without pressure. It's about asking, "How can I help?" rather than feeling burdened by obligation. Jupiter in Cancer retrograde invites us to create space for more nurturing, whether in our relationships, environment, or bodies.

Reflection

1. How can I better nurture my relationships with friends and family? Am I making enough time to check their emotional well-being, or can I offer more support?

2. How can I ensure my home environment supports my loved one's emotional and physical well-being?

3. What changes can I make to my routine to better care for my body, mind, and soul?

Venus in Scorpio biquintile Neptune retrograde in Pisces

This energy allows us the ability to tune into the emotions of others. Sometimes, the actions and expressions of others do not align with what we are intuitively feeling within their energy. Our intuitive abilities are at an all-time high during this period, so if you have something to say but your intuition is telling you that it is not the right time to express it, trust that feeling within you. If you sense that a friend or loved one may be facing an internal struggle now, offer support. If you feel someone is hiding something from you, they probably are, and it may be necessary to do some digging to uncover evidence of what is going on.

This aspect tells us that we can trust our intuition regarding our relationships and connections. We can feel when others are pulling away from us or if someone around us seems to be in low energy and needs extra support. People's behavior and words do not always accurately reflect their true feelings, so trust your intuition if something feels off within your connections allow others the space to open up to you and share their true feelings.

Sun in Scorpio quintile Pluto in Aquarius

In a world overflowing with chaos, we're more cautious than ever about who we take advice from. We're suspicious of the collective, and we have our wits about us when it comes to questioning authority. Many of us are ready to take a stand for social justice, and we're finding new ways to rise up.

This time, it's not about marching in the streets alone; it's about using our social platforms to amplify our voices. We're sharing, exposing, and revealing the secrets that those in power would rather keep hidden. And yes, we're banding together to call out and cancel celebrities who've misused their influence. We recognize that we gave these people a platform and can just as easily take it away.

We're rising up, but not in the traditional sense. This is a different kind of resistance, one that wields the power of technology, social awareness, and collective action to demand change. We're challenging the status quo in a way that's as unpredictable as it is unstoppable.

Mercury retrograde in Sagittarius semi-sextile Venus in Scorpio

This energy exposes the "real ones." When we face setbacks in our lives, it reveals who truly stands by us and who is willing to help us get back on our feet. During these tough times, we discover the friends who show up unannounced with a homemade meal when we're overwhelmed or the family members who drop everything to lend a listening ear. We find out who is genuinely supportive when we lose a job, and someone offers to help polish our resume or connects us with their network, or when we're going through a breakup and a close friend insists on a weekend getaway to help us heal. These moments of hardship expose the people who say they care and prove it through their actions, reminding us who the "real ones" truly are.

Song: "True Colors" by Cyndi Lauper

November 13th

Last Quarter Moon in Leo

In the last quarter moon phase, we are wrapping things up, marking the final push before completing a cycle, project, or manifestation. In the context of a last quarter moon in Leo, this signifies an ending with flair and dramatic expression. Whether concluding a project or a relationship, we are infusing it with creativity and a desire to make a lasting impression. Our actions may be bold and attention-grabbing, leaving others in awe. This energy can manifest both positively and negatively, and the potential consequences or reactions of others may not concern us much during this time. It's a period where we are ready to shock the world, leaving a memorable impact. If others around us seem overly dramatic or intense, it's essential to recognize that this is a collective energy, and allowing them their dramatic moment is crucial to their own self-expression. While we may feel strongly inclined to make everything about ourselves or insert ourselves, observing from a distance rather than getting entangled in unnecessary drama is wise.

Reflection

1. What dramatic or bold actions am I considering to make a lasting impression during this phase?

2. Are there likely any potential consequences or reactions from others during this expressive period?

3. How can I observe and detach rather than insert myself into unnecessary drama during this time?

Mercury retrograde in Sagittarius conjunct Mars in Sagittarius

This energy might have us ready to throw a fit if things don't go our way, so it's essential to be mindful of not over-dramatizing a minor setback. Take a breath and remember that it's not the end of the world. While frustrations can quickly escalate, keeping things in perspective will help you navigate the situation with a bit more grace and a lot less drama.

Song: "Drama Queen" by Sueco

November 15th

Venus in Scorpio sesquiquadrate Saturn retrograde in Pisces

Be cautious of slipping back into old toxic patterns when it comes to your relationships and connections. This energy has a way of tempting us to revisit habits we've already broken. It's the kind of vibe that might bring an ex sliding into your DMs or pressure you to revert to people-pleasing behaviors. You could even be asked to remove a boundary you've worked hard to set. Remember the progress you've made and the effort it took to get here—don't let a momentary lapse undo the work you've already done. Stay strong and stay true to your growth.

Song: "Wicked Game" by Chris Isaak

November 16th

Vesta enters Capricorn

Vesta represents the internal flame within us, the fire that burns deep inside and ignites our souls. With Vesta now entering Capricorn, we're all business all the time. This alignment empowers us with a strong sense of responsibility, whether at work or home. We feel a heightened urgency to be on top of our game and take charge of anything we consider our duty. Sacrifices for success come easily as we eliminate distractions and stay laser-focused on our goals. Our ambition is through the roof, and the energy tells us that with discipline and dedication, we can achieve anything.

However, there's a downside to this relentless drive. We may bite off more than we can chew, and burnout can sneak up quickly if we don't allow ourselves a break. This energy can push us to work into the wee hours of the morning or skip social events to stay on top of what we deem most important. Sometimes, we may even take on other people's responsibilities in addition to our own. If that happens, remember shielding others from handling their own tasks or making mistakes can hinder them from learning valuable lessons. Balance is key, even amidst the hustle.

Reflection

1. What specific distractions could you cut out to stay focused on your goals, and how do you determine whether these sacrifices are truly beneficial or excessive?

2. In what areas of your life do you feel the greatest sense of responsibility? Are there areas where this sense of duty is overwhelming or misplaced?

3. How often do you find yourself taking on others' responsibilities? What impact does this have on your own energy, growth, and ability to achieve your goals?

Sun in Scorpio quincunx Chiron retrograde in Aries

This aspect will likely bring up some fears from the past. We may be asked to participate in something that didn't work out so well for us in the past, so we may not be ready to repeat a painful cycle. We are asked to look deeper at the fears and insecurities coming up for us right now and assess whether we are prepared to release this fear or if we need more time. There is no wrong answer. Some wounds cut deeper than others, and we may need to delve deeper into the pain to feel safe releasing the fears associated with the trigger.

Song: "Workaholic" by 2 Unlimited

November 17th

Mars in Sagittarius sesquiquadrate Chiron retrograde in Aries

This aspect may leave us feeling stifled or held back as if someone or something imposes unfair restrictions upon us. However, it's essential to remember that our limitations are often only as real as we perceive them to be. When we shift our mindset and challenge the beliefs that confine us, we can break free from the barriers that seem to hold us back. The key is recognizing that sometimes, the only thing standing in our way is our perception of what's possible.

Song: "Get Out My Way" by Tedashii

November 18th

Sun in Scorpio trine Jupiter retrograde in Cancer

This energy invites a profound personal experience or revelation centered around letting go of the need to meet others' expectations, embracing your flaws, and recognizing that you are enough just as you are. It may come through moments where you realize you've been bending over backward to gain approval at work, only to see that your efforts go unnoticed, or when you find yourself feeling inadequate in a relationship because you don't fit someone else's ideal. These experiences push you to acknowledge and accept your imperfections as part of your unique story. It's about reaching a place where you can look in the mirror and, despite not being "perfect," feel a sense of peace and completeness because you're finally valuing yourself on your terms.

Sun in Scorpio trine Saturn retrograde in Pisces

Many of us are prone to praying for a miracle or a particular outcome, but what we forget is that many of the things we are praying for, we have the ability to create for ourselves. This aspect asks us to assess what we are still holding onto that conflicts with what we are trying to manifest. Perhaps we wish for more peace in our lives, but we constantly give in to the distractions of others. We may want to generate more income in our business, but we are sleeping until noon. Perhaps we are praying for meaningful connections that can reciprocate the love we are ready to give, yet we are still holding on to connections that cannot provide us with reciprocal energy. What actions are you taking that may be sabotaging your manifestations?

Jupiter retrograde in Cancer trine Saturn retrograde in Pisces

This energy can create a personal dilemma as we're called to extend ourselves toward others or situations that challenge our limits. Maybe you've spent a lot of time and effort learning to assert your boundaries, and now an opportunity arises that tempts you to lower one of those carefully set lines. Or perhaps you've vowed never to revisit a habit you've overcome, but you start to feel confident enough to think you can handle it. This energy serves as a reminder that not everything is black and white, and sometimes it's okay to allow yourself a treat or a bit of flexibility as long as you maintain a sense of balance. It's a lesson in self-control, teaching us that occasional indulgence, when approached mindfully, doesn't mean losing progress—it's about finding harmony in the grey areas.

Mercury retrograde in Sagittarius sextile Pluto in Aquarius

Be mindful of blunt or sarcastic communication, as it can easily be misunderstood, especially if those around you aren't familiar with your sense of humor. Sometimes, a joke or sarcastic remark meant to lighten the mood might come across as offensive or inappropriate if the context isn't right. For example, making a sarcastic comment about how "easy" someone's job is could be taken as criticism if they're actually struggling with it, or joking about a sensitive topic might not land well if others in the room aren't in on the humor. It's essential to read the room and consider who your audience is before letting the sarcasm fly—what may seem harmless fun to you could be perceived very differently by others.

Song: "I Need A Miracle" by Third Day

November 19th

Mercury Retrograde enters Scorpio

As Mercury retrograde shifts from Sagittarius back into Scorpio, it's time to get your popcorn ready. Two things often happen during this alignment, and the first is that people accidentally expose themselves or reveal their true motives. It's as if every one has taken a dose of truth serum and just can't help but spill their innermost desires and secrets. If you've been curious about what those around you are hiding, now is the time to stop investigating and simply listen—you might be surprised at what gets revealed without you having to dig.

The second common occurrence is that those of us who have been working hard to uncover other people's secrets often find out we've gotten it wrong. So, if you've been gathering "receipts" to confirm your suspicions, it's best to hold off on presenting your case, as you could end up embarrassing yourself. It's wiser to do less during this energy and let secrets expose themselves naturally. Otherwise, you risk making false accusations and even drawing suspicion onto yourself.

Reflection

1. When you find yourself trying to uncover someone's true motives, are

you genuinely seeking the truth, or are you seeking confirmation of your suspicions?

2. How often do you listen without judgment or preconceived notions? What steps can you take to become a more attentive listener, especially when others reveal their true thoughts and feelings?

3. What drives your desire to investigate or gather evidence about others? Is it rooted in curiosity, mistrust, or fear of being deceived?

Mars in Sagittarius sesquiquadrate Jupiter retrograde in Cancer

This energy can be challenging, as it often leaves us feeling restricted by the weight of responsibilities at home or within our family. For example, you might feel tied down by the constant demands of caring for a relative or overwhelmed by the never-ending chores and upkeep of maintaining a household. It could manifest as feeling trapped by the need to provide financial support, leaving little room for personal pursuits or relaxation. When family obligations pile up, it's easy to feel your needs are being pushed aside, creating a sense of frustration or resentment. This energy highlights the delicate balance between fulfilling responsibilities and finding time for yourself.

Venus in Scorpio sesquiquadrate Neptune retrograde in Pisces

Trusting your intuition is crucial during this time of heightened sensitivity. If you sense that something is off within your connections, it's worth exploring. Asking appropriate questions to understand others' feelings can be beneficial, but respecting their boundaries is equally important. As you expect your boundaries to be honored, extend the same courtesy to others. This period encourages open communication while being mindful of each other's personal space and comfort levels.

Song: "Confessions" by Usher

November 20th

Venus in Scorpio trine Pisces North Node

Spend less of your time and energy peering into someone else's garden, as the planets are perfectly aligned for secrets to come to light on their own. Instead of exhausting yourself trying to uncover what others might be hiding, do yourself a favor and save your energy. This cosmic alignment also presents a valuable opportunity to look inward and be open and honest about anything you might be keeping hidden. Embrace this time as a chance to come clean, clear the air, and let the truth set you free.

Mercury retrograde in Scorpio opposite Uranus retrograde in Taurus

This alignment is set to uncover truths related to money and finances, bringing hidden matters to light. You might find secrets exposed at work, like discrepancies in payments or issues with compensation, or perhaps you'll discover a hidden fee quietly draining your bank account without you noticing. While this energy can be confronting and may stir up feelings of frustration or shock, remember that it's here to help you rather than hinder you. Bringing these financial truths to the surface empowers you to take corrective action and regain control over your money matters.

Mercury retrograde in Scorpio trine Neptune retrograde in Pisces

Whatever is being exposed right now is happening *for* you, not *to* you, even if it involves your own secrets coming to light. It may be uncomfortable, but these revelations are ultimately in your best interest. While many of us hold on to the idea that ignorance is bliss, being aware and informed is a far more empowering position to be in. Knowing the reality of a situation, even if it's challenging, gives you the clarity to make better decisions and take meaningful action. Embrace the truth as an opportunity for growth and realignment.

Mercury retrograde in Scorpio biquintile Chiron retrograde in Aries

When we discover that others around us have hidden motives or have attempted to betray us, it often triggers memories of past betrayals, reopening old wounds. This can easily lead to feelings of hurt and mistrust, causing us to spiral into thoughts like "I can't trust anyone." However, it's important to recognize that such thoughts are not helpful or accurate. Someone else's inability to be honest is not a reflection of your worth or character. It's crucial to remember that there are still trustworthy people in your life, and one person's betrayal does not mean that everyone is unworthy of trust. Use these experiences to strengthen your discernment, not to shut down your openness.

Song: "Say My Name" by Destiny's Child

November 21st

New Moon in Scorpio

We are delving deep here; this new moon is asking us to consider what has our attention. What are we invested in learning more about? This new moon should have us delving deep into our behaviors, emotions, and experiences; however, it is much more likely to have us hyper-fixated on someone else's journey. We may be asking ourselves, why do they act this way? How do they feel about me? Is it their childhood trauma that is causing them to behave this way toward me? This can have us examining and potentially even diagnosing those around us with all sorts of issues and personality flaws that we are able to identify within them. If we feel someone is gaslighting us, we are viewing it as textbook narcissism. We can quickly find ourselves traveling down a rabbit hole of the different types of narcissism and the common traits to look out for to make sure that we have an accurate diagnosis for their issues.

What I would encourage you to do is to shift your focus onto yourself. What is triggering you right now? Why? Triggers coming up are a good thing because our emotional triggers are like a compass. If we have an emotional response to something, a shadow is potentially hidden within us that needs more attention. Many people want to begin doing shadow work to begin powerfully healing themselves, but they don't know where to start. Allow your triggers to be your guide. Am I triggered by this? Why am I triggered? When was the first time I remember this trigger showing up for me? What do I believe could be the cause of this trigger? Am I ready to heal and release this trigger now, or do I still feel that I need to hold onto it to keep myself safe from harm?

Reflection

1. What currently has your attention, and why do you find it compelling?

2. Are you finding yourself fixated on someone else's journey or behaviors?

3. Can you identify any triggers that have recently come up for you, and what do you believe might be the underlying causes? When reflecting on your behaviors, emotions, and experiences, are there aspects of your shadow self that you feel ready to address and release?

Sun in Scorpio conjunct Mercury retrograde in Scorpio

Sometimes, instead of trying to decipher the truth about what's happening around us, it's more beneficial to examine the truths that lie within us. This requires a high level of self-awareness, particularly when understanding our attachments to other people's behavior. For instance, we might realize that we're constantly disappointed because we expect friends always to be available when we need them, or we feel hurt when a partner doesn't respond the way we want during a disagreement. These reactions often stem from unrealistic expectations we place on others, expecting them to meet needs that perhaps we should be fulfilling for ourselves. By reflecting on our patterns and attachments, we can gain a clearer understanding of how our expectations might be affecting our relationships and learn to navigate them with more empathy and balance.

Uranus retrograde in Taurus sextile Neptune retrograde in Pisces

This aspect brings about a profound self-realization regarding what has been holding you back from attaining the resources and finances you need. Often, it reveals money blocks rooted in long-held belief systems, such as a fear of not deserving abundance or the notion that money is inherently "bad" or corrupting. For example, you might uncover that a belief instilled during childhood—like "money doesn't grow on trees" or "rich people are greedy"—has subconsciously influenced your financial decisions, causing you to shy away from opportunities or undercharge for your services. Recognizing these blocks can be transformative, allowing you to shift your mindset and take practical steps toward financial growth and abundance.

Song: "Bad Guy" by Billie Eilish

November 22nd

Ceres Direct in Aries

With Ceres moving direct in the sign of Aries, the focus shifts from questioning "Who is an ally for us? Who has our back?" to once again reaching out and extending ourselves toward others. The energy encourages us to move beyond seeking support and instead take proactive steps to connect, nurture, and show up for the people in our lives. It's a time to re-engage with the world, offering our assistance and building bridges rather than merely looking for who will stand by us. This alignment invites us to embrace a more outward expression of care and support, rekindling our willingness to take initiative in our relationships.

The Ceres asteroid represents how we nurture others and how we wish to be nurtured in return. Positioned in the sign of Aries, this energy can show up aggressively. This energy encourages us to fight on behalf of the ones we love in order to protect them and stand up for them rather than allowing them to fight their own battles. We expect our loved ones to do the same for us in return. We hope they will have our back when challenged by another and defend us if they witness someone talking negatively about us when we are not in the room.

This energy can show up as you fighting for a cause and becoming a warrior or soldier on the front line in order to create change for those who feel oppressed, or you may find yourself fighting a battle on someone else's behalf. This energy says that if you want to cause harm, you must get through me first. This can also show up as encouraging others around us to be independent and stand up for themselves rather than being intimidated. This energy says there is nothing to fear, and if an obstacle is put in front of us, we will not wait for someone else to remove it but rather make our way around it. We are speaking up and showing great courage and strength within this energy and supporting others to do the same. We will not stand by and watch others be bullied, repressed, or belittled. We will do something about it.

Reflection

1. Do you feel your loved ones adequately support and defend you when you're not around? If not, why might that be?

2. Have you ever found yourself fighting for a cause or defending someone else's rights? What motivated you to do so?

3. How can you balance protecting others with encouraging them to stand up for themselves?

Sun enters Sagittarius

Now that we have created more harmony and balance within our relationships and perhaps kicked some unaligned energies to the curb, it is time to shift our focus to our future. This season, we will be discovering where we are going and what we must do to get there, and we are generally up for the challenge and incredibly optimistic about our ability to achieve our dreams. This is an energy of "I got this, bring it on!" My favorite thing about being influenced by Sagittarius's energy is that we are so vibrant, energetic, and blazing our own path. If anyone comes in to disrupt that peace, we will likely be extremely dismissive, identifying their issue as a them problem. Is someone offended by my newfound confidence or triggered by my success? They'll get over it.

Any challenge that comes towards us during this time, we are ready to face it head-on. We quite enjoy a challenge this time of year. The pace of life is picking up, and we are here for it. There are also more opportunities for adventure, more social events as we get closer to the holidays, and more tasks on the to-do list as the year draws closer. We find ourselves with the energy to catch up with family members and friends for a drink, and despite perhaps indulging in a few too many, we wake up the next day and do some Christmas shopping. We have seemingly endless positive energy. This energy is like being a teenager again, having all the energy to do everything. Nothing will keep us down for too long. Go big or go home.

Reflection

1. Get specific about your vision for the future, and what steps are you taking to achieve it?

2. Reflect on a time when you faced a challenge head-on and emerged stronger. What did you learn from that experience?

3. What opportunities for adventure or personal growth are you currently exploring?

Sun in Scorpio biquintile Chiron retrograde in Aries

At this point, we recognize that our previous challenges have all been helping to ignite the fire within us. We can be more, create more, and have more if we are committed to growth and expansion, and all of these negative past experiences have given us the fuel and the fight to keep going. This energy can make us feel unstoppable and ready to take on the world at our new elevated frequency.

Sun in Scorpio opposite Uranus retrograde in Taurus

We can do more if we give ourselves more of our own energy and learn to prioritize ourselves. This energy tells us that we are worth more than we are currently experiencing and inspires us to push ourselves harder beyond our limits. This can show up as us wanting to learn a new skill, produce more work, hold ourselves more accountable, stop making excuses, rebalance our finances, and make difficult decisions related to investing in ourselves. We can feel the inner transformations and ascension happening within ourselves, and we are increasing our effort to 100% to achieve what we are trying to manifest.

Sun in Scorpio trine Neptune retrograde in Pisces

Shadow work can become somewhat addictive as we begin to feel much lighter, not carrying around all of that resentment and baggage from the past. This aspect is likely to have us feeling a little floaty and very connected to ourselves as we have been able to make peace with our darkness and feel safe and secure in the version of ourselves we are becoming.

Song: "Unwritten" by Natasha Bedingfield

November 23rd

Venus in Scorpio quintile Pluto in Aquarius

This aspect serves as a reminder that knowledge is power, especially when navigating relationships and alliances. If people in our lives have shown themselves to be untrustworthy, this newfound awareness allows us to adjust our approach and interactions accordingly. For example, if a colleague has repeatedly taken credit for your work, you can now be more cautious about sharing ideas with them or take steps to protect your contributions. Similarly, if a friend has been unreliable, you might choose to confide in someone else or seek support elsewhere. Knowing your true allies empowers you to make informed decisions, set better boundaries, and align yourself with people who genuinely have your back.

Mercury retrograde in Scorpio trine Saturn retrograde in Pisces

Mercury retrograde is undoubtedly causing some setbacks, but with the planet moving through Scorpio, these challenges are happening *for* you, not to you. Instead of trying to fight against the obstacles or force your way through them, take a step back and allow yourself to observe. This is a time to be open to the signs and signals pointing out what isn't working or no longer serves you. By doing less and paying attention, you can gain valuable insights into the areas of your life that need change, helping you discover a new direction and make necessary adjustments with clarity.

Mercury retrograde in Scorpio trine Jupiter retrograde in Cancer

Whatever challenge you're currently facing, step back and recognize it as the gift that it is—an opportunity to redirect your energy toward something more meaningful. For example, if that big work meeting you had scheduled gets canceled, embrace the extra time you now have to spend at home with your

329

family. View any missed opportunity as a fresh chance to reconnect with the people who genuinely matter or to finally tackle some tasks on your to-do list that have been lingering. Sometimes, what seems like a setback is really just life, giving you the space to focus on what's truly important.

Song: "Good Riddance" by Green Day

November 24th

Sun in Sagittarius sextile Pluto in Aquarius

This aspect allows us to see our extraordinary potential to make a difference in the collective. Some of us have innovative ideas that could help change the world. Many of us are healers, and the world needs our medicine, whether it be the ability to heal through our words, sharing our talents, or a deep compassion that allows us to create significant change for humanity. Some of us will use this energy to share our wisdom and energy with those around us. Many of us will want to make small changes to help with environmental or political issues or assist those less fortunate.

Song: "Imagine" John Lennon

November 25th

Mercury retrograde in Scorpio quincunx Chiron retrograde in Aries

This energy can feel like a major setback, often triggering negative thought patterns that we've worked hard to overcome. It's important to be mindful of old beliefs resurfacing, such as "I can't make this work," "I can't trust anyone," or "I have to do everything myself." For example, a project at work might hit a snag, and you could find yourself immediately thinking, "I knew this would never succeed," or if a friend disappoints you, it might lead to thoughts like, "People always let me down." It's easy to fall right back into a negative mindset when things go wrong, but recognizing these patterns can help you break the cycle and approach challenges with a more balanced perspective.

Mars in Sagittarius square Pisces North Node

This aspect may stir a strong desire to speak your mind or passionately defend your position, but it encourages you to surrender the need to assert yourself in every situation. For example, if a heated discussion arises at work, you might feel the urge to jump in and set the record straight, or if a friend disagrees with your opinion, you may want to defend your stance aggressively. However, it's important to choose your battles wisely and recognize when it's better to take a step back. Not every disagreement needs to be addressed, and sometimes the most powerful move is to let go and conserve your energy for situations that truly matter.

Mercury retrograde in Scorpio conjunct Venus in Scorpio

In this energy, all that is hidden will come to light, which is why it can often be more beneficial to say less and listen more. The quieter we are, the more perceptive we become, allowing us to notice subtle clues and hidden truths around us. For example, in a work meeting, instead of voicing every thought, you might catch the unspoken tensions between colleagues or notice a detail that reveals a deeper issue. In personal relationships, being attentive rather than jumping into the conversation could uncover someone's true feelings or intentions. By embracing silence and observing closely, we allow the truth to reveal itself naturally without forcing the issue.

Song: "Unfaithful" by Rihanna

November 26th

Venus in Scorpio quincunx Chiron retrograde in Aries

It is not our job to make others understand us. Our job is to understand and embrace ourselves. If others cannot relate to our story and what we have been through to get where we are, then educating them is not our task. This aspect says, "This is who I am, and I am learning to love and embrace my own shadows and darkness so others can either get on board with my transformation or watch me shine from the sidelines." Within this energy, we refuse to identify with our past broken self that needs to be fixed and instead show ourselves some compassion for being perfectly imperfect.

Song: "Born To Try" by Delta Goodrem

November 27th

Venus in Scorpio trine Jupiter retrograde in Cancer

This energy will likely bring a truth to light about your closest relationships, revealing what has been hidden beneath the surface. Your partner might open up about something that's been bothering them for a while, or you may discover that one of your children is struggling in school and needs extra help. You might also learn that a friend or family member is quietly going through a difficult time and could use your support. While potentially challenging, these revelations are opportunities to better nurture and care for those around us. Does your partner need more emotional support? Does your child require a tutor or extra guidance? How can you assist those you care about during their time of need? We can deepen our connections and strengthen the bonds that matter most by addressing these truths.

Venus in Scorpio trine Saturn retrograde in Pisces

This energy signals that we possess the internal wisdom to guide us in making decisions concerning our connections. With a lifetime of experience dealing with relationships, we have accumulated valuable insights. The choices we face might not always align with our preferences, but we can trust our judgment, drawing from the wisdom gained through past experiences and lessons.

Song: "Lean On Me" Bill Withers

November 28th

Saturn Direct in Pisces

Saturn is returning direct, so we are back to experiencing that push-and-pull energy of balancing spirituality and practicality. Pisces says that we can trust in God, the universe, or the divine to take care of us and lead us toward all our dreams, goals, and desires, and Saturn spoils the fantasy party by telling us that it is not entirely true. While we hear the whispers of the universe if we allow space for them, our goals need a practical plan. The universe works by matching the energy and effort that we extend out. So, while yes, the divine does have the capability to shift our whole world overnight by sending us a lotto win; generally, those things only happen to us once we are already thriving rather than when we are down and out, homeless, jobless, and could really use a miracle. If we use everything we have in our arsenal, every resource available to shift our reality, the universe will match that energy.

Saturn likes to apply incredible pressure on us to see what we will do. Will you rise, or will you fall to pieces and just give up? Saturn in Pisces has us on our knees praying for a miracle, and then when that miracle doesn't come or seems to go unanswered, we begin to question our faith and turn away from the divine. When we feel we have no resources left to turn to, no lifeline, we find the resilience to get back on our feet and make a way. We realize that the only person we can count on is ourselves, so slowly but surely, we start moving. We begin rebuilding again, and when we feel as though we are strong again, the universe steps in and says, "Oh, you know that miracle or opportunity that you prayed for? Oh, here it is; sorry for the delay." This can be a very frustrating energy and has us at times feeling as though we are alone on our journey and completely unsupported. But once we recognize that this is how manifestation works, we can begin living a life of abundance, bringing in our desires that once seemed too far away. This energy will be here until 2026, so your miracle and blessing will depend on how long it takes you to learn this lesson.

Reflection

1. How do you currently balance spirituality and practicality in your life? In what ways do you trust in the universe or divine guidance, and how do you practically plan for your goals?

2. Have you experienced moments of praying for a miracle and feeling unanswered? How did it impact your faith?

3. Reflect on a time when you faced incredible pressure or challenges. Did you rise up, or did you feel like falling apart? What did you learn from that experience?

Mars in Sagittarius semi-square Pluto in Aquarius

This energy will have you all fired up, sparking a restlessness and an urge to expand and express yourself. It's a good time to check in with yourself and pinpoint exactly what's fueling this fire. Are you fired up about an exciting upcoming trip or a creative project you're passionate about? Or are you feeling stirred up by drama happening around you, or a perceived need to defend your position? If it's the latter, and you're fired up about something that could disrupt your peace or that of others, it may be wise to redirect this energy toward a more positive outlet. Since this fiery energy isn't going anywhere, you might as well channel it into something productive and meaningful that will benefit you in the long run.

Song: "All Fired Up" by Pat Benatar

November 29th

First Quarter Moon in Pisces

Hello collective, Earth to the collective. Are you there? Are you present? Where did you go? I am sure that we have all experienced times when we are having a wandering thought and just drift off into space for a moment. Before you know it, your mind is still, the thought is gone, and you realize that you are just staring at an empty space at the wall, mouth all agape. We snap back to reality and think, "Wait? Where was I? What was I thinking about?" and can't refocus, no matter how hard we try. Well, that is the energy of the first quarter moon in Pisces.

This is the point of the lunar cycle where we make adjustments to where we are going off course, but it is very difficult to refocus when we are so easily distracted and can't remember the goal or destination. My advice with this energy is just to float, space out, take a nap, binge-watch a reality series—whatever escape your mind is craving (if it's not too destructive, of course). Do that thing. Get it out of your system. You have been working hard all year. You deserve a space cadet moment. This energy will only last for a couple of days, so enjoy your brain malfunction because there is much more that needs to be done. You will snap out of it, so just allow your mind space to wander for now.

Reflection

Use this opportunity to escape your reality. Binge-watch Netflix, do some gardening, play some Xbox, stare blankly at a wall for a while, or take a nap. Enjoy this energy.

Song: "What's Up" by 4 Non Blondes

November 30th

Mercury Direct in Scorpio

With Scorpio's intense and transformative energy moving direct, hidden truths that came to light during the retrograde can now be processed and integrated. This is a time for taking decisive action based on the revelations and lessons learned. Here is a reminder of what to expect with Mercury in its direct position in Scorpio.

334

Mercury in Scorpio always creates an interesting dynamic because we all become very secretive, highly intuitive, and somewhat suspicious. This alignment feels like we are all in a game of Cluedo, trying to solve a murder mystery. So, if there is anything that we have been hiding—be it secret lovers, health conditions, job opportunities, or passion projects that we have been keeping under wraps—it may just be exposed during this time. Everyone around us behaves like an investigator, and they are super suspicious. While usually, we can get away with keeping some things to ourselves, we may find ourselves being interrogated, and it seems like people around us are a little too all up in our business. This works both ways, so if someone around us is keeping something from us, we will feel it intuitively. We are much more perceptive than usual. We feel a need to get to the bottom of what it is that they are hiding. We are all putting on our private investigator hats and will not stop until we have answers.

This energy doesn't just apply to the people around us but also to any topic that we do not have answers to. We may find ourselves getting deep into the occult, using or watching tarot for insight and answers, watching true crime documentaries, or documentaries of any kind. If we want to publish a book but don't know how we will figure it out with this energy present. This kind of investigation is a much better use of our time and energy. Uncovering truths about what everyone else is hiding around us, while satisfying, can lead to further problems within our relationships, and we may just find out something we do not want to hear. Most of the secrets people are hiding are none of our business, and if they are our business, we will find out. These secrets will eventually expose themselves; what is done in the dark will always come to light. Use this energy very wisely and to your advantage rather than getting caught up in something that you have no business being caught up in.

Reflection

1. What secrets or hidden aspects of myself have I been reluctant to share with others?

2. How do I feel about the idea of others uncovering my secrets or hidden truths?

3. How can I respect the boundaries of others while still seeking the truth or understanding in my relationships?

Mars in Sagittarius biquintile Jupiter retrograde in Cancer

This energy highlights areas where we could be doing more, but it does so in a way that inspires and excites us to take action. It's not about feeling pressured; it's a motivating force that encourages growth and self-improvement. Perhaps it's the perfect time to add some education or a new skill to our portfolio, renovate our living space to better reflect our style, or start a workout program that energizes us. This energy invites us to ask, "What would truly nurture my soul right now?" and "In what ways am I excited to expand?" It's all about finding the activities or pursuits that spark joy and bring a sense of fulfillment, making growth feel like a rewarding adventure rather than a chore.

Sun in Sagittarius sesquiquadrate Chiron retrograde in Aries

This aspect indicates that we will likely experience a past trigger at some point. Someone may communicate something hurtful or irritate us by pushing our buttons, and we are somewhat reactive today. My advice is to breathe before you respond. Stop for a moment to assess whether outside influences require a response and if this energy present is distracting you from something more important. Do not allow outside chaos to ruin your vibe.

Venus in Scorpio opposite Uranus retrograde in Taurus

When we take the time to look deeply at ourselves and address our pain, the pain and unhealed wounds within those around us often become glaringly obvious. We can easily recognize the work others still need to do on themselves. Do not fall into this trap of diagnosing the trauma of others. While, yes, it is true that others are likely to have much work to do in releasing their trauma, the only trauma for which we are responsible is our own. This aspect is likely to have us wanting to take a break from looking at our pain and searching for pain points within others, but this is a distraction that will only lead to more resistance in our own healing journey.

Venus in Scorpio biquintile Chiron retrograde in Aries

The most effective way of healing another is to be an example by demonstrating new behaviors and living life with an open heart. If you can do this, others around you will notice. We can all pick up on the subtle vibrations of others, and if you can elevate your frequency to a state of love and peace, others around you will react in one of two ways. They may want to join your frequency, and they might even ask you how you did it, potentially seeking your guidance in healing their own trauma. On the other hand, some may be triggered by your healing and behave outlandishly, attempting to bring you back to your past version. They might see it as a personal challenge to lower your vibration back to one with which they are comfortable. How you respond will determine whether you are ready to accept your new vibration or are tempted to return to past patterns of behavior to protect yourself. We always have a choice whether to respond from a space of love or fear.

Song: "Not My Problem" by TAELA

December Alignments

December 1st

Venus enters Sagittarius

Venus enters Sagittarius is bringing the energy of asserting boundaries and expressing our need for personal space. This period emphasizes relationships that may be limiting or suffocating, prompting a desire to break free. The energy is like receiving messages while out with friends, questioning our whereabouts or return time, causing anxiety and a sense of being restricted. Such connections hinder our free expression and make us feel stifled. Whether it's a boss asking for an extra shift on our day off or more dramatic situations, this energy encourages vocalizing our need to avoid unnecessary drama and setting boundaries to protect our energy.

The adventurous spirit of self-expression during this time may lead to drastic changes in appearance, seeking new experiences like attending a festival or embracing fleeting romances. Every day becomes an opportunity for a new adventure, and consequences are pushed aside. This liberating energy fosters an attitude of doing our own thing and letting others do the same. Maintaining a zero-tolerance policy for drama, many find themselves seeking only good vibes and aligned energies.

For singles, the desire is for someone spontaneous who can keep things exciting; this may lead to interactions with multiple suitors simultaneously. Embracing the single life, enjoying freedom, and inadvertently falling in love become common experiences. Dressing up, feeling social, being open to new connections, and having a carefree vibe will make individuals more attracted to your energy at this time.

Long-term committed relationships may feel the need to break away from routines, introducing spontaneity or creating intimacy in various ways. Boredom with daily habits prompts a desire for change by spending more time outdoors together, planning spontaneous dates, or exploring personal pleasures individually. Partners becoming overly needy or imposing restrictions may be off-putting during this period, leading to a call for more freedom within the relationship.

Reflection

1. Can you recall a time when you felt stifled or restricted in a connection, and how did it affect your overall well-being and self-expression?

2. In what ways do you currently advocate for your own freedom within your connections, and are there areas where you could assert your boundaries more assertively?

3. Consider embracing a zero-tolerance policy for drama and seeking only good vibes. How might adopting this mindset positively impact your relationships?

Venus in Scorpio trine Neptune retrograde in Pisces

As we discover more about ourselves and those around us, we do not always find the answers we want. Sometimes, the illusions we have created about our connections are shattered, and it can feel like we have taken off the rose-colored glasses. It can be challenging to accept the actual reality of a situation; however, clarity given to us through the healing journey is a gift. It assists us in breaking karmic cycles from repeating themselves over and over again, leaving us trapped on a hamster wheel. See any truths revealed to you at this time as a gift from the divine and act accordingly to ensure that you do not repeat the same mistakes of the past and fall back into old habits.

Song: "Accept My Fate" by Andrew Phippen

December 2nd

Sun in Sagittarius sesquiquadrate Jupiter retrograde in Cancer

This energy presents as feeling stifled or restricted by your family or environment, leaving you frustrated and craving more freedom or personal space. Perhaps your family has overwhelming expectations—like needing to follow a specific career path, attend every family event, or live up to their traditions. It might also manifest as feeling confined by your living situation, like sharing a space with roommates or family members who don't respect your boundaries. For example, you may feel smothered by a parent who constantly checks in on you, leaving little room for independence, or perhaps your partner expects you to spend every free moment together, making it hard to focus on personal goals. This energy can also show up as feeling stuck in a town or environment that no longer aligns with your values, with the people around you content to stay the same while you yearn for change. The challenge lies in recognizing where these restrictions are affecting your growth and how you can begin to set boundaries or make changes to create space for yourself.

Song: "Fast Car" by Tracy Chapman

December 3rd

Venus in Sagittarius sextile Pluto in Aquarius

This energy represents the importance of accepting that relationships can evolve, and sometimes that means heading in separate directions or supporting others in their growth, even if it takes them away from us. For example, a close friend may decide to move to a new city for a job opportunity, or your partner may want to explore a passion that consumes more of their time and energy, leaving less room for the relationship to operate as it once did. It can feel unsettling to witness someone you care about grow in ways that change the dynamic between you, but this energy asks us to embrace their expansion rather than resist it. This might mean cheering on a partner who takes a demanding new role at work, even though it leaves you with less time together, or encouraging a friend to travel abroad, knowing that their journey may create emotional distance for a while. The lesson here is that true love and connection come from supporting each other's growth, even when it means navigating new paths and creating space within the relationship.

Song: "I'm Gonna Miss You" by Milli Vanilli

December 5th

Full Moon in Gemini

This Full Moon allows us to clearly communicate what we have discovered after delving deep into anything that has been setting limitations upon us. This can lead to challenging conversations and disruptions with those around us as we communicate what is stifling us or making us feel small. It's a time to examine our relationships and community, assessing how they may impact our ability to reach our full potential. We are putting a stop to anything that we feel is holding us back.

If this energy causes disruption, consider seeking out someone more aligned with your energy for understanding and connection. Remember, there are many others out there with similar frequencies. These connections can be with content creators, guides, mentors, or leaders. The internet allows us to find like-minded individuals with just a click. Whether they inspire, motivate, empathize, or simply radiate positive vibes, they resonate with you for a reason. Take note of the qualities you admire in them, as they will guide you toward finding and expressing untapped potential within yourself.

Reflection

1. Are there relationships or aspects of your community that you feel might be holding you back from reaching your full potential?

2. Make a list of the people you admire most, and what about their energy resonates deeply with yours?

3. How can you embody more of those qualities in order to express parts of yourself longing for expression?

Mercury in Scorpio quincunx Chiron retrograde in Aries

In order to embrace forgiveness, we must first delve back into the pain and emotions of the past and address what went wrong. This energy is here to help us do just that. We are justified in feeling the way that we feel, and we must honor our own emotions. If someone has hurt us, they should be made aware of our experience to ensure that they are clear on our boundaries and the types of behavior that we will not tolerate in the future. There is likely to be some deep communication happening within this energy as we not only express our own emotions but also hold a safe space for others to express their emotions to us so that we can gain a deeper understanding of their experience.

Song: "There's Nothing Holdin' Me Back" by Shawn Mendes

December 6th

Sun in Sagittarius square Pisces North Node

This aspect represents the struggle of trying too hard to force things into place, only to encounter obstacles at every turn, reminding us that sometimes we need to release control and allow the universe to guide us. For example, you may be pushing hard to secure a promotion at work, staying late every night and exhausting yourself, only to find that the opportunity keeps slipping through your fingers. Or perhaps you're planning a big event, meticulously organizing every detail, but unexpected setbacks—like weather issues or last-minute cancellations—keep throwing things off course. These experiences remind us that sometimes, the best path forward is to surrender, trust the timing of the universe, and allow things to unfold naturally.

Mars in Sagittarius trine Chiron retrograde in Aries

This energy represents the powerful opportunity to break free from past traumas and reclaim control over anything that has been holding you back. It might look like finally addressing an old wound—such as ending the grip of self-doubt rooted in childhood criticism by applying for that dream job, even if fear has previously stopped you. For some, it could mean setting boundaries with a toxic family member whose influence has affected your self-worth for years. Maybe you've avoided dating due to the heartbreak from a past relationship, but now you feel ready to open your heart again, reclaiming your power over fear. This energy encourages you to recognize that while the trauma shaped you, it no longer defines you. The past can be a stepping stone, not a prison. By releasing the limiting beliefs and patterns that have weighed you down, you begin a new chapter where you're in charge of your story and free to move forward.

Song: "Free Your Mind" by En Vogue

December 7th

Mercury in Scorpio trine Jupiter retrograde in Cancer

This energy highlights the power of intuition in identifying subtle issues within your home or family dynamics, allowing you to address them before they escalate. It might look like sensing that your child is struggling at school, even if they haven't said anything directly, and deciding to check in with them or arrange a meeting with their teacher. Perhaps you notice tension between family members that others seem to be brushing off, prompting you to initiate an open conversation to clear the air. It could be as simple as feeling that a particular room in your home feels energetically off, inspiring you to rearrange furniture or cleanse the space with sage. This energy encourages us to trust those inner nudges—like noticing that your partner seems distant and surprising them with a thoughtful gesture, or realizing that a family routine needs tweaking to reduce stress. Listening to these subtle cues creates harmony within our homes, addressing issues early and fostering a sense of balance and connection.

Venus in Sagittarius sesquiquadrate Chiron retrograde in Aries

This aspect asks us to examine the moves we have made in the past regarding conflicts with others. Where did we go wrong? Were we too reactive? Were we not reactive enough? Have we allowed others too much influence over our lives or our decisions? Do we need to find our voice within our connections and learn to communicate our needs better? The patterns of behavior we have become accustomed to will be different for all of us, but we all have them. How will we do things differently to break through cycles that prevent us from our most authentic expression? We have been learning how to embrace our highest version and change our behaviors, and it is getting easier with more opportunities to choose a loving response. However, we are tested when we are in a heightened state of emotion. Remember to allow yourself the time to rebalance your emotions and tune into your energetic frequency. If your past pattern of behavior is to cuss someone out, you must allow yourself the space to choose a more loving or dignified response by balancing your emotions first.

Song: "Be Prepared" by Jeremy Irons

December 8th

Mars in Sagittarius quincunx Jupiter retrograde in Cancer

This energy screams, "I can't relate to those closest to me." Perhaps you find yourself at odds with family, friends, or your partner over differing views on important topics. It could be political opinions, lifestyle choices, or personal beliefs that create friction, making you feel disconnected. For example, maybe your family is deeply rooted in traditional values, while you find yourself drawn to a more unconventional way of living, or perhaps a friend passionately supports a cause that you just can't get behind. These differences can leave you feeling isolated as if you're speaking a language that no one else around you understands. The challenge here is not just in having opposing views but in how it affects the connection—leaving you wondering if it's possible to bridge the gap or if you must learn to accept and respect the distance between your perspectives.

Mercury in Scorpio trine Saturn in Pisces

Sometimes, getting obsessive about something can work in our favor. When we channel that intense focus into a goal or passion, it can lead to incredible breakthroughs. For instance, an artist may become so immersed in perfecting their craft that they spend countless hours practicing, and as a result, create their best work yet. Or think of an entrepreneur obsessively tweaking their product until it's exactly right, which ultimately leads to a successful launch. Even in personal development, someone might become fixated on building a healthy lifestyle—tracking their workouts and meals meticulously—which helps them achieve their fitness goals faster than expected.

Venus in Sagittarius sesquiquadrate Jupiter retrograde in Cancer

This energy represents the need to assert our boundaries with those we love, sometimes in a more forceful manner than we might prefer. It could show up as finally telling a friend who always drops by unannounced that you need personal space or firmly expressing to a family member that specific topics are off-limits during conversations. Perhaps you've been lenient with a partner's behavior that has crossed your boundaries, but now you're drawing a hard line, making it clear what is and isn't acceptable moving forward. While setting boundaries with loved ones can feel uncomfortable, this energy reminds us that doing so is essential for maintaining healthy relationships and personal well-being. Sometimes, being direct and firm is the only way others will understand that our boundaries are not just requests but non-negotiable needs.

Song: "Respect" by Aretha Franklin

December 9th

Sun in Sagittarius semi-square Pluto in Aquarius

This energy encourages us to protect our peace by maintaining positive vibes and refusing to engage with anyone whose energy feels misaligned or disruptive. It's the kind of energy where you prioritize your own well-being and set boundaries without guilt. Maybe your friend group is venting about drama, but instead of getting involved, you politely excuse yourself and head out for a walk or enjoy your own company. Perhaps someone at work tries to pull you into office politics, but you decide not to take the bait, focusing instead on your tasks and keeping things lighthearted. This energy reminds us that not every battle is ours to fight—sometimes, the best response is no response. By choosing joy, calm, and alignment with our highest frequency, we free ourselves from unnecessary stress and preserve our emotional energy.

Mars in Sagittarius square Saturn in Pisces

This energy invites you to embrace independence by escaping on a solo adventure or diving headfirst into a new project that excites you. Whether it's a spontaneous road trip, spending the day hiking in nature, or finally starting that passion project you've been dreaming about, this energy encourages you to focus entirely on your own path. Along the way, you may find yourself tuning out negative opinions or unsolicited advice from others. Maybe someone questions the practicality of your new endeavor, but you choose not to engage, knowing that their doubts are a reflection of them, not you. This is a time to trust yourself, follow your intuition, and unapologetically prioritize what lights you up—allowing your adventure or creative work to become a joyful escape from negativity.

Song: "Family Affair" by Mary J Blige

December 10th

Sun in Sagittarius biquintile Jupiter retrograde in Cancer

This energy suggests feeling excited about introducing new ways of doing things within your home and family life. You might feel inspired to rearrange your space, adopt new routines, or try fresh approaches to family traditions. For example, instead of the usual family movie night, you might propose a game night or even a creative cooking competition in the kitchen. Perhaps you've discovered a new time-management system and can't wait to implement it, making mornings smoother for everyone. Or maybe you're ready to introduce sustainable practices like composting or reducing waste, and you feel excited about involving your family in the process. This energy invites you to experiment, innovate, and bring a sense of excitement and creativity into your home, making daily life more dynamic and fun.

Song: "A Spoonful Of Sugar" by Julie Andrews

December 10th

Neptune Direct in Pisces

Neptune in Pisces is a very dreamy and mystical energy in which everything seems possible, and we become experts at envisioning the life we desire. Our imagination expands, and we may find ourselves daydreaming about grand scenarios where all our problems magically dissolve. This energy inspires creativity and optimism, but the challenge lies in grounding these dreams into reality. During this period, it's easy to create illusions about the future that aren't based in truth, leading us to become lost in fantasy rather than taking practical steps toward achieving our goals.

For instance, you might start obsessing over winning the lottery, visualizing what you'd do with all the wealth, yet fail to make tangible efforts toward financial stability. Similarly, you may meet someone who sparks excitement and begin creating a romantic fairytale in your mind, ignoring warning signs or red flags, only to later realize the other person has no intentions beyond friendship. Another common illusion during this period could be fantasizing about quitting your job and traveling the world without realistically planning how to fund such a lifestyle or overlooking the challenges that come with it.

This energy can also manifest as delusions of grandeur. You might convince yourself that you're destined for overnight success without recognizing the hard work and consistency required. Alternatively, you may adopt unrealistic spiritual practices, believing that manifestation alone will solve all your problems without taking concrete action in the physical world. In relationships, you might cling to toxic dynamics, believing that "love will conquer all," even when the situation is unhealthy or unsustainable.

In creative pursuits, Neptune in Pisces can have you starting project after project, deeply inspired, but without ever finishing anything, hoping inspiration alone will carry you through. It can also show up as self-deception—convincing yourself you're fine emotionally when in reality you may be avoiding your deeper wounds and spiritual work. While this energy makes the impossible feel within reach, it is essential to remain mindful, discerning what's real from what's wishful thinking. This period invites us to ground our dreams by balancing inspiration with realistic steps, ensuring that we don't become trapped in a fog of illusion and unfulfilled fantasies.

Reflection

1. Where am I fantasizing about an ideal future but not taking practical steps toward making it a reality?

2. Have I become emotionally attached to a fantasy version of someone or something, rather than seeing it for what it truly is?

3. Is there a creative project or goal that I've started but left unfinished, expecting inspiration alone to carry me through?

Mercury in Scorpio opposite Uranus retrograde in Taurus

This energy is a difficult one that indicates that there may be more to the story. It suggests finding out more information or having more revealed to you, which can potentially set you back. For example, you may have recently quit your job and now discover your rent is increasing. You may have just decided to forgive someone, but now you may be finding out that there was more for which they should have been asking forgiveness. You may have decided to end a long-term relationship and then found out that the person you cared deeply for has entered into a connection with someone else. This energy will affect us all differently and potentially send us spiraling. However, remember that the choices you have made are ones that were in honor of yourself, and any further information you receive now should not be able to sway your decision or trigger an adverse reaction from you.

Mercury in Scorpio biquintile Chiron retrograde in Aries

Pay attention to any negative emotions coming up for you at this time. You may feel an urge to suppress them, thinking that your recent transformation has disconnected you from your past pain. However, that is often not the case at all. If you are feeling triggered right now, take the time to feel into those emotions. Allow your triggers to be your guide as you delve even deeper into the core wounds of your soul. There may be a pain point that you have missed and needs to be addressed.

Song: "Fantasy" by Mariah Carey

December 12th

Last Quarter Moon in Virgo

We have reached the last quarter moon phase again, and the moon is in Virgo, so this is very supportive energy to get things done and wrap things up. We find ourselves with an incredible capability to problem-solve right now. Whenever we talk about moon energy, we must consider the position of the sun because we are assessing the polarity between the two. With the sun in Sagittarius, we ask ourselves which energies create blockages along our path. We all want to expand and grow, and the goal for all of us is financial freedom, time freedom, and not feeling restricted by our relationships or environment. We are assessing what within our lives is preventing us from feeling like we can soar and reach new heights, and we are using Virgo's analytical and practical energy to work out what we will do about it. All restrictions can be eliminated or lessened if we think outside the box. Do we need to rearrange some things in our environment? Do we need to adjust our work schedule? Do we need more self-care or to address a health issue? Do we need to take a vacation to come back fresh and rejuvenated? Are some of our relationships hindering our progress? Do we need to create firmer boundaries or just learn to say no? What needs to change, and what are we going to do about it?

Reflection

1. What aspects of my life create blockages or restrictions along my path to growth and expansion?

2. What steps can I take to create more financial and time freedom now?

3. What practical changes can I make in my environment to enhance my overall well-being and productivity?

Mercury enters Sagittarius

As Mercury enters Sagittarius, a shift occurs in the way we express ourselves. If you've been living life as a delicate wallflower, being mindful of manners, and avoiding rocking the boat, that is about to change. This energy particularly benefits those with a platform, bringing enthusiasm and animation to communication. While it may come off as extra at times, it's ultimately fun. This energy allows us to communicate passionately, and people respond positively to it. We have the ability to speak life into others, making a significant impact with our words. Think of us as motivational speakers, not just offering encouragement but also urging people to stop making excuses, get up, and make a move. The delivery might be blunt and forceful, inspired by Sagittarius' truth-telling nature, but it can inspire significant change by holding others accountable. Sagittarius energy rejects small talk and negativity, focusing on good vibes only. Confronting negativity, we are ready to call out those who refuse to take accountability for their circumstances. It's a season of brutal honesty, bringing forth authenticity rarely seen. This alignment may reveal true feelings, and navigating this transit might be a challenge for those easily offended. Remember, others' opinions are just that—opinions, holding only the power we allow them to have over us.

Reflection

1. Reflect on a moment when someone spoke to you with passion and enthusiasm. How did it impact you, and how might you incorporate a similar approach in your communication style?

2. Consider the concept of being a motivational speaker who encourages action rather than just offering reassurance. How can you embrace a more direct and forceful communication style to inspire change in yourself and others?

3. In what areas of your life could you benefit from a season of brutal

honesty, fostering authenticity and a deeper understanding of yourself and others?

Venus in Sagittarius square Pisces North Node Pisces

This energy can make us feel as though we are too much for others or that someone else's presence is overwhelming us. Perhaps you are excited about a new project, lifestyle change, or opportunity, and your enthusiasm is rubbing others the wrong way. Maybe they tell you to "calm down" or subtly discourage your excitement, making you second-guess yourself. On the flip side, it could be you feeling overwhelmed by someone else's intensity. Maybe a friend or family member is sharing their passions, opinions, or excitement in a way that feels draining or overbearing to you. This energy invites us to examine whether we are being mindful of the emotional space we take up, while also asking if we are dimming our light to fit into spaces that do not fully appreciate our passion. Balance is key—are we projecting too much energy outward, or are we being too quick to judge others for expressing themselves fully?

Mercury in Scorpio trine Neptune in Pisces

There are moments when our obsession with possibility and potential serves as our greatest asset. While others may roll their eyes, saying we have our head in the clouds or that our ideas are unrealistic, this energy reminds us that it's precisely this type of thinking that has driven some of the world's greatest achievements. Fantastical thinking—the ability to dream beyond what seems practical—helps us envision futures others can't yet see.

Song: "Inspired" by Miley Cyrus

December 14th

Mars in Sagittarius quincunx Uranus retrograde in Taurus

This energy propels us to break through restrictions, particularly those related to work and finances. If you've felt stuck in a job with little room for growth, this energy encourages you to look beyond the limitations and explore new career opportunities or side hustles that align with your passions. For example, you might decide to start freelancing in your spare time or finally launch that online shop you've been dreaming of. Perhaps you've been struggling with financial constraints, but now you're inspired to create a budget, cut unnecessary expenses, or develop new streams of income. This could also look like negotiating a raise or asking for a promotion, even if you were previously too hesitant to do so. This energy invites us to take control of our financial future by thinking outside the box and refusing to let past limitations define our potential.

Mercury in Sagittarius sextile Pluto in Aquarius

This aspect ignites a bold, fearless energy, empowering us to take a stand and fight for what we believe is right, even if it means ruffling a few feathers along the way. We are no longer concerned with pleasing others or keeping the peace at all costs. Instead, we feel compelled to speak our truth and advocate for our values, whether that's confronting unfair practices at work, standing up for a friend who's been mistreated, or addressing social issues within our community. For example, you might find yourself leading a protest, organizing a petition, or challenging the status quo in conversations, regardless of the discomfort it might cause others.

Song: "Make It Happen" by Mariah Carey

December 15th

Mars in Sagittarius square Neptune in Pisces

This aspect embodies the power of dreaming so big that others might call you delusional. It's the kind of energy that propels you toward seemingly impossible goals—launching a business with minimal resources, quitting your job to pursue a creative passion, or planning to move across the world with no clear plan in place. Those around you may try to pull you back to "reality," telling you that your dreams are impractical or out of reach. However, this energy teaches us that the most extraordinary achievements often start as ideas others couldn't understand.

Sun in Sagittarius trine Chiron retrograde in Aries

This aspect calls for us not to give in to any fear and has us feeling motivated, inspired, fired up, and supported by the universe. We live life with a sense of adventure within this energy and do not care much about consequences. This energy is like getting a taste of freedom after years of feeling restricted. This energy makes us want to embrace each day as a new adventure and live life with optimism rather than feeling confined by our pain.

Venus in Sagittarius semi-square Pluto in Aquarius

This is a very rebellious energy, one where if someone tells us what to do, we are likely to do the exact opposite just to assert our independence and prove that we are not under anyone else's control. It's the kind of energy that shows up when a friend advises us to play it safe, but instead, we double down and take a bigger risk just to make a point. Maybe a parent or partner suggests we give up on a dream because it's too impractical, but instead, we invest even more time, energy, and resources into it. This energy can make us fiercely resistant to authority, whether it's rejecting a boss's micromanagement at work or disregarding societal expectations about how we should live our lives. While this energy can lead to defiant actions that may surprise others, it also offers an opportunity to tap into our most authentic selves—doing things our way, unapologetically.

Venus in Sagittarius biquintile Jupiter retrograde in Cancer

This energy invites us to bring more fun and excitement into our home and family environment, preventing things from becoming stale or routine. Maybe it's planning a surprise game night, rearranging the living room furniture to create a fresh vibe, or organizing themed dinners where everyone gets to dress up. You might also suggest spontaneous adventures, like going for an impromptu hike or setting up a tent in the backyard for a family camping experience. This energy encourages us to break away from mundane routines and find new ways to connect with loved ones, injecting joy into everyday life. It reminds us that home should be a space filled with laughter, creativity, and shared experiences, where even the simplest moments—like baking cookies together or watching old movies—can turn into cherished memories.

Sun in Sagittarius quincunx Jupiter retrograde in Cancer

This energy encourages us to explore how we can nurture our family relationships and strengthen the bonds that connect us. It invites us to consider: What wild adventures can we embark on together? Whether it's a spontaneous road trip to a new destination, a weekend camping trip under the stars, or simply trying something new as a family—like paddleboarding or taking a dance class—this energy is about creating lasting memories.

It also reminds us that joy is a powerful bonding tool. How can we bring more laughter into our shared spaces? Maybe it's as simple as hosting a family game night, telling silly jokes at dinner, or watching funny movies together. The little moments—tickle fights, inside jokes, and spontaneous karaoke—are just as meaningful as grand adventures.

Song: "Photograph" by Nickelback

December 16th

Mars enters Capricorn

I am hearing the "Eye of the Tiger," the Rocky theme song, as I connect with this energy. This energy tells us that there are no excuses for us not to be successful. We are destined for success. Don't believe me, just watch. This alignment helps us realize that we can achieve almost anything through discipline. If you were to apply more discipline to all areas of your life, you would be miles ahead of where you are now.

You may find yourself cutting out anything, or anyone misaligned with the end goal in this energy. You may be clearing out your schedule of obligations that are no longer a priority. You may be throwing out all the food that will not support your bikini body—removing connections that drain too much of your time and energy. Deleting apps that waste hours of your day. We must make sacrifices to achieve greatness. With this energy, we are taking everything very seriously. We are willing to grind to get where we need to go. This is not only an energy of knowing the following steps to take but also stepping, taking the leap into the life you desire. We are all fired up, making moves, and ready to fight for what we want.

Reflection

1. How can I incorporate more discipline into various aspects of my life to propel me toward success?

2. What are the core priorities in my life right now, and are they aligned with my long-term vision?

3. Are there people, activities, or habits in my life that are misaligned with my goals and need to be cut out?

Song: "Eye Of The Tiger" by Survivor

December 17th

Mars in Capricorn quintile Pisces North Node

While we are entering a phase of intense discipline and productivity, it's essential to apply that same level of commitment to the slower, restorative aspects of life. It's not just about what we accomplish but how we sustain ourselves along the way. Instead of solely focusing on achievements, this energy encourages us to nurture the activities that keep us grounded and connected to something deeper.

Whether dedicating time to a daily spiritual practice like meditation or yoga, spending a few minutes journaling, or scheduling regular walks in nature, these quieter practices create space for reflection and renewal. Consider setting intentions not only for career goals but also for your well-being, such as getting outside every morning or simply pausing to take a few mindful breaths throughout the day.

Sun in Sagittarius square Saturn in Pisces

This is a complicated energy, wanting to push past your resistance and limits to expand beyond fear but also falling back into past patterns of behavior such as procrastination or talking ourselves out of our own greatness. We are returning to bad habits of avoidance or self-sabotage. We are trying to keep our vibes high and remain optimistic, but for many of us, it will feel as if a dark cloud of potential failure is looming, or perhaps we would prefer to reschedule our dreams and goals until tomorrow or a later date. This is the temptation of self-sabotage and self-abandonment. Will you give in?

Song: "Morning Asana" by Londrelle

December 18th

Mercury in Sagittarius sesquiquadrate Chiron retrograde in Aries

It is expected that we will want to fall back into old patterns of behavior and identify with the broken version of ourselves. We become very adept at convincing ourselves of the reasons why we cannot achieve something, replaying the voices of the past telling us that we are not enough. While this aspect can trigger memories of the past, we will likely want to use those as fuel to propel us forward rather than allowing them to overwhelm us or keep us small.

Mercury in Sagittarius sesquiquadrate Jupiter retrograde in Cancer

This aspect brings a powerful urge to break out of old routines and reach new heights in caring for ourselves. We may feel a restless desire to upgrade our approach to health and well-being, pushing beyond the usual boundaries to truly nurture body, mind, and spirit. This could be committing to a more challenging fitness routine, exploring different forms of self-care, or experimenting with healthier eating habits. We may also feel drawn to holistic practices like meditation, journaling, or breathwork to support emotional well-being. This energy asks us to honor that drive, encouraging a proactive approach to becoming the best version of ourselves.

Song: "Mental Health" by Moonlight Scorpio

December 19th

Mars in Capricorn semi-sextile Pluto in Aquarius

This energy invites us to see the power of meaningful commitment. When a goal truly resonates with our purpose, it feels natural to dedicate ourselves fully, turning long-term ambitions into an act of passion rather than obligation. Whether it's launching a creative project, supporting a cause, or working toward a personal dream, we may feel an undeniable pull to put in the effort and make it last. This is a time when commitment feels less like discipline and more like a natural outpouring of enthusiasm and devotion.

Venus in Sagittarius trine Chiron retrograde in Aries

This positive aspect can evoke a sense of nostalgia, prompting us to recall a time when we felt safe and free to express ourselves authentically. It may be a memory of enjoying a particular activity, embarking on a memorable trip, or sharing a connection with a friend where we felt accepted without judgment. This aspect encourages us to strive for those positive experiences once again. We can start saving money for a trip we long for, reintegrate old passions that used to bring us joy, reconnect with friends, or recreate the excitement of falling in love with our partner. Prioritize rediscovering that blissful or adventurous feeling to bring joy and fulfillment back into our lives.

This energy may create a desire to distance ourselves from loved ones if we feel they aren't genuinely supportive or understanding of our needs. For instance, if we're pursuing a new career path or personal goal and receive skepticism instead of encouragement, we may feel inclined to spend more time alone or seek support elsewhere. Similarly, if we're prioritizing self-care routines or health goals but family members don't respect our boundaries, like quiet time or a new schedule, we may feel the need to step back temporarily to protect our energy. This energy encourages us to honor what we need, even if that means creating some space to regain balance and clarity.

Song: "Whatever It Takes" by Imagine Dragons

December 20th

New Moon in Sagittarius

Go big or go home. With both the Sun and the moon in Sagittarius, we are putting no limits on the ways that we can expand and push ourselves beyond our limits. This energy allows us to indulge ourselves in the world of ultimate potential. This is an excellent time for us to consider what we want to bring in for the upcoming year. For some of us, this will be a business goal, our dream job, financial freedom, time freedom, and making money while we sleep. For others, it may be moving home, renovating our home, decluttering our home, or nurturing a sense of safety. Some of us will have health goals as our top priority, such as cutting out certain foods, losing weight, or an exercise regime. It is unlikely to be a goal that you cannot control. We rarely find people creating New Year's resolutions to improve their relationships, as relationships involve other people and their emotions. Too many variables may set us up for potential failure, so most of us steer clear of emotional goals.

Reflection

Sagittarius energy is about going even bigger, so now that you have your goal in mind, what is the next step beyond that goal? What is the one thing you could do consistently to bring you closer to your goal? If your goal is money-related and you are spending all of your money on cigarettes, perhaps yours will be to quit smoking. If you want to move home or declutter your space and living environment, commit yourself to declutter for 30 minutes daily, and you will make significant progress in no time. If your goal is business or health-related, waking up an hour earlier and going to bed at a reasonable time is the small, consistent step that you feel would change everything.

Now, bring in the energy of this moon to go even bigger; whatever commitment you are making to yourself, double it. Push yourself beyond what you feel is possible to achieve, not just the first goal but the goal that lies beyond it. If you were going to declutter for 30 minutes a day, double it to an hour. If you were going to quit a habit to save money, then quit two habits. Sagittarius energy is not about perfection and doesn't care much if we fail but rather influences us to go even bigger, strive even harder, and keep trying.

Set your intentions for the new year, write them down, speak them to the new moon, and begin working on your small, consistent step now. You needn't wait until the 1st of January 2026. The best time to start showing up for yourself is now. So go clean out that drawer, set your alarm an hour earlier, drink some water, eat a banana, or whatever you have decided your small goal will be, then double it. How are you going to commit to pushing yourself beyond your limits?

Sun in Sagittarius quincunx Uranus retrograde in Taurus

This aspect can be a challenge because the part of ourselves longing to be expressed will be louder than ever. We can recognize the limitations we have placed upon ourselves and acknowledge that there is still much work to be done if we are to consistently push through our limits and past programming. The first step in expressing ourselves in the way we wish is giving ourselves permission to do so and changing our minds about what we can achieve.

Song: "Breakaway" by Kelly Clarkson

December 21st

Mercury in Sagittarius square Pisces North Node

This energy brings a powerful sense of possibility, sparking the belief that our dreams are within reach. You may encounter a mentor who seems perfectly aligned with your goals, offering guidance and wisdom that feels like the missing piece. Alternatively, you might come across an influencer online who speaks directly to your aspirations, sharing insights that leave you feeling motivated and ready to take action. This kind of energy reminds us that inspiration can strike from any source and that sometimes, the right words or encouragement come at precisely the moment we need them.

Mars in Capricorn biquintile Uranus retrograde in Taurus

This aspect is a call to get serious about our financial intentions and break free from any limiting beliefs or habits that may hold us back. It encourages us to take a hard look at our relationship with money: Are we overspending, avoiding budgeting, or perhaps doubting our ability to generate wealth? Now is the time to commit to those financial goals, whether it's creating a savings plan, investing in something meaningful, or building new habits that support financial stability. This energy supports us in releasing the mindset patterns that limit us, empowering us to shift our resources and intentions toward a prosperous future. Embrace this moment as an opportunity to redefine your financial story.

Sun in Sagittarius square Neptune in Pisces

It's one thing to dream up exciting possibilities and imagine all the thrilling adventures you'll embark on, but bringing them to life requires action. This aspect urges us to step beyond the planning phase—beyond writing down goals, visualizing, and creating vision boards—and start actively living those dreams. It's time to turn thoughts into reality, to move from inspiration to action.

Song: "Headline" by Folton Lee

December 22nd

Sun enters Capricorn

I love Capricorn season because it makes us feel like we can achieve anything and become the CEO of our own lives. Yes, even the most unfocused procrastinators can achieve something in the upcoming year. The ambition that comes with Capricorn season is the only thing that gets me through the holidays each year. As someone who is clairsentient, I can physically feel the energy of everyone around me. I don't do crowds, like ever. But you will even find me rushing about shopping malls trying to bag a bargain at this time of year. I've got my list. I've checked it twice and will not give up until I have everything on that list. We are all at the top of our game, waking up earlier looking fresh. Not only do we have our whole day planned, but some of us are beginning to plan what next year is going to look like.

Some people underestimate Capricorn energy, but it packs a punch so big that it can turn the most unfocused of us into absolute boss mode. Mercury is in retrograde right now, and with this alignment, we don't even notice. Everything is going wrong, and we are like, "Oh bummer, what's plan B?" That didn't work, so I'll have to go this way. We are too busy and too focused to be thrown off our game. With this kind of energy, we can be a little ambitious, so don't bite off more than you can chew. I am guilty of buying a 12-month gym membership at this time of year, and I'm pretty sure I only went twice, so gamble your time and resources responsibly. What are you doing to boss all the way up this season?

Reflection

1. How can you harness the ambitious energy of Capricorn season to set and achieve your goals?

2. How do you stay focused and determined during the holidays, even in challenging situations?

3. Are there specific plans or goals you've set for the upcoming year, and how do you intend to achieve them?

Venus in Sagittarius square Saturn in Pisces

This energy can be challenging because it often leaves us so focused on our goals and responsibilities that our loved ones may feel sidelined as if we don't have the time or energy to dedicate to them. The drive to stay on track with our progress can make us less willing to shift priorities or hit pause, even if it's to address the needs of those closest to us. Balancing our ambitions with our relationships requires conscious effort, as it's easy in this energy to feel torn between staying committed to our goals and making time for the people who support us.

Sun in Sagittarius quintile Pisces North Node

This aspect encourages us to find deep joy in life's simple, quiet moments. A refreshing sense of playfulness is in the air, urging us to embrace childlike wonder and spontaneity. You may feel inspired to run through a garden sprinkler at the park, reliving a carefree thrill, or feel compelled to do cartwheels on a lush patch of grass you stumble upon. Perhaps you'll even chase butterflies, mesmerized by their beauty, savoring each small moment. This energy invites us to reconnect with the beauty in stillness and find happiness in life's gentle, natural rhythms.

Jupiter retrograde in Cancer square Chiron retrograde in Aries

This aspect can stir up old wounds, bringing to light areas where we once felt neglected or unsupported, and it inspires us to fill those gaps with compassion,

357

either toward ourselves or others. For instance, if you grew up without much emotional validation, you might feel a strong urge now to be more emotionally present and affirming with your children or loved ones, ensuring they feel seen and valued. Similarly, if you experienced a lack of nurturing self-care in your past, you may be motivated to build a routine that prioritizes your mental and physical well-being, filling your life with moments of self-compassion. This energy encourages us to offer the kind of care we once needed, transforming those past absences into acts of love and healing.

Song: "Permission To Shine" by Batchelor Girl

December 24th

Venus in Sagittarius quincunx Uranus retrograde in Taurus

This aspect represents the discovery that others' perceptions should not affect our self-expression. As long as we are not intentionally hurting anyone, we do not need to seek others' approval. Often, we project our feelings of inadequacy outward toward others, but the only approval we truly need is from ourselves. The change begins within us. This energy will likely trigger a deep transformation, moving us into a space of self-acceptance and love, embracing even the parts of ourselves that others perceive as less desirable.

Mercury in Sagittarius biquintile Jupiter retrograde in Cancer

This energy serves as a gentle reminder of the power our words hold in uplifting and nurturing those around us. Simple words of encouragement, like telling a friend, "I believe in you," or reassuring a loved one, "I'm here for you no matter what," can make a world of difference. A kind word, a sincere compliment, or even a short text to check in can provide comfort and support. This aspect emphasizes how much our words can impact others, inspiring them, soothing them, or even helping them heal. When we choose to speak with kindness, we create a ripple effect of positivity and connection.

Sun in Capricorn semi-sextile Pluto in Aquarius

This aspect urges us to step into our authority and take charge rather than sitting back and letting others decide our path for us. Imagine a situation at work where a group project is stalling because everyone is uncertain about the next steps. Instead of waiting for a manager to step in, you might decide to organize a meeting, propose a plan, and get the team moving forward. Or in your personal life, family members have been pushing you toward a particular career or lifestyle choice, but you feel drawn to a different path. This energy supports you in confidently asserting your goals and making your own choices. By taking leadership, you set the direction that feels right to you and avoid being swayed by outside influences, creating a life that truly aligns with who you are.

Venus in Sagittarius quintile Pisces North Node

While stepping up to control specific areas is essential, asserting which responsibilities you will *not* take on is equally important. Imagine you're at work, and a colleague tries to offload tasks onto you that aren't part of your role. Setting boundaries by politely but firmly stating, "This isn't my area, but I'm happy to help find a solution," ensures you're not weighed down by tasks that don't serve your growth. Or in family life, perhaps you've always taken on organizing gatherings, but it's draining you. Communicating that it's time for someone else to step in respects your needs and allows you to focus on areas where you can truly contribute. Saying "no" isn't about shirking responsibility; it's about making space for what aligns with your strengths and priorities.

Song: "I Know Who I Am" by Peachkka

December 25th

Venus enters Capricorn

As Venus enters the sign of Capricorn, we examine our connections and the people around us, asking which connections are here to support us long-term and with whom we can grow and expand. Questions arise about whether we share the same goals with those closest to us, whether our relationships can go the distance, and whether our connections provide a solid foundation of stability and security for the future. We are done playing games and with those in our lives who show constant inconsistency. We are no longer willing to waste time with people who do not take us and our connections seriously; we are now willing to put more time and energy into those connections that are supportive and people willing to reciprocate our energy. We seek consistency and connections that add value to our lives.

For those who are single, the desire is to take things slowly in any new connections to ensure compatibility in goals and intentions. Many singles may focus on career or personal goals rather than getting into a situationship that might distract them from prioritizing themselves. Those open to love will be keenly observant of red flags or areas of misalignment, thinking about their deal breakers and what they truly need from a relationship. Although some singles may have past hook-ups on speed dial, they are less likely to flirt with people from the past during this time, as they need to be taken seriously.

For those in long-term relationships, this placement can open up deep discussions about the future. Questions about the next steps for the relationship, making it official, considering marriage and children, or blending finances may arise. Any areas not aligned or inconsistent behavior within the connection will likely come to a head. Partners are asking each other for more, seeking growth together, and putting in more effort rather than participating in behaviors that pull them apart. The desire is to see progress, commitment, and a sense of safety and stability within the relationship.

Reflection

1. In examining your connections, can you identify those that truly support your long-term growth and expansion?

2. Do your closest relationships share the same goals and aspirations as you, fostering a sense of mutual understanding and alignment?

3. Are you currently involved in connections where consistency is lacking, or are you surrounded by people who take your connections seriously?

Venus in Sagittarius square Neptune in Pisces

This aspect can create tension in our relationships as we assert that we don't want to be placed in a role of importance or seen as a central figure in someone else's life. For example, you may feel overwhelmed by a friend who relies on you for constant advice and emotional support. Expressing that you need space to focus on your own priorities might feel uncomfortable, as it challenges their expectations of you. Similarly, in family dynamics, you might communicate to a sibling or parent that you can't be their go-to person for every decision they face. This doesn't mean you don't care; it's an expression of your boundaries and independence.

Mercury in Sagittarius semi-square Pluto in Aquarius

This aspect reminds us that if we are going to make long-lasting significant change, it is going to require more energy and effort than we are currently putting out. We can make a difference in our lives and the lives of the collective. We can breathe love and light into our community, but it will require consistently breaking old patterns of behavior. This is not an overnight change. We will continue to face our own resistance. Now would be a good time to develop a strategy for coping with obstacles we will inevitably face along the way.

Song: "You Don't Own Me" by Lesley Gore

December 26th

Sun in Capricorn biquintile Uranus retrograde in Taurus

This energy embodies the drive to "boss up" and turn financial dreams into reality. It's a time when many of us feel inspired to establish multiple streams of income, building a foundation of financial independence and security. You might find yourself exploring side hustles, investing, or launching a passion project you've been thinking about for years. Whether it's setting up an online store, investing in stocks, freelancing, or renting out a spare room, this energy pushes us to take concrete steps toward creating wealth. It's about recognizing your power to shape your financial future and bringing your money goals to life.

Song: "I Get Paid Every Day" by Mello Will

December 27th

Venus in Capricorn semi-sextile Pluto in Aquarius

What have we not thought of yet? This is the energy of out-of-the-box ideas that support us in being able to embrace what it is that we truly love. Maybe the hubby can try putting the kids to bed to allow wifey time to work on her passion project. Do we need a mediator or some form of relationship counseling? Do we need a date night that brings us back to the energy of when we first met? Could we each read a relationship book to understand each other better? Have we taken the time to understand the love languages of others around us? Have we lost the spark, and do we need to spice things up in the bedroom?

Song: "Make It Work" by Forest Whitaker & Anika Noni Rose

December 28th

First Quarter Moon in Aries

The first quarter moon phase encourages us to take a close look at our goals and assess the progress we've made. It's a time to recognize what's working well and what adjustments might be needed to stay on track. However, with the moon in Aries, our energy becomes charged with excitement, ambition, and a spark for adventure—but also a tendency toward impatience and distraction. Aries energy loves a fresh start, which means you might find yourself jumping from one idea to the next, eager to begin something new even if it means leaving current projects unfinished. You may wake up with grand ideas, like deciding to start a band (despite not knowing how to play an instrument) or feeling the urge to paint a mural in your home, even though other tasks are waiting.

This playful, "fly-by-the-seat-of-your-pants" energy invites spontaneity and creativity, but it also makes staying focused on finishing anything challenging. It's the kind of time where inspiration is abundant, but consistency might be lacking. To harness this energy, consider writing down each new idea so you can return to it later—without letting it derail the progress you've already made.

Reflection

1. What goals am I currently working toward, and which ones still feel exciting and fulfilling?

2. Are there any projects or commitments that I feel tempted to abandon? If so, why? Is it due to a lack of interest, difficulty, or a new, shinier idea?

3. What excites me most about starting something new? Is there a way to incorporate that excitement into my current projects?

Mercury in Sagittarius quincunx Jupiter retrograde in Cancer

This energy ignites a strong desire for growth and exploration. Many of us may feel the urge to travel, seeking new landscapes and experiences that broaden our horizons and bring fresh perspectives. For others, the call to expand might come through a desire to pursue higher education or delve into new fields of study, eager to gain knowledge and enhance our skills. However, this expansion may require us to make sacrifices or adjust priorities—like spending less time on family commitments or other routines—to fully embrace these opportunities. This energy encourages us to step outside of our comfort zones, inviting us to consider what we are willing to let go of to pursue new paths and experiences.

Venus in Capricorn biquintile Uranus retrograde in Taurus

There are times when we reach an impasse with others, perhaps because they are unwilling to change or give us what we need from them. We must remember that change must begin within us in order to manifest more of what we need. If you are waiting for an apology from someone, perhaps you can reach out and apologize for any negative energy you may have sent their way. If we want

362

someone to treat us with more respect, we can start by showing more respect to ourselves. If we are waiting to receive more recognition at work, then we can increase our efforts so that they become hard to ignore or perhaps begin searching for another company in which our talents and efforts will be valued. It starts with us.

Mercury in Sagittarius trine Chiron retrograde in Aries

This powerful, uplifting energy encourages us to break free from old wounds that once held us back, keeping us in repetitive cycles. Now, we're given the opportunity to transcend these patterns, embracing a new level of strength and resilience. It's a moment of true empowerment, where we can look at past hurts not as barriers but as stepping stones that have shaped our growth. This energy opens doors for us to move forward with confidence, leaving behind the restrictions of yesterday and stepping fully into a future that aligns with our highest potential.

Song: "Let It Go" by Idina Menzel

December 30th

Juno enters Capricorn

This energy brings a heightened desire for stability, maturity, and commitment in our closest relationships. We're drawn to partners who not only provide but also work hard to create a solid, secure foundation. It's not just about having fun together; it's about building something lasting. We want someone who's here for the long haul—someone who can handle our ups and downs and show up consistently, with patience and reliability.

During this alignment, many of us feel a pull toward deepening our commitment and sharing lives in more significant ways, such as making things official, moving in together, or planning for marriage, children, or shared financial investments. We're focused on finding a partner who aligns with our long-term vision, supports our goals, and can be trusted to handle the responsibilities of a shared future. Unreliable behaviors, like overspending or a lack of financial foresight, become particularly frustrating, sparking conflicts or disagreements.

This period encourages us to ask ourselves: Is this someone who will stand by us in the years to come? Can we envision building a life with them, even into retirement? Relationships that can stand the test of time become the goal, making this a powerful time for assessing whether a partner truly fits into our future.

Reflection

1. What qualities do I truly value in a long-term partner, and how do they align with my vision of stability and security?

2. What aspects of my current relationships make me feel secure and valued? Conversely, are there areas where I feel unsupported or uncertain?

3. For those in committed relationships. How comfortable am I with discussing and planning for the future with my partner? Are they equally committed to building a stable future together?

Mars in Capricorn sextile Pisces North Node

This energy brings a strong desire for stability, security, and a sense of comfort in our lives. We recognize our discipline and potential to reach our goals but also crave a path that doesn't feel like a constant uphill battle. We want assurance that our efforts will be met with support rather than endless struggle. This aspect speaks to our need to know that our jobs are secure, our relationships are dependable, and that there will come a time when we can relax, free from the constant hustle. It's a reminder to seek out and cultivate spaces of comfort and stability, allowing us to pursue our ambitions without feeling perpetually on edge.

Song: "I Won't Give Up" by Jason Mraz

December 31st

Mercury in Sagittarius square Saturn in Pisces

This aspect represents a challenge that we are facing. Perhaps we are learning that something requires more investigation or is going to take much more time than we initially thought. This aspect makes us eager to experience more or learn more about a particular topic. However, it also comes with an energy forcing us to slow down and not be too hasty or enthusiastic. Make sure that we are not jumping ahead and completing each step to the best of our ability, as silly mistakes can be made with this aspect present.

Song: "You Learn" by Alanis Morissette

About the author

Gypsy Rose is an intuitive psychic medium, best known for her online antics of singing and dancing as she delivers messages from the spirit realm. She assists others in navigating the twists and turns of their healing journey and reminds them that they are not alone. She guides her clients and followers to embrace their uniqueness and live a life free of restrictions as they align themselves with a higher purpose.

Facebook: @gypsyroseconnectiontospirit
TikTok: @gypsyroseshadowpriestess
Instagram: @gypsyrosepsychicmedium